GW00503537

Gower and South East Wales

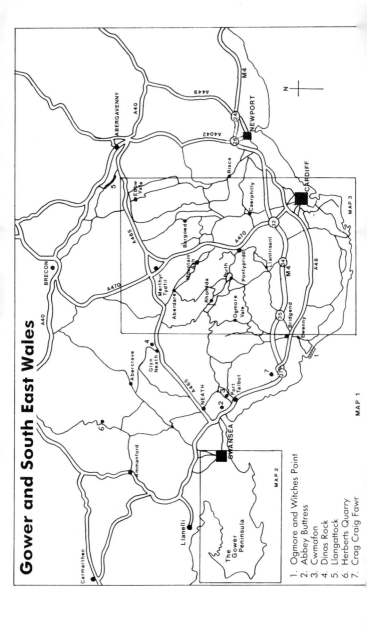

1. Ogmore and Witches Point
2. Abbey Buttress
3. Cwmafon
4. Dinas Rock
5. Llangattock
6. Herberts Quarry
7. Crag Craig Fawr

MAP 1

Gower
& South-East Wales
Wales

Edited by Alun Richardson

Contributors

Chris Allen	John Harwood
Giles Barker	Mick Learoyd
John Bullock	Gary Lewis
Martin Crocker	Pete Lewis
Chris Court	Steve Lewis
Paul Donnithorne	Andy Long
Gwyn Evans	Bob Powles
Alan Giles	Andy Sharp
	Roy Thomas

Crag drawings by Nigel Gerke
Maps by A.Richardson

Produced by the South Wales Mountaineering Club
Copyright South Wales Mountaineering Club

"We live and learn but not the wiser grow."

John Pomfret

This guide is dedicated to my wife and son for the lost hours.
A.Richardson 1991

ISBN 1 871890 11 X

Front cover: Adultress E2 5c Trial Wall
Climber R. Parker   *Photo* C. Ryan
Rear cover: First ascent of Lip Trick E3 6a 6a Dinas Rock
Climber T. Penning   *Photo* P. Littlejohn

Typeset by Parker Typesetting Service, Leicester
Produced by The Ernest Press, Glasgow

CONTENTS

MAPS AND DIAGRAMS

ACKNOWLEDGEMENTS

"Going to the right place, at the right time, with the right people is all that really matters-what one does is purely incidental."

C.Kirkus.

First and foremost I must thank my wife and son for the hours that they freely gave me to pursue this task.

This guide would not have been possible without the hard work of all the previous guidebook writers and editors. I am particularly indebted to M.Danford and G.Evans, who proof read the guide. Any remaining mistakes are undoubtedly my responsibility.

I must also thank the section writers for providing me with the information, allowing me to "tinker" with it and then examining it closely for the many flaws inherent in any manuscript.

There is a cast of thousands who helped behind the scenes, making comments over a pint of beer, going to unheard of places to look at the routes and read very early versions for a giggle; Gwyn Evans and John Bullock, who have scoured Gower in search of gems and gave many constructive comments; Ewan Kellar, for taking over the organisation and typing of the sandstone when all else had failed; Alan Price and A.Long two local climbers able to repeat the hardest routes and make unbiased opinions; Robb Davies, for checking the Morlais section; Dave Hart and Giles Barker, for their early work on the sandstone section; Pat Littlejohn for his helpful criticisms and contributions; H.Collinson, C.Hebbelthwaite, Lucy Gilbert and team, who organised a party and then gave everyone a letter of the alphabet to compile the index; Martin Crocker and Gary Gibson for their criticisms; Jackie Gill for putting her English degree to good use, Paul Donnithorne for checking a lot of the sandstone; John Travelyan for putting his computer knowledge to good use.

I must also thank those SWMC members who kept me going when the flak was flying; Andy Long, Jim Beynon, Chris Allen and especially Roy Thomas. They prevented me sending the whole guide into the National Grid.

Finally, I would not have developed my passion for climbing without the company of such amiable companions as Alan Dance, Clive Curle, Steve Lewis, Adrian Wilson, Andy Long, Jim Beynon, the SWMC "B" Team and many more.

If I have missed anyone I am sorry.

Alun Richardson 1991

INTRODUCTION

"The guide book will be out later this year."

A.Richardson 1988.

"Any new routes should be sent to the guidebook writer if he can be found."

M.Crocker 1988.

"The guide has been in preparation since 1987! I hope it will be ready some time this decade."

J.Harwood 1990.

Well here it is; the guide that has been part of the conversation of South Wales climbers for a few years. It has taken quite a time to prepare, and anyone who has edited or written a guide book will understand why. I certainly underestimated the magnitude of the task when I started as editor and overestimated some people's enthusiasm for the task. I make no apologies for the terse manner in which the guide has been written, to cram more than 1900 routes into a book of this size it was a necessary evil.

There is still much work to be done to unravel the history of climbing in South Wales, and much effort is still needed to sort out all of the routes and variations on Gower. The computer base that the guide now has will eventually lead to the thorough recording of climbing in Gower and South-East Wales.

Gower and South-East Wales have been described as the Third World of British climbing. True, they have rarely been in the forefront of British climbing, but in this guide you will find a variety of climbing unsurpassed in Britain: from the picturesque Gower with its beautiful beaches; Ogmore with its steep advent-urous cliffs; the technical inland limestone; to the recently developed sandstone crags. The area has something to suit all types and ability of climber and it certainly deserves greater popularity.

The recent influx of climbers to Pembroke has brought a steady stream of visitors to South Wales. A detour to the area covered by this guidebook would be a fitting addition or alternative to any climber's trip.

I have been involved in South Wales climbing since 1978 and have followed the development of its climbing over the years with interest. Certainly, in latter years, the "sandstone boom" has revitalised some jaded locals and provided a focus for the talents of many others. The pace of development has been so fast over the last few years that lines have been gobbled up at an alarming rate. This has meant that routes have had to be climbed quickly to protect them from the jackals. Many good routes have been put up with the minimum of fixed gear and with the minimum of human interference, but the Bosch and dangle brigade must be careful that they do not erode the ethics of previous generations. Rather, they should be trying to improve upon them. Attempt the route without fixed gear, if you fail try again and again and then soul-search for the need for fixed gear.

This is not an argument about bolts or pegs, it is about having some pride in the style of the first ascent, and having some soul! I remember the days when people used to pull their ropes through if they fell off! The words of Geoffrey Winthrop Young should still hold true for today's generation; "Getting to the top is nothing. The way you do it is everything". A quote from Craig Smith during 1990 may enlighten a few minds "After climbing my line I was left with the empty feeling that I had previously experienced after creating bolt routes. There's a lot to be said for the traditionalist's approach."

Nevertheless, whatever your ethics or climbing ability, Gower and South-East Wales have something to offer. The area has sea, sun, sand, mountains, bold routes, clip routes, valleys steeped in culture and history, great crags, good crags and even some abysmal crags; everything to make an adventure out of everyone's visit.

An attempt has been made to include at least a mention of all the routes climbed on Gower and South East Wales. I have however, missed out those routes that were so short as to constitute a safe boulder problem rather than a climb. There are quite a few on Gower. For the few routes I have inadvertently omitted I apologise.

Finally, please remember that the inclusion of a crag in this guide does not mean that you have the right to climb there. Please treat any confrontation carefully and do not provoke an incident.

TECHNICAL NOTES

"If you're trying to frighten me you're doing a
bloody good job about it".

W.J.Beynon 1987.

Adjectival Grades
This is an overall picture of difficulty, encompassing 'E' for effort.
If the route is particularly safe or serious this is noted in the
description. For example, it is possible to have two routes given
the same grade which are totally different propositions; one may
be safe but strenuous and the other less strenuous but not so
safe. The route description will distinguish them. The standard
adjectival system has been used:

MODERATE, DIFFICULT, VERY DIFFICULT, SEVERE, HARD
SEVERE, VERY SEVERE, HARD VERY SEVERE, EXTREMELY SEVERE.

The open ended Extremely Severe grade is represented by
E1,E2,E3,E4,etc.

Carrying this guide book on a climb will necessitate the addition
of a grade to the route.

Technical Grades
"It's at least 5c." Every climber I have ever met.

This is an attempt to assess the skill required to overcome the
hardest move on a pitch. There is no direct relationship between
adjectival grade and technical grade, although climbs of a given
adjectival grade are likely to cover a limited range of technical
grades.

The climbs are graded for on-sight leads, but most of the harder
routes have not been led without prior knowledge. The symbol
'+' has been used to indicate routes that have not had sufficient
ascents to reach a consensus about grade and/or quality.

Quality
"The most pleasurable climbs in the world
get three stars and the worst imaginable
get the black spot"

Yorkshire Limestone Guide 1988.

This has been critically examined. Many first ascentionists endow
their routes with star quality. However, for a route to be starred, it
must be of a classic quality that is going to appeal to subsequent
ascentionists. It must have good line, good climbing, good posi-

tions, good rock and/or that sometimes ethereal quality that makes a route a classic.

A three star route must have all, a two star route most, and a one star route some of the above qualities. If it does not deserve stars it may still be a good route, but not a classic one. Poor routes are specifically described as such or have a white spot: .

Some guide book writers have attributed to their area a great number of stars, using the excuse that they are regionally based. This is of no use to visiting climbers for whom stars are most useful. I hope that in this guide you will find that three star routes are in fact classics on a national level, that two star routes are classics of South Wales, that one star routes are classics of the area, and that many of the non star routes are good as well.

Do not dismiss some of the areas on first viewing: try the routes; you will be impressed. This is especially so on sandstone, where some of the crags are a bit esoteric to look at.

Style of Ascent
"For climbers to preplace as many bolts as they feel necessary to allow them to get up the crag, is like my being allowed to play in the first division by tying the opposition's legs together." J.Bass-indale 1988

Maybe the future of British rock climbing lies not in new routes, but in the style of ascent of established ones. It has been impossible to check all the routes and one has to rely on the honesty of the first ascentionists, some are more honest than others! Often, the second ascentionist is in reality the first. Many of the new routes have had very few ascents, especially on sandstone, and are impossible to grade. The first ascentionists came to know them so well in the course of putting them up that they then found it impossible to judge objectively the problems of doing them on sight.

Orientation
In this guide, Gower cliffs have been grouped into sections usually by the convenient approaches and proceeding from W to E. In the South-East Wales section the cliffs have been described individually and have been split into limestone and sandstone areas.

Within each section the routes have been described from L to R, with a few exceptions that are mentioned in the text.

Measurements

After a lot of hard thought it was decided to use the metric system for length. For those dinosaurs who find it difficult, multiply by 3 and add 10% of your answer.

e.g. 45m = 135 + 13.5 = 148.5 ft

Abbreviations

To reduce volume the following abbreviations have been used:

L, LH, LW ....left, lefthand, leftward
R, RH, RW ....right, righthand, rightward
PR, TR, BR, NR.......peg runner, thread runner, bolt runner, nut runner
PB, TB, BB, SB ....peg belay, thread belay, bolt belay, stake belay
PA, BA, TA, NA ......peg aid, bolt aid, thread aid, nut aid
F1, F2 etc ....Friend 1, Friend 2, etc
(R).......................restricted access (appearing in the routes title line)
N, S, E, W ....north, south, east, west
O ....not recommended
+ ....not enough ascents to reach a consensus of opinion on grade or stars.

New Routes

Details of these should be sent to A.Richardson, 24 Penlan Crescent, Uplands, Swansea, SA2 0RL.

First Ascent Details and any other Information

There are many dates and first ascentionists missing. If you have any information on these or anything else that could help us unravel the history of South Wales, please send it to the above address.

ACCESS AND RESTRICTIONS

There are few restrictions on access to cliffs described in this guide, but climbers should bear in mind that many of the cliffs on Gower, and much of the cliff top land, are owned by the National Trust. In addition large sections of the coast lie within National Nature Reserves. Furthermore access is often gained to many crags in South East Wales by way of footpaths across private farm land. Visitors are asked to obey the Country Code and keep to prescribed access paths in other words use common sense.

The Gower coast contains important colonies of sea birds and other cliff-nesting birds. To protect these, a number of restrictions have been agreed between the BMC, local climbers, the National Trust and the Nature Conservancy Council. Failure to abide by these restrictions is likely to endanger access to other, much more extensive climbing areas on the Gower coast.

With the exception of Worm's Head, on which climbing is forbidden, the restrictions refer to the birds' nesting season. In these cases, all affected climbs can be identified by (R) in the title line.

Occasionally, a temporary restriction is agreed and imposed as a consequence of the appearance of a rare and legally protected species. When this occurs, notices will be erected locally and at the site, and the restriction publicised in the climbing press and local equipment retailers.

The specific restrictions are as follows:
1   Worm's Head ....No Climbing at any time.
2   Yellow Wall...............No climbing from the 1st March to 10th August inclusive.
3   Thurba Head ....No climbing from 1st March to 10th August inclusive, on all climbs on the Head.

CLIMBING WALLS AND BOULDERING

CLIMBING WALLS

There are a number of climbing walls in the South East Wales area offering wet weather alternatives for the enthusiastic rock jock.

Swansea University: This is located in the student's sports centre. It is located next to Singleton Hospital on the sea-front A4067. It consists of a 10m by 20m wall with natural rock in place. It provides good bouldering at all levels but is best suited to the lower grade climber. Strictly, it is available only to students and members of the sports club; however, a bit of cunning can usually get one in. It is impossible to use when there is badminton being played.

Clyne Farm Activities Centre: From Swansea centre follow the coast road A 4067, then turn R up Mayals Road, (prominently sign posted Gower). Take the first turning on the R, Westport Avenue, and follow this up the hill. Clyne Farm is hidden on the R at the top of the hill. Described by Clyne Farm as the longest in Britain (it isn't by a long way), its wall provides fingery problems and traverses for the higher grade climber. A large number of the holds are poorly designed and badly maintained; consequently, they are very damaging to fingers that have not been warmed up. There is one wall at an easier angle to provide some climbing for mere mortals. It is very cold in winter, so warm up your fingers before using it.

Cardiff Climbing Wall: Located in the Channel View Leisure Centre, Jim Driscoll Way, Grangetown. It has the best wall in South Wales, providing good training and problems. It is possible to use the wall at most times and there are no restrictions on who can use it. Well worth a visit on those rainy days.

Polytechnic of Wales: This is located in Pontypridd and is very good, but gaining access to it is difficult. It may be worth a try if you are a student or look like one and/or you are stranded in the sandstone area on a wet day. It is rumoured that Climbers Club members have access to it.

BOULDERING

Most climbers have found some sort of bouldering in their local areas to enable them to practice their art when they have not got the time to do real climbing. Some seem to do nothing else.

Swansea: Many of the routes in this area could be regarded as boulder problems and Gower does provide some excellent bouldering in the following areas: Rhossili, Mewslade/Fall Day, West

Tor to Shirecombe and Caswell Bay. On the sea-front opposite the Guildhall is an old stone bridge providing excellent bouldering with soft landings, but beware of glass in the sand.

South-East Wales Limestone: The early construction engineers showed good foresight in using stone that would provide good bouldering for future generations. Cardiff has been scoured by locals and did have a wealth of excellent climbing until the developers moved in. Some good bouldering still remains.

Prostitutes Wall: An excellent traverse with the now famous Yellow Brick Road; follow the yellow dots as your only hand holds . . . desperate. It is located on the other side of the railway line opposite The Holiday Inn in the centre of the city.
Beware of the prostitutes they guard the wall with venom.

Porthkerry viaduct: OS ref 092673 A series of huge stone pillars supporting a railway line. They provide good sustained problems and traverses in a pleasant parkland setting.

Sully Island: OS ref 167670. Situated near Barry Island, this is a good bouldering area but is only accessible at low tide.

Nash Point: OS ref 915685. Situated on the coast between Ogmore and Llantwit Major. The cliffs are composed of blocks of varying stability and have only appealed to one or two local lunatics who have not publicised their routes. There is however some good low level traversing.

Ogmore: At the Southerndown end of Ogmore are some steep problems and traverses that are accessible when the tide is receding. A recently developed bouldering area next to Ogmore is The Trench, developed by Chris Hamper. The landing is sand and the rock excellent, the drawback is that it is only accessible an hour or two either side of low tide. To get to The Trench park at the "pay or be fined" car park at the top of the cliffs just past a cattle grid between Ogmore by Sea and Southerndown. Walk down to the coastal path and proceed eastwards to a bench. The crag is below and gained by scrambling.

Sandstone: The main areas of bouldering on natural outcrops are situated around the Pontypridd area, and are easily accessible.

Ponty Common (OS ref 078903): Overlooking the Pontypridd exit on the A470. Take the Pontypridd exit and follow signposts for Cilfynydd. At the junction at the top of the hill, continue up the hill, towards Pontypridd and District Cottage Hospital, for 50m. A path leads towards a monument. Below the monument and for the next few hundred metres is a series of buttresses housing some good problems.

White Rock (OS ref 078903): Probably the best bouldering area due to its sunny aspect. The problems dry very quickly. Follow descriptions for The Darren but instead of turning R into White Rock Estate continue up the hill towards Llanwonno. Park at the cattle grids at the top of the hill, just past Llanwonno Close. Follow a track to the L from the cattle grids, behind the houses. After 60m bear R to a fence on the L. A small path leads down L to a small pinnacle. 50m L a series of small outcrops provides the remainder of the problems.

Gelli (OS ref 985947): A small series of natural outcrops overlook the B4223 between Llwynypia and Gelli. Car park facilities are available on the LH side of the road. Owing to their N-facing aspect the problems become lichenous, but their pleasant situation overlooking the Rhondda valley compensates for this. The boulders are easily reached in about 15 mins by following the well worn footpath up the hillside behind the car park to the shoulder and then contouring R above the boulders. The crag of Gelli is easily reached, being about 150m further along the hillside.

Trehafod (OS ref 054908): The remains of a bridge provides an excellent wall for traversing. Turn L on the A4058 between Hopkinstown and Trehafod over a small bridge, 400m past the Hollybush pub in Hopkinstown. Follow the unmetalled track RW for approx 300m to the wall.

Cilfynydd: the small natural outcrop above the main crag provides good bouldering.

Penallta: the crag and the outcrops around it provide good bouldering.

Punk Rocks: the bay to the R of the main crag provides numerous short problems.

GOWER

INTRODUCTION

"Gower is that little scrap of green on the map of Wales which juts untidily from the south coast, as though the maker of the mountain block let his finger slip in passing on to the west. Its ragged outline is its chief beauty, the grey bastions of the cliffs cradling broad sandy bays and thrusting seaward again as rugged headlands. It is small wonder that the region bears the distinction of being the first in Great Britain to have been designated an 'Area of Outstanding Natural Beauty' in 1957 by the National Parks Commission.

Stretching along the South coast from the tidal islands of the Mumbles to the tidal island of the Worm, carboniferous limestone cliffs rise in blocky magnificence. Their feet washed by a line of creaming surf, their faces lashed by gales from the Atlantic; but they soak up sunshine where the winds are blocked and reflect an oceanic mildness." From A Natural History of Gower by Mary. E. Gillham.

Gower has, in its small area, just about all the habitats found in Wales as a whole, with the exception of mountains and large rivers. A visit to Gower will not only provide good climbing but will provide a rich variety of fauna and flora in fact large sections of the coastline lie within National Nature Reserves. Gower is the most westerly of the areas covered by this guide and probably contains its largest concentration of rock climbing. It is a good base to use for the rest of South-East Wales as it enables one to camp in a beautiful area with crags on the doorstep and most of the guidebook area no more than an hour's drive away.

All the cliffs have been described using OS references from 1:50,000 sheet 159 "Swansea and the Gower".

There are many campsites in Gower that fill quickly in summer and are closed at other times. For further information on camping and other accommodation it is best to contact the Civic Information Centre, Singleton Street, Swansea (tel Swansea 468321).

The area's southerly aspect and low rainfall permit climbing throughout the year and it is not unheard of for climbers to be seen in T-shirts in the middle of winter.

Finally, remember Gower is a sea cliff area and a lot of the crags are tidal. The rock is constantly being attacked by the sea and so is the fixed gear!

If you have an accident phone 999 and ask for the Coastguard.

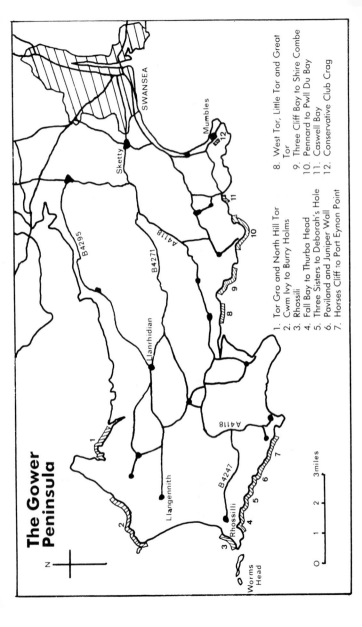

The Gower Peninsula

N

0   1   2   3 miles

Worms Head

Rhossili

B4247

A4118

Llangennith

Llanrhidian

B4271

B4295

Sketty

SWANSEA

Mumbles

1. Tor Gro and North Hill Tor
2. Cwm Ivy to Burry Holms
3. Rhossili
4. Fall Bay to Thurba Head
5. Three Sisters to Deborah's Hole
6. Paviland and Juniper Wall
7. Horses Cliff to Port Eynon Point
8. West Tor, Little Tor and Great Tor
9. Three Cliff Bay to Shire Combe
10. Pennard to Pwll Du Bay
11. Caswell Bay
12. Conservative Club Crag

HISTORY

"When future mountaineers open their eyes and realise what has happened, it will be too late: the impossible (and with it, risk) will be buried, rotten away, and forgotten forever."

Reinhold Messner

Pre-1983 by G.Evans

Gower has a relatively short climbing history, beginning with commando training on the cliffs of Fall Bay during the later war years. This, however, may have been preceded by scrambling and some climbs by the Swansea-born broadcaster and climber, Wynford Vaughan Thomas. The earliest recorded climbs are those of Alan Osborn and Brian Taylor on Boiler Slab in 1949, and of these Dulfer is still worthy of inclusion in any visitor's itinerary. Osborn followed this in 1952 with an ascent of the East Ridge of Great Tor, still probably the best VD on Gower.

During 1954 and 1955, John Brailsford and the St.Athan Mountain Rescue Team developed Little Tor, Three Cliffs and Pobbles Bay, together with the lesser cliffs between Shire Combe and Deep Slade (Pennard). The best route of this period was undoubtedly Scavenger on Three Cliffs, for many years considered a serious route, until the advent of modern protection. J.Brailsford, when climbing new routes, would solo Scavenger at the end of each day to cross check his grades.

During the years following, Jeremy Talbot developed the cliffs almost single handed, and the opening up of Gower for climbing was undoubtedly due to his endeavours. Leaving no section of the coast unexplored, he discovered and climbed literally hundreds of lines. Although it is difficult to single something out of this prodigious effort, perhaps his most noteworthy achievement was the development, with Chris Connick, of Paviland in the 1970's.

The period 1966 to 1969 saw the Swansea University Mountaineering Club (SUMC) actively exploring the peninsula, and turning their attention particularly to the more serious upper cliffs. At the forefront of this was Eryl Pardoe, who brought fresh ideas to the area. With various partners, he opened up Fall Bay Buttress, climbed Pilgrim on the back of Yellow Wall, and also added the fine V-Groove and Power Trap (albeit with aid in places). He was also responsible for the further development of the Pennard Cliffs, and his ascent of Phreatic Line with Martin Hogge is especially worthy of note.

In 1970, Talbot produced the first comprehensive guide, followed later by a supplement containing a further eighty or so routes. The guidebook considerably increased the number of visitors to the area, but development was still dominated by the locals.

The arrival of Pat Littlejohn in 1973, free-climbing the superb Yellow Wall and Transformer, heralded a new era for climbing in Gower. Littlejohn's efforts were followed by Andy Sharp with Muppet Show and then Mick Fowler with the difficult Steam Train. The Yellow Wall now boasts the longest and hardest climbs on Gower and indeed some of the best in South-East Wales.

Elsewhere, local members of the South Wales Mountaineering Club were making an impact. John Bullock and Gwyn Evans began their fine series of climbs at Pennard and Graves End and, while Talbot and Connick were toiling away at Paviland next door, rediscovered Juniper Wall in 1977, where old pegs testified to earlier exploration. First blood went to Mike Harber and John Mothersele, with the excellent Dry Riser. Bullock followed with Hitman and, later, the superb Assassin with Roy Thomas. The older pegs had been left by members of the SUMC in the late 1960's in an abortive post-party attempt on what is now the Jackal Finish. Elsewhere on the cliff it seems that Pardoe may well have led Hitman and a route following the original line of Killer's Route.

In 1981 John Harwood discovered Rhossili's potential for further development and triggered a flurry of activity, recruiting various leaders for free ascents of artificial climbs very much in the modern idiom. The best of these was undoubtedly Lawrence Francombe's ascent of Crime and Punishment with one aid point. Andy Sharp later made a free ascent along with other fine routes in the area. Tony Penning made a contribution here, particularly of unusual route names. 1981 also saw the unexpected discovery and exploration of the Conservative Club Crag by Chris Pound culminating in his ascent of the excellent and popular Out Of The Blue with Pete Saunders.

Finally, work on the 1984 guidebook produced the inevitable crop of new climbs, many surprisingly good for an area already heavily developed. Rhossili, Jacky's Tor Upper Cliff and Pennard provided most of these, all the work of the SWMC. The finest discovery was probably the intricate Secret Combination on Yellow Wall by the ubiquitous Littlejohn, with Steve Lewis. The future will no doubt produce more fine climbs; those interested might care to devote some attention to Thurba Head, which harbours one or two intriguing possibilities in this respect.

Post 1983 by J.Harwood

Almost as soon as the 1984 guidebook was published, activists swooped in to render it obsolete. Andy Sharp led the hardest route then on Gower with Skull Attack, later adding a direct start to make it even more formidable. Sharp and Harwood also added good routes to a selection of crags throughout the area, such as Cut Across Shorty, The Sandpiper, Eastern Promise and the superb Il Bel Camino. They also restarted development at Pennard with the technical Arosfa. At the same time, the crag X syndrome hit the area and after much searching of scattered outcrops the truth came out. Pwll Du Buttress had one route of 1960's vintage and to this were added three more modern ones. Unfortunately, whilst the routes are quite good they do not receive much traffic, the fate of many a crag x.

The historical section in the previous guide ended by drawing attention to possibilities at Thurba Head. Penning was the first to try the obvious smooth corner, resulting in an epic aid climbing session and a Pyrrhic victory. His second had not aid climbed nor been on anything so difficult before, and it took him weeks to recover. However, matters were put right when the old master Littlejohn paid a quick visit and turned the blank corner into Earthly Powers, and another steep line to the R into Summer Wine.

1984 saw the assault on virgin rock continue. Sharp was very much to the fore and, supported by Harwood and Pete Lewis, climbed a number of good routes. Notable were the delectable Treasure, the exhausting Madame Butterfly and the desperate Hairy Dog, which opened up the wall of the same name. On Pennard, Sharp climbed Throb, a harder companion to Arosfa, while Bald Eagle made a frontal attack on the buttress. Bullock swooped in to grab Desperate Dan, the obvious finish to Dan Dare. Meanwhile Alun Richardson and Steve Lewis added to the delights of The Conservative Club Crag with the excellent Hurricane and Cortez The Killer.

However, once again the locals were surprised by a Littlejohn raid. This time he freed Twm Shon Catti on Giants Cave to give Thriller, and then added his Masterpiece, at the time the hardest climb in the area.

New Years Day 1985 saw the usual team in action as Sharp raised standards at Paviland with The Cure. Other new routes on the cliff, such as Talons, increased its appeal for harder climbers. Attention then swung back to the west as Silent Fright and the frightening Executioners Thrill were added by Sharp at Rhossili. At Giants Cave the direct version of Thriller, Can't Buy a Thrill, produced an outstanding pitch, featuring unique leg jams for resting. At Devils Truck, in an effort to get out of a vicious winter wind, Sharp added several climbs, including the technical Saratoga and the excellent Top Of The Form, followed by three exhausting routes on Hairy Dog Wall; King swing, Hound of Hell and King of Pain. Next they rushed to Yellow Wall for a free ascent of Steam Train, just beating Littlejohn who added a variation finish. Mick Learoyd showed his face here and climbed Winter Warmer with its vicious start, a long standing boulder problem.

Suddenly more rivalry appeared on the scene in the shape of Martin Crocker, who used his finger strength to good ends on the incredible hanging arete R of Transformer to give Yellow Regeneration. He also developed a new cliff, Eyeball Wall, with Roy Thomas. Crocker then moved to Thurba Head and added Thin Ice and Thurba Pillar.

On Deborah's Overhang Sharp climbed State Of Grace and, in a new zawn, added Resisting Arrest with Pete Lewis. Sharp, as active as ever, went on to add a number of short but worthwhile routes below Paviland, Liberty being the best, and scoured Gower's cliffs adding routes to Boiler Slab and some hard wall climbs at Graves End Wall. At the same time Bullock returned to old haunts at Pennard to produce Samurai, the best E3 at Pennard, and along with other parties developed Bantam Bay and Pwll Du Quarry.

By 1986 Crocker, supported by Roy Thomas and Matt Ward, had taken over as Gower's pioneer. At Rhossili this team added a number of climbs, of which The Secret and An Audience Of Sheep were particularly notable. Thomas meanwhile used "modern methods" of new routing to beat one dismayed local to the excellent Plot 13 on Jacky's Tor. All of these efforts, however, were overshadowed by the stupendous expedition out of the back of Giants Cave. The Divine Guiding Light remains one of the hardest and wildest routes on Gower at present.

At Catacomb Gully, Crocker discovered some little gems and then added insult to injury by naming the best of them Sharp-Eyed! Sharp was not idle, contributing other short climbs to the gully and starting some controversial developments in the Three Sisters area, with Twilight World being the best and hardest. He also climbed the overhanging horror, Wide Eyed and Legless, naming it after his perspiring second.

At Pennard, Richardson squeezed a few more lines out of the cliff, King Rat being a good eliminate. At Three Cliffs, Steve Lewis, stole The Steal to produce the cliffs hardest route.

The choice of hard fingery problems at Third Sister eventually attracted Crocker, who produced Flaming Fingers and Chilean Flame Thrower before moving to Pennard and producing Five Years To Live with a controversial bolt for protection.

Another development of note at this time was Alan Price's free ascent of Sister Of Mercy.

The systematic development of Gower continued in 1989, but the pace relaxed to a gentle rhythm with two major exceptions, both due to visitors. First, Pete Oxley, fresh from his inspiration with

The Divine Guiding Light, launched himself across the roof to the right to produce Jesus Wept. The line, like its companion, is rumoured to have good holds, though that can hardly be of consolation to anyone suspended halfway along the pitch. Next, local activist Thomas introduced the ubiquitous Gary Gibson to the delights of Yellow Wall. Of course, Gary had to do a new route, and after a weekend's work produced the very steep Man Of The Earth. These climbs showed that big thuggy routes are still to be found if you know where to look!

As the guide comes to fruition, sandstone seems to have focused the talents of many, but Adrian Wilson and Ewan Kellar showed that good lines were available when they stole the traverse of Giants Cave from one irate climber to create Nick'd. As we entered the nineties normality returned with a typical fingery Sharp creation on Third Sister; World In Action. In a last minute rush, as guide was off to the printers, Rhossili provided some little gems to the partenership of Richardson and Jim Beynon, the best being Rhiannon. Although the 'Golden Age' of Gower development has probably passed, it is safe to say that many more routes are still to be discovered on the secluded small crags with which the area abounds. But for all the recent hustle and bustle and occasional controversy which has marked the eighties, Gower will remain an area of great charm and peace where it is possible for climbers of all abilities to enjoy themselves. Let's hope that ruthless men with large egos will not spoil this and that the crags will remain as relatively unspoiled as they are now, so that future generations can take pleasure in the delightful limestone and inspiring scenery.

TOR GRO AND NORTH HILL TOR O.S. ref 457938 and 453938
J.Bullock

SITUATION AND CHARACTER
A good area for climbers bored with Three Cliffs, offering mainly lower grade slab routes in an especially attractive situation. Both cliffs are on the N coast overlooking the Landimore and Llanrhidian Marshes. Unfortunately, the routes are often without the benefit of natural line. The overhanging S wall of North Hill Tor has a couple of harder routes for those with energy to spare. Neither of the crags is tidal, but the access track is underwater during spring tides.

APPROACHES AND ACCESS
See map 2. The crags are reached from Landimore on North Gower, O.S.ref 465930. Park at the end of the narrow lane where it meets the marshes.

Tor Gro
Follow the track W to reach the foot of a slab after about 7 mins. Descent is E down steep vegetation.

Central Slab   45m   VS   4b
D.Jones, R.Owen, et al 1958
Climb a shallow groove on the L until it peters out, then bear slightly R to pass some small overhangs on their R. Climb direct, keeping R of the edge of the slab.

Sycamore   45m   VS   4b
D.Jones, R.Brown et al 1958
Start below a small sycamore at 18m, 6m R of Central Slab. Climb to the tree and move L to finish up a shallow depression, a metre R of the overhangs on Central Slab.

North Hill Tor
About 15 mins walk from the start of the track. In the centre of the main slab is a grassy Y-shaped crack.

Slimline   27m   VD
D.Williams, A.Roche 1982
Start 5m L of the Y-shaped crack. Take a direct line just R of two horizontal cracks low on the slab.

Clean Cut   36m   VD
D.Jones, R.Owen 1958
Start just L of the Y-shaped crack, and climb straight up, finishing over grassy steps.

Slab And Rib   36m   VD
D.Jones, R.Owen et al 1958
Start 8m R of the Y-shaped crack, below a short crack at 6m. Gain the crack, step R and climb to a ledge below a corner. Finish up the R edge.

West Slab   36m   D   *
D.Jones, R.Owen et al 1958
Start 14m R of the Y shaped crack but L of the R edge of the main slab. Gain a hollow at 8m, then a ledge, before going L to another ledge below an overhang . Step L and climb to a large ledge at a corner. A series of steps leads to the top.

To the R of the main slab is a shorter and very smooth slab providing delicate climbing at about VS. The next routes are on the steep wall S of the Tor.

Naughty But Nice   24m   E3   5c,6a
A.Sharp, P.Lewis, J.Harwood 1982
This takes the acutely overhanging wall L of the obvious central

groove. Start at a rib just L of a blackberry bush.
1 12m Climb the rib and continue to a thread belay below the overhanging wall.
2 12m Follow a discontinuous crack L up the wall with difficulty then easy ground and the top.

Windy City 24m E2 5c,5b
A.Sharp, P.Lewis, J.Harwood 1982
G.Evans, J.Bullock Alternative start.
Start at the blackberry bush below the obvious central groove.
1 12m Surmount the overhang and continue to a belay below the groove.
2 12m Climb the steep groove.
Alternative pitch 1: 5c. More directly, gain the obvious borehole slot from the corner on the R.

CWM IVY TO BURRY HOLMS OS ref 436939 to 399926

SITUATION AND CHARACTER
See map 2. This area contains little worthwhile climbing, and few recorded climbs to date. There may be some scope for new climbs however, for the adventurous. Cwm Ivy is a substantial slab of about 18m, overlooking the Forestry Commission plantations about a quarter of a mile N of the hamlet of the same name. The hamlet itself provides the best approach to Hills Tor, and Spritsail Tor. These also provide short clean slabs, good for bouldering but not much else.
Continuing westwards, there is nothing of interest until Bluepool at the E end of the bay, S and W of Minor Point. Here, there is a series of extremely steep cliffs up to 27m , invariably damp but with good rock and some fairly obvious lines. Those tempted should note that access is possible within only 1 hour either side of low tide, at most, and the currents hereabouts are very dangerous.
Burry Holms contains the only recorded climbs in this section. It is the promontary running out W at the N end of Rhossili Bay, and is best approached via Llangennith Burrows. The causeway giving access to it is open within 2 1/2 hours either side of low tide. At the W end of Burry Holms two parallel promentories run out to sea. The N promontory boasts a cliff on its S flank, overlooking the inlet between the two. In the centre of this is an obvious corner. This is the first route.

Great Corner 15m D
Climb the corner.

West Wall 16m HS 4b
Traverse R out of the corner along a fault line to reach a crack which is followed to the top.

RHOSSILI O.S. ref 406877
A.Sharp, A.Richardson

SITUATION AND CHARACTER
Overlooking the beautiful Rhossili Bay and the Worms Head, Rhossili has been recently transformed into an area that boasts a large number of good routes. There is a good mixture of easy and hard routes, and although the sea level crags look small when the tide is in, they grow as the tide recedes. The upper crags face W, whilst the sea-level crags are mainly N facing. A large number of smaller buttresses make the area confusing on a first visit. The sea level crags provide excellent sea-level traversing.

Climbing on the Worms Head is STRICTLY FORBIDDEN. To ignore this ban could jeopardise access to many other cliffs on Gower and it should be strictly adhered to.

APPROACHES AND ACCESS
See map 2. The crags are reached in 10 mins from the car park at Rhossili village by walking W along the narrow private road past the National Trust Shop and coastguard cottages, in the direction of the Worms Head. Just before the end of the road, where the stone wall and cliff edge are closest, cut down RW. The path, obvious once one has gone over the edge, passes beneath a steep SW-facing wall on the R (Trial Wall). The sea cliffs are directly below this and are accessible for between one and three hours either side of low tide. A detailed map of the area on the following page should help you to find the crags, but on a first visit a walk along the beach is recommended.

UPPER CRAGS
These are all situated well above the sea. On your first visit they are best approached from Trial Wall.

TRIAL WALL
This is the steep wall passed on the descent to sea-level. Its easy access, recently renewed fixed gear and fine technical routes have proved popular. It can be sheltered in winter and dries relatively quickly. To the L of the main face, the seaward face has two corners separated by an undercut V-groove.

Laughing Spam Fritter   27m   VS   4b
T.Penning, P.Cresswell et al 1981
Climb the V-groove and ramp to a grass ledge, traverse RW into the cave. Scramble off to the R over some nasty ground.

Some Mothers   27m   HVS   5a
A.Sharp, J.Harwood 1981
This climbs the groove just R of Laughing Spam Fritter, joining it to finish.

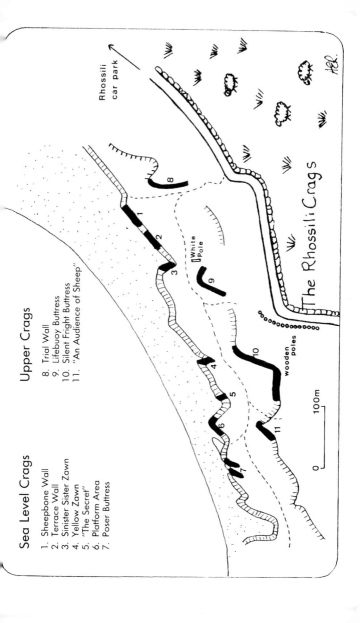

Sea Level Crags

1. Sheepbone Wall
2. Terrace Wall
3. Sinister Sister Zawn
4. Yellow Zawn
5. "The Secret"
6. Platform Area
7. Poser Buttress

Upper Crags

8. Trial Wall
9. Lifebuoy Buttress
10. Silent Fright Buttress
11. "An Audience of Sheep"

Rhossili car park

The Rhossili Crags

White Pole

wooden poles

0   100m

The Adulteress   24m   E2   5c   *
S.Padfield, D.Thomas (Worm Variation A1) 1965
FFA A.Sharp, J.Harwood 1981
Climb the crack just R of the L arete of the main face, through an
overhang, then traverse R along an obvious break and climb the
wide crack to the top.

Blackmans Pinch   24m   E4   6a/b   **
S.Padfield, D.Thomas (The Worm A1) 1965
FFA A.Sharp 1981
A popular testpiece that has recently been chipped. Start just R
of the arete. Climb a RW slanting crack to the overlap. Surmount
this, BR, and gain the break above. Finish as for The Adulteress.

Skull Attack   24m   E6   6b   *** †
A.Sharp, J.Harwood 1985 (top section only)
A.Sharp, P.Lewis 1986
A highly technical wall climb that is rumoured to have some
holds. Start left of Crime and Punishment below a BR. Climb the
thin crack to a roof and go over this to a resting ledge. Step L
and continue up the thin crack and groove to the top, 2PR's.

Crime and Punishment   23m   E4/5   6b   **
G.Hicks, S.Padfield, D.Thomas 1966 (Trial)
FFA A.Sharp, J.Harwood 1981
The first of the original artificial routes to be climbed free. Fine
sustained climbing. Start below a scoop and line of PR and BR
(some old ones) in the middle of the wall. Gain the scoop, then
follow the shallow groove to its top. Move R to a thin crack and
climb this to the overhang. Move past this and reach the top.

Black Wall   21m   E4   6c   *
J.O.Talbot, B.Talbot A2 1961
FFA A.Sharp, J.Harwood 3pts aid 1981
T.Forster, A.Sharp 1988 direct finish †
A vicious, fingery problem, especially when the direct finish is
taken. Start 3m R of Crime and Punishment at a line of rusting
BR. Make a series of difficult moves to below the bulge. Desper-
ate moves lead over the roof to the top. New BR's.

Inch Pinch   18m   E3   6b
A.Sharp, P.Lewis, J.Harwood 1984
An entertaining pitch up a short crack on the R side of the crag.
Boulder the lower wall directly to the PR's on Shake Out. Gain a
crack with difficulty and climb it. Continue more easily to the
top.

The Hant   15m   E4   6b   †
A.Sharp, P.Lewis 1987
Another recently chipped route. Follow Inch Pinch to a good

layaway hold, then move R and over the overlap with difficulty.
Follow a shallow groove and crack to the top.

Shakeout 27m E3 6a **
A.Sharp, J.Harwood 1982
A girdle of Trial Wall from R to L. Start at the R edge of the wall, at
the obvious breakline below the bulges.
1 15m Follow the breakline past 2PR to a hanging stance on
Crime and Punishment.
2 21m Move up 2m and continue LW, PR, to finish up The
Adulteress.

LIFEBUOY BUTTRESS
130m R of Trial Wall is a white pole and 30m further R is a buttress
in the upper cliff. (Below the white pole is Sinister Sister Zawn.)

The Axe 14m E1 5a
T.Penning, A.Sharp, J.Harwood 1985
Climb the LH arete.

Blockbuster 14m E1 5a
N.Williams, P.Williams 1978
The wall 3m R of The Axe. Climb from ledge to ledge parallel with
the arete finishing up a short scoop. PR's missing.

Pulpit 14m HVS 5a
N.Williams, P.Williams 1978
G.Evans, J.Bullock 1982 (finish described)
Not a route to preach about! Climb a stepped corner 9m R of
Blockbuster to a pulpit, move L and up a smooth curving crack for
a metre then L and up a wall into a scoop to the top.

Crunch 24m VS 4c
A.Tyas, J.Pratt, G.Evans 1981
6m R of Pulpit is a corner broken by a grassy ledge. Climb the
corners and the central crack in the upper buttress (escapable).

The area of rock around Lifebuoy Buttress sports some good
boulder problems and short pitches which are best left to the
individual's sense of adventure.

SILENT FRIGHT BUTTRESS
This is located 150m SW along the headland from Lifebuoy Buttress. It has an impressive arete on the L, a lower square-cut
subsidiary buttress in the centre and a prominent overhanging
arete to its R.

Silent Fright 24m E4 5c/6a * †
A.Sharp, P.Lewis 1985
Climb the impressive arete on the LH side of the wall, 2 NR, 1PR,
exit LW with excitement to finish.

Summertime Blues   15m   HVS   5a   †
P.Lewis, A.Sharp 1985
Climb the crack directly up the short steep wall on the R side of the buttress.

Playground Twist   15m   E2   5c   * †
A.Sharp, P.Lewis 1985
The crack just R of Summertime Blues is climbed with interest.

Executioner's Thrill   15m   E4   6b   * †
A.Sharp, P.Lewis 1985
A good testpiece up the technical and bold arete R of Playground Twist.

The following two routes climb the wall 12m R of Executioner's Thrill.

The Mad Mad Mad Lundy Axeman   12m   E3   5c   †
M.Crocker 1988
A poorly protected line. Start from a ledge at 2m, 5m L of two faint parallel cracks in a black slabby wall and follow the tricky slab above, with an awkward move to finish.

Lundy Tilting   15m   E2   5c   †
M.Crocker 1988
Climb the LH of two cracks 5m R of the above route. Gain a ledge at 3m and follow the crack and arete to the top.

Further R, at the R end of Silent Fright Buttress, is a short, over-hanging, knife edge arete.

An Audience of Sheep   15m   E5   6b   †
M.Crocker, M.Ward 1987
Idiosyncratic but wild! Gain a ledge down and L of the stunning arete and then cross RW onto a projecting ledge, TR. Hard moves up the arete, PR, to a jug, BR, lead to amazing moves and a long reach for a jug at the apex, SB.

60m further along is a short slabby wall, recognised by a square-cut window-type notch at the top of the slab.

Wages of Sin   12m   E4   6a
A.Sharp, P.Lewis 1988
A good pitch following the slight groove up the L side of the slab. Good F2 and wires at the top.

SEA-LEVEL CRAGS
The easiest way to find the sea-level crags on a first visit is to walk along the beach. There are stakes in place at the top of some sea-level crags.

SHEEPBONE WALL
This is the sea-level cliff below Trial Wall. Follow the path down to

an area of ledges about 12m above the sea. Immediately beyond the first rocky steps leading down to these, at the first clear ledges, is the top of a chimney-corner (Chimney Crack). At the foot of and a little R of this (facing out) an oval pool is visible. Abseil or walk RW and scramble down and then L to the foot of Chimney Crack. The routes are accessible for 2 hours either side of low tide.

To the L is a steep wall, bounded on the L by a shallow groove in the upper part of the cliff.

First Diedre 10m D
J.O.Talbot 1968
Start below the shallow groove at 8m, bounded on its R by a steep wall. Climb the wall and groove to the top.
The next routes are on the wall to the R.

Mauk Wall 10m S 4a
J.O.Talbot 1968
Climb the L edge of the steep wall, passing a projecting block.

Curving Crack 10m HS 4b
J.O.Talbot 1968
Climb the RW slanting crack just R of Mauk Wall.

Chimney Crack 10 VD   *
J.O.Talbot 1968
This takes the obvious corner and chimney crack R of Curving Crack.

Skull 13m HS 4b
J.O.Talbot 1968
Climb the area of rock between Chimney Crack and Great Diedre.

Great Diedre 12m S 4a   *
J.O.Talbot 1968
This climbs the obvious black corner 9m R of Chimney Crack.

Yellow Edge12m VD
J.O.Talbot 1968
Start just R of Great Diedre. Climb the R wall of the arete until a LW traverse to it can be made. Follow it to the top.

Great Diedre II 15m VS 4c
C.Hird, G.Evans, G.Richardson 1975
Climb the corner 5m R of Yellow Edge, with a tricky overhang at 8m.

Pistas Canute   15m   VS   4b   * †
A.Beaton, C.Allen, M.Danford 1989
Climb Slanting Chimney for 3m, move L into a vertical crack and traverse L across the overhanging wall. Step round an arete and up the centre of the wall.

Slanting Chimney   14m   VD
M.Harber
Ascend the slanting crack R of Great Diedre II.

Rhiannon's Route   17m   HVS   5a   †
A.Richardson, J.Beynon 1992
By hook or by crook I'll be last in the book! The arete R of Great Diedre II. Climb direct through the initial overhang, then follow the R side of the arete to the top.

Recess Crack   17m   VS   4c
J.O.Talbot 1968
Climb the square cut recess 6m R of Great Diedre II and then the crack splitting its back.

Barnacle Ramp   17m   D
J.Beynon solo 1992
The RW-rising crack and ramp to the R of Recess Crack.

Gambolling Gareth's Arete   17m   E1   5b   * †
A.Richardson, R.Lloyd, J.Beynon 1992
Start 7m R of Recess Crack, 3m R of a cave. Climb to the R side of the overhang and traverse to an exposed position at the base of the hanging arete. Climb the arete to the top.

TERRACE WALL
40m SW along the path from Trial Wall or along the beach is an obvious terrace just above sea level, bounded on its R by a deep inlet and R again by a pocketed slab leading to a steep corner.

Deception   23m   S
J.Talbot 1968
Follow the pocketed slab to finish up the steep corner.

Deceit   21m   S
M.Harber 1982
The groove immediately R is gained via the R side of the pocketed slab.

SINISTER SISTER ZAWN
40m further along the beach towards the Worms Head and below the white pole marking Lifebuoy Buttress, is a narrow zawn with a large jammed boulder at its back. Descent is by scrambling down its sides.

Sinister Sister 21m E4 5c †
A.Sharp, P.Lewis 1988
Follow the arete 5m R of the jammed boulder to the break, arrange protection and continue up the arete and groove, TR,

Wiggly Woo 21m HS 4b †
J.Beynon, R.Lloyd, A.Richardson 1992
Climb the gully and obvious narrow pillar R of Sinister Sister. Some loose rock.

60 m further towards The Worms Head is a yellow wall with a distinctive calcite patch. There are a number of PR's but no information on routes is available.

YELLOW ZAWN
80m along the upper cliff path from the white pole or along the beach from Sinister Sister Zawn, is a deep zawn with a cave at its back and a boulder-strewn floor. It contains a 20m high, N-facing wall flecked with calcite, and a yellowish arete. Descent from the upper crags is by an easy scramble.

Turning Japanese 18m E5 6a *
M.Crocker, M.Ward 1987
Start at a large boulder. Climb a finger crack to a horizontal break then traverse R to a good slot on the yellow arete. Climb its L side.

Banzai 15m E4 6a
M.Crocker, M.Ward 1987
A fine steep little route. Climb the arete easily to a sloping ledge at the base of a slender pillar R of the arete. Make hard moves up a thin crack into a groove. Finish up a black wall RW.

60m R of Yellow Zawn and below An Audience Of Sheep are three pillars as you look out to sea. The following route climbs the sheer SW wall on the middle pillar.

The Secret 17m E5 6b ** †
M.Crocker, M.Ward 1987
A direct line up the centre of the smooth wall. Abseil to a good ledge at 3m or scramble in at low tide. Climb LW then back R on white crystal rock, passing a PR with difficulty, to the horizontal break. Continue up the centre of the wall, NR, to finish.

PLATFORM AREA
The following routes are situated on the wall NE of a sea-level platform (frequented by fishermen) overlooked by the stunning arete of An Audience Of Sheep.

Stardust 24m HS 4a **
A.Sharp, J.Harwood 1981
This climbs the wall NE of the platform directly below the arete of

An Audience of Sheep. Abseil or traverse in to gain an overhang 5m R of an arete. Climb to and over the overhang then move up and L to reach a crack near the L edge. Follow this to the top.

Year of The Snail   24m   VS   4b
M.Ward 1987
Start as for Stardust. Continue up the centre of the wall, to the R of Stardust to a small shelf and then a larger ledge. Walk R to block belay.

POSER BUTTRESS
30m W of the sea-level platform, is a deep square-cut zawn with a smooth W-facing wall containing four thin cracks. Approach by abseil to a hanging stance or by descending to a ledge on the LH side of the wall, then down a shallow chimney to a horizontal break that is traversed to a hanging stance. It is possible to start these climbs from lower down when the tide is suitable, but then they are technically harder.

Normal Service   20m   VS   4b
A.Sharp, J.Harwood 1981
The LH crack.

Splash Landing   20m   HVS   5a   *
A.Sharp, J.Harwood 1981
The next crack RW.

Dicky Five Stones   20m   E4   5c   * †
A.Sharp, P.Lewis 1990
A lovely pitch. Start at a ring bolt at sea level! Climb a thin crack to a good break. Thin moves get you established on the wall, continue directly.

The Poser   20m   E1   5b/c   *
T.Penning, A.Sharp, J.Harwood 1981
The third crack RW.

Burning Rubber   20m   E2   5b   *
T.Penning, A.Sharp, J.Harwood 1981
The fourth crack RW.

The following climbs are on the opposite side of the gully.

Chlorophyll Corner   15m   VS   4c
T.Penning, A.Sharp, D.Hillier 1981
Climb a corner crack opposite Burning Rubber, near the back of the gully.

Lobster Song   15m   E2   5b
L.Davies (roped solo) 1988
The arete R of Chlorophyll Corner.

Cincinatti Kid   15m   VS   4c
T.Penning, D.Hillier, A.Sharp 1981
A pleasant climb taking the crack just round the arete to the R of
Chlorophyll Corner, in a narrow wall facing out of the gully.

FALL BAY TO THURBA HEAD OS ref 414874 to 421868
A.Richardson, A.Sharp

SITUATION AND CHARACTER
A beautiful and popular area providing the greatest concentration
of the best routes on Gower and some of its most spectacular. It is
possibly the best area for a first visit to Gower. The area lies
between Fall Bay in the W and Thurba head in the E. It contains a
variety of gullies and buttresses with climbing of all grades; some
are tidal but many are not. At low tide it is possible to walk below
the cliffs, and all beach level routes are accessible for one or two
hours either side of low tide.

APPROACHES AND ACCESS
See Map 2. There are two possible approaches depending on
which end of the area one wishes to visit:
1   For Fall Bay on the W side: From Rhossili, walk to the bottom
(W) end of the large car park (OS ref 415881), turn L (S) through a
gate just L (S) of a public toilet. Continue S across two fields to a
track which leads to a lane, turn R into the lane and take the first
opening on the L. Follow a track with a hedge on the L and at its
end turn R into another field. Walk a short distance with a hedge
on the R, cross a stile and turn L. Follow the edge of the field
round to a caravan, cross the stile and descend an iron ladder on
the R. Fall Bay can be seen below.
Further down the slope a path leads L under the W-facing Fall Bay
Buttress. This path traverses round to the Great Terrace directly
above King Wall (10 to 15 mins from the car park).
If the path is followed into Fall Bay there are a number of short
climbs on good rock in the bay below Fall Bay Buttress.
2   For Mewslade Bay on the E side: From Pitton turn L (S) at an
easily missed crossroads to park after 71m in the field on the L at
Pitton Farm (Honesty box. OS ref 427877). Walk a short distance
down a farm track then bear R past farm buildings to gain the path
leading through a narrow valley to the E end of Mewslade Bay (7
mins walk).

There is a detailed map of the area on the following page which
should aid you in finding the crags.

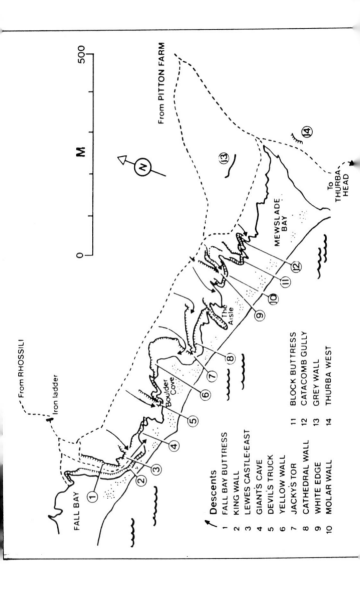

Descents

1 FALL BAY BUTTRESS
2 KING WALL
3 LEWES CASTLE-EAST
4 GIANT'S CAVE
5 DEVIL'S TRUCK
6 YELLOW WALL
7 JACKY'S TOR
8 CATHEDRAL WALL
9 WHITE EDGE
10 MOLAR WALL
11 BLOCK BUTTRESS
12 CATACOMB GULLY
13 GREY WALL
14 THURBA WEST

From RHOSSILI

Iron ladder

FALL BAY

Boulder Cove

The Aisle

MEWSLADE BAY

From PITTON FARM

To THURBA HEAD

N

M

0   500

Fall Bay Buttress (Lewes Castle West)
This is the upper buttress overlooking Fall Bay and is justifiably popular. It provides excellent climbing, mostly at the VS and HVS grades. It is non-tidal and the approach is via the path leading to the Great Terrace (see approach 1). The W face contains most of the routes and is characterised by a series of grooves capped by overhangs. Descent is either L to regain the path or over Lewes Castle East and R to the E end of the Great Terrace. Towards the RH end is a prominent L-slanting groove leading up to the overhangs at their widest point (Osiris). Further L is a prominent vertical corner crack (Isis).

Ket   36m   HVS   5a
E.Pardoe, R.Leigh 1967
Start below a short corner directly above two holes half way along the cliff path. Climb the corner and then a shallow corner slightly L to a cave at two-thirds height. Finish up a broken groove on the L.

Seket   36m   HVS   5b
E.Pardoe, A.March 1968
P.Christie, R.Evans, G.Morris direct finish 1986
Start 3m R of Ket at the foot of a groove below a small triangular overhang at half-height, 4m L of the corner crack of Isis. Climb a groove and slab to an overhang, over this and climb a crack in the wall to the R. Follow broken grooves directly to the top.
Direct Finish 5a: From the corner crack finish directly.

Reptiles and Samurai   36m   E4   6a   **
M.Crocker, M.Ward 1987
A direct line with some committing moves. Start just L of Isis. Climb straight up a white wall and pull over a bulge to a short groove. From the sloping shelf above, pull up direct, PR, to a jug, PR, on the R, and then over the roof, PR. Continue up the short groove to a break. Move L and finish up the broken groove above.

Isis   36m   VS   4c   ***
R.Griffith, E.Pardoe 1966
A classic, high in the grade. Start below the obvious corner crack in the centre of the cliff. Climb a steep wall to gain the main corner crack, which is followed to the main overhangs. Traverse RW to a cave (belay possible), move R and climb the overhang at its narrowest point, then trend L to the top.
Variation start: HVS 5a. R of Isis are two diverging cracks. Follow the L one to a bulge, then traverse L to the corner crack on Isis.

Horus   36m   HVS   5a
P.Hinder, J.Talbot 1975
Start just R of Isis below two diverging cracks. Climb the RH one,

PR, to below a bulge. Step L to a small pinnacle and climb to a break, cross the overhang as for Isis and finish direct.

Rhea   36m   HVS   5a   **
R.Leigh, T.Smith 1967
Start below a short dark slab, 5m R of Isis, with a RW slanting groove/crack above. Climb to a recess and then the groove, PR. Move R onto a rib, follow this and the adjacent groove to a break. Pull through the overhang at the V-groove just L of its widest point.

Lazy Sunday Afternoon   36m   E1/2   5b   * †
G.Evans, J.Bullock 1989
G.Lewis, S.Mundy (the final roof)
Start at the foot of a little steep wall midway between the starts of Rhea and Osiris, beneath the widest part of the overhangs above. Climb the wall and the rib above to belay on Osiris. Continue over the roof at its widest point, TR, PR, and steeply up the wall above.

Osiris   36m   VS   4c   ***
E.Pardoe, R.Griffiths 1966
A fantastic route. Start at the prominent L-slanting groove system towards the RH end of the face. Follow the groove to the overhangs at their widest point (belay possible). Traverse R to pull over the overhang at its weakest point and the top.

Seth   36m   E1   5b   **
J.Talbot the lower crack c1970
A much failed-on route. Climb the lower groove of Osiris for 5m then a steep crack in the R wall to a break (possible belay). Finish as for Osiris.
Variation finish: move L to finish up Lazy Sunday Afternoon E2 5b

Horsis   36m   HVS   5a   *
E.Pardoe, R.Griffiths 1968
Climb the lower part of Osiris' groove then move R to another groove. Follow this past a large block to the overhangs. Finish up the easy groove just R of the overhangs.

Ra   36m   HVS   5a   †
G.Evans, P.Christie 1988
Old bolt holes suggest J.Talbot may have been this way. Start to the R of the grooves of Osiris. Climb the wall to a groove/corner high on the face and swing L onto a rib near the top.

Fall Bay Girdle   85m   VS/HVS   5a,4c,4b   **
R.Griffiths, M.Hogge 1967
An excellent traverse line under the roofs. The first pitch can be avoided by scrambling in from the L. This makes the route VS.

1   24m Climb Ket to the break.
2   31m Traverse R via some awkward moves to gain the arete L of Isis, cross its groove and belay in the cave where Isis crosses the overhang.
3   30m Traverse R until clear of the overhangs then easily to the top.

The lines R of Ra are extremely loose and not described. The front of Fall Bay Buttress is taken by Fallout.

Fallout   36m   VS   4b   O
SUMC 1967
Start at the lowest point of the buttress and climb directly to the top.

South East Diedre   36m   HVS   5a
J.Talbot, P.Hinder 1972
Start R of the base of the buttress below an obvious SE facing corner. Climb the corner until a bulge forces a move LW onto a pinnacle. Go directly to, and climb the final overhung corner, poor PR's in the R wall, to the top.

Continuity Corner   36m   HVS   5a
J.Talbot 1973
This climbs the area of rock R of South East Diedre and is probably best gained from that route.

Lewes Castle East

To the E and separated from Fall Bay Buttress by a gully is another large buttress overlooking the Great Terrace. It has a cave at half-height and an obvious wide crack up on the R. The first route takes the wall R of the gully.

Gethsemane   31m   S   4a
SWMC 1966
Start below the R wall of the gully at a short wall with an open groove above. Tiptoe RW across the wall to gain a ledge at the foot of the groove, follow it to a large ledge and move out R onto a rib which is followed to the top.

Eden   31m   VS   4c
J.Talbot 1971
Start down and R of Gethsemane at two grooves. Climb the LH one to below a triangular overhang, hand traverse L and finish up the rib above the overhang.

The Bottle   31m   VS   4b
J.Talbot, P.Hinder 1974
Start below the cave. Climb a crack and easy groove to the cave, move out L onto a pedestal and follow the steep crack above to the top.

Direct Start: HVS 4b. Gain the steep crack directly via an obvious groove/corner at HVS 5b.

Cave Cracks   31m   E2   4b,5c
P.Littlejohn, A.Davies 1980
1   12m As for The Bottle to the cave.
2   18m Climb to the roof, step R then back L across the lip to gain poor jams. Finish steeply up the obvious crack to the top.

Age Before Beauty   31m   E1   5a   †
G.Evans, P.Christie 1988
This takes the wall between The Bottle and S.W.Diedre. Start at a small cave 3m R of the start of The Bottle. Climb flakes RW and move L into a shallow groove. Follow this and a shallow chimney to a ledge. Finish up the wide crack, avoiding easier ground to the L.

South West Diedre   33m   HVS   5a   **
SUMC 1967
J.Kerry, C.Ryan 1968 (Variation Finish)
A fine route. Start 5m R of The Bottle. Climb a corner and groove to a ledge, step back L and up to a small overhang at three-quarters height. Go over this and finish up the steep crack above. Variation finish: from the ledge below the overhang follow the corner crack to the R instead of. This makes the route VS 4c.

Instigator   33m   HVS   5a
J.Kerry, M.Hogge 1969
Start at a vertical crack 3m R of S.W.Diedre. Climb the crack to a definite widening, bridge up and then climb a groove by its R wall to the recess below the corner crack. Step onto the rib or, better, follow a diagonal line across the upper smooth wall.

Combination   45m   VS   4b
J.Talbot,P.Hinder 1973
Start just L of the front of the buttress. Climb a blocky groove to below the upper wall, hand traverse the curving crack below the upper wall LW and continue round the arete to a recess below a corner crack. Finish up this.

South East Pillar   36m   HVS   4c   †
C.Bonnington, J.Cleare 1964
Follow Combination to below the upper wall, then follow the R side of the headwall. A rockfall many years ago has removed the first ascentionist's line.

Rhydd   36m   HVS   4c
E.Pardoe, R.Griffiths 1968
Start just R of the pillar E of Combination. Climb the corner crack in its entirety past an obvious hole near the top.

Rash Prediction 36m E1 5b †
C.Ryan, P.Greenwood 1970
Takes a direct line up to the small open corner at two thirds
height, 3m R of Rhydd. Care is needed at the top due to loose
rock. Start below the corner and move up to a small bulge. Climb
over this and up to the corner. Continue above until the nature of
the rock demands moving RW near the top.

Twighlight 36m E1 5a O
J.Talbot, P.Hinder 1972
Start 3m to the R. Follow grooves and corners direct to the top.
 R of the last climb the crag becomes very broken. However at the
far R, the upper portion of the cliff becomes more solid and
provides a small buttress giving one further climb.

Till Rock Doth Us Part 12m E3 5c †
E.Kellar, A.Wilson 1990
This takes a central line up the impending white wall between two
areas of yellow lichen. Climb directly up the steep wall until a
good hold on the R can be gained. Finish directly.

Gerontology 58m VS 4b,4b,4b
A.Beaton, M.Danford, G.Richardson 1986
A R to L girdle. Start as for Combination.
1 28m Follow Combination to the recess below the upper wall.
Traverse L along the horizontal crack to belay below the wide
corner crack.
2 15m Step down LW into a groove (S.W.Diedre) then traverse L
to the cave of The Bottle.
3 15m Move L to a pedestal step down and continue traversing
across two grooves to ledges on Gethsemane. Finish up this.

KING WALL
This is the tier below The Great Terrace. It provides a number of
good lower grade routes. Access is for two and a half hours either
side of low water. Descent when the beach is exposed is easiest
by following the Great Terrace RW (EW) into Giants Cave.
Because the first 6m of the wall are easy it is possible to traverse
or abseil into many of the routes. For route identification find
Great Cleft in the middle of the wall. Most routes are related to it.
* Many of the routes here were affected by heavy storms in 1990,
so beware!

Llethrid 26m HS 4a
J.Talbot 1963
A vague route L of Frigg. Climb directly to an indefinite corner
trending RW, move R below it to a scoop then up L to the top.

Frigg 26m VS 4b
J.Talbot, D.Lewis 1963

At the L end of the wall at its highest point, 23m L of Great Cleft, is a shallow blackened groove leading towards the L end of the Great Terrace. Climb the groove trending L near the top where it peters out.

Bolder   26m   VS   4b   * †
J.Harwood, G.Evans 1988
A nice pitch up the slabby wall between Frigg and Beowulf.

Beowulf   29m   VS   4b
J.Talbot, D.Lewis 1963
Climb a groove running RW to a small overhang at three-quarters height that has a light brown stain below it. Traverse L above the overhang to a small pitted slab which is followed via an overhang to the top.

Ragnarok   29m   S   4a   **
J.Talbot, D.Lewis 1963
As for Beowulf but follow the groove to the top.

Trying Lines   29m   VS   4c
G.Evans, J.Harwood 1988
Directly up the wall L of Sweyn.

Sweyn   29m   HS   4b
J.Talbot, D.Lewis 1963
Follow thin white calcite streaks on the broken wall R of Ragnarok, then directly up the wall to the top.

Gefion   29m   HS   4b
J.Talbot, D.Lewis 1963
Start L of the obvious corner recess 12m L of the Great Cleft and 5m above sand. Climb to a small ledge, move up L and back R, finish direct.

The wall is now lower, leading to subsidiary ledges below the Great Terrace.

King Route   21m   VD
D.Jones, J.Talbot 1959
Start immediately R of a corner recess, 9m L of Great Cleft. Climb the wall and indefinite stepped groove slightly RW to the top.

Freya   21m   HS   4a   *
J.Talbot 1964
Climb a shallow groove between the corner recess and Great Cleft.

Valkyrie   21m   VS   5a
J.Talbot 1964
Start 6m L of Great Cleft. Climb to and up a very shallow groove keeping L of a small overhanging block at the top.

Vik 21m HS 4b
J.Talbot 1963
Just L of Great Cleft. Climb the wall and move R into a groove.
Finish up the wall above bearing L.

Great Cleft 21m D
J.Talbot, D.Jones 1959
The obvious broken crack and groove L of a smooth recessed
slab. Climb the wall to gain the crack at half-height. A useful
descent route.

To the R of Great Cleft is a smooth recessed slab.

Vanir 21m VS 4c
J.Talbot 1964
Start below the L side of the slab. Climb up to a scoop and a tiny
calcite knob in a hole. Move up to a shallow groove on the L to
finish.

Balder 21m VS 5a
J.Talbot 1963
Start below the centre of the slab, L of a thin crack line. Climb up
LW to gain a tiny ledge, move R and go up the slab to the top.

Tyr 21m S 4a
J.Talbot 1963
Follow Fafnir until it is possible to move L onto the recessed slab.

Fafnir 21m S 4a   **
J.Talbot 1963
A popular climb that has been affected by rockfall. Climb the
corner at the R side of the recessed slab.

Amble 21m VD
J.Talbot 1961
Climb the pitted wall R of Fafnir via the central crack.

Vorder 21m S 4a
J.Talbot 1963
Climb the arete at the R side of the pitted wall.

Thor 21m S 4a
J.Talbot 1963
Start in the square-cut recess of Odin and climb the crack in the
steep wall on the L.

Odin 21m VS 4b
J.Talbot 1963
A skinny man's route. Climb the obvious chimney/cave, inside if
possible,(it's harder on the outside), then the crack above.

Valhalla   21m   HVS   4c
J.Talbot 1964
Boulder the wall to a ledge and then climb the crack between
Odin and Needle Crack.

Needle Crack   21m   VS   4b   **
J.Talbot 1963
Climb the steep corner R of Odin to easier rock, then pleasantly
up to the final steep section.

Several variations have been climbed in the area of cracks and
slabby walls R of Needle Crack, all by J.Talbot. The following is
the best.

Nimbus   24m   VD
J.Talbot 1963
Start just R of the arete of the corner of Needle Crack. Make an
awkward move to gain the slab just R of the arete and take a
diagonal line up R to a ledge, continue directly to the top.

King Wall Girdle   VS   4c
A R to L girdle. The exact line is not known but it can be girdled
anywhere.

GIANT'S CAVE
This is the enormous square cut cave E of Lewes Castle East. It
contains a high concentration of Gower's harder testpieces, along
with some of its most spectacular. A visit is mandatory just to look
at the routes disappearing through the hole in its roof. Climbs are
accessible for about 2 hours either side of low tide. Minor buttresses flank the cave on either side. L (W) of the cave is a LW
rising ramp with a rockfall. The corner just R of this is taken by
Flake Corner.

Flake Corner   9m   VD   O
J.Talbot 1963
The obvious corner, loose.

Slight   9m   HVS   4c
J.Talbot, D.Lewis 1963
The first shallow corner with a thin crack. Fingery.

Red Admiral   13m   E3   6a
A.Sharp, P.Lewis 1984
Bold climbing on good rock. Climb the arete L of Errant

Errant   13m   E2   5c   *
J.Talbot, B.Talbot aid 1965
A good technical pitch up the clean cut-corner just L of the cave.
Climb the corner to a ledge and belays.

Masterpiece   31m   E6   6b   ***
P.Littlejohn, M.Campbell 1984
A stunning route up the L arete of the cave. Start below the arete.
Climb thin cracks on the arete proper and use painful pockets to
gain proper holds on the break. Follow the groove of Thriller to
the top, lie down and admire the view.

Thriller   31m   E4   6a   **
J.Talbot, B.Talbot 1966 (Twm-Schon-Catti A1)
FFA P.Littlejohn, C.Hurley 1984
An excellent adventure up the L side of the cave. Start at the wide
crack on the LH wall of the cave that leads to the roof. Climb the
crack to the cave roof, traverse strenuously L to gain a hanging
groove and follow this to the top.

Can't Buy A Thrill   31m   E5   6b   ** †
A.Sharp, P.Lewis 1986
A strenuous exposed pitch requiring good footwork. As for Thriller to the roof then launch out along the roof, TR, on buckets and
jams, pull over the lip and finish RW.

The Divine Guiding Light   36m   E7   6b   *** †
M.Crocker, M.Ward 1987
A bat-like escapade. Wild !! One of the most extraordinary and
daunting experiences on South East Wales sea-cliffs. The blowhole in the roof of the cave is gained via the leaning wall and 6m
ceiling. Follow thin cracks 5m R of Thriller and an overhanging
flake, NR, PR, to the horizontal break, TR. Pull up the crack to the
roof, cross it on superb jams and the occasional overhead heel
hook, NR, TR, to a chimney - rest! Squirm across L into the
blowhole and follow the light.

Jesus Wept   E6   6b   *** †
P.Oxley 1989
A line has been climbed starting at the RH side of the back of the
cave and moving RW via some wild climbing to reach the blow
hole. Various insitu gear. Details were not available.

Charlie Don't Surf   18m   E4   6a   *
A.Sharp, O.Jones 1986
Low in the grade. Start below the hanging corner on the RH side
of the cave. A boulder problem start leads to a corner and a steep
exit LW.

Madame Butterfly   18m   E5   6b   *
J.Talbot, R.Corbett 1962 Tablette A2
FFA A.Sharp, P.Lewis 1987
A good strenuous pitch. Some of the in-situ gear needs replacing.
Climb an awkward narrow crack that widens to a large fissure.

Climb the overhanging wall direct to a block overhang. Climb this at its centre and take the steep wall above.

Giants Cave Traverse   A3/4   *
E.Pardoe, M.Hogge, F.Roberts 1968
As for Madame Butterfly to the cave roof. Traverse the underside of the lip and finish as for Can't Buy A Thrill or continue as far as Errant .

Nick'd   30m   E2   5b   * †
A Wilson, E Kellar 1990
A good, airy climb traversing R to L across the lip of the Giant's Cave. Start on the obvious ledges above the corner on the R side of the cave lip. Climb down to the lip where easy climbing LW leads to a blank looking section. Cross this and step down to a large foothold, continue LW past Thriller's final groove to belay at the top of Errant.

The buttress to the R of the cave has been developed with many routes by J.Talbot. The best is described below.

Shannara   15m   HS   4a
P.Hornsby, S.Hornsby 1978
Start below and R of the arete. Climb steeply L to reach a short undercut groove in the arete and continue to the top via the L edge.

DEVIL'S TRUCK
This is the headland E of Giants Cave, with a SW-facing wall at its seaward end rising from a large sloping platform above the beach, and a SE-facing wall round to the R. It provides a number of steep popular routes. The climbs on the SW face are non tidal and the climbs on the SE face are accessible for 2 1/2 hours either side of low tide. Descent is by scrambling down to the L(W).

SW FACE

Legge   9m   S   4a
J.Talbot 1963
Climb the lower wall of The Nose then move L to a small ledge. Move L again and climb the short overhanging wall.

The Nose   15m   HS   4a   *
J.Talbot 1963
Climb the first groove on the L side of the SW face, to a narrow terrace.

Nervus   15m   VS   4c
J.Talbot 1963

Climb the narrow recessed wall just R of The Nose, over an overhang with a red mark below it, then move R to join Transit.

Transit   15m   HS   4b
J.Talbot 1963
Climb the narrow wall to below the overhanging nose. Traverse R and attain the deep cut central diedre. Climb this using the R wall to the narrow terrace.

Aschen   15m   HVS   4c   *
J.Talbot 1963
A steep route in the upper part of the wall. Start in line with the central groove below an overhang at half-height. Climb up to the overhang, move L into the groove and follow it to the top.

Gull Corner   15m   VS   4b
J.Talbot 1963
This takes the crack in the upper part of the SW wall towards its R side. Climb a wall into the crack, which is followed to the top.

White Lime   15m   D
J.Talbot 1963
Start below the crack of Gull Corner. Climb RW and up a slab, just L of the arete of the buttress. Bear L to finish up the crest. It can be combined with The Razor.

The Razor   19m   D   O
SUMC 1968
The arete/ridge above the previous route.

SE FACE

Strogelen   15m   VS   4c
J.Talbot, B.Talbot
This takes the obvious groove at the L side of the SE face, 4m R of the arete on the front of the buttress.

Countdown   15m   HVS   5a
R.Corbett, J.Talbot 1964
Hard for the grade. Climb the short overhang-capped groove just R of Strogelen, step R and finish directly above the overhang.

Endeavour   15m   HVS   4c   *
R.Corbett, J.Talbot 1962
Climb the deep chimney 7m R of Strogelen.

R of Endeavour, at sea-level, a narrow cleft leads to the back of High Chimney Gully.

High Chimney   31m   S
G.Evans, A.Tyas 1983
Climb the narrow chimney in the back LH corner of the gully.

Old Nic   21m   E4   6a   * †
A.Sharp, P.Lewis, J.Harwood 1985
Start 3m R of High Chimney. Climb cracks to a small innocuous looking roof, which can sometimes be climbed to finish up the groove above.

Top Of The Form   21m   E4   6a   * †
A.Sharp, P.Lewis, J.Harwood 1985
Start 4m R of Old Nic below an overhanging groove. Climb the groove and at the roof move out L to continue up the groove.

Saratoga   18m   E4   6b   †
A.Sharp, P.Lewis 1985
Stroll up thin cracks on the L side of the E wall until all hope of progress finishes. Continue for 4m without any holds to the top.

Tom Cat   15m   E3   5c
A.Sharp, P.Lewis 1985
A pleasant pitch, climbing the slim groove 5m R of Saratoga.

SOUTH CRACKED PILLAR
This is the broken S-facing buttress just R of High Chimney Gully. It contains a number of routes too short to warrant recording in a guide but that provide pleasant bouldering with good landings.

HAIRY DOG WALL
Just R of South Cracked Pillar is an acutely overhanging wall with a cave at its R end. This is Hairy Dog Wall. An obvious RW-slanting groove breaks this wall near its R side. The first route takes the deep crack on the L side of the wall. Taped hands or skin like a rhino's bum are advisable on the harder routes and a month of extensive body building would probably help.

Castor   18m   VS   4c
J.Talbot, B.Talbot 1965
Climb the wide crack to an overhang and take this by the crack on the R. Exit RW.

Pollux   18m   S   4a
J.Talbot, B.Talbot 1965
The overhanging crack just R of Castor.

King Of Pain   15m   E6   6b   †
A.Sharp, P.Lewis 1985
A painful pitch up the thin cracks 4m L of Hairy Dog . Climb up

the wall, passing a pocket at 3m, to reach better holds. Move R and finish up the desperate crack.

Hairy Dog   33m   E5   6a,4a   ** †
A.Sharp, J.Harwood 1984
A Rotweiller of a route. Start at a crack with an obvious jammed block at 3m.
1   12m Climb onto the block and continue up the L-slanting crack to large ledges. Now lick your wounds.
2   21m Continue easily to the top.

King Swing   18m   E5   6b   **
A.Sharp, P.Lewis 1985
Another pumper. As for Hairy Dog to the block, move into the R crack and try to climb it and the wall above.

Hound Of Hell   15m   E5   6b   ** †
A.Sharp, P.Lewis 1985
Get in the gym for this one or pray for a rise in the sand. Climb the steep crack in the centre of the wall R of King Swing.

Sense Of Doubt   36m   E3   6a   *
J.Talbot, R.Corbett (Great Cave Corner)1962
FFA A.Sharp 1978
Start below the slanting groove, at the foot of the overhanging wall. The difficulty of this pitch depends on the level of the sand. Gain the groove and follow it to its end. Finish up the loose wall on the L.

Without A Doubt   35m   E5   6c
A.Sharp, P.Lewis 1987
The groove 3m R of Great Cave Corner. A boulder problem start leads to good holds at 4m (these can be lassoed). Follow these holds to a break, traverse L and finish up King Swing.

GREAT BOULDER COVE
This is the very impressive boulder-filled cove to the R of Hairy Dog Wall. It contains Gower's showpiece, Yellow Wall. If steep, spectacular and adventurous routes are your game then this is the place for you. During the breeding season it can be a spectacular arena for watching the birds, especially if a Peregrine arrives on the scene. Access is easy at low tide, from E or W, along the beach. It is also possible to scramble down rocks overlooking the cove on its R (E), (this is Jacky's Tor) or from the top of Yellow Wall by scrambling down L(W), but this is a little harder. It is possible to gain access to the landward routes on Yellow Wall at some high tides.
There are two main walls: Yellow Wall and Eyeball Wall

YELLOW WALL
This is the E-facing wall. It is very steep, seamed with grooves and overhangs, and contains some of Gower's finest routes, rivalling the best in Britain. In the winter it is a sun trap but from 1st March to 14th August it is a breeding ground for sea birds and there is a ban on climbing between these dates.
For the first 4 routes it may be advisable to leave a rope in place from the top of the cliff to make the long, muddy slope finish bearable.

5 Minutes To Kill   24m   E3   6a   (R)
A.Sharp, R.Powles 1987
A vague line up the grooves L of Winter Warmer. Climb up and LW to a good ledge, step R and climb the arete and wall to gain a sloping ramp. Climb the R wall past a large flake then follow poor rock to the top.

Winter Warmer   24m   E3   6a   (R)
M.Learoyd, R.Thomas 1985
An enjoyable route with a vicious start taking the shallow groove systems just L of the corner of Skylark. Climb the bulge just L of SkyLark, via a crack, to a ledge. Climb RW into a groove then back L to gain a LW-sloping ramp. Join Muppet Show to finish.

Skylark   39m   E2   5c   * (R)
C.King, S.Monks 1978
Start below an overhang above which is a blackish clean-cut corner. Climb to the large overhang at 4m, move to its L end, then over it RW. Traverse RW into a clean-cut corner, climb it to a ledge, step R into a short groove, then climb the wall above to finish up a crack in the steep wall just L of the arete.

Muppet Show   39m   E1   5a   * (R)
A.Sharp 1976
P.Littlejohn, C.King 1977 direct finish.
A fine route. Climb a groove below a small jutting prow under the lowest line of overhangs, to the horizontal break at 4m. Climb LW to below the bulging groove then traverse L to reach easy ground at the top of the corner of Skylark. Finish up loose rock above.
Direct finish: A much harder but better finish is to climb the top part of Enigma. Instead of traversing LW to Skylark, move up the steeper grooves until they blank out then LW (E2 5b).

Enigma   39m   E4   6a/b   * (R)
J.Talbot, R.Corbett (Red Slab) 1962
FFA P.Littlejohn, S.Lewis, C.Curle 1981
Direct Start A.N.American, A.Richardson 1985
A good route with some in-situ gear that needs renewing. Start as for Muppet Show to the horizontal break at 4m, then follow a line of undercuts up LW to an overhang. Climb through the small

overhang via a thin crack, then move R into Muppet Show. Continue straight up the bulging groove above until it becomes blank. Traverse L on sloping holds to the arete and follow it delicately to the top.
Direct start: Gain the small overhang and thin crack from directly below. This makes the route more sustained.

Enigma Variation   E5   6b   *   (R) †
M.Crocker, M.Ward 1987
The final bulging groove is taken directly, PR. A belay at the base of the groove is advisable (Heroin belay).

Secret Combination   39m   E4   6a,5c   ** (R)
P.Littlejohn, S.Lewis 1982
Steep! Start as for Muppet Show at the small prow.
1   15m Surmount the prow and traverse R to make steep moves into a shallow groove leading to a small cave.
2   24m Climb the steep wall above the cave until it is possible to traverse L and swing around the arete into the groove of Enigma. Finish as for Enigma.

Heroin   49m   E5   6a,6b,5b   *   (R)
M.Crocker, M.Ward 1986
A route to get high on.
1   24m Follow Enigma or Secret Combination to a large ledge in the groove of Enigma just L of the arete.
2   12m Move R onto the wall, PR, swing onto the arete and climb the wall L of the arete, PR, then move back onto the arete which leads to a ledge. SB and PB.
3   12m Climb straight up the arete, above exiting L to finish.

Yellow Wall   45m   E3   5c,5c   *** (R)
J.Talbot, R.Corbett 1962 A2
FFA P.Littlejohn, A.Houghton 1977
Superb. Start 4m R of Muppet Show beneath the groove at the lowest point of the bottom break. It is capped by a triangular overhang.
1   33m Climb the first groove to the overhang, move L to a possible belay in a cave. Move diagonally RW, PR, to the obvious corner. Climb stylishly or fight your way to a large ledge.
2   12m Climb the LW-leaning groove on the LH side of the ledge. A bold start leads to slightly more secure climbing and the top.

Hard Liner   45m   E6   6b,5b   ** (R) †
M.Crocker 1991
A tiring and technical start leads to a wild excursion up the arete between Yellow Wall and Steam train. Start as for Steam Train.
1   33m Follow the groove of Steam Train to the roof. Continue direct up the overhanging grey groove, PR, and reach the main rising break (junction with Steam Train). Pull into the groove of

1. 5 Minutes to Kill
2. Winter Warmer
3. Skylark
4. Muppet Show
5. Enigma
6. Heroin
7. Yellow Wall

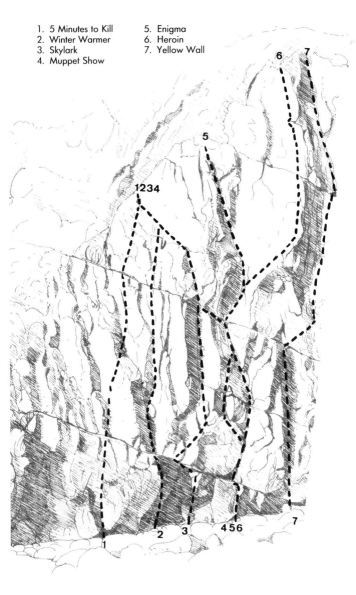

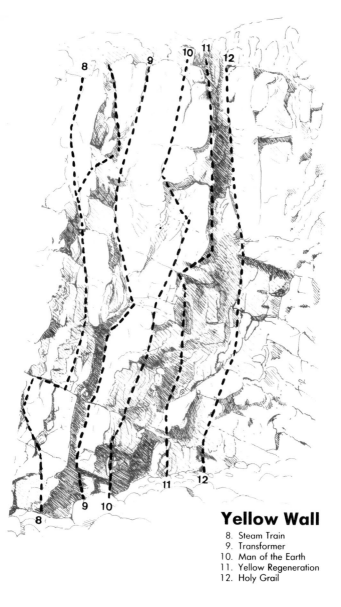

Yellow Wall

8. Steam Train
9. Transformer
10. Man of the Earth
11. Yellow Regeneration
12. Holy Grail

Steam Train, then swing L into a bottomless groove. Climb the groove, PR, to gain a break above in the arete. Ignore the RW escape and make two long moves up the final arete to the Yellow Wall belay ledge.
2   12m Climb the cracks and flakes towards the RH side of the backwall to the top.

Steam Train   45m   E4   6a,5b   ** (R)
M.Fowler, M.Morrison 1977 1pt of aid
FFA A.Sharp, P.Lewis 1985
Direct finish P.Littlejohn, L.Foulkes 1985
This takes the narrow groove and crack R of Yellow Wall. Start at a large boulder 1m R of Yellow Wall.
1   33m Step R from the boulder and follow a shallow groove with a red L wall to the overhangs. Traverse R 3m and step up to another groove. Move up deviously to reach a horizontal break and a ledge.
2   12m From the R end of the ledge, traverse RW around the arete to gain a red slab which is traversed to a groove (Transformer). Move up the groove 1m, then traverse L to another short groove which leads to the top.
Direct Finish: From the ledge climb the middle of the wall above (E4 6a).

Transformer   48m   E3   5c,5c   *** (R)
P.Littlejohn, A.McFarlane 1978
C.King, S.Monks (finish described) 1978
Utterly brilliant! Big muscles will make the route feel a grade easier, especially the top pitch. The route takes the prominent slanting grooves on the R side of the wall. Start 6m R of Yellow Wall beneath a block overhang at the base of a corner.
1   27m Climb awkwardly round the roof, follow the corner and RW-slanting groove until moves LW lead to a thin long ledge.
2   21m Step RW into a groove and follow this to the obvious deep crack on the R wall. Muscle up this to the top.
Variation Finish: Instead of taking the crack, traverse L into a stepped groove system . . .
Wimp!

Yellow Regeneration   51m   E6   6b,6b   *** (R) †
M.Crocker, R.Thomas, M.Ward 1988
A magnificent route up the overhanging wall and arete between Transformer and Holy Grail. Start 6m R of Transformer.
1   27m Climb a narrow groove to roofs, pull out L, TR, to gain a diagonal ramp, PR, then cross the overhung wall LW to jugs, TR. Stand up and follow the diagonal crack LW to move up onto an angular block, SB.
2   24m If strength permits, climb up RW on good holds, poor BR, to a narrow footledge below the arete, PR. Climb the arete, TR, then a long reach leads to easier ground.

Man Of The Earth 40m E6 6b,6b *** (R) †
G.Gibson, R.Thomas 1989
A breathtaking route of the highest quality. Start at a slim groove
between Transformer and Yellow Regeneration.
1 20m Climb the groove, PR, to a break, then cross the overhanging R wall, PR, into a shallow groove, TR, leading to good
holds. Swing up LW, PR, through overhanging rock to gain overhung ledges, PR. Power through a bulge, TR, to reach a break, TR.
Climb past another break to a PB.
2 20m Climb a shallow groove above, old BR, then swing L and
climb a thin crack in the headwall, PR, TR, to good jugs. Finish
awkwardly.

Skyhedral Wall 45m E6 6b *** (R) †
M.Crocker 1991
Totally unrelenting and strenuous but with three good shakeouts.
Take plenty of long slings and a normal rack with Friends.
Start at a small cave 3m R of Yellow Regeneration. Climb overhanging layback cracks, TR, PR, and swarm over a capping bulge
on the L to reach a hand rail leading RW to a good rest. Climb
diagonally L, PR, to a niche with plentiful jugs. Take a slim groove
on the R to another niche, TR. Power over the bulge above, 2PR's
and continue up a thin L-facing groove to a horizontal break.
Hand-traverse L and from a thin short crack crank over a bulge,
PR, to a juggy rising break. Rockover into a shallow niche, reach a
good break and bear LW to finish at a small L-facing groove.

Holy Grail 45m E2 5b ** (R)
P.Littlejohn, J.Harwood 1980
Worth searching for, more solid then it looks. This takes the
broken corner formed where Yellow Wall meets the shattered
face at the back of the cove, to reach the prominent acute corner
high up on Yellow Wall. Start at a jutting block below an overhang
at 21m. Climb deviously LW to gain a small ledge. Move L to the
corner and up to the overhang. Move LW to gain the superb final
corner and the top.

Gafaelwy 45m E2 5b,5c * (R)
E.Pardoe, R.Griffiths 1960
FFA S.Lewis, P.Littlejohn 1980
Start R of the previous route, below a jutting block.
1 27m Gain the jutting block, then up and L to the corner crack
and overhang on Holy Grail. Over this and RW to a stance below a
wide chimney crack.
2 21m step L and climb a thin crack via overhangs to the top.

Pilgrim 42m E1 5b,5b O (R)
E.Pardoe, L.Costello 1966
1 27m As for Gafaelwy.
2 15m Climb the obvious wide crack that trends R to the top.

Germany Calling   50m   E3   5c,5b,5a   * (R)
A.Sharp, P.Lewis 1987
The obvious R to L break at one third height. Start as for
Man Of The Earth.
1   20m Traverse to a belay on Yellow Wall.
2   18m Traverse to Muppet Show.
3   12m Finish up Muppet Show.

Transverse   30m   E2   6a,   5a   (R)
S.Lewis, G.Lewis 1985
The traverse line below Germany Calling.
1   21m Start as for Transformer. Climb to the first break and
move L to gain the traverse line which is followed to Skylark. Belay.
2   9m Finish up Skylark or continue traversing past Winter
Warmer and down L to a ledge. Climb a thin crack to a sloping
stance and the top.

Opposite Yellow Wall and to the L of Eyeball Wall is a black slab.
This must be one of the few cliffs in Britain to be threatened by a
conglomerate cornice !

Don't Look Up   22m   E2   5c   †
R.Thomas, J.Bullock 1990
Start just R of an earthy crack on the L side of the slab. Climb to a
narrow ledge, move up a steep section, PR, and continue to a
lower off point, PR, TR.

A Shadow Hanging Over Me   22m   E1   5b   †
R.Thomas, J.Bullock 1990
Start at the RH earthy crack. Climb up the crack then step out L
onto the slab, up a short steep crack until moves over calcite
encrustations, 2PR, lead to the steep upper section. Lower off.

EYEBALL WALL
The smooth crack-seamed wall opposite Yellow Wall provides a
number of shorter routes. An abseil rope in place would make
belaying easier.

Contact 10.10   12m   E4   6b   †
M.Crocker, M.Ward, R.Thomas 1986
Climb the black scoop and thin crack on the L side of the face,
exiting R from the crack via a shallow groove.

Fovea 40   12m   E3   6a   †
R.Thomas, M.Ward, M.Crocker 1986
Climbs the scoop and crack between Contact 10.10 and Specky
Four Eyes, TR.

Eyeline   12m   E3   5c   †
R.Thomas, M.Ward, M.Crocker 1986

Climb the scoop and crack between Fovea 40 and Specky Four eyes. TR.

Specky Four Eyes   12m   E2   5c   †
M.Crocker, M.Ward, R.Thomas 1986
Start at the foot of a diagonal fault running to the headland. Climb a scoop moving R to a jug, then move up R and back L to a crack leading to a belay.

Eyeball to Eyeball   12m   E2   5c   †
M.Ward, M.Crocker, R.Thomas 1986
Start at the R side of the face. Climb to the L side of the diagonal fault line, TR, then move up to stand on another fault. Move over the bulge to a vertical slot then up to a break above and a short wall to easier ground.

JACKY'S TOR
This is the prominent headland to the R(E) of Great Boulder Cove. It provides a number of good quality climbs. There is a large deep cave L of the large front buttress and a lower subsidiary buttress L of this. Access is possible for 1 1/2 hours either side of low tide. It is possible to gain the more westerly routes via a scramble down the W side as for Great Boulder Cove.

Subsidiary Buttress
There is a large sloping platform at the foot of the buttress. 2m above this and running along the L side of the buttress is a ledge. The first climb starts below the RH end of this.

Red Corner   21m   VD
J.Talbot, D.Lewis 1963
Gain the ledge and climb a groove above to a recess. Surmount the overhang and follow the slabby groove above to the top.
The front of the buttress is split by a groove.

Kinder   24m   S
J.Talbot 1963
Start a metre L of the groove below a steep juggy wall. Climb the wall direct to a large recess below the groove in the upper half of the buttress and take the corner to the top.

Guardian   24m   S   *
J.Talbot, D.Lewis 1963
Start below the groove, climb it to the large recess and traverse R to the arete. Follow this to the top.

To the R is a gully containing a cave. The LH wall has many short easy climbs that provide good bouldering.

Chantilly Lace   21m   HVS   5b   **
A.Sharp, J.Harwood 1982

A cracker, taking the steep corner L of the cave with good protection and good rock.

Possessed   22m   E4   6a   *
J.Talbot, P.Perkins 1964 (Cave Overhang)
FFA A.Sharp, J.Harwood, D.Hillier 1982
A sustained pitch with plentiful but indifferent protection. Start R of the cave. Climb a flake crack to a small ledge, step L to gain a thin crack, PR, and climb this, PR, to easier ground.

Damned   22m   E2   6a
A.Sharp, D.Hillier 1982
A good and varied route. As for Possessed to the small ledge, move R and climb the crack to a small roof. Battle up the corner crack above and finish along the traverse line of Cave Traverse.

Cave Traverse   39m   HS   4a   *
R.Owen, C.Andrews, C.Edwards 1960
An exposed route. Climb into the cave and traverse RW to the first corner crack. Follow this to a recess, level with the top of the wall above the cave. Traverse L to ledges, 2 PR.

The main buttress of Jacky's Tor is to the R (E), with massive overhangs on its R, seaward side. The upper half is very loose and routes avoid it. The wall R of Cave Traverse has been developed by J. Talbot but is very loose and broken. The next route described takes the groove on the RH side of this face.

Agamemnon   27m   VS   4c   O
E.Pardoe, L.Costello 1969
Follow the steep broken groove just L of the front of the buttress taking care with the rock, to a RW traverse line at 27m. Belay. Either finish direct or traverse R to reach easier ground.

V Groove   27m   E2/3   5c   **
E.Pardoe, D.Ellis 1966
Delicate and technical at first then more exposed and strenuous, one of Gower's earliest classic hard routes. Start below the rib L of the overhanging corner in the front of the buttress, climb it and the thin crack to gain the V groove. Exit LW from the notch and climb a shallow groove above to a ledge, TB. Traverse RW to easy ground.

Plot 13   27m   E4   6a   ***
R.Thomas, J.Bullock, L.Moran 1987
A good modern addition at the top end of its grade. Start at the overhanging chimney just R of V Groove. Bridge up the constricted chimney until it is possible to step down R below a sharp fin of rock. Climb the thin crack on its L side to the overhang. A hard move, NR, leads to a hidden hold above the overhang. Step R to

the arete, PR, then move LW onto the face and make hard moves up and L, NR. Continue up the face to the top.

R of the main face of Jacky's Tor is a bulging wall with a thin crack on its L side and a shallow groove at its R.

Crank The Hummer   24m   E3   6a   *
A.Sharp, J.Harwood, P.Lewis 1984
This takes the thin crack mentioned above. Climb to the start of the crack, PR, move over a small overhang and follow the crack to the top.

Cut Across Shortly   19m   E3   6a   *
A.Sharp, J.Harwood 1983
The groove L of Red Diedre. Gain it by climbing the arete. Poor PR.

Red Diedre   18m   VS   4c   *
J.Talbot, D.Lewis 1963
A steep corner skirts the overhang area to the R. Climb easy rocks to gain the corner and climb it directly.

Mittel   18m   VD
J.Talbot, D.Lewis 1963
This moves R from Red Diedre to finish up the arete.

CATHEDRAL WALL
R of Jacky's Tor is a wide gully with a steep L wall and two obvious grooves at the back. Access is possible 1 1/2 hours either side of low tide and descent is via ridges and chimneys either side of the gully.

Prima   15m   S
J.Talbot, R.Corbett 1961
This takes the corner at the L end of the steep L wall.

Hades   15m   HS   4b
J.Talbot, R.Corbett 1962
The crack 1m R of Prima.

Kalk   18m   S
J.Talbot 1962
Start up Owch but move L as soon as possible and climb the centre of the wall.

Owch   15m   S
J.Talbot, R.Corbett 1961
This takes the prominent crack in the middle of the wall, 3m R of Prima.

Dulfer 18m S 4a   *
J.Talbot, R.Corbett 1962
The bulging groove and crack 3m R of Owch. Climb a steep wall
on jugs to the groove, surmount a bulge, step L to a recess and
follow the crack to the top.

Dolce Vita 18m VS 4c
R.Corbett, J.Talbot 1962
As for Dulfer to the bulge then follow a steep and shallow groove
up R, bear L and finish direct.

Cyntaff 18m HVS 5a   **
P.Dyer, R.Corbett 1962
A certain amount of determination is needed to climb the fine
corner R of Dolce Vita.

Faint White Hope 18m E2/3 6a   *
A.Sharp, J.Harwood 1980
The boldness of this route will depend on the level of the sand.
Start at a short groove in the R wall of Cyntaff. Climb it to an
overhang, make bold moves LW and finish steeply up the wall
above.

At the back of the gully are two obvious grooves reached by easy
scrambling.

Adam 12m S 4a
J.Talbot, R.Corbett 1962
The LH groove.

Eve 12m S 4a
R.Corbett, J.Talbot 1962
The RH groove.

THE PULPIT
R of Cathedral Wall is a slabby broken buttress. This is split to the
R of centre by an easy broken groove (useful descent). Just R of
the buttress is a deep recess with a square black hole just below
half height at the back.

Smoove 15m VS 4c
R.Corbett, J.Talbot 1962
This climbs the smooth overhanging groove in the seaward end of
the L wall of the recess. Climb the groove and pull out R on good
holds to a ledge below another groove capped by an overhang.
Take this and exit L.

Gold Kappel 18m VS 4c
J.Talbot, R.Corbett 1962
Start as for Smoove, then move delicately R and over a smooth

sloping bulge to a ledge. Climb the R edge of the groove to the top.

Canalog   15m   VS   4c
R.Corbett, P.Perkins 1962
Climb the steep wall L of the black hole.

The Beak   18m   VD
J.Talbot, D.Jones 1961
Start below the black hole. Gain the hole and traverse LW to a ledge below the upper groove of Smoove, now climb the steep wall on the L.

Checkmate   13m   VS   4b
J.Talbot 1963
As for The Beak to the hole, then climb the corner above.

Font   13m   VS   4b
J.Talbot 1963
As for Checkmate to the upper corner, then move R and climb the narrow pillar.

THE AISLE

This is the low promontory running out to sea R of Cathedral Wall. It is detached from the mainland and it is possible to pass behind it by a narrow gully and in front at low water. The area around The Aisle has been explored by J.Talbot. The routes are too short to be included here, but they provide excellent bouldering with good landings.
Behind The Aisle is a hole. Go through this to reach the next routes, which are situated on the R (W facing) wall of the overhung gully. They can also be accessed by abseil.

Boom Boom Boris   15m   E4   6b   †
A.Sharp,O.Jones 1986
A hard and bold pitch. Start 3m L of Treasure. Climb the wall on pockets to an overhang. Move out L and finish, crux.

Treasure   15m   E2   5c   *
A.Sharp, J.Harwood 1984
A good climb high in the grade. Gain a thin crack line and, using many excellent small holds on the wall, gain the top.

JACKY'S TOR - UPPER CLIFF

Above and behind Cathedral Wall is an extensive, non-tidal, upper tier of cliffs with a grass ramp at its foot. It provides a number of worthwhile climbs. At the foot of the cliff, towards the centre, is a detached pinnacle about 2m high, above and R of which, in the middle of the wall, is a large shield of rock bounded on the L by a crack. About 22m R of the pinnacle is a small cave. R again is a distinct bulging buttress, Rolly Bottom Buttress. Access is best from the top of the cliff via a grassy slope to the E of the cliffs.

Codpiece 21m HS 4a
A.Beaton, G.Richardson et al 1982
Start 11m R of the detached pinnacle. Climb a crack leading up and R to a ledge at half-height, traverse R to the detached shield and gain its top. Finish LW up the wall.

Thanksgiving 21m HVS 5a   *
P.Littlejohn, A.N.Other
Start at a groove 13m R of the detached pinnacle. Climb the groove LW to the overhangs, passing a ledge at half-height (Codpiece). Now take the continuation groove through the L side of the overhangs to finish.

Raindrops 21m HVS 5a
G.Evans, G.Richardson 1981
Start 2m R of Thanksgiving, directly below the shield. Climb cracks bearing RW for 3m, then continue direct to the R side of the shield. Surmount the shield and continue RW up the wall above. Finish up the wide crack in the L side of the bulges.

All There 24m VS 4c   *
G.Evans, J.Bullock, R.Thomas 1982
Start as for Raindrops. Climb cracks bearing RW to gain a shallow niche. Climb a crack leading to a bulge below the R side of the highest overhangs, traverse R and break through at the weakest point. Finish direct.
Variation finish: Loose. From the bulge move L and gain the top of the overhangs. Climb these RW (HVS 5a).

A Bit On The Side 26m VS 4b
G.Richardson, M.Danford 1982
Start 4m R of Thanksgiving, below a crack leading to a shallow recess at 6m. From the recess climb the broken cracks above to a small line of overhangs, traverse R and finish up a steep groove.

ROLLY BOTTOM BUTTRESS
This is the prominent buttress at the RH end of the cliff. It has an obvious black-stained wall up its centre.

Rolly Bottom Buttress 30m VS 4c
G.Evans, G.Richardson 1977
G.Evans, L.Moran 1990 independent finish as described
A little loose in places. Start at the LH side of the buttress, climb steep rock to gain a groove. At its top continue up a thinner crack in the same line to the top.

Mewslade Bay and Thurba Head, Gower

Photo A. Richardson

Muppet Show E1 5a Yellow Wall *Climber S. Eggert*   *Photo C. Ryan*

The Sandpiper   30m   E3   5c   *
P.Boardman, G.Williams, W.Hurford 3pts aid 1970
FFA A.Sharp, J.Harwood 1983
A sustained and worthwhile pitch. Climb straight up the black
streak and the middle of the wall above until a blind pull around a
small roof leads to looser but easier climbing.

Sidewinder   30m   HVS   5a
A.Sharp, J.Harwood 1982
Climb a short corner on the R side of the buttress and step L into a
broken groove. Avoid it by taking the jamming crack on the R to
finish up a clean corner.

Below and R of Rolly Bottom Buttress is a cave with a slab above it.

Trivial Pursuit   18m   VD/S
G.Evans, J.Bullock 1988
Climb the R side of the cave to a ledge, step onto a block at the
foot of the slab before continuing to the path, (very escapable).

MOLAR WALL AND WHITE EDGE
47m R (E) of the Aisle is the obvious feature of White Edge, a high
narrow pillar. Below it is the broad low buttress of Molar Wall
(characterised by calcite flecks), the L (W) facing facet of which is
very steep. To the R the buttress is more broken and gradually
loses height. Access is via the beach 3 hours either side of low
tide or by descending grassy slopes to the E of White Edge.

MOLAR WALL WEST
The small but clean W-facing facet.

Bochlwyd   12m   HVS   5a
J.Talbot 1964
This takes the thin LW-trending crack at the L side of the W facing
facet.

He Man   12m   E2   5c   †
A.Richardson, S.Lewis 1987
Climb the crack-seamed wall directly up the centre.

Muscle Man   12m   E1   5b   †
A.Richardson, S.Lewis 1987
Climb the slab 3m R of He Man, then up the overhanging wall and
overlap via a long reach.

Christa   13m   HS   4b
J.Talbot, B.Talbot
Start at the R side of the wall where rocks project into the sand.
Climb L of a corner to below an overhang, cross it RW or, much
harder, LW (5b).

SOUTH FACE
On the S face are two easy scrambling routes, both climbed
by J.Talbot, 1963 Right Buttress and Left Buttress

Straight Crack   9m   VD
J.Talbot 1963
Where the wall projects out SW, is a narrow recessed wall with a
deep narrow crack. Climb it.

Recessed Wall   15m   VD
J.Talbot 1963
The wall R of Straight Crack.

Sharp Corner   12m   VD
J.Talbot 1963
The corner L of Blocky Corner.
In the centre of the S facet is a recess with a cave at the back and a
square-cut chimney groove to its R.

Blocky Corner   12m   VD
J.Talbot 1963
This takes the corner L of Curving Corner.

Curving Corner   12m   HVS   5a
D.Baines 1963
Fun. Climb the steep smooth corner L of the cave until it is
possible to gain the arete on the R.

Cavity Crack   15m   S
J.Talbot 1963
Climb the square cut chimney groove R of the cave. A harder
variation is to move L at half-height and climb its L edge.

Deception Crack   6m   S
J.Talbot 1963
Start at an easy recessed slab and climb a vertical narrow crack.

Two Step Wall   13m   HS   4b
J.Talbot 1963
Start on the R side of the wall and strenuously climb an overhang
to a ledge. Climb the second overhanging section by a committing move R to a slippery ledge then LW to the top.

MOLAR WALL EAST
The wall to the E.

Hairline   7m   S
J.Talbot 1962
Follow the smooth wall NW to where a cleft is formed by a

pinnacle. Climb a shallow blind corner crack on the L wall just before entering the cleft .

Thrutch   7m   HS   4b
J.Talbot 1963
4m L of Hairline is a definite concavity. Climb to the overhang direct and then up to the upper ledges.

First Corner   7m   S
J.Talbot 1963
The first corner in the upper wall L from Thrutch. Gain it by the smooth wall below.

Second Corner   9m   S
J.Talbot 1963
The corner just L of First Corner. It merges into a bulge higher up.

Twist   12m   HS   4a
J.Talbot 1963
Climb Second Corner to the bulge, then traverse L across a steep wall to reach another corner. Follow this to the top.

Third Corner   9m   S
J.Talbot 1963
4m L of Second Corner, bear LW at the top.

WHITE EDGE
The obvious pillar of White Edge is above Molar Wall.

White Edge   36m   VD   *
J.Talbot, D.Lewis 1964
A good route marred by some loose rock. It takes the knife-edged pillar directly with short excursions R or L. Bear LW at the top.

On the W flank of White Edge is the following route:

Ha He Verschneidung   27m   VS   4c
J.Talbot 1970
Takes the central groove in the upper half of the W flank. Move R at the top.

On the E flank are the following routes:

White Whale   21m   E1   5b
J.Bullock, L.Moran 1987
6m L of White Elephant. Start below three black streaks high on the buttress. Climb straight up via two ledges to reach a steep crack leading to the top.

White Elephant   21m   E1   5b
L.Moran, J.Bullock 1987

At the extreme RH side of the E flank is a prominent corner bounded on the L by a clean wall. Start at the centre of the wall. Climb straight up past an old PR to a ledge, step R and climb the groove.

Pidgeon Crack   21m   VS   4c
J.Talbot 1970
The prominent corner on the R side of the E flank.

BLOCK BUTTRESS
This is the impressive, conspicuous buttress at the seaward end of the headland E of White Edge. Below and L of the highest point is a deep gully. Access is via the beach 1 1/2 hrs either side of low tide. Descent is towards the E.

Piz   12m   HS   4b
J.Talbot, R.Corbett 1962
Climb the groove at the seaward end of the L(W) wall of the gully.

Kleine   12m   VS   4c
J.Talbot, R.Corbett 1962
A poorly protected line up the wall R of Piz and L of Thing.

Thing   21m   HVS   5a
J.Talbot 1964
Follow the water worn groove 7m R of Piz, and just L of the seaweed covered rock. Take the easier corner above to finish.

Cima   36m   E1   5b   ** †
J.Talbot, R.Corbett 1962
A large rockfall has removed the upper part of this route. There used to be a massive overhang in place at the top! Start at the foot of the L of two cracks at the back of the gully. Climb the crack via a bulge to a recess (belay possible), step R and climb a rib to gain a corner. Follow this to the overhang which is turned on the L. Finish up the corner exiting R. SB.

Kaiser   39m   HVS   5a,4a   **
R.Corbett, D.Jones 1962
1   15m As for Cima to the recess.
2   24m Step R onto a rib, then into the corner on the R. Follow this until it is possible to gain a traverse line on the R wall. Follow it to, and finish up the arete.

The Limping Limpet   31m   E5   6a   †
M.Crocker, M.Ward 1987
A bold undertaking between Kaiser and Power Trap. From the niche of Power Trap, reach over the bulge to a good hold in the base of a faint runnel. Pull up and climb directly, poor NR, to the traverse of Kaiser, finish up Power Trap.

Power Trap   36m   E2   5c   ***
E.Pardoe, R.Griffiths 1966
FFA P.Littlejohn, S.Jones 1970
Exposed and fierce climbing, a determined approach will work
wonders at the start. Start at a steep crack system in the R wall of
the gully. Climb the crack, past a niche, then take a diagonal line
LW avoiding the arete to finish just L of the arete.

South Pillar Rib   36m   S   **
J.Talbot, R.Corbett 1962
This takes the narrow RH pillar of the gully. Various starts are
possible; the best is described. Climb the LH groove and gain the
pillar front. Continue up the pillar until it narrows to an arete.
Finish RW taking care with the rock.

To the R of these routes is a cave at half-height.

Burn The Boss   24m   HVS   5a
A.Sharp, J.Harwood 1983
Start in the cave. Move up the L rib of the cave and enter a crack.
Follow it to the top as for South Buttress.

South Buttress   61m   S
SUMC 1969
A long but poor route. Take a line R of a cave at half- height to a
narrow rib, then trend LW to reach the centre of the wall above
the cave. Finish direct.

Deep Crack   61m HS
J.Talbot 1963
Climb the deep crack R of South Buttress to join that route.

On the upper E face of Block Buttress, overlooking Trident Gully,
is a pair of cracks near the sea-ward edge.

Picket Line   18m   E1   5b
G.Evans, J.Bullock 1984
Climb to the cracks and follow them to the top. This route is best
gained via The Soft Mouthed Brown Mullet.

TRIDENT GULLY
This is the deep inlet immediately R(E) of Block Buttress. Access is
via the beach or by scrambling down R of the gully, 1.5 hrs either
side of low tide.

The Soft Mouthed Brown Mullet   12m   E2   5c   *
A.Rowby c1960
A good pumpy problem climbed by all and claimed by many. It
takes the steep cracks in the LH side of the W wall of the gully. It
can be linked with Picket Line to create a good outing.

Groundswell 15m E3 6a   †
M.Ward, M.Crocker 1987
This takes the centre of the white wall R of the previous route.
Start at the foot of the ramp of West Pillar Corner. Climb sharp
rock to twin undercuts at half-height. Tackle the wall above.

Sharma 15m E3 5c   †
M.Crocker, M.Ward 1987
This takes a line of cracks in the RH side of the wall. Start as for
West Pillar Corner. Climb up to a spike, then climb awkwardly
over a bulge onto a steep wall. Climb RW then straight up .

West Pillar Corner 24m S 4a
J.Talbot, R.Corbett 1961
This climbs the ramp running up RW in the L wall of the gully and
finishes up the corner above.

Central Crack 24m VD
J.Talbot, R.Corbett 1961
Just R of the ramp is a chimney. Climb the arete R of this and the
broken crack in the wall above.

Meander 24m D
R.Corbett, J.Talbot 1961
Start as for Central Crack, climb up and R to the arete overlooking
the gully and follow this to the top.

Kopf Out 26m HVS 5b
A.Richardson, S.Door 1989
At the base of the arete where the gully gets very narrow is a short
crack. Climb it and move RW to an obvious flake. Move RW again
and climb the centre of the steep wall. Using the back wall is
cheating!

At the back of the gully is a smooth pillar in a gloomy recess.

Balm 12m VS 4c
G.Evans, J.Bullock 1980
The L edge of the pillar and the crack on the L.

Malm 12m VS 4c
J.Talbot, B.Talbot 1966
The R edge of the pillar to the roof, move R to a ledge, then take
the wall above.

Trident Wall 21m E1 5b   *
J.Talbot, M.Hicks 1969
Start at the centre of the concave R wall of the gully by a short
water-worn groove. Climb up and L below the bulges before
breaking out onto the upper wall and thence to the top.
Direct finish: go directly over the bulges(E1 5b).

South West Diedre   21m   HS   4b
SUMC   1967
Climb the short groove on the seaward side of the gully's R wall
and then traverse easily along the flake to finish.

Pillar Crest   20m   D
J.Talbot 1961
An easy pleasant scramble up the crest of the buttress on the R (E)
of the gully.

CATACOMB GULLY
This lies above and behind Trident Gully. It is non-tidal and access
is by scrambling down from the E or ascending Pillar Crest from
the beach.

Celtic Uprising   12m   E1   5b
M.Crocker 1987
Steep climbing 4m L of West Corner Crack. Climb to a line of
LW-trending finger flakes and follow them to their end. Pull up to
an obvious pocket and finish as for Relics.

Relics   15m   E3   6a
M.Learoyd, H.Griffiths 1986
A technical pitch 3m L of West Corner Crack. Climb past an old BR
to twin vertical slots in the centre of a brown-streaked wall.
Continue up and finish out LW, NR.

West Corner Crack   15m   HS   4b
J.Talbot, R.Corbett 1961
This takes the corner crack, widening to a chimney, half-way into
the gully on the L wall.

Ribbery   15m   VD
J.Talbot, R.Corbett 1961
Climb the wall R of West Corner Crack, just L of the arete.

Ribald   15m   HVS   5b
H.Griffiths, M.Learoyd 1986
Climb the overhanging and E facing wall of Ribbery to join it at the
top.

Rib and Crack   15m   HS   4a
J.Talbot, R.Corbett 1961
A nice pitch taking the corner R of Ribbery, the second in the L
wall.

The Jewel   15m   VS   4c   *
A.Sharp, J.Harwood 1981
A little gem following the shallow groove in the wall R of Rib and
Crack, moving RW at the top.

Sharp Eyed   15m   E5   6a   * †
M.Crocker, M.Ward 1987
A good wall climb between The Jewel and Crypt; difficult protection. Start 3m R of the arete. Climb on widely spaced pockets, LW
at first, to a vague break, TR on a spike. Move up R on better
holds to the obvious flake. Finish LW.

My Wife and I   15m   E5   6a   †
M.Crocker 1987
Start R of the start of Sharp Eyed. Climb over a bulge in line with a
hairline crack to good finger edges, make a long reach and continue straight up through bulges to the top.

Crypt   15m   E2   5b
J.Bullock, G.Evans
An entertaining pitch, often wet. Start at the base of the brown-
stained corner crack. Climb it and the overhangs above.

The Dungeon   15m   E4   6b   †
M.Crocker 1987
A good route up the slender pillar R of Crypt. Start as for Crypt
then climb straight up the pillar on good holds to a bulge. Pull
into a thin crack and then gain a good break below a roof. Swing R
and continue more easily.

The next routes are on the W-facing wall.

Left over   15m   D
J.Talbot, R.Corbett 1961
Climb the L edge of the W-facing wall trending R at the top.

Gunpowder   18m   E3   6a
J.Talbot (Futility A1) 1963
FFA A.Sharp 1982
Start at the L end of the overhang which runs across the R wall of
the gully. Pull through the overhang, old BR's, to a break and
continue directly to the top.

Franceschi   15m   E2   5b
J.Talbot, B.Talbot 1965
FFA A.Sharp, J.Harwood 1982
A.Sharp 1987 (direct finish)
Start underneath the centre of the overhang, directly below a
shallow groove in the upper wall. Surmount the overhang and
finish up the groove RW.
Direct finish: after the roof finish direct. Bold! (E2 5c).

Treason   15m   E4   6b   †
A.Sharp 1987
Move through the roof at its RH end and make a long reach to
painful holds, PR. Finish up the groove.

Banana Man   15m   E4   6a   †
A.Forster, A.Sharp 1988
Start just R of Franchesci's roof at a PR with a long sling. Make
difficult moves past the PR to the top.

Nemesis   12m   E3   6b   †
A.Sharp, A.Forster
Climb the wall to the R. The exact line is not known.

Gamma   11m   VS   4c
R.Corbett, P.Perkins 1982
Follow the groove running up the R side of the overhang and pull
up L above the overhang. Finish up the groove.

Trubble   11m   HVS   4c
R.Corbett, P.Perkins 1962
Climb directly up the wall L of Gamma. Finish over the roofs.

Beta   11m   HS   4a
R.Corbett, P.Perkins 1962
The crack to the R of Gamma.

Midel   11m   VD
R.Corbett, P.Perkins 1962
Climb the pillar between Beta and Alpha.

Alpha   7m   D
J.Talbot, R.Corbett 1962
The R most crack.

FOURTH GULLY
This is the gully below and R of Catacomb Gully, with an obvious
hanging block at the back, above a cave.

Ramp and Slab   11m   VD
J.Talbot, R.Corbett 1961
Climb a narrow ledge on the L wall of the gully, rising steeply to a
short crack. Finish up this. It can also be climbed direct at VS.

Overhanging Corner   7m   HS   4a
J.Talbot, D.Lewis 1962
Follow a rising corner on the R side of the gully which merges
with a crack below the R side of the overhang. Exit up this.

THIRD GULLY
This is situated below and R of Catacomb Gully. The centre of the
gully is divided by a steep pillar rib and at half-height is cut by a
wide flat square ledge. To the R of the rib is a narrow deep cleft.

Rough!   11m   VS   5a
K.Snook, L.Moran,et al 1978
Short, painful but good. Climb the obvious crack at the seaward end of the L(E) wall, moving RW at a small roof.

Herzog Kamin   18m   S
J.Talbot 1963
This takes the deep chimney crack at the back of the LH side of the central pillar rib.

Buhl Riss   12m   VS   4c
J.Talbot 1969
In the back of the deep cleft is a narrow crack cutting the smooth R wall. Climb to a tiny flake then go up a crack to the top. The route is much easier if the back wall is used.

West Diedre   15m   VD
J.Talbot, R.Corbett 1961
The corner L of the central pillar running up just R of Herzog Kamin.

SECOND GULLY
This is the narrow deep cut cleft R of Third Gully.

Botzong   12m   S
J.Talbot 1961
This climbs the steep smooth chimney crack at the back, behind a large distinct jammed block.
To the R of these last routes the cliffs peter out rapidly, providing bouldering and short scrambles mostly explored by J.Talbot.

GREY WALL
At the back of Mewslade Bay is the valley providing access from Pitton. Just L(W) of the valley is Grey Wall on the upper slope. The rock is loose. The LH side has a large overhang at half-height.

Quergang   30m   VS   A1
J.Talbot, B.Talbot 1966
Start in a line just below the L side of the overhang and climb a wall directly up to a ledge. Traverse R below the overhang, and continue across the wall R at the level of a horizontal crack to reach an obvious corner. Finish up this.

Direct   30m   E3   5c
P.James 1984
Start in a line just R of the overhang and L of Ermintrude. Climb direct to the horizontal crack of Quergang, then to the top.

Ermintrude   13m   E1   5b
M.Jones, P.Murphy 1982

Take a broken fault 3m L of PMC 2 to a niche before continuing direct to a horizontal crack and a small ledge then the top.

P.M.C. 2   13m   HVS   5b
S.Vince, J.Makin
The groove L of South East Chimney.

South East Chimney   15m   D
J.Talbot, D.Thomas 1959
Follow the obvious chimney to the top.

Wall and Corner   13m   VS   4b
J.Talbot, D.Thomas 1959
Start 2m R of an easy chimney L of centre.Climb a wall RW to a ledge, then a corner on the R wall to the top.

THURBA WEST
Opposite Grey Wall, overlooking the bay and strictly speaking on Thurba Head, is the prominent outcrop of Thurba West. A few short climbs exist on its LH side at up to S, and an artificial route (South Wall A2), following a line of rusty bolts, on its RH side.

THURBA HEAD
This is the impressive headland at the E side of Mewslade Bay. It offers less climbing than might be expected, but what is there is excellent. It is extremely tidal and access for most routes is for 1/2 hr either side of low tide. From Thin Ice onwards the tide hardly ever clears the base and a traverse in may have to be made. There is a restriction on climbing from March 1st to August 14th.
Access is via Pitton (see access 2 at the start of this section). From the mouth of the valley, cross the wall at the stile and follow a path diagonally to the top of the headland, which narrows and becomes an arete at its seaward end. Abseil from blocks 9m below the top, down the W side to the sloping platform; not advisable unless it is near low tide. It is also possible to traverse into the W facet from Mewslade Bay, but this is only possible at very low tides.
The E flank of the cliff can be reached from the E side of the headland via a traverse and some scrambling, but the E side is very tidal and it is almost impossible to reach the base of the cliff except on spring tides.
The most obvious feature of the cliff is the steep pillar overlooking the sloping platform, bounded on the L by a gully and chimney topped by large overhangs, and on the R by a large corner with a chimney at its foot.

Central Cleft   42m   S   (R)
M.Hogge, E.Pardoe 1969
A disgusting route after the nesting season, but a useful escape. Start below the gully and chimney L of the main pillar. Climb the

chimney and groove bearing LW below overhangs to easy rocks, then climb the obvious deep groove above and L.

Right Crack   48m   E2   5b   ** (R)
E.Pardoe, M.Hogge 1969
FFA P.Littlejohn, J.Harwood 1980
Perversely, this route takes the thin crack and groove in the L side of the central pillar. Start just R of the gully below a thin barnacled crack.
1   39m Climb the crack and groove to an overhang, over this directly, and continue to a bulge and tiny overlap of brown rock. Follow a diagonal line RW across the top of the pillar.
2   9m Easy climbing remains to the top.

The Thurba Pillar   45m   E5   6b,4a   *** † (R)
M.Crocker 1985
A powerful and superb pitch up the splendid square cut pillar between Right Crack and Earthly Powers. Start as for Right Crack.
1   36m Climb steeply up the L arete of Earthly Powers. At 6m pull round L to the base of a crack line on the face. At its end swing up L to a shallow niche below the slim section of the pillar. Climb the pillar using the R arete until better holds are gained slightly L. Continue up the leaning wall via a line of hairline cracks and a short angular groove to a belay.
2   9m Climb the arete easily to the top.

Earthly Powers   45m   E5   5b,6a   *** (R)
T.Penning (first Pitch) 1981
T.Penning, P.Littlejohn 1983
A superb route on magnificent rock, attempting to climb the striking black groove line on the main pillar. Start beneath the groove an hour either side of low tide.
1   15m Climb steeply on good holds directly to a small stance beneath the black groove.
2   30m Climb RW to the arete and move up to the band of overhangs. Traverse L beneath the overhang till above the blank section of the groove, then climb straight up very steeply to reach the broken crest of the buttress. Finish easily up this to block belays.

Thin Ice   24m   E4   6a   ** † (R)
M.Crocker, G.Jenkin 1985
Exposed and technical wall climbing up the thin crack in the wall R of the arete. Start as Barnacle Bill. Traverse L from a good ledge in the chimney on sharp rock to a bulge and pull over it to a small slot. Move up L to better holds in the crack and climb it to finish R of the arete.

Barnacle Bill   24m   E1   5b   ** (R)
R.Griffiths, P.Peck 1pt aid 1971

FFA J.Bullock, C.Lownds 1982
Another good climb taking the big corner R of the central pillar.
Start at a hanging belay below the short chimney, climb it and the
corner to the top.

Summer Wine   24m   E3   6a   ** (R)
P.Littlejohn, T.Penning 1983
A strenuous, well-protected pitch; a real pump; 1m longer and it
would be E4. Start beneath the thin groove R of Barnacle Bill at
dead low tide or traverse in from the R (E). Climb to the overhang,
move LW around this and follow the thin crack and groove to the
top.

5m R of Barnacle Bill is another, higher corner.

Junior Jaws   21m   E1   5b   * (R)
T.Penning, D.Hope 1982
Start at high-tide level, below and slightly R of the upper corner.
Climb up to the foot of the groove on the R, pull up L and around
the arete to gain the foot of the corner and climb it.

Laughing Gear   18m   HVS   5a   (R)
T.Penning, J.Harwood 192
As for Junior Jaws to the groove then follow it to the top.

Wimp   18m   S   (R)
G.Richardson, M.Danford 1982
Start below the open groove in the upper RH part of the cliff, just
L of a deep chimney crack which bounds the cliff on the R . Climb
to the steep broken groove and the top.

THREE SISTERS TO DEBORAH'S OVERHANG   OS ref 427867 to 434863
A.Richardson

SITUATION AND CHARACTER
This was an area neglected by previous generations. It has, however, come under close scrutiny by local climbers in more recent
times and the number of routes has increased dramatically.
The Three Sisters to Deborah's Hole area comprises a group of
cliffs lying high above the sea mid-way between Thurba Head and
Paviland. The cliffs are not yet popular and loose rock is still
encountered, so care should be taken.

APPROACHES AND ACCESS
See map 2.

1   Approach from Pitton as for Thurba Head, (approach 2 in the
Mewslade to Fall Bay section). From the top of Thurba Head
follow the cliff top E for approximately 15 mins past a wall and stile

until an obvious valley is reached leading to the sea. This is Ram Grove (430866). The Three Sisters are immediately E from here.
2   An alternative, possibly faster approach to the Third Sister is from Paviland and takes 30 mins from Pilton Green car park (see Paviland section). Follow footpaths across fields (as for Paviland) and after reaching the stile at the head of the valley, take the first stile in the wall on the R. Gain the cliff top and follow the path past a stone wall running down a valley to another valley, also with a stone wall running down its length. At the mouth of this valley is a shattered pinnacle up on the R (W), Deborah's Overhang is below this. Shortly after this is another valley, follow this down R to a rickety fence and the Third Sister.

RAM GROVE CRAG
As the pebble beach of Ram Grove is approached (see approach 1), there are a number of small compact cliffs to the W. The first cliff contains a number of short climbs. It is characterised by two R-facing grooves that divide the cliff into thirds. The RH groove is Insatiable Appetite.

Standing Guard   21m   HVS   5a
N.Williams solo
The groove/chimney which bounds the L side of the main part of the cliff.

Snowstorm   18m   E3   5c   †
P.Thomas, J.Harwood 1989 1 pt aid
This climbs the wall just L of the second R-facing groove line. Start below a TR at 7m. Climb to the overhang, TR, step L and surmount the bulge. Continue up the cracks and groove above.

Taste of Tradition   18m   E4   6a   †
P.Thomas, J.Harwood 1989
An interesting pitch immediately L of Beth. As for Beth to the bulge, move L and then make a sustained series of moves up to a poor PR under the roof. Move over the roof and onto the slabby wall above, move L to gain a ledge. Continue up the cracked wall above to the top.

Beth   16m   E2   5b   †
P.Thomas, J.Harwood 1989
This tackles the steep rock L of Insatiable Appetite. Start 7m L of Insatiable Appetite. Climb easily up to a bulge, PR, move slightly R over the bulge to a groove which leans LW. Continue on better holds to the top.

Insatiable Appetite   13m   E1   5b
N.Williams
The obvious R-facing groove about 21m from the RH end of the

crag. Climb up to a bulge and make an awkward move to enter the groove. Continue with less difficulty to the top.

Honey   13m   E1   5b
A.Richardson, L.Moran 1988
Start 6m R of Insatiable Appetite below an obvious square cut overhang at the top of the crag. Climb a wall until a move can be made LW to a groove below the overhang. Continue up the groove at its R side.

Sugar   12m   E1   5b
A.Richardson, L.Moran 1988
Climb the vague grooves just R of Honey.

50 Franc Menu   12m   VS   4c
N.Williams solo
Just L of Entre where the concave strata meets the ground. Climb the shallow yellow groove and then move RW into the groove above.

Entre   9m   VS   4c
N.Williams solo
Start just R of where the concave strata and the rubble meet. Climb the cracked wall to the top.

Appetizer   8m   S
N.Williams solo
The short broken groove on the far R of the crag.

There is a loose cliff closer to the sea that has yet to receive an ascent, surprise, surprise!

FIRST SISTER
From the beach at Ram Grove follow the lowest path EW; the First Sister is seen as a compact cliff having an overhanging face marked to the R by a Y-shaped depression.

Sister of Mercy   21m   E4   6a
J.Bullock, G.Evans 1987 1pt aid
FFA A.Price 1988
The clean, snaking crackline in the centre of the buttress. Climb steeply to the second of 2 PR's. Climb the groove to an easier crackline which leads on dubious rock to the top.

South East Wall   21m   E1   5b
J.Talbot, B.Talbot 1966
FFA J.Bullock, G.Evans, 1984
Climb into the Y-shaped depression at the R side of the cliff, then traverse R to a groove/crack which is followed to the top.

Brothers in Arms   21m   HVS   5a
G.Evans,J.Bullock 1987
Climb the obvious RW-slanting corner/crackline on the R of the crag.

SECOND SISTER
This is the buttress adjacent (E) to the First Sister. It has an attractive S wall, with an overhang at three-quarters height and an obvious corner on the L.

Barney Rubble   18m   VD
C.Allen, solo 1987
This climbs the loose rock L of the fin of rock.

South Wall   33m   VS   4c   *
E.Pardoe, J.Talbot 1969
A.Richardson, J.Beynon 1989 variation start
A fine climb once the loose start is overcome. Start on the subsidiary ledge at the centre of the crag and make a LW rising traverse to reach the corner crack. At the next break go over the roof to the top.
Variation start: misses out the loose start. Gain the corner crack from the L, below the sharp fin HS 4b

Arrow   33m   HVS   5a
G.Evans, P.Clay 1978
This supersedes an earlier indirect route: Harrow. It climbs the lower slabs R of the start of S.Wall, via a slanting crack line to the RH side of the overhang and over this to the top.

Topless Admirer   33m   HVS   5a
L.Davies, P.Thomas 1987
This takes a line of slabs and grooves 4m R of South Wall. Finish as for South Wall.

Sister Sledge   33m   E1   5a
G.Lewis, P.Thomas, A.Richardson 1988
Start as for Topless Admirers, then finish up the obvious grooves further R .

THIRD SISTER
A popular venue during the last few years for the hardman. Situated 5 mins walk E of the Second Sister, this is a series of solid bulging and overhanging walls rising in a LW direction, separated by bedding planes. The routes all start from a grass terrace running up L at two-thirds height from just above a rickety fence. The most obvious feature is the shallow cave 4m up French Undressing, but beware the nest is thought to belong to a Pterodactyl.

Flaming Fingers   18m   E5   6b   ** †
M.Crocker unseconded 1988
An impressive pitch taking the unlikely bulging wall 9m up the
terrace from French Undressing. Safe but strenuous. Swing R, PR,
to an obvious jug and then climb straight up the wall in wild
positions, 2 PR's, to the break. Step L and climb a good flake crack
to easier ground.

Popped In Souled Out   21m   E5   6b   * †
A.Sharp, P.Lewis, J.Harwood 1988
A well protected desperate in a unique position. Start 7m up the
ramp from French Undressing below a PR and BR line. Pull up, PR,
then make a long reach to a BR. Crazy moves RW lead to a rest,
PR. Continue direct, PR, TR. Belay on a large block.

Chilean Flame Thrower   15m   E5   6b   * †
M.Crocker 1988
The uncompromising leaning wall 3m L of French Undressing.
Climb the centre of the leaning wall moving slightly L, PR, to good
holds in a vertical slot. Move back R to jugs in the break, then
reach over the bulge and finish more easily.

French Undressing   18m   E4   6b   * †
A.Sharp, P.Lewis, J.Harwood 1987
A nice pitch with one very hard move. Start below the shallow
cave at 4m. Climb up the steep wall to the cave, PR, move L then
straight up, PR, to an easy finish.

Twilight World   18m   E4   6a   * †
A.Sharp, P.Lewis et al 1987
Another good pitch with ample old in-situ gear. Start 2m R of
French Undressing. Climb a crack , PR, move L, TR, then straight
up, TR, to an easy finish.

South East Wall   18m   E2   5b   **
J.Talbot, R.Corbett aid 1963
FFA A.Sharp, P.Lewis 1987
A very good pitch following RW slanting ramp /crackline marked
by old PR's up the steep wall R of French Undressing. Start as for
Twilight World, climb the crack, then move RW to gain the RW
slanting crack and a steep finish.

Fiesta   21m   E2   5c   *
A.Sharp, P.Lewis, J.Harwood 1987
A good pitch on perfect rock. Start 3m R of South East Wall. Climb
the yellow streak steeply on pockets into a shallow groove, then
follow this via a step L at 12m. Finish as for South East Wall.

Bob's Your Uncle   18m   E3   6a   *
A.Sharp, R.Powles 1987
Start 4m R of South East wall on the R side of the buttress. Gain a
RW slanting crackline and follow it up the prow to the next
rampline.

Ten Bears   12m   HVS   4c
R.Powles, A.Hughes 1987
A vague line. Climb the discontinuous crack system in the prow
6m R of Bob's Your Uncle. Finish with care.

The next two routes lie on the tooth of rock on the path between
the Third Sister and Deborah's overhang.

Dentist's Chair   18m   E3   5c
A.Sharp, P.Lewis, J.Harwood 1987
Climb the groove on the L side of the tooth to a small overlap,
step L into the main groove and follow this to the top.

"Open Wide Please"   18m   E5   6a   †
A.Sharp, P.Lewis 1987
A bold and sustained pitch up the centre of the tooth, 4m R of
Dentist's Chair. Climb LW up the bulging wall into an open
groove and follow this with difficulty until easier climbing leads to
the top.

DEBORAH'S ZAWN
This zawn is situated just below the path which runs beneath
Third Sister. Easy scrambling leads to the bottom. The routes are
only slightly tidal but after a heavy sea are likely to remain damp
for some time. The most obvious features are the RW-rising
traverse line of Silent Echo and the steep LW-leaning crack of
Resisting Arrest.

Silent Echo   19m   HVS   * †
A.Sharp, P.Lewis 1985
R.Powles, A.Hughes 1987 Direct start
A nice pitch. Climb steeply to the RW traverse line then follow it
across the face to PB and BB. Abseil off.
Direct start E1 5b: Climb the steep wall in the centre of the face to
the traverse on the original route.

Bolder Boulder   18m   E4   6a   * †
A.Sharp, P.Lewis, J.harwood 1987
A good pitch on excellent rock. Start at a small overhang 6m R of
the direct start of Silent Echo. Climb through the overhang, PR,
move up L on good holds and finish as for Silent Echo.

Wide Eyed and Legless   18m   E6   6c   †
A.Sharp, P.Lewis, J.Harwood 1987
One of Gower's more technical test pieces, sadly chipped by one

misled local. Start at the slanting crack 4m R of Bolder Boulder and, struggle up the initial wall, NR. Hard climbing leads past a PR, then easier climbing leads to the traverse and finish of Silent Echo.

Resisting Arrest   19m   F6   6h   * |
A.Sharp, P.Lewis 1985
A good climb. Follow the crack 3m R of Wide Eyed And Legless past a TR with difficulty. Continue to the PB and BB on Silent Echo. Abseil off.

Debbie Reynolds   15m   E5   6a   * †
M.Crocker 1988
A committing pitch. Start below the flake in the leaning brown-coloured wall on the LH side of the zawn and climb straight up the back wall to a bulge. Gain the flake strenuously and finish up the leaning wall. PB back L.

DEBORAH'S OVERHANG AREA
This is the wildly overhanging concave buttress 185m E from the Third Sister. It can be approached from the Third Sister along the coastal path via an exposed step across a gap, or via the E side down an obvious valley.

State of Grace   45m   E4   5c,6a   * †
A.Sharp, P.Lewis, J.Harwood 1985
The second pitch takes the large roof on the L of the crag and is characterised by two large holes.
1   21m Climb a shallow groove to below a crack and a large ledge PB.
2   24m Move L from the ledge and follow pockets past two holes to good belays well back, 3 TR.

Deborah's Overhang   45m   A3
J.Talbot, B.Talbot 1967
A future free climber's problem. This route crosses the roof to the R of State of Grace. Only the holes for 12mm and 10mm bolts are present.

Deborah   21m   E4   6b
A.Sharp, P.Lewis 1985
Start on the beach directly below a large hole. Climb the roof, NR, PR, to a ledge, then easily to a roof. Traverse off R to finish.

At the far RH end of the overhang are two routes:

Three Minute Hero   18m   E5   6b   *
A.Sharp, P.Lewis 1985
Start on the far L of the central terrace below some small over-hangs, ancient BR. Pull over the roof, PR, and enter a small hole, TR. Continue up the crack above to finish.

Ground Control   15m   E4   6b
A.Sharp, P.Lewis 1985
The crack and groove 3m R of Three Minute Hero. Climb the roof via the crack and up the short corner to the top.

PAVILAND AND JUNIPER WALL OS ref 437859 to 438858
A.Richardson

SITUATION AND CHARACTER
Paviland and Juniper Wall are amongst Gower's best cliffs, providing sound climbing on surprisingly good rock. Set in rugged surroundings, they provide a good selection of middle-grade routes with the odd hard one thrown in to keep the chalk and tights brigade satisfied. Paviland appears vegetated at first sight, but this disguises the fine climbing to be had there. The main cliffs are non-tidal. There is an ideal cave to have lunch and shelter in if one happens to get caught in a rain shower.

APPROACHES AND ACCESS
See map 2. The area is best approached from Pilton Green on the B4247. Cars can be parked on open land on the N side of the road opposite a large white house. To the L of the house is a sign post for Paviland Cave. Follow the footpath (S) through fields until a stile is reached at the head of a valley. Approaches diverge here.
1   Paviland Far West and Far Far West: Cross the stile and bear R(W) up a slope to reach open cliff top, then head for the headland to the R(W) of the Valley. Paviland Far Far West is the narrow tidal zawn just to the R (W) of the headland and Paviland Far West is the more seaward zawn just below the W extremity of Paviland Main cliff.
2   Paviland: From the stile follow the wall/fence down the valley and traverse around the back of the inlet to the seaward buttress on the R(W). An exciting but easy traverse past some blow holes leads to the front of the cliff: 20 mins from Pitton Green.
3   Juniper Wall: From the valley bottom scramble round the L(E) side of the inlet and along ledges to the grass slope at the foot of the cliff.

PAVILAND FAR FAR WEST
This crag should provide some entertainment for those climbers wanting to get away from it all. See approach 1. This non-tidal gully has a steep E-facing wall 15m high. It is reached by abseil from pegs or slings at the top or by scrambling in along the E side of the zawn. It is advisable to belay to an abseil rope because of the chossy top. The routes are described L to R relative to a large jammed conglomerate chockstone at the base of the cliff. The rock has a tendency to seep after rain.

Hung Over   15m   E1   5b   †
J.Bullock, R.Thomas 1988
Start 9m L of the chockstone just L of a rock pedestal. Climb a
short overhanging wall to reach large holds, TR, then up past a
small overlap with a hole. Climb the wall above, TR, to a horizontal break. Finish directly.

Threadbare   15m   E1   5b   †
J.Bullock, G.Evans 1987
Start 1m R of Hungover. Step off the top of the rock pedestal past
a hole and a small overhang, then trend LW to reach a depression
with black streaks. Exit RW to belay.

Nematode   15m   E2   5b   †
R.Thomas, J.Bullock, L.Moran 1988
Start 1m R of the rock pedestal. Climb steeply, TR, past a hole
containing a TR to reach a calcite area, TR. Finish straight up, TR.
Belay on the abseil rope.

Rock Bottom   15m   E1   5c   †
J.Bullock, G.Evans 1988
Start just L of the chockstone. Step off the E side of the zawn and
climb to a small scoop, TR, move L into a shallow groove, PR.
Finish directly.

Chock A Block   15m   E1   5b   †
R.Thomas, J.Bullock 1988
Start at the chockstone. Pull up steeply, TR, then up the steep
wall, 2TR. Finish up the short wall above. PB.

Off The Peg   15m   E2   5b   †
J.Bullock, L.Moran, R.Thomas 1988
Start 2m R of the chockstone at a TR above a small hole. Climb
past the TR and up the wall to a small overhang, TR. Move over it,
PR and up the wall above. Belay to the abseil rope.

Scarface   15m   E1   5c   †
J.Bullock, L.Moran, R.Thomas 1988
Climb the wall 6m R of the chockstone, TR, to reach a shattered
groove. Follow this to the top. Abseil rope belay.

Stonewall   15m   E1   5c   †
J.Bullock, L.Moran, R.Thomas 1988
Start 9m R of the chockstone. Climb to a diagonal RW-sloping
ledge then straight up LW, TR, to the top. Abseil rope belay.

PAVILAND FAR WEST
This is the zawn immediately W of Paviland main cliff. Approach
as for Far Far West (approach 1) but go down over a rock bridge
and scramble down. The routes are only accessible at low tide.

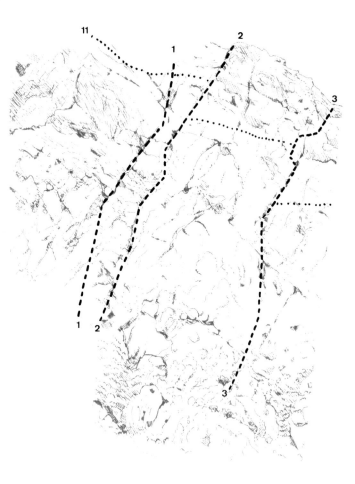

1. Armageddon
2. Gimli
3. Middle Earth

Paviland

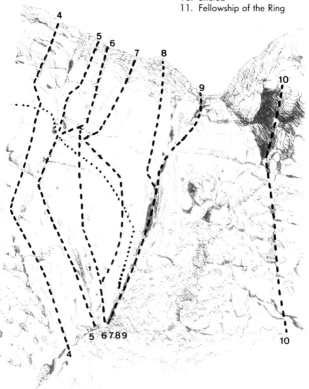

The cliff is characterised by a smooth overhanging white wall at its landward end. Access is by scrambling down the E-facing wall.

Rorkes Drift   21m   E1   5b   †
A.Sharp, J.Harwood 1985
Climb the centre of the wall 4m L of Smuts, moving R to finish.

Smuts   21m   VS   4c   †
A.Sharp, J.Harwood 1985
Abseil onto a large ledge below the obvious corner in the wall at the W end of the cliff and climb the corner.

SEA-LEVEL CRAGS
At the end of the wall/fence (approach 2) there is a gully leading to the sea. It contains a few short problems on the obvious E-facing wall as one enters the gully, all the obvious lines were climbed by C.Hebbelthwaite and A.Richardson during 1989.
The next routes are only accessible an hour each side of low tide, by following the gully, mentioned above, seawards until access can be gained to a gully to the W.

West Wall
This is the E-facing wall of the gully.

Simple Minds   12m   VS   4c
P.Lewis, J.Harwood 1985
Start just L of the overhangs guarding the base of the crag and climb the RW corner ramp.

Liberty   12m   E2   5c   **
A.Sharp, P.Lewis 1985
A strenuous, well-protected pitch. Follow the broken cracks just L of Simple Minds.

Metal Fatigue   12m   E3   6a
A.Sharp, P.Lewis, J.Harwood 1985
From 3m up Liberty, move LW into a small hole and follow this past a roof, exiting RW.

East Wall
This is the W-facing wall of the gully.

Yanks   12m   E4   6c   †
A.Sharp, J.Harwood 1985
This takes the thin flake crack in the centre of the E wall. Try to climb the flake crack to a spike (this can be lassoed), then trend RW up the wall to finish.

PAVILAND MAIN CLIFF
This is gained by following approach 2. The first feature to be

seen is a large cave (Paviland Cave). High above and to the L is
Shelob's Cave. Immediately L is an obvious groove/gully with
numerous holes; this is East Gully Groove. The majority of routes
are described from R to L since this is the direction of approach.
There are many variations but only the major ones are described.
The slabby buttress above Paviland Cave is loose and not recommended although routes have been recorded.
The first route described is situated on the E face, above blow
holes at the base of the cliff.

Polly's Route   45m   VD
R.Cole, P.Cole 1976
Climb the yellow slab trending LW.

The next route climbs through Shelob's Cave high above Paviland
Cave:

Shelob   36m   HS-,4b
J.Talbot, C.Connick 1976
An exposed and often hilarious route at the top end of its grade.
Start L of Paviland Cave.
1   24m Climb easy vegetated slabs to gain the cave. A belay here
makes it easier to watch the leader's antics on the next pitch.
2   12m Climb up the R side of the cave, round the back and
across the L wall to gain the hole, exit and belay.

East Gully Groove   36m   VS   4c   *
J.Talbot, C.Connick 1976
A good, well-protected route. Climb the gully in its entirety,
passing J.Talbot's workshop at half-height. Finish RW at the top.

Talons   32m   E2   5b,5c
M.Learoyd, G.Royle, R.Thomas 1984
Short fingery pitches up the R side of the steep smooth wall.
1   16m Climb Half Dome to the break then climb down to reach
EG Groove, or climb EG Groove to the first big hole.
2   16m Climb up the groove until it is possible to swing onto the
overhanging L wall. Follow a line of pockets up the wall; several
TR's and old PR's.

The Cure   33m   E4   6a/b   *
J.Talbot, C.Connick (Cancer A1)
FFA A.Sharp, J.Harwood 1985
As for Half Dome to the break. Just R of the second pitch of Half
Dome strenuously follow a faint crack line/weakness in the upper
wall to the top.

Half Dome   36m   E2   5b,5c   **
J.Talbot, C.Connick 1977
FFA A.Sharp, J.Harwood 1981
A justifiably popular route, sustained and pockety. Start a metre

or two up East Gully Groove.

1 17m Climb the wall to an old TR then move RW to gain an obvious foothold. Continue slightly LW to gain holds on the break and move LW to an obvious niche/ledge (The Ring Stance).

2 19m Traverse back to the R end of the ledge, move up RW to gain a good hand hold, R again to a crack, then steeply up to gain an old TR. Finish direct. Do not confuse this pitch with the top of Babylon: it follows a line R of Babylon .

Babylon   42m   HVS   5a   **
J.Talbot, C.Connick 1977

This takes a line R of and parallel to The Ring. Start at a deep slot at the foot of East Gully Groove. Climb cracks in the wall 1m R of The Ring to reach the ledge (variations possible) . From the R end of the ledge climb the cracks directly above, 2TR. Bear LW at the top.

Variation Finish: It is also possible to break through the roof just R of the top pitch of The Ring (5a).

The Ring   42m   HS   4b   **
J.Talbot, C.Connick 1976

The calcite-encrusted line rising from the foot of East Gully Groove. Climb to an obvious hole and follow the calcite line to the niche, possible belay. Climb the crack/groove above to the top.

Liang Shan Po   45m   HVS   5a   **
J.Talbot, C.Connick 1977

Fine climbing. Start L The Ring. Climb the wall anywhere via a tiny overhang at half-height, following a line roughly parallel to The Ring. Take the overhang direct via an obvious crack L of the arete, PR, and finish directly.

Middle Earth   45m   VS   4c   *
J.Talbot, C.Connick 1977

Another good route up the deep central groove and crack leading through the high central overhang L of Liang Shan Po. Start below the faint black-stained wall just R of two small recesses. Climb the wall anywhere to gain a deep groove and follow this to an overhang split by a deep crack. Move LW to gain a vague pedestal, up to a bulge then R to gain the crack above the overhang or take it direct (5a). Follow the crack to the top.

Black Widow   45m   HVS   5a
J.Talbot, C.Connick (first half) 1977
G.Evans, D.Hopkins (complete route) 1987

Start midway between Middle Earth and Gimli. Climb the wall fairly directly to about mid-height then move up and R to a shaky pillar, on Gimli. Go up L to below the roof and pull R on a good hold to the top.

Gimli 42m VS 4c   *
J.Talbot, C.Connick 1977
This climbs the crack and groove up the R side of the high central
overhang. Start in the recess containing a hole, directly below the
R side of the big roof. Climb cracks to the R end of the overhangs,
move steeply up the groove until below a final overhanging crack,
move up L and back R to the top. The crack direct is 5a.

Armageddon 42m VS 4c   *
J.Talbot, C.Connick 1978
This takes the wide crack near the R end of the big roof. Start in
the recess as for Gimli, climb a ramp on the L wall of the recess
and follow a crack to a steep bubbly wall beneath the roof. Take
the wide crack through the overhang, then the steep wall above
to the top.

Balrog 42m HS 4b
J.Talbot, C.Connick 1976
The LH overhangs are comprised of a big upper roof and a smaller
one below and L. Climb a groove and corner to the L side of the
smaller roof, traverse R below it to the corner and climb this to
the big roof. Move steeply L then back R to a niche above the
roof. Finish direct. (The first roof direct is 4c).

West Arete 45m VD (O)
J.Talbot, C.Connick 1977
A loose monster at the far LH end of the face. Climb to an overlap
and move RW into a vague corner, then LW to the skyline arete
and finish up this.

A few loose routes have been recorded L of this but are held in
place by beams from outer space and are not recorded here.

Fellowship Of The Ring 42m HVS 5b,5a,4c   **
J.Talbot, C.Connick 1977
A fine high level girdle of the cliff. Start by scrambling up the easy
lower part of East Gully Groove to the obvious LW rising traverse
line.
1   9m Move LW and traverse with difficulty to a ledge and belay
(The Ring).
2   12m Move slightly up and L and traverse steep rock to reach a
deep groove (Middle Earth). Belay at the bottom of this.
3) 21m Climb the groove to the overhang. Move onto the pedestal
L of the groove and continue traversing L to the next groove
(Gimli). Climb this for about 3m before stepping L onto the
undercut wall below a small overhang. Traverse below the overhang to reach a crack (Armageddon) and then the top.

Red Lady 48m E1 5a,5b
J.Talbot, C.Connick c1977
FFA J.Bullock, G.Evans 1980

A rather indefinite rising traverse. Start as for Half Dome.
1   25m Climb onto the wall and make a LW rising ascent to the quartzy crack of The Ring. Traverse L to Liang Shan Po and follow this for a short distance to the level of a small hole. Traverse L to Middle Earth and belay in the crack below an obvious niche.
2   23m Move LW to the crack of Gimli and swing L onto the wall above the large overhang. Swing L to Armageddon, up which it is advisable to finish.

The downward continuation of East Gully Groove leads to a non tidal gully with a short E-facing wall. It contains a number of micro routes.

Mouse House   9m   E2   5c   †
P.Donnithorne,1988
This takes a line near the LH end of the wall, 2 TR's.

Ferrit   9m   E1   5b   †
P.Donnithorne 1988
The wall 2m R of Mouse House.

Shrew   9m   E1   5b   †
P.Donnithorne 1988
Climb the wall 2m R of Ferrit.

Rat   9m   E4   6a   †
P.Donnithorne 1988
R again. Climb to an overhanging flake crack and follow it with difficulty.

Ice Age Zawn
This is the very small narrow zawn below the L side of Paviland Main Cliff.

Ice Age   15m   E3   5c   †
A.Sharp, J.Harwood 1985
The obvious layback crack in the L side of the zawn. Finish directly.

Down Under   21m   E5   6a   * †
A.Sharp, P.Lewis, P.Thomas 1985
A strenuous number. Start 6m R of Ice Age and climb an obvious line of LW trending flakes over a roof to the top.

Squeeze Please   18m   VS   4c
P.Thomas, P.Lewis, A.Sharp 1985
The chimney at the back of the zawn, finishing behind the chockstone

JUNIPER WALL
Follow approach 3. At first sight this cliff appears slabby and

Juniper Wall

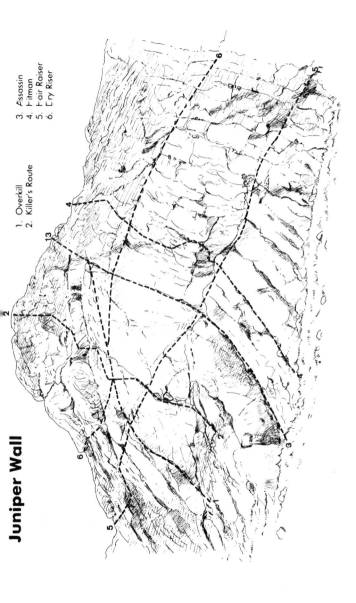

1. Overkill
2. Killer's Route
3. Assassin
4. Hitman
5. Hair Raiser
6. Cry Riser

broken, but the routes are not easy-angled. The buttress is triangular with prominent overhangs at its apex. A large overlap
runs down L from a corner beneath the centre of the main
overhangs. In the centre of the crag below the overhangs is a
slightly R-slanting groove and thin crack. This is crossed at one-
third and two-thirds height by two cracks rising LW across the
crag, parallel with the R skyline. In the L side of the main overhangs is a prominent nest. This should be left alone, not only for
ornithological reasons, but also because of the dire con-
sequences of disturbing the resident.

The lines, although good, tend to be a bit difficult to follow, so
read the descriptions carefully. Belays on the top of the cliff are
positioned well back and descent is by an easy gully to the W or
grassy slopes and scrambling to the E.

Overkill   48m   HVS   4c,4c
M.Harber, D.Parsons 1981
Start at the L side of the cliff just R of some black-stained rock and
below a RW-slanting crack which rises to meet an overlap.
1   24m Climb the crack to the overlap. Continue RW beneath it
until it is possible to traverse R to a poor stance (The Junction),
PR, 4m below the main overhangs.
2   24m Traverse R for 4m and pull steeply up R before continuing
the traverse to below the R end of the overhangs. Climb up
bearing RW to finish.

Killer's Route   42m   E2   4c,5b   *
C.Elliot, T.Oliver 1977 (pitch 1)
G.Evans, J.Bullock 1977 (pitch 2)
Start below and L of the slightly RW-slanting shallow central
groove by a wide slanting crack and slab.
1   20m Climb up L to a large triangular niche. Surmount the
overhang above and continue up a crack to a poor stance (The
Junction).
2   22m Climb up and L to a small overhung ledge in a corner. Pull
over to another overhung ledge, quit it on its R and continue up
steep but easy ground.

Barracuda   38m   E5   6a,5c   *
A.Sharp, J.Harwood 1982
A bold hard route up the wall between Killer's Route and
Assassin.
1   18m Climb directly up to the black-streaked wall from the start
of Killer's Route, sprint for the gear and make it snappy, to the
same belay as Killer's Route.
2   20m Move slightly R from the stance and climb to a small
overhung ledge in a big corner in the overhangs above. Finish
easily as for Killer's Route.

Assassin   45m   HVS   5a   **
E.Pardoe, 1968/69
FFA J.Bullock, R.Thomas 1978
Superb initial climbing up the RW-slanting groove in the centre of
the cliff. Climb the crack and slab that lead to a groove and a
shallow niche at 21m. Continue using the twin cracks above,
move R around the bulge and then L to a broken groove. Follow
this with difficulty to a ledge, and then easily to the top.

Perch   35m   E1   5b   †
G.Evans, J.Bullock 1989
This doesn't quite have the bite of Barracuda! Climb to the overlap as for Hitman then continue up a pair of thin cracks to the
break of Dry Riser. The wall above is climbed to the top finishing
about 3m R of Assassin.

Hitman   33m   VS   4c
J.Bullock, G.Evans 1977
A sustained but vague line. An obvious wedged block above the
lower LW-slanting diagonal crackline and R of the groove of
Assassin is the first objective. Start below the block. Climb to the
L of the block and awkwardly onto it, step up L into a small niche
and follow the crack above to a shallow depression on the upper
diagonal crack (Dry Riser). Move diagonally RW across a steep
wall to gain a broken crack and follow this slightly L to the top.

Rattle And Hum   35m   VS   4c   O   †
C.Allen, L.Cain 1986
Start 2m R of Hit Man. Climb a RW slanting crack to the top.

Task Force   36m   VS   4c
M.Harber, C.Horsfield 1982
Start at a small recess below and slightly R of the wedged block of
Hitman. Climb a crack in a vague groove slightly RW, until it is
possible to step R into a small recess in the upper diagonal line on
the face (Dry Riser). Step up L and climb the steep broken crack as
for Hitman.

Hair Raiser   44m   HVS   5a,4c
M.Harber, S.Robinson 1982
This follows the lower of two LW slanting cracklines across the
face. Start at the RH end of the crack.
1   24m Follow the crack to the apex of the easy angled slab below
Assassin, follow it along the steepening crack and strenuously
across a bulging wall to a niche (Killers Route). Continue for 4m to
belays in a small recess.
2   20m Move L to an overlap and follow it down for 4m. Pull up L
at a slight break, to another overlap. Traverse L beneath this to
finish at the gully.

Ninja   30m   VS   4b   *
C.Allen, M.Danford, A.Beaton 1990
Start just L of Hair Raiser. Climb directly to a hanging block at 3m,
follow a zig zag crack to a shallow niche on the upper diagonal
line. Continue up and L through a black stained bulge, to another
shallow niche. Bear R to finish.

On The Horizon   24m   VS   4b
G.Richardson, J.Pratt, C.Lownds 1981
A.Beaton, C.Allen, M.Danford direct start 1990
Start at the bottom RH end of the lower diagonal crack. Follow
parallel cracks RW until they peter out, move R and up to a recess
taking care with the rock. Finish directly.
Direct Start 4c: The crack 3m R of the normal start.

Socialist Worker   27m   VS   4c
L.Moran, K.Snook, G.Richardson 1977
It keeps going left. Start at a shallow black-stained scoop 4m R of
On The Horizon. Climb a crack line trending slightly LW to a
junction with the upper diagonal crack (Dry Riser). Continue in
the same line up the crack above to a vegetated depression. Move
L and finish directly.

Dry Riser   67m   HVS   4c,4c   **
M.Harber, J.Mothersele 1977
A girdle taking the higher of the two diagonal cracks. Start at the R
side of the cliff where the crack meets the ground.
1   36m Climb the crack to below the main overhangs. Traverse
6m L to the poor stance of Overkill (The Junction).
2   31m Traverse L for 7.5m and break through the overlap just L
of a tiny corner. Continue up and L to easy ground.

The Jackal Finish   E1   5b
J.Bullock, G.Evans 1982
From the belay on Dry Riser move up and L into a corner where
the overlap meets the main overhang. Climb the corner, moving L
below a PR to a rib. Continue L for 3m to a rest, then back R and
follow a groove through an overhang and up steep rock to finish.

HORSES CLIFF TO PORT EYNON OS ref 442856 to 468844
A.Richardson

SITUATION AND CHARACTER
A complex stretch of coastline offering much rock, but with the
exception of the excellent Boiler Slab, little climbing . . .as yet.
The area abounds in small isolated buttresses and is a pleasant
place to walk and explore away from the hordes.

Scavenger VS 4b Three Cliffs *Climber* H. Griffiths

Photo G. Evans

Foxy by Proxy E5 6a Fox Hole Crag *Climber* A. Long   *Photo* A. Richardson

APPROACHES AND ACCESS
See map 2. It is possible to approach this section as for the approach to Paviland, or from Overton.
1   Horses Cliff and Yellow Buttress: From the stile at the head of the valley leading to Paviland and Juniper Wall (see the previous section), bear L (E) across open cliff land until a fence is reached running down to the sea. Follow it down a deep gully to reach the cliffs.
2   Overton Cliff and Boiler Slab: Follow the A4118 to Port Eynon but just before entering it turn off R to Overton village and follow a lane (OS ref 455853) W along the cliff top. There is parking along the length of the lane but it is constantly used by farmers so please park carefully. Cross the stile and take the first valley on the L for Overton cliff and the second valley on the L for Boiler slab. The cliffs are to the L (E) when facing out to sea.
3   Port Eynon Point: Park in Port Eynon and follow coastal paths W to the headland.
4   Oxwich Point: Head for Oxwich Green (limited parking so do not obstruct the turning area for buses). To the R of a barn is a path between high hedges. Follow this past a caravan park to a sewage farm and over two stiles to the cliff top. Follow a limestone ramp down LW to the coastal path and follow this EW to an obvious buttress on the skyline 20 mins from Oxwich Green.
An alternative approach is to park at Oxwich and follow the path through the woods on the W side of the bay past a chapel and then round the headland.

HORSES CLIFF AND YELLOW BUTTRESS
At the base of the gully (Approach 1) Horses Cliff is seen to the W and Yellow Buttress to the E.

Horses Cliff
Horses Cliff is a narrow ridge running down towards the sea with a prominent tower at the seaward end.

South Ridge   45m   D
J.Talbot 1963
A mountaineering route. Start at the base of the ridge of Horses Cliff and follow it to the top.

The Corner   9m   S
J.Talbot 1969
This takes the short corner on the W flank, via a steep overhang, to reach the South Ridge.

Yellow Buttress
Yellow Buttress is more impressive than Horses Cliff, with a steep narrow ridge on the L and a series of grooves to the R. There is a prominent saddle at its base.

South West Diedre   18m   S
J.Talbot 1969
A good line L of the ridge. Some rock requires careful handling.

The steep bulging E face has two obvious groove lines:

Left Groove   15m   S
The LH groove is gained by a traverse from the ribs on the L.

Right Groove   15m   E1   5a
The RH groove is much steeper than it looks. Gain it from below and slightly R.

DEVIL'S CWM
45m S from Yellow Buttress is a great rocky hollow falling for approximately 30m to the sea. It contains extremely friable rock and none of the climbs can be recommended.

WHITE PILLAR
Not an easy cliff to find. From the end of the lane (approach 2) follow the cliff top to a gate with sheep pens just on the R. Beyond this the path leads to another gate and stile with a valley on the L, and thence to a second, wider valley, 10 mins from the end of the lane. White Pillar is to the W of the mouth of this valley, and is reached by scrambling down to a big sloping ledge at its foot.
The cliff has a wide slabby section rising to a series of overhangs and tapering to a pinnacle trending L.

Crack and Slab   27m   VD
J.Talbot 1967
Lacks the quality of West Kante. Climb the crack/fault on the L side of the cliff to join West Kante at the raised slab. Finish R instead of climbing the final wall.

West Kante   30m   S   **
J.Talbot 1967
A good climb. Start on the L by a sentry box at 6m. Climb to it, then take thin cracks to a broken groove. Follow this via an overhang to a short slab below the final wall. Climb this direct to a groove and the top.

Grey Slab   27m   S
J.Talbot 1967
Start R of West Kante and climb the slabs R of a chimney/crack, then traverse R below overhangs to a groove breaking through them on their RH side. Step L at its top to another groove and finish.

Sizzler   27m   E1   5b   †
J.Harwood 1987
Start just R of Grey Slab. Climb to the overhangs and pull through

onto a small smooth hanging slab and over the next overhang to reach a crack leading to easier ground and the top.

Bermuda Shorts   24m   VS   4c   †
J.Harwood 1987
Start below the midpoint of the overhangs. Climb up to the overhangs and move 2m R along Grey Slab. Move over the overhang at a break to reach a groove L of the finish of Grey Slab. Follow this to the top.

BLACK HOLE CRAG
Looking E from White Pillar or W from Boiler Slab, there is an obvious low rocky promontory running out to sea. Just W of this, at the foot of a large dome-like headland, is a wall 91m long with a large pool at its E end. The cliff is accessible for about 2 hrs either side of low tide. There are many easy routes with so many variations that it is not possible to describe them: J.Talbot has stepped on every hold.

BOILER SLAB
This is the best cliff in this section, containing some excellent middle-grade routes. It is reached by following approach 2. It has a broad slabby face with a broken buttress to the L and a large overhang at its centre top, with, more overhangs below R. The cliff is named after the wrecked ships boiler which can be seen at low water. It is popular with groups so be prepared to share the cliff.
The broken buttress to the L has been climbed on by many outdoor centre instructors for years, but no routes have been claimed.

Classic   19m   VD   **
A.Osborne, B.Taylor 1949
Climb the obvious corner on the L side of the main slabby face, keeping to its RH slab.

Column   19m   S   4a
J.Talbot 1967
Start a metre R of Classic. Climb directly up the R side of a shallow pillar just L of a groove, to a shallow depression with a patch of ivy. Climb over this and follow ledges to the top.

Dulfer   19m   S   4a   **
A.Osborne, B.Taylor 1949
An excellent route with continually interesting climbing. Follow the obvious corner R of Column until it peters out. Step R and continue to the bulges above, step L and climb the break in the bulges, then climb directly to the top.

Swirtler   21m   HVS   5b
T.Moon, C.Maybury 1973
Climb the R edge of the smooth slab 1m R of Dulfer to the bulges above. Go through these in a direct line between Dulfer and Direct route.

Direct   21m   VS   4b   *
J.Talbot 1968
Start 5m R of Dulfer. Climb a distinct black slab with ivy, up L to a curving overhang and surmount this trending L. Follow the slab above to a small roof and pass it on the L. Finish direct through the bulges.

Termination   21m   HVS   5a
P.Hinder, V.Rees 1970
A good, steep, but poorly protected pitch. Start 3m R of Direct below a patch of ivy on the overhang above. Climb to it, over it and up the thin crack until it peters out. Traverse LW and exit over the bulging blocks L of the main overhang.

Nuclear Arms   21m   E2   5c   *
A.Sharp, J.Harwood 1985
A one move wonder. As for Termination to the traverse, continue to the large roof and finish over this on its L side, PR.

Middle Age Dread   21m   E4   6a
A.Sharp, P.Lewis 1985
Start 4m R of Termination. Climb an orange groove and slabs to the main overhang at its widest point, PR (missing). Explode through the roof to the top.

Nemo   18m   VS   4b
P.Hinder 1970
Climb a short broken corner, 6m R of Direct, to the L end of an overhang with a black-stained slab below it. Surmount it using a thin crack, move RW and continue direct to a groove through the block overhangs above. Follow this taking the jutting overhang at the top directly.

Tokyo   21m   E2   5c   *
A.Sharp, J.Harwood 1985
An eliminate between Nemo and Ayesha, offering good climbing. Start just R of Nemo, below the widest part of the overhang. Climb to the overhang and make a long reach over it. Continue with interest to the top bulges and climb through the middle of these to the top.

Tokyo 11   VS   4b
G.Evans, K.Snook 1988
The thin crack through the overhang between Tokyo and Ayesha.

Ayesha   21m   VS   4c   *
J.Talbot 1971
Start at the foot of a slab below the RH end of the overhang and just
L of the obvious groove of Pinnacle Crack. Climb the overhang at
its RH end, continue to the overhangs above and take these on
good holds on the R rib to the top.

Pinnacle Crack   24m   VD
J.Talbot 1969
This takes the obvious broken groove at the R of the main face.
Follow the groove to a bulge, step L taking care with the rock, then
follow a continuation groove to the top.

Girdle   27m   VS   4c
G.Evans, G.Richardson 1977
Start up Classic and follow the obvious horizontal crack at half-
height. Finish up Pinnacle Crack or Ayesha.

Overhang Traverse   36m   VS   4c
A.Bevan, R.Bowen, D.Jones A1 1960
FFA C.Maybury, T.Moon 1973
Climb Dulfer to the obvious horizontal crack then go up to the next
crack. Move RW to below a small roof then go up to the main roof.
Follow the horizontal crack RW and exit up a deep cut to the R.

OVERTON CLIFF
A minor crag reached by taking the first valley on the L from the end
of the lane of approach 2. The cliff is to the E of the mouth of the
valley and at first sight is impressive, but unfortunately the routes
start from a grass ledge at the level of the cave on the S face,
reducing the length to 14m.

South West Corner   14m   D
A.Osborne, B.Taylor 1952
This takes the corner L of the centre of the crag.

West Wall   14m   S
J.Talbot 1969
This climbs the R wall of the corner.

Black Widow   14m   HVS   5a
T.Moon, C.Maybury 1973
This climbs the groove on the upper face, R of West Wall.

South wall   14m   E1   5b
J.Talbot 1968
FFA G.Evans, G.Richardson 1978
This follows the line of bolts just L of the cave. The upper part of the
line of bolts can be reached from the R side of the cave at the same
grade.

Cave Crack   14m   HS   4a
T.Moon, C.Maybury 1973
This climbs the rib at the R of the cave, over a small overhang and up the groove to the top.

PORT EYNON POINT
Follow approach 3 to the headland, OS ref 471845. The only recorded climb here is in a cave reached just after passing Port Eynon headland, 5 to 10 mins from Port Eynon car park via the Youth Hostel. Access is only possible at low tide.

Port Eynon Cave Climb   18m   S
D.Lillicrap 1957
Start at the back of the cave and climb the R wall to a black hollow. Go up and out R then traverse delicately to a tiny ledge, and move up and across R to where the overhang eases. Climb the overhang direct to a good ledge and an easy wall.

OXWICH POINT
A pleasant series of buttresses that are not often visited. They are exposed to the wind and are therefore cold in winter. Follow approach 4.
A minor buttress, easily recognised by its prominent overhanging nose, is passed en-route to the headland. The first routes described are situated here.

Mortuary Crack   9m   D
B.Winterburn et al 1971
This follows the obvious crack running up behind the blocky nose.

Vampire Wall   11m   VS   4c
J.Procter, B.Winterburn 1971
Start at the inner edge of the wall R of the above. Traverse to a small ledge in the middle. Move onto the nose and over it.

Next is a prominent buttress on the W side of the headland. It is characterised by bulging walls split by a series of steep corners.

Far South West Corner   12m   VS   4b
R.Owen, D.Jones 1959
The furthest corner to the L.

Lichen Wall   12m   HVS   5a
J.Talbot, D.Thomas Aid 1959
FFA E.Kellar, A.Richardson via direct start 1959
Climb the centre of the wall L of South West Corner.

South West Corner   12m   HS
R.Owen, D.Jones 1958
This follows the next corner R of Far SW Corner. Loose in its upper section.

South West Chimney   12m   HS
R.Owen, D.Jones 1958
Further R. Steep bridging up the wide chimney crack to the top.

Oxbow   12m   VS
J.Bullock, G.Evans
The crackline just around the arete from South West Chimney.

Benbow   12m   VS
J.Bullock, G.Evans
The steep crack line on the R side of the overhanging face .

OXWICH BAY QUARRY OS ref 507858
Overlooking Oxwich Bay on the N side of the headland containing
Oxwich point, is an old quarry that has seen some recent activity
but no details are available.

WEST TOR, LITTLE TOR, AND GREAT TOR
OS ref 519878 to 529876
A.Richardson

SITUATION AND CHARACTER
A pleasant area of crags rising from spacious sandy beaches to the S
of the village of Penmaen. Great Tor is the very prominent feature
at the end of the headland separating Oxwich Bay from Three Cliff
Bay. Little Tor is a smaller headland set back a couple of hundred
metres W across the beach and West Tor is a little further W and
well above the beach.
The climbing is generally in the lower grades and this is an ideal area
for families or educational groups, when the tides are favourable.

APPROACHES AND ACCESS
See map 2. Approach from Penmaen. There is a small car park on
the A4118 at the Post Office and village store. Take the path
through the wide gate leading E past the village store. At the end of
the sunken lane fork R. Soon the back of Great Tor can be seen.
Descend slightly R to the beach, between Great Tor on the L(E) and
Little Tor on the R(W). West Tor is gained by walking past Little Tor
and scrambling up.

WEST TOR
This is the white slab situated well above sea-level. The Tor tends to
be vegetated in its upper part but the clean grooves to the R offer
some interesting climbs. The first routes in this area are found at
sea-level.

Fartlek   9m   E1   5c
P.Lewis, A.Sharp 1985
Start at beach level below the slab containing Curving Crack.

Climb a short thin crack.
The next routes are on the short slab above beach level.

Curving Crack   11m   VS   4c   *
J.Talbot, D.Corbett 1958
The deep cut in the slab above Fartlek. Difficult climbing involving acrobatic, out of balance moves; the lowest part is the hardest.

Smooth Operator   11m   E3   6a
A.Sharp, P.Lewis 1985
An eliminate line up the centre of the slab between Curving Crack and Innocent Savagery.

Innocent Savagery   11m   E1   5b
P.Lewis, A.Sharp 1985
Climb the series of cracks R of Curving Crack.

Popsi's Joy   11m   VS   4c
Climb the thin crack on the R edge of the slab.

Traverse   12m   VD
J.Talbot,G.Jones 1959
This takes a rising traverse line L across the slab .

Further R and higher up again is the Great Slab, on the E side of the Tor.

Notched Rib   15m   S
J.Talbot, D.Thomas 1959
This follows the rib on the L of the slab.

Cooking The Books   11m   E2   5b
A.Sharp, P.Lewis 1985
Climb the R arete of the slab.

Central Route   11m   E3   6b
J.Kerry 1971
FFA A.Sharp, P.Lewis 1985
Climb the thin cracks in the centre of the slab.

LITTLE TOR
This is accessible for 4 hrs either side of low tide. Descent is W across ledges and down to the beach. To the L (W) of the main cliff is a short wall with three obvious cracks.

Central Crack   9m   VD
J.Talbot, G.Jones 1959
The first crack.

Thin Crack   9m   S
J.Talbot, G.Jones 1959
The narrow crack R of central crack.

Right Crack   9m   VD
J.Talbot, G.Jones 1959
The wide crack to the R.

The main buttress is next.

Right Corner   15m   S
J.Talbot, G.Jones 1959
The steep corner on the L side of the buttress.

Left Edge (Tri Cornel)   18m   VD
J.Brailsford, St.AMRT 1954/55
Start at the L edge of the slab and follow cracks then tiny corners
to ledges and the top.

Centre Route   18m   VD
J.Talbot, G.Jones 1959
This vaguely climbs the corner and wall to the R. Many variations
are possible.

Central Flake   18m   S   4a   *
J.Brailsford, St.AMRT 1954/55
Climb the middle of the raised central slab.

Flake Corner   15m   VD
J.Brailsford, St.AMRT 1954/55
Climb the corner and wall R of Central Flake.

Direct Centre   18m   VD
J.Brailsford, St.AMRT 1954/55
Ascend directly up the wall R of Flake Corner.

Right Edge   18m   VD   *
J.Brailsford, St.AMRT 1954/55
Climb the R edge of the Tor.

LITTLE STAR WALL
This is the short wall lying further back R (E) of the previous routes.

Scout Crack   12m   S   **
J.Brailsford, St.AMRT 1954/55
A popular route up the smooth crack in the L side of the wall.
Using the ledge is cheating . . . so I've been told.

Superdirect   12m   E1   5c   *
SUMC 1965

FFA A.Sharp, J.Harwood 1980
A popular problem directly up the wall 2m R of Scout Crack.

Twinkle   12m   VD
J.Brailsford, St.AMRT 1954/55
The diagonal crack running up R via a distinct white calcite mark.
It is possible to go direct at 4c from the calcite mark.

Stella   12m   VS   4c
This takes the wall between Twinkle and Twin Crack L.

Twin Crack Left   9m   VD
J.Brailsford, St.AMRT 1954/55
A metre R. The L of two cracks via a peapod recess.

Twin Crack Right   9m   D
J.Brailsford, StAMRT 1954/55
The RH crack.

GREAT TOR
This is the obvious large headland situated further E.

UPPER TIER
This consists of a broad vegetated S face on which no worthwhile
routes have been found, and a narrow W face and E ridge. The
routes here are unaffected by the tide and can be approached by
bearing L(E) onto the headland leading out to the Tor rather than
descending to the beach as described in the approach section.
There is an obvious saddle between the Tor and the headland. On
the W side of the saddle, on the overhanging wall facing inland,
some routes have been described.

Southern Freeze   18m   HVS   5a
J.Harwood, A.Sharp 1980
The cracks on the L.

North Corner   39m   HVS   5a
R.Owen, C.Andrews 1959
The stepped corner to the R. Climb the quartz-flecked slab until it
is possible to move L to the foot of the corner. Finish up the final
slab.

The next two routes are on the narrow W-facing edge of the Tor.

Direct   42m   HVS   4c
R.Owen, C.Andrews 1959
Start below the narrow W face at an easy-angled calcite-flecked
slab some way up the beach. Follow a direct line up the centre of
the W face with poor protection.

South Edge   42m   HS   4a
J.Talbot, D.Thomas 1959
Start as for the previous route. Climb the R edge of the slab to its top. The rock needs care in the upper reaches.

East Ridge   73m   VD   **

A.Osborn, S.Osborn 1952
A well positioned route up the E-facing ridge of the upper Tor. Start on a platform well above the beach, below an E-facing wall at the foot of the ridge.
1   18m Climb the crack in the wall, move R and follow ledges to a large grassy terrace.
2   18m From the L end of the terrace climb a groove in the seaward face of the ridge before continuing up the arete to a stance by a flake. (The crack in the centre of the wall can be climbed at 4c).
3   13m Climb onto the flake and follow the arete to a grassy stance.
4   24m Climb the centre of the wall.Continue up short slabs to the top.

Just to the R (NE) of the saddle immediately behind the Tor is a series of E-facing corners which can be climbed at about S/HS.

LOWER TIER
At sea-level the S face is dominated by The Great Flake, behind which is a bubbly slab of similar height that contains all the routes described here.The climbs are tidal and best approached at low tide.

West Chimney   15m   S   4a
D.Jones, R.Owen 1954/55
The obvious leaning chimney, 5m L of the Great Flake, below and slightly L of the upper W face of the Tor.

Left Edge   18m   VS   4c
J.Talbot 1960
This follows the L edge of the bubbly wall. Start at the L end of a small ledge, climb the wall then a distinct corner. Finish up the sharp edge.

Bubbly Wall   18m   HVS   5a
J.Talbot, D.Thomas 1960
Start as for West Corner. Climb up for a metre, then traverse L onto the wall to reach a crack, which is followed to the top

West Corner   12m   D
A.Osborn, S.Osborn 1952
This climbs the distinct stepped corner just behind the L edge of the Great Flake.

Barnacle   12m   VS   4c
J.Talbot 1960
Start 3m R of West Corner below a distinct hole in the rock. Climb past the hole and continue very steeply to a good ledge. Finish up the yellow wall above.

Preuss Crack   12m   VS   4c
J.Talbot 1960
Start at a distinct short crack in the lower wall, 3m R of Barnacle. Climb the crack to reach good holds. Bear L and climb the crack above exiting RW.

Curving Corner   18m   VS   4c
J.Talbot 1960
A steep and delicate route a metre or so R of Preuss Crack. Climb a short crack in the lower wall and make an awkward mantleshelf on to a narrow ledge. Follow this up LW to its top, then climb a thin wall to a shallow scoop. Move into this then layback up a finger crack to the top.

Direct   18m   HVS   4c
J.Talbot 1960
As for Curving Corner to the ledge but take a thin crack and the steep smooth wall above to the top.

Right Curving Corner   21m   VD
J.Talbot 1960
As for Curving Corner to the ledge, traverse R to below a corner and follow it up RW to the top.

Brown Slab   21m   VD
J.Talbot 1960
This takes the wall R of Right Curving Corner.

Holey Wall   24m   VD
J.Talbot 1960
Climb the wall and short crack R of Right Curving Corner.

Y Wall
The slightly recessed wall to the R.

Right Corner   15m   VD
J.Talbot, D.Thomas 1959
Climb the LH crack then move RW to the top using a crack and corner

Left Corner   15m   VD
J.Talbot, D.Thomas 1958
Start as for Right Corner but exit the crack immediately and climb direct.

Block Wall   16m   VD
J.Talbot 1959
Just R of the previous route at a pool. Climb the lower crack of Y Wall, then traverse R above the pool and climb direct.

Central Crack   16m   VD
J.Talbot, D.Thomas 1959
Start at the R side of the pool and climb a crack to the top.

There are a number of obvious boulder problems to the R. These have all been climbed by J.Talbot.
To the E of Great Tor is a vast area of climbable rock with many short routes, far too numerous to record here. It is an area ideal for groups and the scrambler. E of the saddle of the Tor and well above the sea and Odin's Wall is a small crag with a cave at its base. The next route takes the wall/rib R of the cave. A preplaced rope belay is advisable.

Obscenities   12m   E4   6b   †
E.Kellar, A.Wilson 1990
Climb the rib direct, 1TR, 2PR's, to the roof, Pull through the roof into the groove via very thin moves until a 'thank God' hold can be reached. Continue direct to the top.

ODIN'S WALL
Amongst the array of buttresses E of the Tor and some 73m back from the seaward-end, is a prominent S-facing wall with a cave at its L side. Other than at near low tide, this is approached by bearing L (E) onto the headland leading out to the Tor, rather than descending to the beach as described at the beginning of this section. Follow the backbone of the headland and at the first pronounced saddle turn L(E). Odin's Wall can be seen below. Bear R over steep grass and then follow rocks down to the beach. The routes are accessible for two hours either side of low tide.

Cave Crack   18m   HS   4b
R.Owen, D.Jones, A.Bevan 1959
Start at the cave on the L side of the wall. Climb the corner L of the cave until it is possible to traverse delicately R into the hollow above the cave. Then climb the crack which runs diagonally R to the top.

Cave Crack Direct   18m   VS   4b   *
J.Talbot 1959
As for Cave Crack to the hollow, then climb the crack directly above to the top.

Direct   21m   VS   5a   *
J.Talbot, D.Thomas 1959
Start at the recess just R of the cave. Gain the crack above the

recess and follow it to the top. A wet landing awaits those who fail on the first two moves.

Fiechtl   18m   S
J.Talbot, D.Thomas 1959
Start at a small cave on the R side of the main wall. Climb the wide crack until it is possible to step into the crack immediately L. Climb this to a sentry box and then the top.

Wide Crack   18m   D
R.Owen, D.Jones 1959
Start as for Fiechtl. Climb the wide crack, chimney and corner to the top.

Girdle Traverse   18m   VS   4c
A R to L girdle at half-height.

Further E at beach level are a number of short walls all climbed on by J.Talbot. The start of the climbs can be identified by a small rock outcrop isolated from the mainland and rising from the beach. One route here is worthy of a mention.

Hole Slab   9m   D
J.Talbot 1959
Climb a distinct corner for a short way then climb a slab to an obvious hole. Finish direct.

THREECLIFF BAY TO SHIRE COMBE O.S ref 538878 to 548873
A.E.Richardson

SITUATION AND CHARACTER
Set in one of Gower's most scenic areas, this has become one of its more popular venues, providing pleasant slab climbing on good rock, almost exclusively in the lower grades. The Three Cliffs themselves lie at the end of the headland in the SE corner of Threecliff Bay separating this from the smaller Pobbles Bay to the E. Shire Combe is the prominent pillar projecting into the sea at the E end of Pobbles Bay. Unfortunately, it is a popular area for groups, who often do battle over their favourite routes.

APPROACHES AND ACCESS
See map 2. There are a number of possible approaches:
1   For Three Cliffs: Just before Penmaen, when approaching from Swansea, is a telephone kiosk. Turn R (N) into a National Trust car park. From here head towards North Hill Farm and signposts for the beach, cross the river via obvious stepping stones. The rear of the Three Cliffs is visible ahead.
2   For Three Cliffs and Pobbles Bay: Just past the Golf Club (do not park here) at Southgate, is a lane. At its end follow an obvious path W through the sand dunes that lead to Pobbles Bay. Please

park carefully if using this approach.
3 For Pobbles Bay and Three Cliffs: From the National Trust car park at Southgate, follow a private road W. Near its end a path breaks off LW, follow this along the cliff top past Shire Combe and around the back of Pobbles Bay (20 mins).
4 For Shire Combe: Park as for approach 3. Follow the private road from Southgate until an iron stake is seen at the cliff top. 60 to 70 metres beyond this is a rocky ridge descending from a promontary overlooking Pobbles Bay; this is Shire Combe. Descend a vague path to reach the E side of the headland. The slab containing Anemone wall is about 100 metres further E.
5 For Watch House Crag: Park as for approach 3. Follow the private road from Southgate to its end at 'Watch House' and then head for the sea.
6 For Watch House East: Park as for approach 3. Follow the private road from the car park, take the first broad track on the L and cut down through a col before crossing the grass to the W. A short stretch of gorse-lined path leads to a small clearing. The crag is below. Continuing around the back of the cove brings one down onto a grassy promontory from which the cliff can be seen.
7 For Fox Hole Crag approach as for Watch House East but go E for 50m after reaching the foot of the grassy col to reach several spike belays 4m above the top of the crag. It is best to leave a spare rope to belay/ lower off. Scramble down easily over grass either side to reach the cave. OS ref 552873.
It is also possible to reach the Watch House Crag to Fox Hole Crag area at low tide by walking directly towards the sea from the National Trust Car park and heading W. This is preferable for those new to the area.

THREE CLIFFS
This is the prominent cliff on the E side of Three Cliff Bay, it has three pinnacles and a large through-cave that lies between the highest pinnacles. Descents follow easy ledges and grooves either LW (W), or more difficult RW (E). Climbing is possible for 3 hrs either side of low tide.

Cleft 11   11m   D
J.Brailsford, St.AMRT 1954/55
Below the L pinnacle is a raised slab and to its R is an obvious cleft. Climb the cleft and the slab above, keeping L of a small block overhang.

Wall Climb   11m   VD
J.Brailsford, St.AMRT 1954/55
The slab R of the cleft can be climbed anywhere.

Three Cliffs

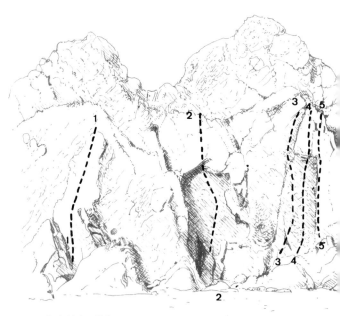

1. Initiation Flake
2. Inverted V
3. Joggled Wall
4. Joggled Wall Direct
5. Perseverance

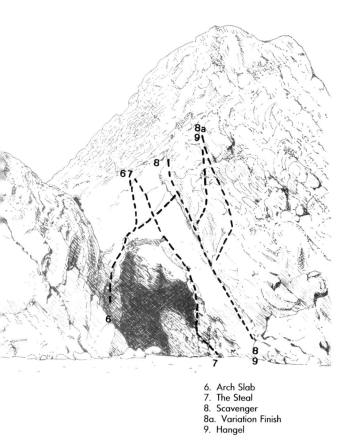

6. Arch Slab
7. The Steal
8. Scavenger
8a. Variation Finish
9. Hangel

Left Corner   11m   D
J.Brailsford, St.AMRT 1954/55
Further R is another raised slab. Climb the L corner of the raised slab.

Initiation Flake   12m   S   *
J.Brailsford, St.AMRT 1954/55
Climb the raised slab in its centre.

Right Corner   12m   D
J.Brailsford, St.AMRT 1954/55
Climb the R corner of the raised slab

Meander   12m   D
J.Brailsford, St.AMRT 1954/55
Take any line up the pocketed slab R of the raised slab.

In the recess between the first and second pinnacles is a smooth slab topped by an inverted-V overhang.

Left Corner   16m   D
J.Brailsford, St.AMRT 1954/55
Climb the corner L of the recessed slab area.

Inverted V   16m   HVS   4c   *
R.Owens, C.Edwards 1959
A short bold route. Climb the smooth slab to the overhang's apex, over this and delicately up the slab above.

Spouse Crack   16m   S
J.Brailsford, St.AMRT 1954/55
Climb the thin crack in the RH side of the slab to a short groove on the R. Take this to the overhang and pull over to an easy groove or move L and climb the crack system above the overhang.

Quartz Corner   16m   HS
J.Brailsford, St.AMRT 1954/55
This follows the narrow slabby corner R of the recessed slab. Climb this to a calcite slab then move R over an overhang and go up a crack to the top.

Joggled Wall   18m   VD   *
J.Brailsford, St.AMRT 1954/55
This follows the rough brown slab that forms the corner of Quartz Corner, avoiding the overhang on its L side. The L edge can be climbed at the same grade.

Joggled Wall Direct   18m   HS, 4b   *
C.Edwards, R.Owens, C.Andrews 1959
Takes the overhang Joggled Wall avoids.

Perseverance   18m   HS   4b/c   *
J.Brailsford, St.AMRT 1954/55
Follow thin disjointed cracks in the grey raised slab R of Jogggled
Wall Direct, moving L at the top and avoiding the R edge. It can
also be climbed on the L arete at the same grade.

Right Corner   18m   M
J.Brailsford, St.AMRT 1954/55
The obvious corners to the R are useful for descent.

Arch Slab   24m   VS   4c   **
R.Owen, C.Edwards, C.Andrews 1959
Start on the L wall of the cave below a groove. Climb the groove
until just above the lip of the cave, traverse RW (the lower your
feet the harder it is) to the apex and then go directly up the slab or
finish up Scavenger or its variation finish.

Under Milk Wood   21m   VS   4b
R.McElliot, R.Hoare 1984
Start inside the cave. Climb across the L side of the arch of the
cave and exit through a small hole.

The Steal   24m   E4   6a   **
S.Lewis, A.Richardson, C.Curle 1987
A good modern addition requiring arms like Twizzle (ask your
mum and dad) for the crux. Start directly below the bottom of the
small subsidiary slab that runs down from the cave apex. The start
is problematical and best approached from the R, PR. Gain the
roof and go over it onto the subsidiary slab. Climb this delicately
to the cave apex, PR, over this and finish directly.

Scavenger   26m   VS   4b   ***
J.Brailsford, St.AMRT 1954/55
J.Kerry variation start 1970
A pure line with perfect climbing. Start below the obvious corner/
slab R of the cave. Ascend it with a mixture of crack and slab
techniques, to a large ledge below the top. PB.
Variation start: start in the cave 4m from the normal start. climb to
gain a spike on the edge of the slab then join the slab.
Variation Finish: From a point when the route reaches the cave
apex struggle RW up a steep wall to easier ground.

Hangel   27m   VS   4c
R.Owen, C.Edwards, C.Andrews 1954/55
Climb Scavenger for half its length to a point level with the start of
a small recessed slab on the L. Move out R by an overhanging
ramp ledge to below a slab. Climb direct up its L edge to the top.

Plumb Line   45m   D
J.Brailsford, St.AMRT 1954/55

Start on a slabby buttress at the foot of the third pinnacle. Climb the buttress and then the narrow raised slab to more broken slabs which are followed to the top.

Disappointment   45m   D
J.Brailsford, St.AMRT 1954/55
Start at the foot of the obvious broken groove on the SE facet of the pinnacle. Climb the groove and step R into the more narrow continuation groove; thence the top.

Traverse of The Three Pinnacles   76m   D   *
A good scramble from L to R keeping to the crest and taking in all the summits.

POBBLES BAY
A pleasant small bay immediately E of Three Cliff Bay. The routes are short but interesting and run from the Three Cliffs to Shire Combe. A good area for a family visit, or as an alternative to Three Cliffs when that is full.

West Crag
Round the corner from Three Cliffs is a cave. R of the cave is a small crag with three overhangs and a raised pillar on the R.

Gwyn's Route   11m   HS
Climb the three overhangs direct.

Main Wall   11m   S
J.Talbot, R.Corbett 1954/55
From the corner of Gwyn's Route move L onto the wall and up.

Left Corner   11m   VD
J.Brailsford, St.AMRT 1954/55
Climb the corner R of Gwyn's Route.

Left Pillar   11m   VD
J.Brailsford, St.AMRT 1954/55
Climb the L side of the raised slab R of Left Corner.

Pillar Route   11m   D
J.Brailsford, St.AMRT 1954/55
Climb the R side of the raised slab.
Moving R (E) from these routes is an obvious small gully.

East Fissure Wall   11m   VD
J.Talbot, R.Corbett 1954/55
Climb the back wall of the gully.

Shy Slab   9m   VD
J.Brailsford, St.AMRT 1954/55
Climb the steep slab on the R side of the gully over two bulges.

Square Cut   9m   D
J.Brailsford, St.AMRT 1954/55
The slab to the R.

Right Edge   9m   D
J.Brailsford, St.AMRT 1954/55
The next slab to the R.
To the R(E) is a deep gully.

Little Corner   9m   VD
J.Brailsford, St.AMRT 1954/55
Climb the slab on the inside of the gully.

Fissure Direct   9m   VD
J.Brailsford, St.AMRT 1954/55
Climb the fissure and the slab.

Fissure Route   9m   D
J.Brailsford, St.AMRT 1954/55
Climb the deep fissure to the R.

Soap Gut   9m   D
J.Brailsford, St.AMRT 1954/55
Climb the slabby wall just R of the fissure.

Scoop   9m   D
J.Brailsford, St.AMRT 1954/55
Go up from the obvious scoop at ground level.

First Slab   9m   D
J.Brailsford, St.AMRT 1954/55
The most easterly slab. Climb it direct.

Girdle   9m   VD
J.Brailsford, St.AMRT 1954/55
The obvious line girdling the crag.

The remainder of rock on the E of Pobbles Bay has been explored and a number of short routes recorded, but they are left for people to rediscover but not to reclaim.

SHIRE COMBE
There is climbing in two areas here: Shire Combe itself, located at the far E of Pobbles Bay; and The Slab, about 100m E of the headland (see Approach 4).

SHIRE COMBE
The climbing is on a slab of rock resting against the headland with a cleft behind it. Access to the routes is by descending down the W face of the headland and traversing in.

East Face   36m   D
J.Talbot, D.Thomas 1954/55
This climbs the L arete of the E-facing wall of the buttress, continuing up RW via short walls from the ledge at one-third height.

The Jackal   27m   HVS   5a
N.Williams, P.Williams 1980
Start at the foot of the overhanging corner on the E-facing wall. Climb the corner until able to move L across the overhanging wall to gain a ledge on the arete. Continue easily up the wall LW to the top or, harder, finish up the twin cracks on Eastern Promise.

Eastern Promise   27m   E2   5C   *
E.Pardoe, P.Kokelaar 1965
FFA A.Sharp, J.Harwood 1983
A fine pitch. Start as for The Jackal but continue to the overhang, go over this LW and finish up twin cracks.

The next routes start inside the cleft.

Il Bel Camino   27m   HVS   4c/5a   **
A.Sharp, J.Harwood 1983
A superb route, excellent rock and a unique atmosphere. The route is approached by scrambling through the cleft from the W. Start directly below a boulder choke formed where the slab rests against the headland. Climb the cleft to the choke then move RW around the choke to the top.

Painters Paradise   27m   VS   4c
C.Hebbelthwaite, J.Beynon 1988
This climbs the slab R of Il Bel Camino to join it at its top. Approached by scrambling in from the E.

THE SLAB
This is the slab 100m E of the headland.

Great Chimney   23m   VS   4b
R.Owens, D.Jones 1959
Start at the L end of the ledge at the foot of the slab. Gain the chimney from the rib bounding the slab on the L and climb it, taking care with blocks at the top.

Honesty   18m   VS
J.Kerry, A.Randall 1970
Climb to the rib of Great Chimney then move R onto the slab and climb it direct.

Pickpocket   21m   HVS   5a/b
J.Kerry, A.Randall 1970
An artificial but enjoyable route directly up the slab between Great
Chimney and Anemone Wall. Using the crack is forbidden.

Anemone Wall   21m   VS   4c   **
J.Brailsford, St.AMRT 1954/55
Start where the crevasse closes and traverse L to the obvious
diagonal crack. When it peters out at a pocket, climb direct.

Alternate   18m   S
J.Brailsford, St.AMRT 1954/55
Start R of Anemone Wall. Follow discontinuous cracks and water-
worn grooves direct to the top.

The more broken slab to the R of Alternate gives a number of easier
climbs following indeterminate lines. Two of the best ones are
described below.

Respite   18m   VD
J.Brailsford, St.AMRT 1954/55
Start a metre R of Alternate and climb the slab direct.

Wide Crack   13m   D
J.Brailsford, St.AMRT 1954/55
Follow the wide crack to the top.

Girdle Traverse   22m   HS
J.Brailsford, St.AMRT 1954/55
Traverse the slab from L to R.

WATCH HOUSE CRAG
A minor, scrappy crag for the jaded locals. After reaching the sea
(approach 5) move W until a narrow gully well above the sea is
found. The first route starts on the L side of the steep slab.

Mr Angry   15m   VS   4b   O
E.Alsford, P.Donnithorne 1988
Very poor rock makes this a route for those with a death wish. Start
at a LW slanting groove, with some sandy rock at its base. Climb the
groove for 6m then move RW to finish straight up over a tiny
overlap.

Fob   15m   E1   5c   †
G.Evans, M.Lewis 1986
Start 3m R of Mr Angry. Make awkward moves up a thin crack, then
continue directly, taking care with loose undercuts on the overlap.

Mainspring   18m   E1   6a   †
G.Evans, N.Lewis, J.Bullock 1986

Start 3m down the slope from Fob. Mantleshelf with difficulty over the initial bulge and continue directly, PR, to a grassy ledge. Finish diagonally up the final wall. Belay well back.

Chronometer   18m   E1   5a   †
J.Bullock, L.Moran 1986
Start at a slot below the L side of the bulges in the middle of the cliff. Climb to the bulges and follow these LW.

Escapement   18m   E2   5b   †
J.Bullock, L.Moran 1986
A strenuous line through bulges just L of a calcite streak.

Alarm Clock   18m   E1   5a   †
L.Moran, J.Bullock 1986
This takes the rib and slight bulge R of the calcite streak. Loose.

WATCH HOUSE EAST
This is the steep buttress 300m E of Watch House Crag and is of interest to local climbers only. The cliff is barrel shaped and has an obvious depression in its upper section with a wide corner crack leading up RW. To the R the crag is severely undercut and a groove line running up to the L gives the line of Clip Joint. The routes can be attempted at all but the highest tides. It is best to lower off the routes and a PR in a small rock outcrop and a sling around a stout gorse bush just below the clearing are provided.

Straining Pitch   18m   E2   5c   †
J.Bullock, G.Evans 1989
Start just L of a small flying buttress at the LH end of the crag. Climb steeply, TR, to reach a ledge, TR. Step R to a layback crack and climb this, 2PR, to a ledge. Climb straight over the overhang above to a PB. Lower off.

Jump To Conclusion   18m   E3   6a   †
J.Bullock, M.Kydd, G.Evans 1989
Start 6m R of Straining Pitch below a brownish overhang at 16m. Climb to the base of the overhang and lurch/jump/dyno for a jug up L. Pull over and continue straight up to reach a ledge at the foot of a L-slanting groove. Climb the R arete of this to reach large holds. Lower off.

Pump Action   21m   E3/4   6a   †
J.Bullock, R.Thomas 1989
Start 3m R of Jump To Conclusions at a prominent red and white stratified niche. Climb this to ledge, step R and continue steeply, 2 PR, to a large pocket below the final problem! Over this to reach good finishing holds and a further niche, PR. Step R and climb a groove and corner crack to reach belays in a small rock outcrop.

Clip Joint   21m   E3   6a   †
J.Bullock, G.Evans 1989
Start where a red-tipped rock meets the cliff. Climb an overhang-
ing crack, TR, with increasing difficulty to reach a good incut, PR.
Move R to reach a chockstone, bridge up the groove onto a slab,
TR, and continue up a rounded arete to the R of a corner crack

The Road To Nowhere   E2   5b   †
G.Evans, J.Bullock 1989
The obvious lower R to L traverse line. Not as innocuous as it
appears. Start at the niche of Pump Action. Climb to an undercut
area of white rock and follow the traverse line by horizontal
techniques until it is possible to become vertical again. Teeter up
to the second TR on Straining Pitch before continuing up the
hollow flakes to reach a rounded spike where a grass cornice
abuts the crag. Lower off a sling around this.

Hue And Cry   E2   5c   †
G.Evans, J.Bullock 1989
A mid-height traverse. Above the rounded spike at the end of The
Road To Nowhere is a TR. Start from this thread, reached by
abseil. Move R to the layback crack of Straining pitch and follow
this to good holds. Descend RW to the ledge of Jump To Conclusions and continue steeply R to the slab of Clip Joint. Finish up
this.

FOX HOLE CRAG
Tucked away, this good crag is extremely steep and non tidal. It is
formed by the walls and upper roof of a large cave about 183m E
of Watch House East.The routes start at the narrow buttress
formed by the junction of the large cave and a smaller subsidiary
cave on its R.

The Hooker   21m   E4   6a   * †
J.Bullock, R.Thomas 1990
Climb steeply up the LW-leaning crack in the narrow buttress,
2TR, to reach the RH end of a terrace. Move straight up the
bulging wall, PR, and use a cemented hold to reach large holds,
PR. Difficult moves up allow good finishing holds to be gained,
PR, and provided some arm strength has been retained, the top.
SB.

Foxy Lady   21m   E4 6a   * †
J.Bullock, R.Thomas 1990
Start as for The Hooker. Climb RW past a hole and back L to a tiny
cave, PR. Swing L and, using a large cemented hold, gain the
terrace. Traverse L for 3m to an area of conglomerate, climb up,
PR, and back R, to reach a fine finger slot, PR. Layback furiously
upwards in an impending situation to reach good finishing holds,
PR, TR. SB.

Foxy By Proxy   21m E5 6a   * †
A.Long, A.Richardson 1991
A combination of the above routes making a bigger pump. As for
The Hooker to the cemented hold, reach up, PR above, climb
down and L to reach the finish of Foxy Lady at the layback, 2PR's,
TR. SB.

DARK SIDE OF THE MOON ZAWN
At sea level below Fox Hole Crag is a narrow zawn, with an
overhanging N facing wall.

The Illywhacker   8m   6c
A.Long Unseconded 1991
Climb the wall directly on painfully small holds, 2 PR's.

PENNARD TO PWLL DU BAY OS ref 567868 to 570866
A.Richardson

SITUATION AND CHARACTER
This is a series of impressive steep limestone buttresses overlooking the sea, E of Southgate. It is very close to Swansea and
therefore, popular. All the cliffs are non-tidal and lie on NT land.
The rock is sometimes loose but traffic has improved the situation
on most climbs, and it now sports a number of good challenging
lines.

APPROACHES AND ACCESS
See map 2. From Swansea follow the B4593 to Southgate, where
parking is available in the National Trust car park.
1   Heatherslade Buttress: Follow a muddy path E along the
coastal path for 5 mins. The crag forms the E side of the second
obvious gully to the R(S).
2   Pennard and all other cliffs: Follow the narrow road E for 10
mins to a valley running to the sea from Hunts Farm (there is a
prominent horse-worn circle). There are two possible approaches
from here:
a   A path leads down the valley to the coastal footpath and along
the base of the cliffs (10 mins from the road).
b   A better, but not so obvious, approach is to follow the cliff top
path past two huts on the L. Just past these a prominent rocky
headland is seen (there is a pond on your L). Go just past this
headland and descend towards the sea. High Pennard is to your L
(E) and Pennard Buttress is to your R(W).

HEATHERSLADE BUTTRESS
See approach 1.

GBH   13m   HVS   4c
R.Small, P.Carling 1974

Start below a grassy ledge on the L side of the cliff. Gain a ledge and pull into a depression on its R side. Continue LW then RW to the overhang. Take this then move RW to the top.

Felony   13m   HVS   5a
D.Butler, C.Davies 1975
Start below and R of the grassy ledge. Climb to a bulge and gain a small ledge below an overhang. Traverse R to a loose groove, climb it and bear LW over the next overhang.

Indecent Exposure   11m   HVS   4c
R.Small, P.Carling 1974
Start 6m R of an indefinite corner bounding the buttress on the L. Climb to small ledges at the foot of a corner capped by a block overhang. Gain the overhang, traverse L for a metre or two and finish direct.

Petty Larceny   11m   S
P.Carling, R.Small 1974
Climb the indefinite corner on the R and the loose groove above.

Bandolier   24m   VS   4c
R.Small, P.Carling 1974
A L to R girdle at half-height.

PENNARD BUTTRESS
This is the first of the main Pennard cliffs (see approach 2). It consists of a prominent buttress low on the L, with a lower wall of overhang-capped corners to its R. Above the lower wall rises another steep but more broken wall, which forms the R flank of the upper part of the main buttress.
The first climbs described are on the prominent buttress low on the L.

The Throb   45m   E5   6b,5a
A.Sharp, J.Harwood 1984
A pitch for steel fingers, serious and friable. Start below the slim groove L of the large rounded bulge on the LH side of the lower wall.
1   30m Climb steeply on pockets to a subsidiary bulge above and L of the main bulge, move R to gain a groove which is followed to belays.
2   15m Finish as for Arosfa.

Five Years to Live   15m   E5   6b   †
M.Crocker 1988
A micro route up the improbable bulge and arete between The Throb and Arosfa. It once sported a BR and has not been led without it. Start below the bulge. Climb to gain a pocketed crackline, TR, then cross the bulge RW to gain the arete, BR

(removed). Continue straight up the arete, TR, PR, past a break to a step L and the belay of Throb. Scramble off LW.

Arosfa 45m E4 6a/b,5a   *
E.Pardoe, R.Griffiths 1968 Tintack
FFA A.Sharp, J.Harwood 1984
1   33m Start below the groove R of the bulge. Climb over the bulge, PR (missing), to reach a short corner below a square-cut overhang. Swing R and climb broken cracks to good ledges.
2   12m Turn the large overhangs above on the L, and continue up the wall, PR, to join Alpha. Finish as for that route.

Alpha 36m HVS 4b,5a
H.Insley and others 1958
Start at the foot of the buttress just R of Arosfa, below an overhang-capped corner.
1   18m Climb a rib to the corner, turn the overhang on the R and follow a rib to the upper of two ledges, PR.
2   18m Traverse R for 3m and climb the wall steeply to a groove which leads to the impressive square-cut corner and the top.
Alternative pitch 1   4c. Move up L from the capped corner and turn the overhang on the L, then move R and continue up the wall to the belay.

Beta 16m VD
H.Insley and others 1958
Start at the foot of the wide crack R of Alpha, which separates the main buttress from the lower wall. Climb it to a niche below a bulge, move R and continue to ledges.

Beta Plus 14m HS 4b
R.Griffiths, E.Pardoe 1966
The corner 4m R of Beta. Turn the overhang on its L.

Knucklefluster 11m E2 5c   *
A.Sharp, P.Lewis 1984
A popular technical pitch up the wall just R of Beta Plus. Climb the wall until a move RW gains a good hold, TR, then move steeply to the break. Step L and finish up Beta Plus or, harder, over the roof.

Knuckleduster 11m E3 6a   †
A.Long 1989
A bold eliminate squeezed in between Knucklefluster and Gamma Minus. Climb the wall and overhang directly, PR.

Gamma Minus 12m HVS 5a
E.Pardoe, R.Griffiths 1967
This climbs the prominent corner R of Knucklefluster to the black bulge. Make an interesting move onto the R arete, follow this and the crack L of the overhang to the top.

Kiwis Can't Climb 12m E1 5c
A.N.Other, B.R.Other 1864
This takes the rib between Gamma Minus and Gamma. Where Gamma moves L, step R and pull over the roof. Finish direct.

Gamma 12m HVS 5a   *
E.Pardoe, R.Griffiths 1967
A tough little route. The next corner, trending LW. Climb to the bulge, move L to the arete (Gamma Minus), move RW and struggle over the roof.
A variation: from below the bulge gain the groove to the R, 4c.

Trundleweed 12m E2 5b
Climb the rib and short groove a metre R of Gamma.

Delta 13m S 4b
M.Hogge, J.Birch 1967
The steep and delicate groove R of Gamma.

Delta Minus 12m D
SUMC 1966
Takes the next obvious break slanting LW.

Vandal 9m S
J.Brailsford et al
A direct line up the short steep wall just R of Delta Minus.

Girdle Traverse 53m HVS 5a,4c,4b   *
J.Williams, P.Kokelaar 1967
A R to L girdle of the lower wall.
1 18m Start as for Delta Minus. Climb into the overhung corner of Gamma and make delicate moves to the arete. Enter the corner L and hand traverse below the overhang to a ledge on Beta Plus.
2 14m Descend LW to below a bulge then move up to the foot of the corner of Alpha.
3 21m Traverse 3m under overhangs before pulling onto the wall above. Continue L across two grooves before stepping down onto a grass ledge and belay in the gully.

Directly above the lower wall is an impressive sheet of rock which forms the R flank of Pennard Buttress. It has a band of loose and overhanging rock above and R.

Tom Tom 24m E3 6a   †
P.Donnithorne, E.Alsford 1988
This takes a line 3m to the L of Dan Dare. Climb on flat holds, TR, to a large ledge on the L. Continue up the centre of the R wall of the corner above.

Dan Dare 21m E2 5c   **
J.Bullock, G.Evans 1981

A fingery and sustained route at the top end of its grade. Start from the small bush below the centre of the blank sheet of rock. Gain the vague hollow and move R to the foot of a scoop, follow this past a fragile rock spike and hopefully the break. Traverse L to an open groove and follow this to the top.

Desperate Dan   6m   E3   5c   **
J.Bullock, G.Royle 1984
A direct finish to Dan Dare taking it into serious arm-pumping territory. Instead of moving L at the break move R and launch up to reach an overlap and, strength permitting, the top.

White Feather   21m   E4   6a   **
A.Sharp, O.Jones 1986
Just L of Timorous Tarzan is a steep crack. Follow this, TR, to a roof, PR. Finish boldly up the groove above, hidden PR. An alternative finish that makes the route E3 is to join Desperate Dan at the break.

Timorous Tarzan   36m   E1   5a
P.Littlejohn, J.Harwood 1980
J.Harwood 1pt aid 1980 (direct finish)
FFA Direct finish A.Sharp, O.Jones 1986
This climbs the calcite-encrusted layback crack on the R side of the wall. Climb the crack to its finish, then traverse R on loose-looking holds to an obvious groove. Climb this to the top.
Direct Finish E2 5c: Climb the wall above the layback crack and clip the second PR on White Feather.

Bald Eagle   24m   E4   6a   *
A.Sharp, J.Harwood 1984
This climbs the rib R of Timorous Tarzan then steps L and climbs the groove of White Feather.

In the R side of the steep wall, R of the wide central groove, are two holes in a broken crackline.

Digby   22m   E2   5b
J.Bullock, G.Evans 1981
J.Bullock, G.Evans 1987 direct finish
Start below the holes and follow the crackline to a ledge. From the RH end of this climb straight up, 2TR, to the top.

The broken crack containing the holes provides a poor climb at VS 4b.

HIGH PENNARD

Above and to the E of Pennard Buttress is an impressive crag containing Pennard's best routes. Once loose it now sports some of the most solid routes . . . well almost!

Left Edge 24m E1 5b
E.Pardoe, D.Barker 1968
A bit loose, but exciting, this takes the pillar that bounds the cliff on the L side. Climb the LH side of the pillar for 3m, then traverse R to a hole. Move up l past a PR and move R to a corner leading to the top.

Blood First 24m E3 5c   †
E.Kellar, P.Nicholas 1989
Climb direct to the hole on Left Edge, then climb past it trending slightly RW, PR, until it is possible to step R into the corner groove of Loony Left

Loony Left 24m E1 5c
J.Bullock, L.Cain 1987
2m R of Blood First. Climb direct to the R side of the overhang R of Left Edge, TR, over the roof via a baffling move and finish up the corner above.

Sudan 24m E1 5b   *
R.Leigh 1967
FFA P.Littlejohn, J.Harwood 1980
Start at the base of the pillar R of Left Edge. Climb up R to the overhang under the nose of the front of the pillar. Take the thin crack L of the nose then move R onto the pillar. Continue directly and boldly to the top.

Wandering Star 24m E1 5c O   †
A.Richardson, N.Gyerke 1987
An indefinite line attempting to climb the shallow hanging groove R of Sudan. Start just R of Sudan and climb to the break, move R and attempt to gain the groove with a brief excursion into Skive at its start. Finish over the roof between Skive and Shogun.

Skive 24m HVS 5a   ***
R.Griffiths, E.Pardoe 1966
A great route. Start 3m R of Sudan. Climb the obvious crack through two roofs. At the third, traverse L for 3m and climb deteriorating rock to the top.
Skive Direct 24m E1 5b ***: At the third roof finish direct up the final groove of Shogun.

Shogun 24m E2 6a   **
J.Bullock, G.Evans 1982
A route requiring a certain amount of inner self to surmount the roof. Climb direct to the obvious weakness in the roof just R of Skive, levitate over the roof, PR. Move L and climb a vague arete to reach Skive at the horizontal break. Finish up the groove above taking care with the rock.

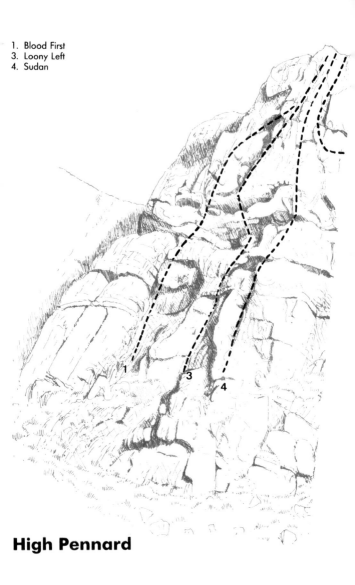

1. Blood First
3. Loony Left
4. Sudan

High Pennard

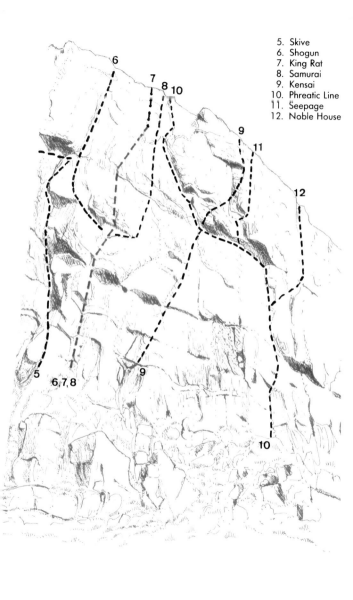

5. Skive
6. Shogun
7. King Rat
8. Samurai
9. Kensai
10. Phreatic Line
11. Seepage
12. Noble House

King Rat   24m   E3/4   6a   **

A.Richardson, A.Long 1987

A diretissima giving good climbing. Follow Shogun over its roof to a horizontal slot in a small overlap, climb the wall direct, joke TR, to the horizontal break. Continue directly by a hidden layback flake, finish directly, PR.

Samurai   24m   E3   6a   ***

J.Bullock, L.Moran 1987

The best route at Pennard. Follow Shogun over the roof to the horizontal slot as for King Rat, then step R to a shallow groove. Climb this past a small overhang, PR, and continue directly to the top.

Kensai   27m   E3   5c

J.Bullock, L.Moran, G.Evans 1986

Start directly below the upper groove of Phreatic Line. The initial groove is very serious. Climb to an obvious RW-curving overhang and follow it to a junction with Phreatic Line, below the layback groove. Pull straight over via a finger crack then step R into Seepage, finish LW via a curving crack.

Kensai/Phreatic Line Combination   E3   5c   **

Climb Kensai to join Phreatic line.

Phreatic Line   24m   E3   5c   *

E.Pardoe 1968

FFA P.Littlejohn, J.Harwood 1980

Takes the layback groove in the upper wall R of Samurai. Start at the R side of the crag below the overhang running LW in the upper part of the wall. Climb to an obvious ledge and perched flake, gain the overlap and traverse line above. Move LW to the layback groove and continue to the top.

Seepage   24m   E1   5b

E.Pardoe, C.Knight 1969

From the perched flake on Phreatic Line climb the wall direct to the overlap, TR. Step slightly L and pull over the bulge into a groove which is followed to the top.

Noble House   24m   E1   5b   O

J.Bullock, G.Evans 1982

Climbs the loose groove and upper wall R of Seepage. Climb RW to the perched flake on Phreatic Line, go diagonally RW to cross and gain the top of a shattered groove, move onto a wall above the overhang, step L and climb to the top.

The Amazing Bugblatter Beast Of Zarg   36m   E2/3   6a   *

A.Richardson, N.Gerke 1987

A good R to L traverse. Follow Phreatic Line to the overlap and climb L along the obvious break to belay in Skive. Continue the traverse to Left Edge and finish as for that route, or better, finish up Sudan.

To the R the cliffs deteriorate and although lines have been recorded the rock is poor and not recommended.

The Great Tower
This is the obvious pillar R of High Pennard. It has two routes, but take care with the rock.

Triattsdyfai   18m   E1   5b   O
E.Pardoe, R.Leigh 1967
A well-positioned but friable route up the L side of the face. Start below and slightly R of the obvious crack at 6m. Climb the wall and crack. From the top of the crack make a hard move up and L onto the edge. Follow the wide crack above to the top.

South East Edge   18m   E1   5b
H.Insley et al 1958/59
Variations J.Talbot 1968
J.Bullock, G.Evans 1981
High on the R side of the tower is a clean crack. Climb the R edge of the wall, just L of the ivy, to a corner level with the bottom of the crack. Traverse L onto the face and up to a good ledge. Follow the crack and groove to the top.

To the R of The Great Tower is a grassy gully and a small clean buttress that has a few short problems on it.

GRAVES END WALL
To the E of The Great Tower, looking up the grassy gully, is a short wall with a larger wall on the terrace above. It has an obvious horizontal break at about 4m, with the upper wall bulging gently. The climbs are described relative to a small cave at the bottom LH side of the main face.

Over Easy   13m   S   4a   *
M.Danford, G.Richardson 1978
The wall and groove 3m R of the small cave.

Too Late   13m   S
G.Richardson, M.Danford 1983
The wall and broken crack 3m R of Over Easy.

Marguerite   13m   VD
G.Evans, J.Bullock 1981
The obvious broken crack 9m R of the small cave.

Vertical Smile   13m   VS   4c   *
G.Evans, J.Bullock 1981

N.Low, M.Low (direct start) 1987
A popular route. Start just R of Marguerite. Climb the wall to a ledge, traverse R and follow a groove to the top.
Direct start: Gain the groove/ crack from directly below. E1 5b.

Helter Skelter   13m   E2   5b
H.Jones, A.Healy 1984
Climb the wall below the top crack of Vertical Smile, to a small ledge. Climb onto the wall above via a flake and continue up a crack above.

Sun Fix   15m   E3   6a
A.Sharp, J.Harwood 1985
A nice pitch up the cracks in the wall L of Toetector. Climb through the roofs L of Toetector, step R at the break and climb directly up the wall.

Toetector   15m   HVS
J.Bullock, G.Evans 1978
Start 7m R of the broken crack of Marguerite, where there is a thin crack with block overhangs at 4m. Climb to and through the overhangs and move R onto a flake. Finish with an awkward move L from the top of the flake.

Laissez Faire   15m   E3   6a
A.Sharp, J.Harwood 1985
The strenuous curving crack 3m L of TR1.

Thickhead   15m   E3   5c   *
A.Richardson, A.Giles, et al 1987
Climb the bulging crack 2m L of TR1 to a break, then step L and climb twin cracks to the top.

Fever Pitch   15m   E3   5c   †
A.Long, A.Richardson 1991
Climb the wall and bulge between Thickhead and TR1 to a break, then climb the bulging wall above to join TR1 at the recess.

TR1   15m   E2   5c   *
J.Bullock, G.Evans, G.Richardson 1982
Start 9m R of Toetector at a corner capped by a triangular block overhang. Climb the corner and overhang onto the obvious break, step L and up into a small recess, and then direct to the top.

Mental Floss   15m   E5   6a   * †
A.Sharp, J.Harwood 1985
Climb the steep wall 2m R of TR1 to the break, move R and finish directly up the wall.

Solar 15m E4 6a   * †
A.Sharp, J.Harwood 1985
Climb the shallow corner 4m R of TR1, then the pocketed wall and scoop above.

6m R of TR1 the wall is recessed with an obvious flake up on the L and a jammed block overhang high on the R.

Left Corner 13m VS 4c
J.Talbot, G.Jones 1959
The initial steep wall leads to a wide crack defining the flake, monkeys may use the ivy.

Right Corner 13m HS 4b
J.Talbot, G.Jones 1959
The steep corner R of the recess leads to a half-way ledge. Follow the crack in the wall above.

The next route is round the corner on the L edge of a cave.

Left Pillar 16m VS 4b
J.Talbot, G.Jones 1959
Climb the pillar L of the cave via the steep groove. Finish R, above the cave.

Kamin 13m VS 5a
J.Talbot, G.Jones 1958
A popular problem. Climb out of the back of the cave. Finish direct from the ledge.

Chasm 13m D
H.Insley et al 1958
A useful descent route just R of the cave.

Crevice 9m S 4b
Hinsley et al 1958
Climb the smooth crack R of Chasm.

The short wall to the R of Crevice has a crack and two wide corner cracks.

Ivy Saviour 8m VS 5a
K.Wood, G.Evans 1974
The first crack.

Cycle Track 8m 4c
G.Evans, K.Wood 1974
The wide corner crack.

Monkey 8m 4b
N.Williams
The next corner.

A short white wall to the R has been bouldered, top roped and soloed all over, and recently it even suffered the ignominy of having its ivy torn away and some futile TR's put in place on problems that had been done a long time ago. Enough said!

GRAVES END EAST
From Monkey either walk 100m E along the cliff top to an easy gully descent or, if the blackthorn is not biting, traverse below the cliffs. Graves End East has buttresses either side of the easy descent gully.

Baboon Traverse   27m   VS   4c
N.Williams 1980
To the W of the gully is an entertaining traverse following the obvious break line. Start from the foot of Cornel.

Cornel   15m   VS   4b
J.Bullock, G.Evans 1977
This takes the corner rising above the L end of Baboon Traverse.

Nettlebed   15m   HVS   5b
K.Wood, G.Evans 1974
At the middle of Baboon Traverse gain the break and the broken crack above.

Restful   15m   E3   5c
G.Evans, J.Bullock 1pt aid 1985
FFA M.Learoyd, R.Thomas 1986
Mistaken by many for Nettlebed! To the R of Nettlebed is an obvious curving flake gained via a problem roof/corner. It is poorly protected.

To the E of the descent gully are four definite buttresses. The first has only scrambles but the second has a number of good routes.

Marmite   15m   VS   4c   *
G.Evans, J.Bullock 1977
This takes the central groove on the W face, finishing over the obvious flake.

Taipan   15m   E1   5b
G.Evans, J.Bullock 1982
A poor eliminate requiring will power to avoid using holds on Marmite. Climb the thin cracks R of Marmite.

Graves End Arete   15m   E3   5c   †
M.Crocker, R.Thomas 1989
An exciting pitch up the leaning arete of the second buttress. Start below the arete R of Taipan and climb up the bulging wall to ledges at 4m. Gain the crack in the arete, which is followed intrepidly to the top.

Coffin Crack   15m   VS   5a   *
J.Bullock, G.Evans 1977
This takes the wide crack/groove on the E side of the buttress.

Cleansing Agent   12m   VS   4c
G.Evans, J.Bullock 1978
The thin crack L of the jammed boulder cave. Gain and follow the
crack steeply to a ledge, then continue up the groove above.

Marmolata   13m   VS   4c
J.Talbot, G.Jones 1959
Start R of the jammed boulder cave. Turn the jammed boulder to
the R and finish up the crack above.

Breakout   13m   HVS   5a   *
N.Williams,P.Williams 1979
A real stopper at its old grade of VS and still one at HVS! Climb
the obvious crackline on the front face of the buttress E of Marmolata.

BANTAM BAY CRAG
A short crag, situated in a small bay approached by walking along
the coast from Pwll Du Bay or from Pennard. It is not easy to find
and is the sort of crag that only a local or seasoned Gower visitor
would be interested in finding (OS ref 574866). It does tend to
become dirty from underuse and the finishes are atrocious, but
the climbing is good. A rope left in place is advisable.
The cliff has a small wall characterised by a corner crack on its R
side.

Egged On   18m   E2   5c
M.Learoyd, R.Thomas 1985
Take the cracks on the L side of the crag, moving R after the roof.

Rampant Cockeril   18m   E2   5c
C.Parkin, P.Blackburn 1985
Climb to the obvious roof, move R and pull over it strenuously.
Continue up the wall above.

Don't Count Your Chickens   18m   E2   5c
P.Blackburn, J.Kitching 1985
Start just L of Ruffled Feathers. Hard moves gain a crack which
leads to hard moves L onto a ledge. Move back R and to the top.

Ruffled Feathers   18m   E2   6b   *
M.Learoyd, R.Thomas, G.Royle 1985
A good route when clean, taking the thin cracks in the wall R of
the arete below the finish of the previous route.

Gift Horse   18m   E1   5b
G.Royle, R.Thomas, G.Royle 1985
The obvious corner crack.

Wide Eyed and Legless   18m   E1   5b
P.Blackburn, J.Kitching 1985
The thin crack in the short wall of the big corner crack. Step back
L and follow the groove above.

PWLL DU QUARRY

This is the scruffy quarry situated on the W side of Pwll Du Bay
(OS ref 570866).

Ashes to Ashes   21m   E3   6a
R.Thomas, J.Bullock, L.Moran 1pt aid 1986
This takes the obvious LH crackline. A problem move leads to a
PR, moves back R and up lead to the base of a groove, PR. Climb
this, then cross L to the arete and climb the hanging crack, PR, to
just below the top. Use a nut for aid and step L to finish or, better,
lower off the nut.

Dust to Dust   21m   E4   5c   †
M.Crocker, R.Thomas 1986
This takes the line of shallow grooves in the centre of the crag.
Start just L of an unclimbed layback crack, climb the first groove,
PR, to a jug. Move up the slabby wall to the next groove and roof,
swing L into a crack and the top.

The Flight Of Icarus   21m   E3   5c   †
A.Berry, J.Bullock 1990
A dirty poorly protected route taking the layback crack just R of
Dust to Dust. Climb the crack past an overhang. Finish via large
ledges and a mossy pull over. SB.

PWLL DU BUTTRESS

Situated to the R of Pwll Du Quarry and originally called Lower
Goonland Rocks, probably a better name. In its centre is a clean
buttress with a slanting crack on its R and a wide chimney on its L.
Descent is LW over boulders.

DT's   15m   E1   5b
G.Evans, G.Richardson 1983
Climb a thin crack to reach the wide chimney, which is followed
to the top.

Star Trek   15m   E1   5a
J.Bullock, G.Evans 1983
Start R of DT's and 4m down the slope. Climb the wall to a bulging
crack, move R to a ledge below two cracks, climb the L crack and
boldly layback over a bulge to the top.

Llareggub   21m   E1   5b
G.Evans, J.Bullock 1983
From the lowest point of the buttress gain a rib and then a groove.
From its top move R to the crack and layback to the top.

Where Eagles Dare   18m   HVS   5a
J.Kerry, A.Marsh 1970
This takes the obvious hanging flake on the R side of the buttress.
Start R of Llareggub and climb the steep crack to a ledge at
half-height. Layback the flake before moving L at the top.

CASWELL BAY OS ref 591876
A.E.Richardson

SITUATION AND CHARACTER
A pleasent slabby series of cliffs with some fine climbing for the
lower grade climber. Situated within easy reach of Swansea and
only 5 mins from the road, it is Gowers most populated beach in
summer and is not the crag for the self concious climber.

APPROACHES AND ACCESS
See map 2. From Swansea go towards Mumbles, at the mini
roundabout in Mumbles (White Rose pub on the corner) turn R
and head up the hill. At the top of the hill turn L at signs for
Caswell Bay and follow the twisting road to the Bay. Park in an
obvious "pay or be fined" car park opposite the beach. The
climbing is on a series of slabs on the W side of the bay. Descent
is via a path W for a short distance then down easy slabs and
corners, or E if the tide is high.Access is possible for a few hours
either side of low tide.
The most notable feature is the central slab with a narrow rock
neck at its foot. A through-cave runs behind it. The slabs 27m
seaward and to the L of the central slab can be climbed anywhere
at D standard.

Purple Haze   21m   VS   4b
P.Thomas, R.Bennett 1985
L of the central slab is a narrow slab widening towards its top.
Start up the slab but break LW onto ledges and finish via a short
slab.

Sibling Arete   27m   E1   5b
S.Lewis, G.Lewis 1982
Climb the R arete of the narrow slab in its entirety. No protection.

Once In A Blue Moon   27m   HVS   5a
D.Butler, C.Davies 1976
Between Sibling Arete and the gully to the R is another narrow
slab, which peters out at three-quarters height. Start in the corner

bounding the slab on the L, climb the slab and corner and finish up the earthy crack above.

What Not   22m   VD
G.Evans et al 1977
Start below the central slab, at a narrow slab leading up to an earthy gully on its L. Climb the narrow slab to its top then traverse R on obvious pockets to the L edge of the central slab. Follow the edge to the top.

Plasticene Dinosaur   21m   E1   5b   †
D.Butler, C.Davies 1976
A.Berry, J.Preece, D.Naylor 1990 reclimbed after a rockfall.
Reach the cave apex via the huge block overhang and obvious large hole, climb the slab to the overlap. Finish up the slab above.

Nat Not   21m   VS   4c   **
G.Evans, M.Danford, G.Richardson 1977
The best route at Caswell. Start on the rock neck below the Central Slab. Traverse deviously into and climb the R wall of the through cave to its apex. Pull over this onto the slab above and continue directly.

Great Slab   21m   HS   4b
Climb the centre of the central slab linking up the two obvious holes. Not well protected.

Right Edge   21m   VS   4b
Follow the RH side of the slab. Poorly protected.

Mac the Knife   22m   E4/5   6b   *
P.Littlejohn, C.Hurley 1984
This painfully attacks the overhanging crack in the R wall of the central slab. A mega pump with a bold finish up the central groove to the top.

Antic Corner   20m   E1   5b
D.Butler, C.Davies 1pt aid 1976.
A.Barley, G.Evans, C.Hird 1974.
A.Berry,1989 direct start.
Start in the RH entrance to the through- cave.Chimney up and pull onto the slab at the foot of the corner. Follow this via an overhang, to the foot of a grass tongue. Climb the rib on the R to the top.
Direct start: Start as for Shufflebottom Crack and pull round an overhanging prow to join Antic Corner, (5c).

Shufflebottom Crack   22m   HVS   5a
G.Evans, P.Clay 1981
A fun route requiring unique contortions. Start at the foot of a

wide smooth crack R of Antic Corner. Climb the crack to the overhang and shuffle up it to the slab. Move up and over to the R edge and finish up this. Belay well back across the path.

The wider cracks and slabs to the R give a number of pleasant short climbs.

LIMESLADE CRAG OS ref 617868
Between Langland bay and Limeslade bay is a steep W facing wall that has seen some activity over the years with approximately 5 routes up to E3/4 in standard. All the lines were climbed by University college Swansea MC but no details are available.

CONSERVATIVE CLUB CRAG OS ref 620877
A.E.Richardson

SITUATION AND CHARACTER
The cliff is a splendid sheet of limestone adhering to the hill behind the Mumbles Conservative Club. Once dirty, its cleaning has revealed a small number of excellent routes. It is set in woodland and the lower third can be slow to dry out. The top is vegetated and descent is via abseil from an obvious tree. Beware of midges in the summer and be prepared to clean the slab early in the year, but please do not use a wire brush because the rock is very soft.

APPROACHES AND ACCESS
See map 2. From Swansea go into Mumbles and park opposite The Conservative Club. The crag is just visible through the trees, up and R of the club. Follow the path along the side of the club, then scramble up an earthy bank to reach the cliff. It is in the middle of a residential area so please act accordingly.

Cortez The Killer   27m   E2/3   5c   *
A.Richardson, S.Lewis 1984
A technical start up the L arete leads to a bold LW step to a ledge, PR. Move back R onto the wall, PR, and up the crack to an exciting layback on the final arete, PR.

Out Of The Blue   27m   E2   5c   *
C.Pound, P.Saunders 1981
Start 3m R of Cortez The Killer at parallel cracks, climb these past an overlap and continue up the obvious crack, PR.

Hurricane   27m   E4   6a   **
S.Lewis, A.Richardson 1984
Good technical slab climbing with a run out finish. Start as for Blood On The Tracks. After a metre or two step L to an n-shaped depression, move L and back R to gain a hole, then climb deviously up the slab to the top. 3 PR's.

Blood On The Tracks   27m   E2   5c
C.Pound, P.Saunders 1981
A poorly-protected climb taking the twin cracks 4m R of Out Of The Blue. When the cracks finish climb the slab and the corner L of the overhangs.

Energy Crisis   27m   HVS   5a
P.Saunders 1981
A vegetated route.Start 3m R of Blood On The Tracks. Climb vegetated cracks to the overhang R of the hanging rib, step L onto the rib, pull over the overhang and follow a narrow crack to the top.

Antelope Special   27m   HVS   5a
C.Pound, G.Lewis 1982
Climb the corner on the R side of the slab to the overhangs. Percy Thrower country! Traverse across the R wall to the arete and finish up the dirty rock above. A route that will improve with traffic, especially a JCB.

Floating Voter   27m   E3   5c   *
A.Long, C.Hebblethwaite 1989
A.Richardson Variation 1991
A sort of traverse. From the second peg on Cortez The Killer traverse RW to gain the first PR on Hurricane climb to the second PR and then step R into Blood On The Tracks to finish.
Variation: From the crack of Out Of The Blue climb diagonally RW to gain the second PR, 6a.

SOUTH EAST WALES

INTRODUCTION
"Inland South Wales has no climbing . . . For those who insist on
seeing climbing at its most absurd an essential itinerary would
include Llangattock, Vaynor, Taff's Well, Dinas Rock, the sum
total of their climbing potential is rather less than that of the
Cromlech boulders"

J.Perrin 1973

Surely the crags have changed since 1973, maybe climbers
attitudes have changed or maybe Jim Perrin was out to confuse us
all again, whichever it is, the above quote is not true today. This is
the fourth climbing guide to South East Wales and depicts the
development that has proceeded since 1983. New routes are still
being discovered on the varied cliffs of South East Wales and
although the space between routes is getting smaller there are
still a few interesting and challenging gaps left. Please do not
erode the few challenges left by greed.

South East Wales has a plethora of good cliffs, providing climbing
for the adventurous spirit on the sea cliffs at Ogmore, climbing
for the new breed of "sports climbers" at Taffs Well and Dinas
Rock, many excellent crags for the beginner and a whole host of
routes for the seasoned explorer to discover.

The popularity of some cliffs comes and goes lets hope this guide
inspires you to discover the variety and wealth of good climbing
that South East Wales has to offer.

Dinas Rock, Cefn Coed, Morlais Quarry, Taf Fechan, Baltic
Quarry, Twynau Gwynian Quarry are covered by sheet 160
"Brecon Beacons"; and Llangattock by sheet 161 " Abergavenny
and the Black Mountains". For Ogmore and Witches Point sheet
170 "Cardiff and Newport" covers Taffs Well East and West and
Wenvoe.

HISTORY

Pre 1983 By T.Penning

Early Developments
Climbs must have been made prior to the sixties, but there are
scant details available.(Anybody with any information should forward it to the editor).

The Middle Tier at Morlais was one of the first cliffs to receive attention; in the early sixties by Barry Powell, Harold Insley and other members of the SWMC and later by Mike Danford and Pat Wood. Unfortunately many of the names of early routes have been lost, and new names were given to include them in the first South East Wales guide. Also during this early period John Bradley, Alan Barney and Tom Dodd were developing Pant-Y-Rhiw at Llangattock. Meanwhile Powell climbed the classic Pine Tree at Taffs Well and later, Ken Hughes made the first breach of the Shield with Nero.

One of the discoveries of the sixties was Taf Fechan, which was worked out in one massive drive. The principal climbers were Cled Jones, Dave Parsons, Peter Leyshon, Phil Watkin and Derek Taff Ellis. In a supplement to Taf Fechan, in 1969, one of the climbs, Monument to Insanitary, appeared with the following written below it, "A hangover, wet rock, cold feet, a watch stopping at the start of the climb, the nearby sheep carcass, the flight of a large black bird and the erection of a large memorial cairn by watching friends, defeated a previous attempt by another party!" yet another, The Coffin, had written beneath it, "A block fell onto D.Parsons head". These early pioneers knew how to enjoy themselves!

Dinas Rock also saw some activity but was originally thought to be to loose for good free climbing. The Strider by Phil Thomas and Jeepers Creepers by Phil Watkin, were pointers to what the future really held there.

Towards the end of the sixties Clive Horsfield and Thomas discovered Cefn Coed and although routes were climbed the next stage was to prove more significant.

Into The Seventies
Horsfield, John Kerry, Thomas and Watkin were just some of the climbers to descend on Cefn Coed and practically work the cliff out. Such was the pace of development that only a handful of climbs have been made there since. One route, Aphrodite, nearly put paid to two of the leading pioneers, when Thomas became airborne clutching a block which then nearly decapitated Horsfield.

As interest was slackening at Cefn coed, John Mothersele discovered Ogmore and climbed several routes including the crux of Explosure Explosion. Kerry arrived quickly on the scene to take a few of the routes, including Megalopolis and Gremlin, while Thomas and Horsfield (always in the thick of things) climbed such routes as Abbey Road and Siren.

The Heard brothers Charlie and Richard, climbed Griffin with its exposed finish, and Andy Sharp produced Finger print, Fast Reactions and Norwegian Wood. But Ogmore still remained the most undeveloped cliff for its size in South East Wales, until Pat Littlejohn came along. As well as free climbing routes such as Dracula and Fools Fantasy, he added many of his own, including Wounded Knee, Spellbinder, Phaser, Hunchback and Sorcery his first E6 and perhaps Britains boldest route at this time. One of the more outstanding events was Littlejohns solo of Bigger Splash on the first ascent. Although he could not recommend it as a solo he said " If you catch the tide right, there's up to eight feet of water covering the jagged rocks below". Littlejohn was active in another area as well. At Llangattock he climbed Cold Snatch and Hangman with Dick Renshaw; at Dinas Rock, Slickenside and Springboard "free" using a dead tree to surmount the overhang and at Taffs Well, Diamonds with Steve Lewis and Skywalker, unseconded. Throughout Littlejohns activity, Sharp was also at work, and with Pete Lewis traversed The Shield at Taff's Well to give Changes. At Dinas, he climbed the technical Sense of Humour. The other main event of this time was On the Broadwalk by Chris Connick and Dylan Hughes, a fine discovery.

Latest Developments

Tony Penning and John Harwood paid a visit to the Eastern Edge of Llangattock that not only confirmed the quality of Littlejohns new routes, but revealed much unclimbed rock to which they added routes of their own. Penning made leads in other areas as well, with Pete Cresswell, Sharp and Dennis Hillier. These included Blade Runner at Morlais, Wild Magic at Dinas and Johnny Cum Lately on Pant-y-Rhiw, Llangattock. The latter was named because Harwood turned up a week too late to be on the first ascent.

Sharp continued to look for difficult problems, and found them; Dead Red and the terminal Exile at Morlais; and Acid Rain at Llangattock, the hardest route to date on the inland crags.

Littlejohn's fascination for the overhanging wall beneath Bigger Splash at Ogmore continued, and Zardoz was born. This was the fourth desperate on this particular piece of rock.

Meanwhile back at Morlais, Hillier had climbed To The Batmobile, and at Llangatock several short routes including the excellent Wildest Dreams.

South East Wales has never been popular with climbers from other areas, which in a way is fortunate for the locals. When they have visited however, they often leave with a favourable impression. Lawrence Francombe and friends came for a visit and snatched three climbs at Dinas Rock including the difficult Under The Broadwalk. There is so much still to be done in the area that visits like Francombe,s are refreshing. Let,s hope others will come, with an eye for lines and the desire to climb them.

History 1983 onwards
J.Harwood

1983 began quietly as though even the locals needed to take a hard look at the new guide book and then the crags. Andy Sharp was the first to take up the challenge and having freed Lindas Wall of its aid point put up the hard Partners In Crime in cold windy conditions. He also added Mean Green to Llangottock, made more notable when the second ascentionists pulled out the peg runner.

Then Littlejohn made his mark with typical audacity he attacked the 8m roof in the main overhang at Dinas to produce Giant Killer. Twice he got to the lip only to rest on a runner on the final ascent. This is one of the areas best climbs and was one of the most outrageous overhangs in the country at that time. It waited for almost a decade to see the first free ascent by Marrtin Crocker but only after the removal of a loose flake and the placement of a bolt on the upper wall by an earlier aspirant. Littlejohn and Penning also added the excellent Lip Trick traversing along the lip of the main overhang.

At Ogmore, always a favourite with Littlejohn, he added the very steep Flying Wizard with Penning. The same team then moved onto Taffs Wells and cleaned Painted Bird and Gladiator, two pitches previously described as loose and unclimbable. The very hot weather, lack of chalk and a sizable fall onto a dodgy Friend 1 dictated dawn starts before they were climbed. In 1984 Llangatock started to attract some belated attention, Chris Court added many routes to Chwar Pant Y Rhiw and Craig y Castell, White Tiger, Gold Rush and Julia Andrea were probably the most notable. Penning was also active and added a number of good climbs to Llangatock, his best being Winning, a delectable groove. Gary Gibson was also active adding Mad Hatter.

Mention of Gibson brings us to a controversial event in 1984. Sharp had managed the only traditionally protected line up the Great Wall at Morlais but whilst locals agonised over the possibilities to its left, Gibson, on his first visit to the area placed a bolt and climbed Rogues Gallery. All hell was let loose, the hanger was stolen and replaced several times but that seems old hat now that bolts have been accepted on many cliffs now (only by a small minority of active climbers. Ed).

At Cefn Coed a flurry of activity broke out on Bridge Cliff. Penning began events with the now popular Death of A Salesman, but it was left to Sharp to produce a series of finger searing problems, of which Tough Of The Track is probably the best. A much looked at problem The Great Arete was finally climbed by Penning at quite a reasonable grade.

Back at Dinas Rock Penning was responsible for the much eyed overhanging crack in The Cave Area, Imperial Girl, and for opening up the Bridge Cliff with Torrid Nights.

Meantime at Ogmore, a host of good pitches were being added to the traditional part of the cliff, mainly by Mick Learoyd and Thomas. Hired Gun is perhaps the best of these. Around this time Littlejohn weighed in with a typical hard and excellent climb Right Little Raver. In the winter months an as yet unnamed party were discovered trying to ascend what later became Warlock, with a ladder! (names will be revealed for a small fee). Meanwhile Thomas was seeking his own perverse adventure and with the support of J.Bullock and G.Royle produced several horrors up the biscuit rock of Ogmore. Sleepless Nights and Information Received being typical examples.

As 1985 dawned and the supplementary guide was about to appear there was a flurry of activity at Dinas Rock, firmly establishing the cliff as the premier inland crag for hard routes in South East Wales. Gibson visited again and added the excellent Spain. Spurred by this Littlejohn attacked the huge corner to create The Big Time accompanied by Penning and Harwood.

Sharp and Lewis then climbed two steep and difficult routes to the right; Salem's Lot and Harlem. Finally just in time for the 1985 supplement, Penning with Sharp and Learoyd added several pleasant pitches to the Cave Wall of which Cats is probably the most enjoyable.

Ever controversial and completely unrepentant from his drubbing of the previous year, Gibson returned to Morlais and climbed the difficult No Mercy for which he added another bolt. Then at Dinas Rock he added Berlin which gave excellent climbing up an impressive line but used two bolts. It was now clear to the locals that if they were not to lose out on some of the remaining challenges then they were going to have to use bolts as well. With superkeen new routers such as Gibson and Matt Ward willing to attack any unclimbed line ruthlessly there seemed little alternative. A stand by a few against all bolts did not have widespread support especially after a bolt chopping escapade at nearby Wintours Leap. The current situation is a mess with a whole spectrum of opinions as to where bolts are or are not allowed.

Crocker visited Llangatock where he ascended Vendetta and The Roaring Eighties, two excellent additions. Chris Court was again active here and did Liberator and a host of other routes. But the most notable series of climbs was at Ogmore where Crocker took over where Littlejohn had left off.

Usually seconded by Matt Ward he climbed Mantra and the

Uncanny up the exhausting wall left of Sorcery. The latter included a Crocker dyno which gave considerable problems when Pete Oxley made the second ascent, snapping the first protection peg. Crocker also added the superb hanging arete right of Zardoz, Daughter of Regals free ascended Warlock and climbed Burn Em Up on the cracked wall left of Fire. All of these routes were of the highest standard and difficulty.

Next year he continued his onslaught by moving further along the cliff and added Motor Torpedo, Sonar and Ultra Virus. He crowned his achievements for the year with Twenty First Century a major and acutely overhanging climb on the wall left of Davey Jones' Locker. Other efforts of note were Littlejohn's lead of Astrobrain and Sharp and Lewis's ascent of Brothers in Arms.

As winter approached the search was on for suitable crags to keep fit on. As a result of the dry weather several worthwhile places were rediscovered or redeveloped. In the latter bracket was Taf Fechan, a product of the seventies, and feared by most for its man eating blocks after the first 16m. Crocker and Ward swept in and added some lines with lower off points to improve the crags offering.

Another discovery that winter was Wenvoe Quarry. Here Gary Lewis and Dave Meek got things underway with The Meek The Mad And The Ugly, but then Crocker, Ward and Thomas blitzed the crag. Thomas finished the year by adding Here Comes The Sun which contains some classic home made fixed gear, it is rumoured that Chouinard closed down after seeing the pegs.

The next development was from Sharp and Lewis who had spied a slab opposite Taffs Well. After mammoth gardening sessions they climbed three good routes which are the hardest slab routes in South East Wales. On the main cliff Crocker worked on the desperate Spuriously Yours which was shortly afterwards given a more reasonable companion with Crime Of Fashion by Sharp and Lewis.

At Llangatock, Gibson revisited to produce Hitman while Crocker grappled with the flowstone to yield the excellent Wonderlands a contender for best pitch of the crag. At Ogmore he returned to add the space walking route Roof Of The World only the proximity of gear will reduce the fear quotient on this route.

Meantime Sharp and Lewis seized a dry spell to climb Stay Hungry and Party to the overhanging back wall of Taffs Well West. Sharp was so pleased with the routes that he let the cat out of the bag. A fatal mistake! In two weekends Crocker and Gibson had cleaned up with the best being Its A Black World by Gibson and Streaming Neutrinos by Crocker.

Meanwhile, storms were creating havoc at Ogmore and a massive rock fall removed some of last year's creations. The winters storms were definitely responsible and not as some wag suggested, the weight of Crockers fixed gear.

1988 was the start of the sandstone boom (see later section) and the other crags were nearly forgotten, although Crocker made several forays onto worse and worse rock at Taffs Well to prove he could still keep his head together. However a big route was in the wings at Ogmore, Davy Jones' Locker. This had been the scene of a first ascent epic when Charlie Heard was benighted and drenched under the cave roof (The Locker), He and his brother returned the next day to complete the ascent by difficult and precarious aid climbing. Local climbers were stunned to hear that Crocker had freeclimbed the 22m roof. It was no surprise to hear that there were two no hands rests on the big pitch enabled by diving head first into the holes in the roof. For sheer impressiveness the ascent brought Littlejohn's bold products of a decade earlier up to date and has thrown out the challenge for the next 10 years.

Penning had not been idle during this period and was adding some good routes to Llangatock the best being Heaven Can Wait and I.Q.Test.

A the guide neared fruition and the nineties loomed ahead South East Wales history ended with more adventure down at the much maligned crag of Ogmore. A heart stopping abseil led Thomas to a hanging stance above a roaring sea where he watched Crocker force the spectacular Skull Thuggery through the roofs L of Davy Jones's Locker. The last word in the history goes to Gibson who climbed Hawaiian Choice at Dinas Rock, however the bolt he placed has reduced the committment on nearby Spain highlighting a further problem with bolt protected routes.

So we can take stock and ponder the wealth of attractions that the area now holds for climbers. Everything from serious leads on overhanging Ogmore or crumbling Taffs Well, easy beginners climbs on solid limestone, extremely technical test pieces. Visitors from outside the area are still relatively rare but hopefully the new guide will change that. The Eighties have been a period of change and not a little controversy. By now, however, a code of ethics is emerging and one hopes that visitors and locals alike will respect the area and its crags, enjoy their climbs and contribute positively to development. Above all let's remember future generations and leave them fine crags and routes so they can gain as much pleasure from climbing as we all have.

HERBERT'S QUARRY OS ref 733188
P.Donnithorne

SITUATION AND CHARACTER
Situated in the Carmarthen Fans (Black Mountains) N of Swansea they are an esoteric series of walls ideal for those climbers wanting to go where few have gone before.

APPROACHES AND ACCESS
See map 1. From Brynamman follow the A4069 Llangadog road for 3 miles until a car park is reached just below the crest of the hill. A track on the R leads to the quarry.

West Wall
Towards the RH side of the cliff is a pinkish groove.

Wooly Bully   15m   HVS   5a   †
P.Donnithorne, E.Alsford 1988
Climb the pink groove, 3PR's.

Doochie Coochie   12m   E4   6b   †
P.Donnithorne 1988
Start 4m L of a muddy corner. Climb a wall, 2PR's, difficult moves lead up and L to finish.

East Wall
This is the large quarry, furthest from the road. A 24m wall is topped with blocks.

Nine Below Zero   24m   E4   6a   *†
Start just L of Can't Do My Homework. Climb up, PR, then move L and up, TR, 2 PR's, BR, continue to a horizontal break, then go LW over blocks to a BB. Lower off.

Can't Do My Homework   12m   E1   5b   *†
The line just L of Mojo, 2BR's.

Mojo   12m   VS   4c   *†
E.Alsford, P.Donnithorne 1988
Climb a crack on the RH side of the vertical wall, TR, to a bay at half height, PB. Abseil.

DINAS ROCK (CRAIG Y DDINAS) OS ref 913080
S.Lewis
"If in doubt . . . run it out" A.Price 1989

SITUATION AND CHARACTER
Dinas Rock, like many limestone crags throughout the country has evolved from a cliff once considered only suitable for aid climbing into a free climber's paradise. It is a brilliant crag and definately worth a visit.
With the advent of modern equipment, techniques and attitudes Dinas Rock now sports some of the finest free climbing in South East Wales, with routes that rival those in other parts of Britain. The climbing is often very steep up smooth faces and mostly in the upper grades, many of the harder routes become dusty and require brushing.

APPROACHES AND ACCESS
See map 1. The cliffs run along the Afon Sychryd, one kilometre E of Pont Nedd Fechan. It is approached from the A465 and Glyn Neath Road via the B4242 to Pont Nedd Fechan, from where an unclassified road follows the river upstream to a sharp R turn at a bridge. The steep main face with its slanting crack lines is immediately visible on the L above the main car park. A track leading to the R from the car park gains access to the other areas.

THE MAIN FACE
This is flanked on the R by easy slabs that can be climbed any-where at up to VD standard. The first route starts from the track above the car park on a short wall on the L side of the face. The wall has a good abseil tree and is best used to clean the routes prior to an ascent.

Evening Wall   6m   VD   O
Climb a crack in the LH side of a short wall.

Flake Wall   39m   HS   4a   O
Very loose. Climb a short wall L of the arete to a tree. Continue up via a flake to the top.

Slickenside   41m   E2   5c   *
P.Leyshon, D.Parsons (S A1 Slowcoach)
FFA P.Littlejohn, D.Renshaw. 1979
Thin climbing. Start on the LH side of the face just R of the arete at thin cracks. Climb the cracks to a ledge at 18m. Continue more easily until it steepens, then follow a crack, PR, to the arete and the top.

Churchill   38m   E4   6b   *
P.Leyshon, D.Parsons S A1
FFA P.Littlejohn, S.Lewis 1980

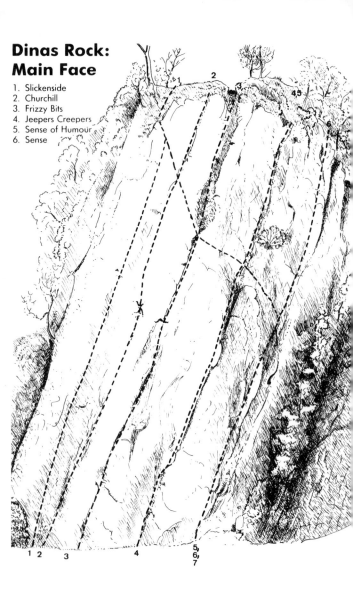

Dinas Rock:
Main Face

1. Slickenside
2. Churchill
3. Frizzy Bits
4. Jeepers Creepers
5. Sense of Humour
6. Sense

Sustained for the first 13m. Start at the first groove R of Slickenside. Climb the groove past several PR's to a small hole at 13m, step R and finish up a crack and open groove above or finish up Slickenside.

Frizzy Bits 38m F2/3 5c *

D.Parsons, P.Leyshon (A2 Helen)
FFA A.Sharp, P.Lewis. 1979

A good pitch that is often dirty. Start at cracks 1.5m R of Churchill. Climb the cracks to a shallow groove/pod and continue up the finger crack. Finish up the dirty groove or step L to join Slickenside.

Angus Anglepoise 38m E3 6a †

P.Donnithorne, T.Meen 1987.

An eliminate route taking a thin crack between Frizzy Bits and Jeepers Creepers in its entirety. Start 3m R of Frizzy Bits.

Jeepers Creepers 38m HVS 5a

P.Watkin, C.Jones c 1970

A good but often dirty route. Climb the obvious groove in the centre of the face.

Sense of Humour 38m E2 5c **

P.Josty, A.N.Other (S A1 Josty)
A.Sharp, P.Lewis 1979

A popular climb. Start at thin cracks 2m R of Jeepers Creepers. Climb the cracks until a difficult traverse L (a metre or two below a tree) can be made into Jeepers Creepers which is followed to the top alternatively lower off the tree.

Sense 38m E2 5c **

S.Lewis, G.Lewis. 1982

A direct version of Sense of Humour, more committing. Follow Sense of Humour to its traverse L, then continue directly up the cracks in the arete passing a tree to the top.

Frisky 45m E2 5c

A.Sharp. 1980

A diagonal R to L traverse taking little newrock. Follow Sense of Humour to its junction with Jeepers Creepers then continue LW to finish up Slickenside.

The Coffin 30m VS 4a O

C.Jones, D.Parsons 1967

Advisable to have a priest and undertaker present. Climb the wide groove on the R of the face with poor rock and protection.

Porth Crawl 33m E2 5b

A.Sharp, J.Harwood 1980

Start just R of the Coffin. Climb the wall for 6m then the groove for 6m. Traverse R onto a sloping ledge, then L to a crack which is followed to the top.

THE GREY WALL
This is the second wall, 150m along the track leading from the car park to the upper cliffs.

The Dented Cavalier   21m   E2   5b
T.Penning, J.Harwood 1982
Scant protection and poor rock. Climb to a scoop in the lower wall, traverse L for a metre or two and up R to a ledge and sapling. Move R, then back L over a bulge and climb to an overhang, traverse L then back R above the overhang to below a tree at the cliffs top.

IVY BUTTRESS
This is the next section of cliff a further 50m along the path from Grey Wall. The routes have proved very popular. The routes are described relative to the obvious corner of For The Love Of Ivy.

South West Guru   12m   E1   5c
A.Sharp, P.Lewis 1988
Start at an obvious rib 12m L of For The Love Of Ivy. Climb the rib to a roof and pull over, BR, to a BB.

Deadly Nightshade   12m   E4   6a
A.Price solo 1988
Start as for South West Guru and trend RW up the slab to an overlap. Cross it with difficulty then continue more easily to a BR and follow good holds straight up. Then move L, BR into the belay of South West Guru. The BR's were added after the first ascent

The Inflated Roundhead   15m   E4   6a
M.Crocker, R.Thomas 1988
A technical pitch. Climb direct to a diagonal break and pull straight over a bulge to gain a series of good holds, from the top most of these, BR, move L over a bulge and back up R to finish up a shallow groove. Abseil.

Bob's Birthday Party   12m   E2   5c
R.Powles, A.Sharp, P.Lewis 1988
Start at a large boulder 6m L of For The Love Of Ivy. Climb past a small tree, up the slabs above, BR, until a step L can be made, traverse R and lower off the situ gear.

The Running Man   24m   E4   6b   *
A.Sharp, P.Lewis 1988
Start at a thin crack between Bob's Birthday Party and For The Love of Ivy. Climb the crack to a ledge, up slabs to another ledge

and move up, BR, by desperate moves, then better holds. Another hard section leads to a tree and PB. Lower off.

For The Love Of Ivy   30m   HVS   5a
C. Connick, D. Hughes 1979
Perhaps the scene for a future Harrison Ford adventure. Climb the obvious corner to the jungle above.

Beware of Poachers   21m   E2   5c   *
P. Donnithorne 1988
A. Price, A. Long 1988 direct version
This starts just R of For The Love Of Ivy. Climb to the roof past a TR, BR, move R and over the roof to a good hold. Finish up the flake crack, tree belay.
Direct version 6b: from the BR at the roof climb direct to the good hold.

Squash The Squaddie   21m   E3   5c
A. Price, S. Elias 1988
Start 3m R of the previous route. Bold moves lead to a good crack, up this to a roof and move L and into a groove. Climb this and over some overlaps to a final tricky move to a BB. Lower off.

Thousand Yard Stare   12m   E4   6a   *
A. Price, S. Thomas 1988
Good clean climbing R of Squash The Squaddie. Ascend a vague groove to an overlap, BR, cross this and continue boldly up a wall above. Then use a hidden hold in a scoop to reach a belay station.

Unnamed Route 1   30m   E1   5b
L. Francombe, A. Reed 1981
Start R of the obvious corner at a boulder. Climb the slabs RW to a groove which is followed to an overhang. Climb this moving L and follow the groove to the top.

Hermen Munster   18m   E4   6b
A. Sharp 1983
Named because a fall before the peg will result in a flat head. Start 6m R of the last route. Climb up for a metre and then move L into a shallow groove (technical). Continue, PR, to an abseil station.

BLACK SLAB
Further up the track is a black slab set above the path in a clearing.

Gypsy   9m   HVS   4c
T. penning, J. Harwood 1985
Climb the middle of a small black slab.

Moth   9m   E1   5c
P. Donnithorne, T. Meen 1986
The slab a metre or two R of Gypsy.

KENNELGARTH WALL
Further along the path one reaches an impasse with a good but short overhanging wall on its L and the cave area across the river on its R. Ahead is a series of short waterfalls. There is a BB on the ledge above (no hanger).

Technitis   7m   E1   6b
P. Donnithorne, T. Meen 1988
A boulder problem up the far LH end of Kennelgarth wall BR, TR.

Out Come The Freaks   7m   E4   6b
A. Sharp 1988
Start 2m R of the last route. Hard moves lead past an overlap to moves RW past a BR.

Fings Ain't What They Used To Be   9m   E5   6b
A. Sharp, P. Thomas, P. Lewis 1988
Raving hard pal!. Steep and sustained climbing with excellent protection. Climb the crack and wall L of Kennelgarth, 3PR's. BB.

Kennelgarth   9m   E4   6b
A. Sharp, P. Lewis 1pt pt aid 1985
Fierce climbing up the rightmost crack. Struggle past a PR to gain better holds, TR. Use this to finish, BB. This has recently lost a block and may now be impossible.

THE CAVE AREA
This is situated across the river from Kennelgarth Wall. Some of the routes are becoming overgrown and would benefit from some ascents.

In Like Peter   27m   VS   4a
T. Penning, P. Cresswell 1980
This climbs the obvious layback crack on the wall facing Kennelgarth wall.

Imperial Girl   21m   E4   5c   **
T. Penning, J. Harwood
A strenuous climb taking the jam crack on the L side of the cave. Start as for In Like Peter. Follow this, then traverse R to a TR at the start of the crack. Struggle up the crack TR to easier ground. The E is for effort.

Smeagol   24m   A2   S
P. Thomas

Climb the roof crack 1m from the L edge of the cave to finish up the wall above.

Rat on a Hot Tin Roof 21m E5 6a
A. Sharp, P. Lewis 1pt aid 1984
Start R of Smeagol. Climb up to the hand traverse crack (good thread) in the back of the cave. Follow this to good holds on the lip. Using a NA, pull into the scoop, NR. Abseil off.

Apathy 24m A2
P. Thomas, C. Elliott 1975
Climb the next roof crack to the R and the wall above.

Strider 39m HVS 4c   *
A good climb taking the obvious chimney and arete to the R of the cave. Climb the chimney, then slabs and a shallow groove on the L to a niche. Step down R, then move up and R across a steep slab to the arete. Traverse R to finish up a groove.

Strider Direct 39m HVS 5a
Start at a crack just R of the chimney. Climb this, moving L then R onto the face of the buttress. Continue past two small trees to a steep slab, then move R to the arete which is followed with some loose rock to the top.

CAVE WALL
These routes start from a vegetated ledge above and to the R of The Cave Area.

Cats 15m E2 5b   *
T. Penning, M. Learoyd, A. Sharp 1985
Enjoyable climbing. Start from the L end of the ledge. Tiptoe LW to reach a TR and good holds. Swing L and climb more easily to the top.

Evita 13m E3 6a   *
T. Penning, M. Learoyd 1985
Technical climbing on good rock. Start below a small corner at half height on the L end of the ledge. Climb past a PR at 4.5m and continuer to a ledge. Finish up RW.

Picnic at Hanging Rock 13m HVS 5a
M. Learoyd, P. Lewis 1985
Start from the middle of the ledge and climb the obvious corner.

The Horror Show 9m E3 6a   *
A. Sharp, P. Lewis 1985
Start from the R end of the ledge. Climb the bulging wall to a good rest below a thin crack, climb the crack and abseil off from the second of 2 TR's.

THE BRIDGE CLIFF
This is the cliff at the top of the waterfall just past two iron spines gained from a traverse along the top of Kennelgarth Wall or during a dry spell by climbing the waterfalls.

Kick The Dog Next Door   24m   E2   5c
R. Thomas, M. Crocker 1988
A serious route. Start 3m L of the chimney of Continental Touch at a cleaned face. Gain a small tree and ledge, then climb more steeply up the centre of the wall above.

Continental Touch   27m   E1   5b
A. Sharp, J. Harwood 1985
Climb the chimney/groove on the L side of the main buttress to the top, PR.

Torrents Of Spring   26m   E3   5c
R. Thomas, J. Bullock, G. Royle 1988
Start L of Torrid Nights beneath the large cave reached by scrambling up vegetated slabs. Climb L out of the cave then up a short shattered wall to a horizontal crack, TR, up more steeply into a groove below an overhang. Traverse R beneath the overhang to finish L of the finish of Torrid Nights or use 2PA and climb the roof.

Torrid Nights   42m   E3   5c   *
T. Penning, J. Harwood 1984
Climb easily for 9m then step up R and back L to a sapling, move R into a corner, then R again to an arete. Pull over a bulge and up L to a small corner. Finish up L.

New Human   42m   VS   4b
C. Connick, D. Hughes 1979
Start just L of the lowest overhang in the centre of the face. Climb across the overhung slab moving L under the roof to a cave. Trend RW to another cave and follow the groove above to the top.

Bitterstrain   13m   E1   5c
P. Donnithorne, N. Ashcroft 1988
Scramble up to a belay area directly above the old fallen tree on the path between New Human and the Main Overhang Area. Start 6m L of an enormous wedged boulder. Move boldly up on sloping holds to a crack, then move up and L to large blocks. From here a difficult move gains a PB. Abseil.

Obscurities   15m   E1   5c
P. Donnithorne, E. Alsford 1988
Start on some blocks above the large jammed boulder. Make a difficult move over an overhang, PR, step up L to a small tree then

past a TR to another small tree. Step up and R, PR, to yet another small tree, finish directly.

Black Fox   33m   E4   5c   6b
A. Sharp, P. Lewis 1985
Start at a small slab 6m R of Torrid Nights.
1) 18m Climb the slab and groove above, moving L to a TB.
2) 15m Climb the overhang above the belay and continue up the slab above, 2 PR's, to a holly tree. Abseil off.

Cool Hand Fluke   21m   E3   5c
A. Sharp, J. Harwood 1985
Start 4m R of Black Fox. Climb the Slab/wall and go through the L side of a roof with difficulty. Abseil off the trees above.

Running Blind   21m   E4   6b
A. Sharp, P. Lewis 1985
Climb the slab and groove 3m R of Cool Hand Fluke to a roof. Go over this to a tree. Abseil off.

MAIN OVERHANG AREA
Further along the path one meets "the main attraction".

Descent Route   45m   D
Not the best of descents!. Start at a large jammed block reached by scrambling up L from the L side of the main overhang. Climb the R side of the block, then a short crack before moving R into a gully leading to the top.

Ivy Nest   24m   VD
Climb the deep cleft 12m L of the main overhang.

Stray Cats   24m   E4   6a
P. Tilson, M. Daniford A2 (Sisyphus) 1972
FFA A. Sharp, J. Harwood 1984
Good steep climbing. Start just R of Ivy Nest. Pull over a small overhang with difficulty to good holds. Move R, BR, to a groove and follow this to the top.

The following seven routes have the same start at the remains of a large tree at the L end of the main overhang.

Each Way Nudger   15m   E3   6a
G. Gibson et al 1985
Climb up for 4m, then via a shallow groove and a thin crack on the L gain the bulge. Pull over this LW to a situ belay. Abseil off.

Gentle Push   18m   E4   6a   *
P. Littlejohn, C. Court 1985
Sustained and technical. Follow a groove on the L over some

bulges until level with a smooth wall leading R. Traverse R for 3m to a thin crack and make hard moves up the wall to gain good holds above the bulge. Finish up L.

Unnamed Route 2   18m   HVS   5a
L. Francombe, A. Reed 1981
Climb up R to a small overhang, pull over this and move R to a big flake. Climb this and the groove above, on the L, to the top.

Wild Magic   24m   E3   5c
T. Penning, P. Cresswell 1982
Good exposed climbing. Traverse a horizontal scoop RW to the arete on the lip of the overhang, TR. Climb up and traverse R to a shallow corner, PR. Climb this to the top.

Finger Pinch   18m   E3   5c
P. Donnithorne, T. Meen 1986
Follow Wild Magic to the TR, Climb the obvious line above to another TR. Step L at the overhang, PR, and then climb up and R over a bulge to the top.

Lip trick   42m   E3   6a, 6a
T. Penning, P. Littlejohn 1983
A wild trip on the very lip of the overhang. Start at the large tree.
1) 21m Follow Wild Magic to the PR. Continue traversing (crux), PR, to a PB.
2) 21m Climb up then R to a groove. Climb this for 3m until it is possible to move R to a crack (Gastro). Follow this passing old PR's to the top.

Cautious Lip   48m   E6   6a   6b   6a   ***
A. Sharp, P. Lewis 1985
A brilliant L to R girdle on the lip of the main overhang in outrageous positions. Start at the large tree.
1) 18m As for Wild Magic.
2) 12m Move R into the crack of Gastro, NR, and climb down this for 4.5m. Traverse R into Bangkok and Belay.
3) 18m Traverse R and finish up Caution To The Wind.

Giant Killer   42m   E6   6b   6a   ***
P. Littlejohn, T. Penning 1pt aid 1983
FFA M. Crocker, R. Thomas 1988
Now free of its one rest point. Until the ascent of Davey Jones' Locker it was probably the largest and most spectacularly free roof climb in South Wales. Very strenuous with good protection (if you can hang on long enough to place it). Start below and L of a short corner on the LH end of the Main Overhang.
1) 21m Climb up for a metre or two and move R into the short corner. Climb this to the roof and traverse R to the groove/crack line splitting the roof. Follow it across the roof and pull over the

lip, BR. With bulging eyes and muscles, gain a PB above.
2) 21m Climb up and R into an obvious groove above. Follow this to the top.

Gastro 51m A3, E3 6a
C. Mortlock
Start near the centre of the main overhang at a thin, crack and groove line running across a subsidiary overhang. Dangle and bash your way up it.

Bangkok 21m E5 6b
A. Sharp, J. Harwood, P. Lewis 1985
Abseil into a TB on the lip of the roofs, 4.5m L of Caution To The Wind. Follow the line of pockets up the arete above, moving R to finish, 2TR's, PR.

Caution To The Wind 21m E4 6a *
A. Sharp, P. Lewis 1985
Abseil to the main groove on the R side of the lip of the roof. Climb the groove, NR, TR, to a PB.

Sai Finish 21m E5 6b *
A. Sharp, J. Harwood 1985
From 3m above the belay on Caution To The Wind, move L to finish up a slim groove.

Springboard 42m A2 E3 6a 5a
P. Watkin, C. Jones A2
P. Littlejohn, M. Harber FFA from the lip 1979
The direct start is a future project. Good climbing above the overhang. Start below a crack splitting the roof on the LH end of the Main Overhang. It is also possible to reach pitch 2 via an abseil to the lip of the overhang.
1) 24m Use aid to gain the lip of the overhang (A tree was climbed to avoid this, but it has vanished). Free climb to gain the groove above and follow this to a tree stump and belay.
2) 18m Step L and climb to exit L on to vegetation.

Spore Wars 36m E6 6c 6a **
M. Crocker, R. Thomas 1 pt aid 1988
A superb unusual route. Start below the RH end of the main overhang.
1) 15m Pull up to the roof and using a BA gain a big jug over the lip, NR, crank up L, BR, then traverse L along the lip, BR into a deep groove, TR. This leads to a small stance where the groove deepens, BB.
2) 21m Move up R onto the arete and continue on good holds to a niche, PR, (Subversive Body Pumping). Blind moves RW leads to bold climbing up a grey/black scoop to a break, PR, pull up R to a tree and abseil.

Subversive Body Pumping   24m   E5   6c/7a   **

M. Crocker, R. Thomas 1988

The holdless, bottomless groove on the R edge of the main overhang is gained via a desperate move, BR. Bridge up, BR, swing L to better holds and the base of the crackline above, NR, follow it past 2PR's to a semi rest next to a white niche, PR. Pull blindly out R into a grey/black scoop and climb up R to a tree, lower off.

Powers That Be   30m   E6   6c   ***

M. Crocker, R. Thomas 1988

A tremendous diagonal line with all insitu gear. From the second BR on Subsersive etc, swing R to a concreted jug, TR, gain the hanging slab above, BR and leg pump RW across it, BR, TR, to a rest on Berlin, NR. Step up as for that route, BR, then make precarious moves R, BR, to good footholds L of the arete. Move up to the roof, PR, and make a long reach, PR, to a jug in its apex, pull over and up to a tree. Abseil.

Berlin   21m   E5   6b   ***

G. Gibson, M. Croker 1985

An excellent pitch, technical and strenuous. Start beneath a series of staggered grooves 3m L of the main groove of Big Time. A dyno start, or stand on a boulder, leads to a break, TR. Make a trying move over the bulge, PR, to gain the slab above. Step L then climb thinly and boldly to a BR and continue through the bulge into a V groove. Step R and climb past a BR, PR, then swing L into the final groove. Abseil from BB.

Big Time   30m   E6   6a   **

P. Littlejohn, T. Penning, J. Harwood 1pt aid 1985

A bold pitch that may need cleaning first. Start beneath the obvious corner in the middle of the face (BR at 6m). Climb steeply to reach the second of two bolts and use it for aid to reach a small ledge. Climb up, old BR, and follow the corner passding two poor PR's, bold and sustained, to the overhang PR. Traverse R to a short V groove which is climbed to a ledge on the R. Abseil of trees.

Angel Heart   22m   E6   6b/c   ***

A. Sharp, P. Lewis 1pt aid 1985

Follow Big Time to just above its BA, step L and climb the groove ibn the arete on a series of undercuts to reach a good ledge. Move L and finish as for Berlin, or better finish over the roof as for Powers That Be. 3BR's, 1PR. Abseil from a BB.

Crock of Gold   30m   E6   6b/c   ***

M. Crocker, R. Thomas 1988

A fantastic, sustained and direct line. Start 6m R of Big Time below a small sapling on ther lip. Climb through the roofs, TR, 2 PR's,

NR, with wild moves to gain the sapling on the lip, PR, and a resting place on thge R. Move up and intricately L, BR, and then directly to a narrow, sloping footledge, BR. Make further hard moves up the crackline, PR, to join the traverse of Big Time and move R Along this to abseil off trees.

Salem's Lot   30m   E6   6b   ***
A. Sharp, P. Lewis 1985
Yet another excellent pitch which accepts the challenge of initial overhangs and blank walls above. Start as for Crock Of Gold. Muscle past a PR to gain the sapling. MOve up, 3m then R to follow a series of small incuts up the wall (bold). Tree belay.

Harlem   30m   E6   6b   **
A. Sharp, P. Lewis 1985
FFA. M. Crocker 1988
An impressive route up some very steep rock. Start at a small recess between two trees growing out of the rock. Climb strenuously through the first overhang, TR on massive pockets to gain a good finger ledge above the bulge, PR. Get established on the finger ledge! Extending moves lead through the next roof, TR, BR, to a superb pocket. Pull onto the slab and move L into a shallow groove, climb it and the wall above, NR, to easier ground and BB, PB. Abseil.

Hawaiian Chance   24m   E5   6c   **   †
G. Gibson, R. Thomas 1991
A varied route. Start just L of Spain. Climb to the roof and a tree stump, then power through the roof, TR and BR, to an arete, BR, leading up to a junction with Spain and a good rest. Continue into a groove, 2TR's where a complex series of blind moves lead LW, BR, round the arete onto the front face and good holes, BR. Pull up LW to a crack and follow this to a niche, TB's. Lower off.

Spain   24m   E4   6a   ***
G. Gibson 1985
Arguably the best route of its grade in South East Wales. Exceptional climbing in exciting positions. Start beneath a Tube at 9m. Climb to a small tree and pull over the bulge into a scoop, step up and move L to the arete and climb steeply past 2TR's to gain a rest in the hanging groove above (unfortunately a poorly positioned BR on Hawaiian Choice can reduce the commitment of the next moves). Reluctantly step R onto the lip of the overhang and traverse RW to a groove in the arete, 2TR's. Step up and swing L, PR, pull wildly over the roof to gain the crack above, TR. Finish up the crack to tree belays.

Groovy Tube Day   24m   E1   5b   *
C. Connick, D. Hughes 1978
A unique route which explores the obvious tube. Start as for

Spain. Follow Spain into the scoop. Step up and move R into the tube (possible belay). Exit from the top of the tube and climb the corner above to the trees. Abseil off.

On the Boardwalk   65m   E1   5a   5b   5c   **
C. Connick, D. Hughes 1979
FFA A. Sharp, R. Powles 1981
Nice climbing in good positions. Start as for Spain.
1) 13m Follow Spain and belay in the Tube.
2) 18m Traverse R from the top of the tube and move up onto the slab to a crackline. Follow this, then move R to a small foot hold on the lip of the overhang. A long low step to a mantle shelf leads to good holds. Move R to a small tree and PB.
3) 18m Traverse R and up and R again to a small tree and TR out R. Swing R onto a large block and continue to a large tree. Abseil off.

Venice   11m   E4   6b
A. Sharp, P. Lewis et al 1985
Short sharp and dirty. Requires major cleaning. Start 3m R of Spain. Climb the crack and roof, situ wire and PR to a small tree. Abseil off.

Dr Van Steiner   22m   E5   6a
G. Gibson, 1991
A scary route with poor protection. Start 5m R of Groovy Tube Day. Climb via a small tree through the initial overlap, BR, to the main overlap, F3. Pull through this, PR, onto the upper wall, PR, and climb direct to join Groovy Tube Day at the tunnel. Bridge out and pull onto the face above to join Spain at its twin TR's. Finish up Spain.

Day Screamer   22m   E3   5c
A. Sharp et al 1985
A dirty start leads to good climbing above. Start 8m R of Spain. Climb the overhang and crack above to a ledge. Step L and climb the slab and the overlap above to a tree belay. Abseil off.

Access to the following routes is gained by scrambling up to two small caves on an earthly ledge 65m R of Spain.

Dream Academy   22m   E2   5c/6a   **
T. Penning, J. Harwood 1985
A nice pitch on good rock, hard for the grade. Start on the LH end of the ledge by a tree or climb the start of Day Screamer. Climb a short wall to a narrow ledge, move up and L to gain the RW slanting crack leading to an overhang. Go L on undercuts, and gain good holds above, climb up R then L beneath the second overhang, PR, pull over this, TR, and climb the wall above to a tree belay on the L. Abseil off.
Variation Finish: Climb up and R over the second overhang to a TB. 6a.

Incidentally X   18m   E5   6b   †
G. Gibson 1985
This line had not had an ascent since a rockfall removed part of it,
its grade is suspect. The superb overhanging wall to the L of the
cave, committing and strenuous. Climb the easy wall to the
break, PR, make hard moves using side holds to gain a hidden
jug, PR. Extend for a hold above, and pull desperately to the final
bulge, PR. Lurch over this for good holds and the belay. Abseil
off.

Brazilian Blend   21m   E4   6a   **
G. Gibson 1985
Excellent climbing on perfect rock. Climb a groove between the
two caves, step R, pull back L and go over the bulge, PR, onto the
slab above, climb straight up and over two bulges to the top.
7TR's and PR mark the way.

Let's Tango In Paris   21m   E3   6b   *   †
G. Gibson 1991
Follow Brazilian Blend up the groove to the first TR. Stand up and
L and make powerful moves LW, BR, to twin finger jugs and a
tricky move onto the face above. Continue up to the slim groove
above and follow this without deviation to good holds at the top.
Move R to a tree and abseil.

Sverige   21m   E3   6b   *
G. Gibson, T. Penning, C. Court 1985
A well protected problem. Climb the groove R of Brazilian Blend
and pull over the bulge, PR, onto the slab above, 2TR's. Climb the
overlap above 2PR's by a difficult sequence and finish easily over
the final bulge, 3TR's. Abseil.

Breakout   21m   E4   6a   **
A. Sharp, J. Harwood 1985
Start on the block R of Sverige. Climb the wall, TR, then move up
L to the roof, PR, continue up the groove and slab to a tree.
Abseil.

Vitamin Z   21m   E4   6b
A. Sharp. P. Lewis et al 1985
A nice pitch. Start at a corner to the R of the caves. Climb the
corner, step R and make a hard pull over a bulge, poor PR. Pull
past this with difficulty and continue to an abseil tree.

Under the Boardwalk   27m   E3   6a
L. Francombe, A. Reed 1981
Start as for Vitamin Z. Climb the corner to some large blocks on
the R. Move up L over the bulge to the horizontal break. Climb L
to an obvious groove and follow this to a tree belay. Abseil.

OGMORE OS ref 868741 to 88273
R.Thomas

"There's more fun to be had at Sully Island" J.Perrin 1973

SITUATION AND CHARACTER

Ogmore contains the greatest concentration of South East Wales' best routes and many that rank alongside the best in Britain. It is wild, steep, exciting and seriously underrated. You will either love it or hate it but whichever it is you must encounter "the Ogmore experience".

Ogmore is a limestone sea cliff situated between Ogmore by Sea and Southerndown. It offers climbing of a strenuous nature; on steep and overhanging rock that is generally well supplied with holds. The rock is mostly good but some of the finishes and occasionally entire routes are not exactly stable. It can suffer from seepage and is extremely tidal, with the tide rising 6m to 9m up the cliff, so beware of in-situ gear and purchase some tide tables. It is a great crag for those who value adventure and excitement in their climbing. It has been neglected over the past few years and deserves a lot more attention from visitors and locals alike.

APPROACHES AND ACCESS

See map 1.

1   The climbs are usually approached from the W (L) side of the cliffs. Follow the road from Ogmore by Sea (B4524) towards Southerndown (Dunraven Bay) until it reaches a sharp bend passing West Farm (just after the sign marking the boundary of Southerndown). Park above the cliffs in a grassy area bounded by concrete posts. The Old Stable Tea Shop is ideally situated here for those who have cocked the tides up or require a 'pick me up' after their route. Descend a grassy gully towards the sea to reach a narrow path running W. At the base of the gully, to the L(E) is a pinnacle which is the start of Exposure Explosion and further L along the cliff top are the abseil stakes above Elephant Wall.

Follow the path W for approximately 80m then descend to a rock platform at the top of Route 1. Abseil or reverse the route.

It is also possible to traverse further W and scramble down easy rocks to reach the LH side of the crag.

2   On spring tides, access is also available from Dunraven Bay along the base of the cliff and is a better way to reach Phaser Wall and the crags to its E.

Knowledge of the tides is essential as there is a large tidal range, rucksacks are best left at the top of the cliff (local knowledge tells us that they end up in Padstow, Cornwall!). Climbs can be reached from the beach two hours after high tide. Two cut off points are the ridges below Scutch and Davy Jones Locker. These may not be passable at all on neap tides. Once a knowledge of the cliff is gained, access to most areas can be made by abseil and abseil posts are noted in the route descriptions.

The Left Hand Crag
At the L end of the crag is a large square cave with a prominent rock scar to its R. The following three routes are on the wall L of the cave. They lead to a large ledge with stake belays that are also useful for abseiling. These routes are 100 m to the L(W) of the descent route (Route 1).

Spangle Texture　18m　VS　5a
S.Blackman, M.Eden 1984
Start 4m L of the cave. Gain the first horizontal crack, traverse L then directly up to a belay on the large ledge.

In Dispute With Nappy Rash　18m　HVS　5a
G.Lewis, S.Lewis 1983
Start 3m L of the cave. Climb easily onto a ledge, continue to the upper horizontal break and traverse slightly LW until a line of holds lead to the large ledge.

Raw Energy　18m　E2　5c　　　　　　　　　　　　　　　　　*
M.Learoyd, R.Thomas, G.Royle 1984
Start just L of the cave and climb via an undercut ledge and flake crack to the roof. Pull up L onto the obvious nose, move L up the wall, PR, and continue over the small roof to the large ledge.

The Pursuit Of Happiness　19m　E4　6a　　　　　　　　　　　†
S.Bartlett, S.Kennedy 2pt aid 1980
FFA A.Sharp, O.Jones 1986
This climbed the R side of the prominent white buttress forming the R side of the square cave a significant rockfall has removed the lower part and the finishing blocks.

The long wall to the R of the square cave has few notable features and contains two routes.

Chill Factor　18m　HVS　5a
P.Littlejohn, S.Lewis 1981
Another route that has been affected by storms. Start R of the cave just L of a grey arete. Climb up for a metre or two before moving R onto the arete and up to an overhang. Step L to a ledge then back R and climb the roof to the top.

Side Step　24m　VS　4b
J.Harwood, C.Horsfield 1978
Start just R of a shallow cave at the featureless wall. Climb diagonally L for 15m to follow a weakness in the upper wall.

The obvious buttress to the R(E) is Twinkle buttress and house the descent route. 18m L of the descent route (Route 1) is a line of overhangs high on the wall.

Kite   18m   E1   5b
S.Lewis, J.Harwood 1978
Climb to the lower overhangs 4m from their L end. Follow a crack round the first overhang then move L over the top overhang to finish.

Swing Wing   18m   E3   5c
P.Littlejohn, T.Penning 1983
Start as for Kite. Climb to the first overhang and pull over this. Move R to a short corner, then LW and back R to finish over the top overhang.

Mighty Steel   18m   E5   6c   †
M.Crocker, M.Ward 1987
Direct and desperate. Start from a recessed ledge R of Kite. Climb to the first roof, PR, undercut through the break in the roof, NR, to better holds, then direct, PR, through the roofs to a recess and an exit LW.

Storm Damage   18m   E2   5b   †
M.Crocker, R.Thomas 1987
Start below a white slabby rib. Climb to the R side of the roofs. Continue directly over these to the top.

Christmas Cracker   18m   HVS   4c   *
P.Thomas, J.Mothersele 1972
Start 9m R of Kite below the R side of the overhangs, at a shallow groove. Climb the R rib of the groove for 9m then move up R to a bulge. Climb back L above the bulge, surmount the overhang and finish up the obvious groove to the L.

Christmas Hangover   18m   HS   4b
J.Mothersele 1972
This climbs the groove just R of Christmas Cracker. Climb diagonally L to a ledge then follow the line of least resistance up R to finish.

Slippery Jim   18m   VS   4c
J.Harwood, P.Thomas 1974
Start just R of Christmas Hangover at a shallow overhung corner. From the L climb to the shallow overhung corner then move up RW to finish up the groove.

Strategic Zap Attack   18m   E2   6b   * †
M.Crocker, M.Ward, R.Thomas 1987
A superb roof problem. Start just L of Twinkle Buttress and surmount the large roof at 12m. A long reach is needed to get over the roof at its widest point, PR.

Ogmore: Main Cliff; Left-hand Section

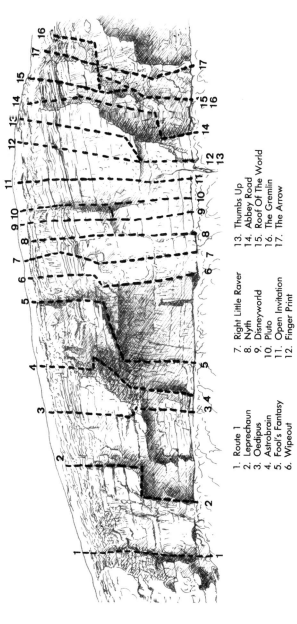

1. Route 1
2. Leprechaun
3. Oedipus
4. Astrobrain
5. Fool's Fantasy
6. Wipeout
7. Right Little Raver
8. Nyth
9. Disneyworld
10. Pluto
11. Open Invitation
12. Finger Print
13. Thumbs Up
14. Abbey Road
15. Roof Of The World
16. The Gremlin
17. The Arrow

Twinkle Buttress
The small prominent buttress standing out from the general line of the cliff. Descent is possible by route 1 or there is a large spike at the top for abseil if required.

Pillock   15m   VS   4c
P.Thomas 1972
This follows the overhanging chimney and shallow groove just L of Twinkle.

Twinkle   12m   D
J.Mothersele 1972
This takes the easiest line on the L edge of the buttress.

Route 1   12m   D
J.Mothersele 1972
This takes the obvious corner to the R of the buttress.

Canute   12m   VD
C.Horsfield 1972
To the R of Route 1 is a wall with a shallow corner on its R. Climb the crack on the R and move round L onto the wall. Follow a shallow groove up to the L.

Canute Right Hand   12m   HVS   5a
P.Thomas 1972
Climb Canute until it is possible to step R under a bulge to the foot of a shallow corner. Finish up this.

The next feature is the obvious corner and roof of Leprechaun.

Leprechaun   18m   E1   5b   *
J.Kerry 1 pt aid 1973
FFA P.Littlejohn, J.Harwood, J.Mothersele 1977
Start 9m R of Route 1 at an obvious corner capped by a large overhang. Climb to the overhang then move R to gain a bottomless corner. Climb up to a flake crack then move L across blocks to the top.

The next two routes have been affected by storms.

Oedipus   18m   E3   6b   †
P.Littlejohn, A.Sharp 1978
Gymnastic. Climb the L side of the blunt arete R of Leprechaun to bulges, then move up R and back L to gain a ledge above the roof. Move onto the face above and finish.

Oedipus Variation   18m   E3   6b
M.Learoyd, G.Royle 1984
As for the last route to the ledge, continue L beneath a nose.

then move back onto the nose and climb the crack above to finish.

Astrobrain   18m   E6   6b   * †
P.Littlejohn, R.Thomas 1986
Start just R of Oedipus. Climb steeply up R to a crack and into a pod. Traverse R to a block then up R again until a few moves lead to a PR. Bold moves up and L lead to an exit.

Fool's Fantasy   33m   E4   6a   *
P.Thomas,C.Horsfield aid 1974
FFA P.Littlejohn 1977
A spectacular mind blowing pitch which follows the lip of the shallow but large cave 20m R of Leprechaun. Climb a groove L of the cave to the first roof. Traverse RW around this and continue to beneath the main overhangs. Traverse R to pull round the R end of the roof and climb direct to a groove.

Wipeout   27m   E4   5c   *
P.Thomas, C.Horsfield aid 1974
FFA P.Littlejohn, J.Mothersele 1977
A strenuous route. Climb the LH of two overhanging grooves R of Fool's Fantasy, past a bulge, until it is possible to swing R and finish up a short wall.

Right Little Raver   27m   E5   6b   ** †
P.Littlejohn, M.Moran 1984
Immaculate wall climbing between Wipeout and Nyth. Climb on good holds to a good NR where the face is smoother and steeper. Continue to a small flat hold, then move up L to an obvious short crack. Move L and finish as for Wipeout.

Nyth   27m   E4   6a
P.Thomas, J.Harwood 1 pt aid 1975
FFA P.Littlejohn, J.Mothersele 1977
This climbs the RH of the two overhanging grooves R of Fool's Fantasy. Slightly bolder than Wipeout. Climb the wall, keeping L of the crack, until level with the base of the groove. Climb the groove to the top.

Disneyworld   27m   E5   6c
M.Crocker, R.Thomas 1991
Boulder problems in the sky. Climb to large TR's on the L wall of Pluto, step round L and make problematic moves over the roof, continue up the wall above, 2 PR's.

Pluto   27m   VS   4c   ***
C.Horsfield, P.Thomas 1972
A good line through some spectacular terrain, a must for any aspiring Ogmore leader. Climb the V-chimney a metre or two R of

Nyth, swing L near the top to finish up the arete.

Pluto marks the L side of a shallow bay 95 metres across. The bay is split into two by a subsidiary buttress.

Open Invitation   27m   E5   6b   * †
M.Crocker, M.Ward 1985
The smooth wall between Pluto and Finger Print gives a technical, fingery and sustained climb. Ascend the easy crack just L of Finger Print and continue direct up the steep wall to a horizontal crack. Move R up to the next horizontal break, then make a hard move to a small overlap and climb the thin crack in the leaning wall to the top.

Finger Print   27m   E3   6a   **
A.Sharp, S.Lewis 1977
A classic roof problem. Start under an overhang on the wall R of Pluto. Climb to the overhang, PR, power over it and continue steeply up the crack to finish.

Thumbs Up   27m   E3   6a   *
P.Littlejohn, A.Richardson 1pt aid 1983
P.Littlejohn, J.Mothersele 1984
A fine pitch. As for Fingerprint to above the overhang then traverse R above the lip to a small ledge. Climb the wall above to the top.

To the R of Pluto is a series of R facing corners (Abbey Road to Megalopolis) trending to the R, with overhangs at their base.

Brothers In Arms   27m   E6   6b   **
M.Learoyd, R.Thomas 1pt aid 1985
FFA A.Sharp, P.Lewis 1986
If you have arms like Garth 'Go for it' The obvious crack in the impending L wall of the corner of Abbey Road. Climb to a small roof and move over this into the thin crack above, PR, then up and into the crack, which splits a larger roof above. Continue through the roof and the crack above to the top.

Abbey Road   27m   HVS   5a   **
P.Thomas, C.Horsfield 1972
Airy climbing up the first of the R facing corners. Bridge up the cave for 4m then traverse R onto the wall, climb to the overhang and follow the RH groove to the next overhang step L and up to finish.

Roof Of The World   24m   E5   6c   ** †
M.Crocker, M.Ward, R.Thomas 1987
A tremendous route with a complicated roof section and good protection. Follow Gremlin to the roof at 12m, step L and climb R

Ogmore: Main Cliff; Right-hand Section

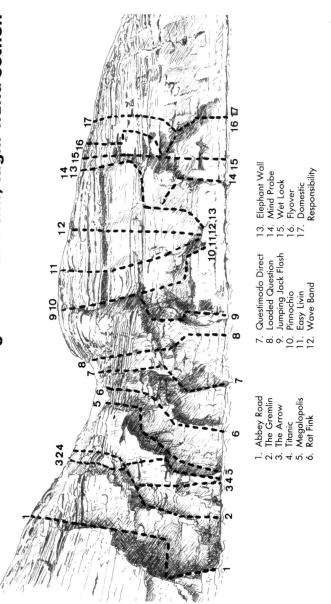

1. Abbey Road
2. The Gremlin
3. The Arrow
4. Titanic
5. Megalopolis
6. Rat Fink

7. Questimodo Direct
8. Loaded Question
9. Jumping Jack Flash
10. Pinnochio
11. Easy Livin
12. Wave Band

13. Elephant Wall
14. Mind Probe
15. Wet Look
16. Flyover
17. Domestic
Responsibility

through the roof using a concealed pocket on the lip, PR. Step R above the roof and climb the wall just L of the arete to the top.

The Gremlin   27m   E1   5a   *
J.Kerry 1972
A metre R of Abbey Road are two shallow grooves which meet at a more obvious V groove. Climb the L, cracked groove and continue RW round the overhangs to a niche. Traverse R under the bulging wall to a groove and the top.

The Arrow   27m   E2   5c   **
J.Kerry aid 1972
FFA A.Sharp, J.Harwood 1977
A good pitch with a taxing move to gain the smooth groove/ corner. Climb to a small roof a metre or two R of Gremlin. Move L onto the wall. Gain the smooth groove/ corner, then pull out L at the roof and continue round the overhanging blocks on the L to finish up a short corner on the R.

Titanic   27m   E4   6a
J.Kerry aid 1972
FFA A.Sharp 1979
Start as for The Arrow. Climb the R groove to the roof, then traverse R to the edge. Gain a bottomless crack which is followed to finish as for Gremlin.

Mauritania   27m   E5   6b   †
M.Crocker, R.Thomas 1988
Climb to the roof as for Titanic then struggle out R over the roofs until it is possible to swing back L, TR, to the top.

Megalopolis   33m   E1   5b   **
J.Kerry 1972
A little L of centre of the L part of the bay 12m R of Abbey Road is a clean wall bounded on its L by a continuous overhang and a roof at the top. Bridge the cave to gain a corner crack leading to the roof. Traverse R then climb the overhang to a niche. Traverse R to the foot of another overhang which is climbed to finish out R.

Rat Fink   27m   HVS   4c   *
P.Thomas, C.Horsfield 1974
A direct version of Megalopolis, bold for its grade. Climb the centre of the wall R of Megalopolis and move R to gain a thin crack, climb it to a break in the overhang. Climb over this to finish out R.

Rat Fink Direct Start   E1   5b   *
P.Thomas, J.Harwood 1987
Start 3m R of the original start. Climb steeply and pull over the roof using a large hold to gain the upper wall of Rat Fink.

Many of the routes in the next section have been affected by storms.

Questimodo   24m   E4   6a
P.Littlejohn, A.Sharp 1977
Strenuous and sustained. Start 9m R of Rat Fink, below a blank groove rising above a shallow cave. Climb for 12m then move R into the groove which is climbed for a metre or two to a crack. Traverse L and continue up L to gain easier ground and the top.

Questimodo Direct   24m   E5   6a   * †
M.Crocker, M.Ward, R.Thomas 1988
This is unaffected so far by storms. From where Questimodo traverses out L continue directly up the smooth groove to finish easily. Bold but low in the grade.

A Sugar Free Diet   24m   E5   6b   †
M.Crocker, R.Thomas 1989
The whole upper section is missing. A supercharged eliminate. Start as for Questimodo. Climb to the cut away roof, swing L to gain sloping holds in a shallow groove above the roof. Pull up to a pocket and then climb straight through the bulges above to reach good holds, PR. Finish easily.

Drill For Glory   24m   E5   6c   * †
M.Crocker, M.Ward, R.Thomas 1988
The lower section is storm damaged. Problematical climbing up the bulging arete R of Questimodo. Start below and R of the rib. Climb easily up a shallow groove, then bear L across a roof to the rib, 2TR's. A desperate sequence over the first bulge, PR, gains better holds, PR, pull up and slightly R over the second bulge, TR, and finish more easily up and LW.

The next section is characterised by three obvious flat roofs at 22 m (Jumping Jack Flash to Pinnochio).

Loaded Question   27m   E3   5c   *
P.Littlejohn, J.Mothersele 1977
An interesting pitch. Start below and to the L of the three large roofs, in the centre of the L part of the bay. Climb the wall to a ledge at 9m and traverse L for 3m to a slab between two bulges. Finish directly up a crack above.

Jumping Jack Flash   33m   E1   5c   *
P.Thomas, C.Horsfield 1974
FFA A.Sharp, J.Harwood 1977
This takes the chimney between the two LH roofs. Climb a groove 5m L of a round cave to a niche below an overhang. Pull onto the L wall and continue to a recess below the overhang. Move R to blocks then L to a chimney. Climb this and the crack

on the R to finish. A better finish is to join the second pitch of Griffin.

Griffin   32m   E3   6a,5a   *
C.Heard, R.Heard aid 1976
FFA A.Sharp, J.Harwood 1980
Start just R of Jumping Jack Flash at a round cave.
1   21m Climb to a vertical cave at 7m, then traverse across its L wall to a hanging groove. Up this to easier ground and a stance on the L below the main overhang.
2   11m Traverse R a metre or two to a short corner, then surmount the overhang to finish up L.

Pinnochio   36m   HVS   4c   ***
J.Kerry, C.Horsfield 1972
This should be on every S.E.Wales climber's tick list. The Climb finishes up a short chimney on the R side of the three overhangs. Climb a LW rising crack/corner line below and R of the overhangs to a ledge beneath a steep wall. Traverse L past a crack above and climb the bulging wall to a chimney. Climb the chimney, step L along the lip of the overhang with your stomach in your mouth and continue up L to a crack which is followed to a pinnacle, sit down and consider those who were at their limit when it was graded VS!.

The Flasher   84m   HVS   4a,4b,4c,5a,4c
S.Robinson F.Lunnon 1979
A poor R to L girdle which starts at the pinnacle as for Exposure Explosion. The only good pitch is above Fingerprint at 5a.
1   7m Move around the outside of the pinnacle and descend a crack and chimney to belay in a confined area under an overhang.
2   21m Follow the break out L to a corner, (Megalopolis).
3   22m Continue along the break into a corner via a steep hand traverse, (Abbey Road).
4   16m Traverse around the arete and descend slightly before reaching the top of a crack, (Fingerprint). Continue into a corner then move out L onto the arete.
5   18m Traverse L to a swing across a bottomless corner, then cross a grassy groove and climb a crack on the L to finish.

Exposure Explosion   84m   HVS   4a,4b,4c,4c,4a,4a,5a   ***
P.Thomas, C.Horsfield 1st complete ascent 1974
An brilliant L to R girdle that has seen its fair share of epics with people being lowered into the sea, complete with Rollei cameras and watches, due to poor rope work and an inability to communicate. The route is best climbed when "the waves are crashing below slobbering and sucking like some disgusting animal". It starts from the pinnacle described in approach 1.
1   7m From the R (E) side of the pinnacle descend a crack and chimney to belay in a confined area at the start of the traverse.

2 20m Follow the break out R to a stance on the arete prior to entering Wet Look cave. (This is the top of Elephant Wall pitch 1)
3 8m Traverse round the arete to the cave of Wet Look.
4 11m Climb RW out of the cave to belay on good ledges outside the cave.
5 26m Continue R to belay on a small stance on a prominent buttress (this is part of Scutch).
6 7m Traverse R around the arete to a belay in a corner/chimney (Siren).
7 8m Traverse R for 5m then make hard moves up to gain the top.

ELEPHANT WALL AREA
This is the rather featureless pale wall to the R, Pinnochio takes the L side of it. The following four routes may be climbed when the tide is quite high, by abseiling to a small ledge below a fine wall split by two horizontal breaks. There are 3 SB in place at the top. Large Friends are useful and above the second break the rock should be treated with some care. The wall is sunny in the evenings and usually free of seepage.

Easy Livin'　36m　E2　5b　　　　　　　　　　　　　　**
P.Littlejohn, J.Mothersele 1977
Start just R of Pinnochio on the L side of the face. A fine steep climb. Ascend rough rock to ledges below smoother rock, then move LW into a groove leading to the first horizontal break. Pull around the L side of an overhang and climb the steep wall to the second, more friable, break. Finish up the final wall.

Wave Band　36m　E2　5b　　　　　　　　　　　　　　　*
P.Littlejohn, J.Harwood 1977
Start below the faint cracks in the smooth steep rock R of Easy Livin'. Climb easily to the ledges below the smooth steep rock. From their R side climb directly up the smooth wall crossing two breaks to the top.

Slime Crime　36m　HVS　5a
J.Harwood, M.Rhodes 1980
As for Wave Band to the ledges. Follow a short corner on the R side of the face to a horizontal break, pull into the hanging corner and continue directly to the top.

Elephant Wall　35m　VS　4a,4b　　　　　　　　　　　　*
J.Harwood, P.Watkin 1972
Start as for Wave Band.
1 15m Climb to the ledges. Step R and climb the knobbly wall to the horizontal break and an airy stance.
2 20m Step up and R at the break and climb a short groove and steep wall above.

Mind Probe   33m   E1   5b   *
A.Sharp, P.Thomas 1972
Steep and strenuous. Climb the chimney 8m R of Elephant Wall
and just L of an arete, for 5m then move L to a crack in the arete.
Climb the crack then traverse L onto the front of the buttress and
continue to the horizontal break. Finish up the groove in the
arete.

Wet Look   33m   HVS   4c,4c   *
P.Thomas, C.Horsfield 1971/2
This gains the usually wet cave high up on the crag.
1   15m Climb the bulging wall below the L side of the cave to
gain the cave.
2   18m Traverse L on small holds to reach good horizontal
cracks, use these to climb a chimney and reach easier ground.

A metre or two to the R is a square cut chimney taken by Tusker
Chimney, and a prominent black prow taken by Domestic Bliss.

Tusker Chimney   33m   HVS   5a,5b   **
C.Horsfield, P.Thomas 1972
A route of character with two contrasting pitches. Start below the
square cut chimney in the R part of the bay.
1   22m Climb the LW slanting crack and square cut chimney to a
roof. Step L onto a small slab and traverse R under the roof, then
move up to a belay ledge.
2   11m Climb easily up and R then take a steep wall on large
holds at first, to a crescent shaped overhang. Make a hard traverse R then finish up a groove.

Flyover   36m   E2   5c,5b   **
R.Thomas, G.Royle 1986
Fine positions on the exposed top pitch. Start 2m R of Tusker
Chimney.
1   18m Climb a groove until a traverse L can be made, PR, to a
good hold. Take the wall above then move R to belay as for
Tusker Chimney.
2   18m Pull up the wall to reach a LW traverse above the lip of the
cave and beneath a small roof. Follow this to a crack splitting the
roof which leads to a ledge and easier ground.

Domestic Bliss   30m   E1   5b,5a
M.Learoyd, R.Thomas, G.Royle 1984
Start as for Flyover.
1   18m Climb the hanging groove as for Flyover, then swing R
onto the prow. Climb steeply up to the Tusker Chimney belay.
2   12m Climb the steep wall L of Tusker Chimney, trending back
R after overcoming the bulge.

Domestic Responsibility   30m   E2   5a,5c   *
G.Lewis, C.Hurley 1983
Start on the R side of the black prow.
1   18m Step onto a crinkly wall and move up and L to good holds on an arete. Pull around L at a horizontal crack and move up to belay as for Tusker Chimney.
2   12m Move up and R below the finish of Tusker Chimney then make a long reach for a hidden jug. Finish steeply up the wall above.

Tusker Right Hand   33m   HVS   5b
C.Horsfield 1972
Climb the chimney and crack 6m R of Tusker Chimney to the horizontal break, then climb directly up the wall a metre L of an obvious crack (Flash Harry).

Flash Harry   24m   HS   4a   **
P.Thomas 1972
The best route of its grade at Ogmore. Start 13m R of Tusker Chimney. Climb via a groove to an obvious crack a metre or two R of Tusker Right Hand, thence to the top.

Yorkshire Pud   24m   S
M.Rhodes, J.Harwood 1980
This follows the easiest line up the cracked arete R of Flash Harry.

Tim's Route   24m   VD
J.Mothersele 1972
Start just L of the obvious corner on the R side of the bay and follow the easiest line up the grooved arete.

Mordred   24m   VS   4b
B.Davies 1972
This climbs the obvious corner 9m R of Flash Harry on the L side of a seaward facing buttress.

NB * The toe of the buttress at this point may be difficult to pass except at very low tides.*

The Dribbling Douh What   24m   HVS   4c
P.Thomas, A.Sharp 1975
Climb the arete R of Mordred. Poorly protected.

Scutch   27m   HVS   5b   *
P.Thomas, J.Harwood 1974
Climb the buttress mentioned above to a steep crinkly wall. Move L to its centre and gain the horizontal break with difficulty. Continue carefully to the top.

Ogmore: Tiger Bay Area

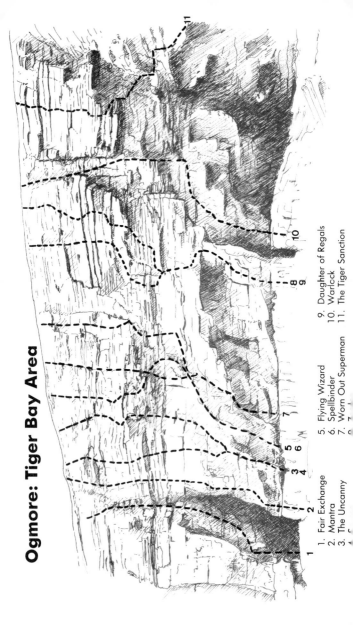

1. Fair Exchange
2. Mantra
3. The Uncanny
4.
5. Flying Wizard
6. Spellbinder
7. Worn Out Superman
8.
9. Daughter of Regals
10. Warlock
11. The Tiger Sanction

Cold Front   27m   HVS   5b
M.Learoyd, R.Thomas 1984
As for Scutch but keep to the R side of the face. Step onto the arete 3m below the horizontal break and climb a groove above the break to finish.

TIGER BAY
The RH face of the buttress has steep barnacle-encrusted rock on its lower part and is bounded on the R by the prominent chimney of Siren Direct, which exits from a large cave. To the R of the large cave of Siren is a wall of steep compact reddish rock, Sorcery Wall, bounded by the shallow groove and projecting ledge of Sorcery. To the R of Sorcery Wall is a long sweep of crag leading into the back of a bay where there is a huge cave. On the R side of the bay is the stratified Fire Wall. The following 4 routes take the RH face of the buttress. The tides can be beaten by abseil approach from stakes above Fire wall.

Quick Draw   27m   E4   6b   ** †
R.Thomas, J.Bullock 1987
An appropriately named route. Start at the LH side of the face. Climb to a deep crack and follow the curving line R, TR, to join Hired Gun, hard moves up and L, PR, gain a small ledge. From here climb a groove to a PR, move L, TR, pull over a small overhang, PR, and continue to the top.

Hired Gun   27m   E4   6a   * †
M.Learoyd, G.Royle 1984
A sustained pitch. Start at the ramp of Siren and climb a green crack to broken blocks below the overhang, PR. Swing L over an overhang, and continue more easily to the top.

Siren   33m   VS   4c
C.Horsfield, P.Thomas 1972
This follows a ramp line which joins a chimney above the large cave. Gain the ramp directly or from the L and follow it until it narrows. Make blind moves R and climb the chimney/corner to finish.

Fair Exchange   30m   E3   6a
R.Thomas, J.Bullock 1pt aid 1984
FFA A.Sharp, O.Jones 1986
Climb to the ramp of Siren then make a strenuous hand traverse to a jagged flake crack and climb it, TR's. Swing along the flake to join the chimney of Siren Direct.

Siren Direct   21m   VS   4c
M.Learoyd, H.Griffiths
Start on the R of the cave and climb the overhanging, narrowing chimney to join Siren.

Bigger Splash   73m   E3   5c,5b   ***
P.Littlejohn pitch 1 solo 1977
P.Littlejohn, A.Sharp, S.Lewis 1977
An excellent, sustained girdle from L to R. Start from the chimney of Siren and finish above the huge sea cave above Tiger Sanction. Muscles are needed on the first pitch and a cool head on the second. Start 9m down the chimney of Siren
1   45m Traversing R along a line of weakness 2m lower than the final pitch of Exposure Explosion. Move R around the arete and climb strenuously until the angle eases (possible belay and escape). Climb up and R and continue the traverse to a projecting ledge on the arete.
2   27m Traverse into a corner formed by the back of the zawn. Climb up and traverse R along the lip of the huge roof until it is possible to climb up for 3m to a line of flat holds. Step R to a crack and climb this and the break above to finish. SB well back.

SORCERY WALL

Mantra   36m   E5   6a   ** †
M.Crocker, M.Ward 1985
A superb pitch up the L centre of the wall, strenuous and intimidating. Climb the RH side of a rib on the R edge of the cave to a small slot. Pull R round the bulge to some small ledges, then climb steeply and boldly diagonally RW to good holds in a horizontal break. Continue direct to the Bigger Splash break then, in the same line, via a thin crack to the top.

The Uncanny   36m   E6   6c   ** †
M.Crocker, M.Ward 1985
A desperate pitch up the L arete of Sorcery. Start 9m R of Siren below a projecting ledge at 7m. Climb to the ledge, move L and then steeply up to a tiny roof on the arete, PR. Pull over the roof and dyno up R to a good hold. Another hard move gains The Bigger Splash break, from where a direct line up the thin crackline, L of a shallow scoop in the headwall, leads to the top.

The Uncanny Direct   36m   E6   6c   ** †
P.Oxley 1988
Start just L of Sorcery. Climb easily to a recess at 3m, TR, possible belay, then cross bulges, PR, TR, to join the original route 1m L of the projecting ledge.

Sorcery   36m   E6   6b   **
P.Littlejohn, S.Robinson 1979
A committing climb taking a shallow overhanging groove 9m R of Siren, possibly the first E6 of this type in Britain. Start beneath the projecting ledge of The Uncanny. Climb into a niche then break up R on razor rock to the ledge, then up R to a slot and a groove. Move up this until it is possible to move R to gain a horizontal

break (Bigger Splash).Traverse L for 3m then go directly through the overhangs via a groove to the top.

Spellbinder   42m   E4   6a   ***
P.Littlejohn, A.Sharp 1977

A superb climb. Start beneath the RW rising ramp line R of Sorcery. Climb to a big slot, then traverse R and up to a smaller slot. From its R end climb straight up to reach a horizontal break (Bigger Splash). Continue directly over the overhang and steep wall above to a groove by a detached block. Gain ledges before finishing up the arete of the large corner on the R.

Flying Wizard   42m   E4   6a   **
P.Littlejohn, T.Penning 1983

Wild, wild, wild! Start up the ramp of Spellbinder until below the widest part of the roofs, then break out L over the roofs and climb steeply to the top.

Worn Out Superman   30m   E6   6b   *** †
M.Crocker, R.Thomas 1990

"Does this routes name allude to the first ascentionist or the former laird of Ogmore?" A staggering line. The grade is reduced to E5 if a stance is taken on Bigger Splash. Start 4m R of Spellbinder beneath an overhanging scoop. Chimney up the scoop, swing RW along a break and over a small roof, 2TR's, to gain the Spellbinder ramp. Step R and from a short crack go through the bulge above, PR, to reach Bigger Splash. Break through the ceiling above via a notch, PR, and trend LW then RW up the committing headwall to the top. SB.

Zardoz   45m   E5   6b,5c   **
P.Littlejohn, A.Richardson 1982

A bold climb. Start beneath the broad white to the R of Spellbinder, just to the R of a roof.
1   24m Climb to ledges beneath the roof. Move R to gain a small sloping ledge then make devious moves LW over a bulge to gain a shallow groove leading to good holds beneath the next set of overhangs. Break L then go straight up to a small hanging stance where the angle eases (Bigger Splash).
2   21m Climb RW to a line of overhangs and traverse R to stand on the obvious projecting strata. Climb straight up the compact upper wall for 4m before bearing slightly R to the top.

Daughter of Regals   45m   E5   6b,6a   *** †
M.Crocker, M.Ward 1985

A high grade classic up the hanging arete R of Zardoz.
1   27m As for Zardoz until after the groove below the second roof, then traverse R for 3m to a narrowing and pull over to a ledge and a hanging stance.
2   18m Climb the 2m roof above the stance slightly R of the belay

to a good break, then trend R to an arete and finish via a thin crack on its L side.

Warlock   51m   E6   6b,5b   *** †
R.Thomas, C.Parkin A2/E1 1985
FFA M.Crocker, M.Ward 1985
A magnificent route. Start 6m R of Zardoz from a narrow platform just L of the huge cave and on the R side of a narrow rift.
1   24m Climb the bulging wall, TR, and shallow groove, PR's, to below the roof. Traverse R along a narrow wall until a series of hard moves up R gains a jug on the hanging arete, PR's. Climb a short corner to a good stance, PB.
2   27m Traverse L to a thin crack and follow this and an easy groove to a projecting ledge on the R. Finish up a wide crack.

The Tiger Sanction   57m   E5   6a,5b   †
M.Crocker, G.Gibson 1985
An exacting and daunting expedition into the cave at the back of Tiger Bay. Start on its R side 6m L of the corner of Fury
1   33m Climb up to a LW pointing block ledge, step R then climb the wall to a TR below the roofs. Move L, pull over the roof and swing L round a rib. Traverse L, low at first, PR, then at a slightly higher level to a projecting shattered rib just R of the huge crack line, PB. Place a high runner to protect the second.
2   30m Pull up L then traverse L on 'biscuits' to a short bottomless groove. Up the groove, then step L onto a balanced block and pull over the roof onto the headwall. Climb the headwall stepping L to exit at a short crack.

FIRE WALL

Fury   30m   E3   5c   *
P.Littlejohn, C.Heard 1983
Climb the big obvious corner on the L side of Fire Wall then move up and pull around an overhang to a ledge. Climb the compact wall on the R, continue carefully up the steep stratified rock to a small ledge, step R then climb straight up on good holds.

Burn Em Up   33m   E4   6b   *** †
M.Crocker, R.Thomas 1985
A brilliant pitch up the centre of Fire Wall, good rock and protection. Start at the central crack/groove between Fire and Fury. Climb the groove to ledges below the first roof, swing R and climb a steep thin crack to the second roof. Traverse L and go through the roof on good holds, PR, and climb the smooth wall above direct to the top.

Fire   30m   E4   5c   **
P.Littlejohn, J.Mothersele 1977
An exacting pitch in its upper part. Climb a vague crack 6m from

Ogmore: Castle Area

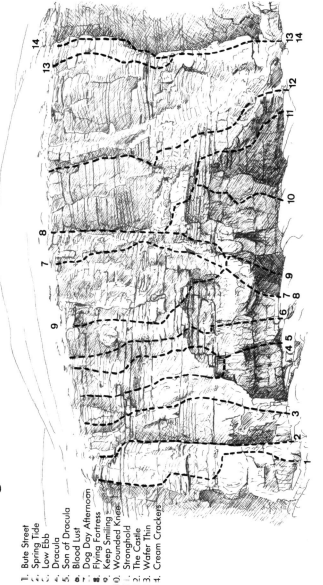

1. Bute Street
2. Spring Tide
3. Low Ebb
4. Dracula
5. Son of Dracula
6. Blood Lust
7. Dog Day Afternoon
8. Flying Fortress
9. Keep Smiling
10. Wounded Knee
11. Stronghold
12. The Castle
13. Wafer Thin
14. Cream Crackers

the R edge of Fire Wall to a roof, over this then up the wall above to smoother rock and a rest. Climb on dubious conglomerate rock with little protection until the angle eases and the top is thankfully reached.

Deep Fry   36m   E5   6b   †
M.Crocker, M.Ward 1986
A direct start to Brimstone. Start a metre or two R of Fire. Climb a groove to where it starts to overhang. More difficult climbing, PR, leads to good holds enabling the crack of Brimstone to be gained. Finish up this.

Brimstone   30m   E1   5a   *
P.Littlejohn, J.Mothersele 1977
This climb gains the shattered crack on the R edge of Fire Wall via a traverse from the corner around to the R. Climb the L wall of the corner to a crack 2m R of the arete, move up to good holds and traverse strenuously L around the arete to the base of the crack. Climb it.

Kickenside   30m   E1   5b
S.Lewis, J.Harwood 1978
This route has been superseded by others. It linked up the start of the Knave with the finish of Well Blessed.

The Knave   27m   E2   5c
M.Learoyd, R.Thomas 1985
Climb the arete between Brimstone and the Bishop to meet the hand traverse of Brimstone. Hard moves up R lead to a groove. Up this, then L to large holds R of Brimstone. Finish direct.

Well Blessed   27m   E1   5b
R.Thomas, G.Royle 1984
Climb the easier lower section of the Bishop until it is possible to move L to horizontal holds below a small pod. Move past it and climb the RH groove up to the overhangs. Move through these carefully to the top.

The Bishop   27m   HVS   4c,4b   *
C.Horsfield, P.Thomas 1972
FFA P.Thomas, A.Sharp 1975
On the R side of the bay is an impressive protruding buttress. This climb takes the chimney and cave on its L.
1   13m Climb easily to the cave, bridge up this, pull over the roof to gain a small square chimney and belay.
2   14m Traverse R to the arete and continue up a groove taking care near the top.

Cone Country   27m   HVS   5a   *
P.Lewis, J.Harwood 1980

Climb the middle of the wall R of The Bishop to the overhang, traverse R a metre and pull over just L of the arete. Continue up the groove as for The Bishop.

Bute Street 30m E2 5b
A.Sharp, P.Thomas c19/'i
Climb the L side of the seaward face of the buttress to an overhang. Step R into the centre of the face, surmount the overhang on friable holds and climb up for 3m, then traverse L to join the groove of The Bishop.

The buttress now returns in a high wall to the obvious corner crack of Poseidon.

Spring Tide 27m E2 5b   *
R.Thomas, G.Davies 1984
Climb just R of the L edge of the wall until a band of high horizontal cracks is reached. Pull over these until a final smoother wall leads to the top.

Low Ebb 30m E3 5c   **
R.Thomas, J.Bullock 1984
Excellent, sustained climbing with the crux at the top. Climb the finger crack a metre or two L of Poseidon, then move onto steep horizontal strata. Follow these directly up the centre of the face to the bottom of a smooth steep headwall. Up this to finish.

The last two routes can be linked by an obvious hand traverse along the horizontal bands below the headwall.

Poseidon 27m HVS 5a   *
P.Thomas, J.Mothersele 1972
This follows the obvious corner crack. Climb the initial groove and step L into the corner. Follow this carefully over a small overhang to a larger overhang. Traverse R to a ledge and continue to the top.

Poseidon Direct Finish 12m E1 5a
R.Thomas, R.Haslum 1983
From the overhang on Poseidon continue straight up the corner and exit with great care.

THE CASTLE AREA
There is now a broad sweep of crag continuing to a small sea stack (The Castle). The bottom part of the crag is mostly good rock but care should be taken with some of the exits. Large stakes provide an exciting abseil approach.

Scorcher 30m E3 6a
P.Littlejohn, C.Heard 1983

Start 3m R of Poseidon at a crack. Climb direct for 6m, move R to a runner slot, step up R and climb to the overhangs, over these via a thin crack. Continue for 3m then move R and up to a corner at an overhang. Turn it on the L to a final crack and the top.

Dracula   42m   E2   5c,5b,4b   *
P.Thomas, C.Horsfield 1974
FFA P.Littlejohn, C.Ward-Tetley 1977
A good route but arrange the pitches so that pitch 3 is your mate's lead. Start below a pod like recess R of the large cave.
1   9m Climb to the recess then out of it before making a hard traverse L to reach a stance above the roof.
2   21m Move L and reach a hanging groove/crack which cuts through the roof. Up this strenuously to better holds, and continue until able to move R to the middle of a long ledge.
3   12m Traverse L and pull into the obvious groove/chimney leading to the top.

Son of Dracula   35m   E4   6a,5a   **
P.Littlejohn, J.Mothersele 1977
Start as for Dracula.
1   21m Climb into the recess as for Dracula. Move out R onto the face and climb the wall and shallow overhung grooves leading through the overhang on the L to a ledge. Belay just above.
2   14m Traverse R for 3m then climb up L above an overhang finishing up the slab.

Blood Lust   36m   E4   6b,4c   * †
M.Crocker, R.Thomas 1985
Quality climbing up the wall and overhanging groove just R of Dracula.
1   24m Climb the wall trending L at the top, to a break. Move up and R into a groove, PR. Follow this and the wall above the roofs, moving L to ledges and a belay.
2   12m Climb a crack and groove to the top.

Dog Day Afternoon   39m   E1   5b,4b   *
P.Littlejohn, J.Mothersele 1977
A fine first pitch, steep and interesting. Start 4m R of Dracula and 13m R of the corner of Poseidon below a RW slanting line.
1   27m Climb to a horizontal crack at the base of some smoother rock. Move up RW to a white niche, follow the groove above and finish RW taking care with some holds.
2   12m Climb the corner crack on the L to the top.

Flying Fortress   39m   E1   5b,4c
S.Massey, S.Bartlett 1979
1   24m As for Dog Day Afternoon to the white niche. Climb up RW to a corner, then R onto the arete. Continue up a loose groove to belay on the L of a large ledge.

2 15m Climb the slab just R of the arete for 6m, move L and climb a groove to the final overhang, which is turned on the L.

Keep Smiling 39m E2 4b,5b,5c
D.Cuthbertson, P.Littlejohn 1981
This crosses Dog Day Afternoon on a counter diagonal line. Start beneath a large cave at 8m.
1 7m Climb to the cave.
2 21m Traverse to the arete and move up to a small cave. Traverse L for 6m past a groove (Dog Day Afternoon) to reach a crack leading to a huge detached flake overhang. Climb diagonally LW from the flake overhang to a stance, TR.
3 11m Climb to the final large roof and surmount it via the widest and most central crack.

Wounded Knee 42m E3 5b,4c   *
P.Littlejohn, J.Mothersele 1977
Strenuous and committing climbing weaving through the overhangs L of Stronghold. Start 3m L of the overhung cave 12m L of the arete opposite The Castle.
1 27m Climb the wall on good holds, then traverse R below the overhangs to the crack rising from the cave. From its top gain the arete and climb direct through the overhangs to reach a crack leading to ledges. Belay as for Stronghold, on the largest ledge to the L.
2 15m as for pitch 2 of Flying Fortress.

Stronghold 42m HVS 5a,4c   *
P.Littlejohn, J.Mothersele 1977
Start 4.5m L of the arete opposite The Castle at a leaning wall of conglomerate rock that gives surprisingly solid climbing.
1 27m Climb up and L to some conspicuous slots, up for 3m then diagonally LW to reach an area of ledges.
2 15m As for Flying Fortress.

The Castle 44m VS 4b,4b
J.Kerry, C.Horsfield 1972
Start opposite The Castle, at a boulder below obvious grooves in the upper wall.
1 22m Climb to a flat ledge, continue up R, then L to another ledge. Take care with the rock.
2 21m Climb a groove and pull over a bulge to a ledge, follow a groove for 3m to a chockstone, traverse L to another groove. Climb this to an earthy groove and finish up the crack on the L.

Western Shoot Out 39m HVS 4c,5a
S.Robinson, F.Lunnon 1979
A not so classic uncleaned route from the on-sight era when men were men. It takes the lower arete and LH crack high on the wall.

1 16m Climb the arete on the L to an overhanging cleft. Take this on the R to a flat ledge.
2 22m From the ledge move LW following a broken crack and smaller ledges to a large ledge (escape possible LW). Move up a thin crack in a short steep wall making an awkward mantleshelf on the R. Follow the dirty crack in the wall to a large niche, exit carefully past the overhang.

Weakhold 45m HVS 5a
G.Lewis, et al c1984
A wandering R to L girdle. Climb the arete opposite the Castle for 10m, traverse L into a bay and finish up The Castle.

Wafer Thin 36m E2 5b   †
R.Thomas, J.Bullock 1988
1 18m Climb to the ledge as for Cream Crackers.
2 18m Move up L onto a rocking block, pull over to a small ledge, PR, and continue up the crack above.

Cream Crackers 42m E4 5a,5c   †
R.Thomas, G.Royle, J.Bullock 1988
This takes the L side of the upper arete R of Western Shoot out.
1 21m Climb the lower arete to a ledge, PB.
2 21m Pull directly over the prow at the start of the arete, PR, then move L onto the L side of the arete. Continue up this, 2PR's, to finish as for Information Received.

HOB NOB BAY
The next bay is composed of horizontal strata of brittle yellow rock; the Ogmore biscuit variety, and is characterised by routes from the "well-cleaned" era.

Information Received 42m E4 5a,5c   †
R.Thomas, G.Royle 1986
A true biscuit route.
1 21m As for Cream Crackers.
2 21m Climb easily to a ledge above. Swing up horizontal bands, TR, and pull around to the R side of an arete. Climb a short wall to beneath a small overhang, PR, up the crack on the R, PR, then back L, PR, to a scab of rock, PR. Climb just R of the arete, PR, and then the actual arete to the top, SB.

Takes The Biscuit 45m E4 5c   * †
R.Thomas, J.Bullock lower section 1988
R.Thomas, M.Crocker 1988
A strenuous and demanding route R of Information Received. Start 3m L of the arete by a large boulder with a chimney above. Climb the chimney until it is possible to move L onto the wall, TR. Continue up the wall, PR, to gain the horizontal break, PR's, possible belay. Move L to gain a steep crack, follow this, PR, TR,

to more horizontal bands. Move R, PR, to reach a continuation crack which is followed, 3TR's, to the top.

Here Today 45m E3 5b,5b †
R.Thomas, G.Royle, J.Bullock 1988
The chimney, yellow slab and steep headwall R of Talioc The Biscuit. Start at a green cave.
1 15m Climb out of the cave, NR, and go up the steep chimney, PR to exit L to a ledge. PB.
2 30m Climb the yellow slabby wall, PR, then a steep crack.

Mother Earth 45m E2 5a †
R.Thomas, J.Bullock 1989
At the back of the bay is an earthy chimney providing the longest, most entertaining chimney pitch in S.E.Wales. Start L of the chimney and climb conglomerate rock until it is possible to step R into the chimney. Follow it past numerous threaded chockstones until an escape can be made RW just below the top to avoid the final mud slopes.

The next routes are on the large concave wall R of the earthy chimney. Several stakes are in position above the yellow wall and Quimble.

Sleepless Nights 39m E4 5c * †
R.Thomas, G.Royle 1987
A route of character approached easily by abseil at all but the highest tides. Friends are useful in the upper section. Start 5m R of Mother Earth. Climb a steep red hollow flake line, TR, PR, and move onto the wall above, PR. Climb this to easier angled rock, 3PR's, 1TR. Follow the upper wall just L of a shallow niche, PR, then continue up a disjointed crack, poor TR, over several bulges. Belay below the top on the abseil rope.

Best Of Friends 39m E2 5a †
R.Thomas, G.Royle, G.Davies 1987
Technically easy but serious. Large Friends are useful. Start 3m R of the last route at a pile of conglomerate rock. Climb the rubble to a large jammed boulder, then over a small roof and follow a faint crack to the easy angled section, PR. Move RW then climb the steep upper wall over several bulges to gain a crack just below the top, exit RW, SB.

Floozie 42m VS 4b,4b
G.Lewis, S.Robinson, F.Lunnon 1980
Looser than it looks! This takes the upper arete of the concave wall.
1 21m Climb the rubble as for the last route and follow a RW rising traverse and a sharp broken corner, then move carefully RW to belay on the arete.
2 21m Move R around the arete, following steep corners to the top.

Further R is a high yellow wall with a block strewn ledge at half-height. The finish to some routes is a steep earth bank, and it is advisable to leave a rope in place. Brushing of the holds may be needed. The routes start from the large ledge which is best approached by abseil.

Suspended Sentence   22m   E4   5c   O   †
R.Thomas, G.Royle 1986
The LH crack in the wall. Start at the LH side of the ledge. Climb a shattered crack to a smaller ledge, step R to the main crack, 2TR's, and up it to a small overhang, PR. Pull out R to finish.

No Reprieve   22m   E3   5c   †
R.Thomas, J.Bullock, M.Learoyd 1986
Start at the ledge, L of the RH crack. Climb a short wall to a ledge, move up L and follow a line of ledges to a LW rising flake traverse leading to a crack. Climb the final wall and thin crack, PR, TR. Belay on a rope.

Have Mercy   21m   E4   6a   †
M.Crocker, G.Gibson, M.Ward 1985
Climb the thin crack in the R side of the wall exiting RW, SB.

Quimble   30m   VS   4b
R.Crockett, M.Harber 1980
The first route up this dubious section of cliff: a useful escape route. Start below the prominent L-facing corner on the R side of the yellow wall. Climb to a niche, step L, move up to a ledge and climb the corner with little protection.

On the R side of the bay are the remains of several large sea caves. Huge rockfalls have decimated the routes in previous publications. The following remain.

Towaway Zone   13m   HVS   5a
L.Foulkes, P.Lewis 1980
Only the first pitch remains! It is possible to combine this with pitch 2 of Motor Torpedo. Start on the L side of the first, smaller, cave. Climb a shallow groove and crack to a small roof then traverse R to a ledge.

Motor Torpedo   48m   E4   6a,5b   †
M.Crocker, R.Thomas 1986
A wild route breaking through the L side of the roofs of the largest cave. Start at the L side of the cave.
1   27m Climb a short, sea washed wall, then a steeper compact wall RW to a small ledge in its centre. Move back L to some small ledges, PR, traverse L along the lip of the roof to good jams, PR, up to a horizontal break, then move L to a good stance as for Towaway Zone.

2   21m Traverse back R, avoiding the blocks, to a crack in the headwall, and climb it on good holds over a small roof. Trend L up the wall exiting directly.

Goodnight Cowboy   30m   E2   5b   †
J.Mothersele, J.Kerry 1974
A.Dance, A.Richardson 1984
R.Thomas, J.Bullock 1989
A line that has had three first ascents but only the last has stayed in place. Start at the sea-washed rocks between the caves or abseil into the cave. Climb smooth rock to gain a crack leading to the cave. Traverse L onto a very small ledge below a faint groove. Follow the groove to ledges then up a steep wall on incuts, PR, to gain a larger ledge. Take the groove above, 2PR's, until it is possible to escape with care up earthy ledges.

R of the rockfall is the cave from which the now defunct route, Aids, exited. On the buttress to the R are the following routes:

Ultra Virus   30m   E4   6a   **   †
M.Crocker, R.Thomas 1986
Brilliant climbing through the roofs. Climb easily to a ledge below the widest part of the roof, over the roof on the R, 2PR's, then climb direct up the overhanging wall, PR, to a ledge at its top. Step R and climb the final wall LW.

Last Buck   24m   E1   5b
C.Heard, R.Thomas 1980
This takes a faint groove in the LH side of the steep smooth white face to the R of Ultra Virus. Gain the groove easily and follow it strenuously to ledges. Finish direct.

Fast Buck   24m   HVS   5a
P.Littlejohn 1977
Start on the L of the face almost below Last Buck. Climb easily RW until the wall steepens, continue R again to reach a detached block. Climb carefully to the top.

Trusty Blade   27m   E2   5b
R.Thomas, J.Bullock 1983
Start from the L edge of the cave on the R end of the wall. Climb up and onto the black prow, move steeply up to the base of a groove, PR, and follow this until it is possible to exit onto a ledge. Climb the loose chimney on the L.

DAVY JONES' LOCKER
R of Trusty Blade is a large cave and R again is the huge sandy floored cave of Davy Jones Locker.

At all but the lowest tides the point to the E of this cave is impassable.

Fast Luck   27m   E1   5b   *
R.Thomas, G.Royle 1984
Start at the buttress 15m L of Davy Jones' Locker, below an
obvious corner high up. Climb easily at first then move boldly to
gain the corner and follow this to the top.

Delirious   30m   E6   4b,6b   †
M.Crocker, M.Ward 1986
A gruelling route, possibly the most serious undertaking at
Ogmore. Start on the L side of the cave housing Davy Jones'
locker, L of a chimney.
1   9m Climb the groove and rib to a good ledge.
2   21m Pull into a short R groove and follow it strenuously to
good spikes, then diagonally R to a large roof. A long reach, TR,
heel hook along the lip and over it leads to a bulging wall. Finish
straight up this.

Twenty First Century   45m   E5   5c,6a   ** †
M.Crocker, R.Thomas 1986
A tremendous route. Starting just R of Delirious and L of a
slanting chimney in the L retaining wall of the cave.
1   24m Climb a groove L of the chimney, swing L to a ledge at a
break, climb steeply to a slot below a roof and pull over on jugs.
Move up R, PR, and RW along a traverse line to a good stance on
the edge of the cave.
2   21m Traverse L at a higher level and climb a short groove, PR,
over a roof on jugs and straight up the wall. Move out and out,
4PR's, until it is possible to pull over to easier ground and the top,
SB.

Skullthuggery   45m   E5   6a   ** †
M.Crocker, R.Thomas 1989
Sensational climbing low in its grade. Start as for Davy Jones'
Locker at low tide or abseil down Twenty First Century and clip its
gear.
1   24m Follow Davy Jones' Locker to the top of the corner, swing
up L and walk to the stance of Twenty First Century.
2   21m Cross the ceiling, above the belay, RW, PR, NR, to gain a
ledge. Climb direct, 2PR's, and where the good holds run out
make fearsome moves to overcome the final roof, PR, then move
LW across to easy but loose rock.

Davy Jones' Locker   51m   E7   6a,6b   *** †
G.Andrew, C.Heard (A3)1978
FFA M.Crocker, R.Thomas 1989
Those who are widely travelled enough to have walked into the
bowels of the great sea cave of Davy Jones' Locker will agree that
the cave roof represents to the free climber, one of the most
spectacular challenges in Southern Britain. Is it Britain's biggest
free roof? Start from the rear L of the cave at low tide, retreat is

Bishop HVS 5a Ogmore *Climbers* E. & P. Littlejohn

Photo C. Howes

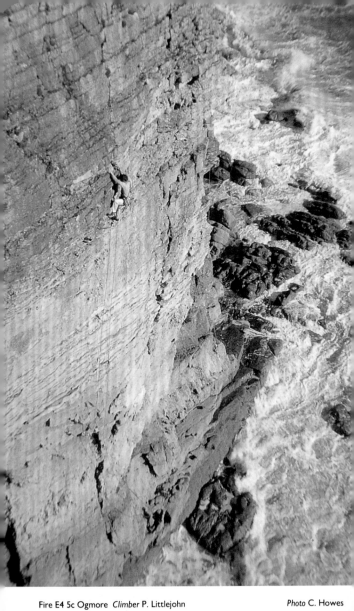

Fire E4 5c Ogmore *Climber* P. Littlejohn

Photo C. Howes

cut off within 3 hours. Timing is important to ensure that the second climber is battling his way across the final roof as the sea thunders into the back of the cave.

1 27m Climb fairly steadily up the face R of a RW trending crackline to a deep break. Pull up a short groove to good holds on a beak of rock. Make committing moves into the roof capped groove above and traverse RW, on the lip of the first low level ceiling which the aid route ascended, to 'the keyhole stance'. Spare a thought for the late Charlie Heard who was benighted here on his own during the first ascent.

2 24m Cross the first 2m ceiling, PR on the lip, and grapple greasily around to jugs, TR. Above is an aven where a no hands rest may be gained. Drop out and with deft handwork extend around the 2m ceiling to move awkwardly up to another aven, The Aven Haven, for another no hands rest. Some fifteen to twenty minutes later fight across the 11m stepped roof on jugs. Keep enough strength for the final stretch, many PR's. From the lip scramble up to the top. SB.

From the small sandy shelf that forms the floor of the cave it is possible to scramble up a short wall on the R to reach ledges and a rock platform. There are large stakes in place above The Hatch for a convenient abseil approach.

Automatic 24m E4 6a * †
M.Crocker, R.Thomas 1985
A fine strenuous route. Start 3m L of the overhanging crack of Fast Reactions at the R edge of the cave. Pull over the first roof to an obvious jug, pull over the next roof, PR, and trend LW over the bulges above to a slight niche. Continue more easily up the wall, SB.

Fast Reactions 26m E2 5b *
A.Sharp, P.Lewis 1977
Start from the ledge at the bottom of the corner crack of The Hatch. Climb a strenuous LW slanting, overhanging crack splitting a series of small stepped roofs.

The Hatch 24m HS 4a *
P.littlejohn solo 1975
Gain the obvious corner and climb it direct.

Here Comes The Rain 24m VS 4c †
M.Ward, M.Crocker 1986
Start as for The Hatch. Climb the groove to a ledge, traverse R along the lip of the overhang then climb the arete.

One Cool Vibe 24m E3 5c †
M.Crocker, R.Thomas 1986
This attacks the same arete as Here Comes The Rain, from the RH

side. Start 6m R of The Hatch. Climb RW on ledges then back L to the arete, continue straight up keeping just R of the arete to exit slightly LW.

Crushproof   21m   HVS   5a
A.Sharp, J.Harwood 1977
Start 7m R of The Hatch, just L of a jutting prow. Climb the wall over an obvious flat block, continue direct to easier ground. Belay well back.

Cold Steel   21m   E2   5b
P.Littlejohn, A.Davies 1980
Start below the overhanging prow R of Crushproof and L of an overhanging crack. Climb to a ledge and pull past the first overhang, move R to a bottomless groove and climb direct until the angle eases and the top is reached.

Phaser Wall
To the R of the prow is a bay of overhanging rock. This area can be approached by abseiling down The Hatch.

Glycogen   24m   E1   5a   **
A.Sharp, J.Harwood 1977
Brilliant, energy sapping climbing, it is possible to lie down in the horizontal strata to rest, but be sure to photograph the antics as he or she tries to get out again! Climb the overhanging crack on the L side of the bay, 3m R of Cold Steel, over two roofs, and finish up the chimney and crack above.

Overboard Man   27m   E4   5c
P.Littlejohn, P.Boardman 1977
Strenuous and not easy to protect. Start a metre or two R of Glycogen at a vague crackline. Climb to small overhung ledges, then work L for a metre before climbing to a small overhang, move R then up to finish.

Brawn Drain   27m   E4   5c   †
P.Littlejohn, S.Robinson 1979
Start between Glycogen and Phaser at a vague weakness. Climb up to and past the first overhangs, moving slightly L to a horizontal break at 9m. Traverse R to good holds and continue R to a ledge above the main overhang. Climb diagonally L and break through the roofs to a steep wall. Climb direct for 3m before moving L to easier ground.

Drain Wave   36m   E3   5b
S.Lewis, C.Curle 1981
A wandering line. Climb Brawn Drain until it is possible to traverse R to a large ledge (Phaser). Continue diagonally R to a crack then up to a large ledge on the R. Finish diagonally RW.

Phaser 30m E3 5c ***
P.Littlejohn, J.Harwood 1977
A Wild Pitch. This takes the next obvious crack R of Glycogen.
Climb from the L through the roof to gain a ledge below the
crack, and power up it.

Whatever Next? 30m E5 5c †
P.Littlejohn, R.Thomas 1986
Start a metre L of the green chimney/cave of Butch Cassidy.
Committing and strenuous. Climb up a deep crack, hand traverse
L and move up L, PR, pull over the roofs and climb the very steep
wall using a series of horizontal holds to gain a large ledge. Finish
direct, belay well back.

Butch Cassidy 36m VS 4b *
J.Harwood, C.Elliot 1977
Start below the large roof with a vertical cave. Gain the roof and
continue up the R side of the chimney to a ledge. Go behind a
large chockstone to the arete on the R and continue to the top.

Stray Dog 33m VS 4c
F.Lunnon, S.Robinson 1980
Start as for Fashoda Chimney. Climb to the top of the main
overhang and traverse L along the lip. Move up on steep rock to a
doubtful block and L to a niche. Continue up the L slanting crack
to the top.

Fashoda Chimney 35m VD *
C.Heard, R.Heard 1975
A pleasant climb taking the obvious corner/chimney R of Butch
Cassidy. Climb a slab, then a corner to a large ledge and up the
wide chimney to an overhang. Traverse R to the arete and final
corner, taking care with the rock.

DIRTY HARRY SLABS
RW the crag forms three long slabs divided by corner cracks. The
routes make up in length and adventure what they lack in rock
quality and reasonable/ sensible protection in other words they
are serious.

First Slab

General Gordon 35m S
J.Mothersele, G.Jones 1971
This follows the friable L edge of the slab R of Fashoda Chimney.
Climb a crack to an overhang, traverse L to a ledge and finish up
the corner.

Khartoum 42m E1 5a
C.Heard, C.Pound, R.Thomas 1983

Start at the featureless slab to the R of General Gordon. Climb the centre of the slab marked by a vague crackline until it steepens below the headwall, PR, then follow horizontal bands to finish up a steep crack.

Never Again   42m   HVS   4b
G.Royle, R.Thomas 1986
A poor, loose, route 12m L of Lady Jane. climb the lower slab to reach a crack in the steeper upper half.

Lady Jane   45m   HVS   4a,4c
J.Kerry, C.Horsfield 1972
Start below a corner crack on the R of the L slab. Serious in its upper section.
1   21m Climb the slab past the first overhang to a ledge.
2   24m Climb up to a second roof, taking care with the rock. Step L to finish up a corner.

No Shadow of Doubt   45m   E3   5c,5c   †
R.Thomas, J.Bullock, M.Learoyd 2 pts aid 1985
A spectacular outing. Start as for Lady Jane.
1   21m Climb the slab of Lady Jane, hand traverse R above the first roof and move up the bulging wall above, PR, to the arete. Climb this to a ledge. Large Friends are useful.
2   24m Move 3m L up to a roof then use 2PA to gain the wall above and the top, PR, TR.

Second Slab

Camptrail   39m   HVS   5a
P.Littlejohn, J.Mothersele 1977
This takes the L edge of the slab, loose. Climb 3m R of the arete to a ledge on the L. Continue in the same line to finish.

Jermyn Street   44m   E1   5a
P.Littlejohn, J.Harwood 1977
This route climbs the middle slab 7m L of Falls Road. Start at a ledge 4m up the corner crack of Falls Road. Climb up LW for 6m to a slight ridge, continue up for 18m then trend L to reach a faint crack leading to the top.

Red Light   42m   E1   5a
P.Littlejohn, M.Price 1980
Start about 4m L of the corner crack of Falls Road and climb until 6m from the top. Traverse R and finish up a crack line. A serious pitch.

Falls Road   45m   HVS   4c
C.Horsfield, P.Thomas 1974
The obvious corner/crack on the R of the slab.

1   12m Climb to a ledge in the corner/crack.
2   33m Climb the corner for 21m then move onto an earthy ledge. Follow a groove to exit R above an overhang. This section is uncleaned and has poor protection.

FALSITY WALL
The crag now faces W again.

Norwegian Wood   45m   E2   5b
A.Sharp, J.Harwood, P.Lewis 1977
Start at a shallow corner 1m R of Falls Road. Climb a shallow groove to the ledge on Falls Road, follow a RW trending calcite line over a small roof using friable horizontal bands. Gain a ledge in the middle of the wall, PR, possible belay. Follow a calcite line RW to finish up the arete.

Yesterday's Hero   42m   E2   5b
L.Foulkes, P.Lewis 1980
A more direct and solid line gaining the ledge of Norwegian Wood. Start at a thin crack between Norwegian Wood and the initial corner of Falsity. Climb the crack to a break, step L, then through the roof and up to ledges, PB possible. Continue as for Norwegian Wood.

The upper reaches of Falsity wall contains two black streaks.

Black Looks   42m   E3   5b,5c   †
R.Thomas, M.Learoyd, G.Royle 1984
A serious pitch. Leaving a rope for the final grass section is advisable.
1   24m As for Falsity to the ledge and PB.
2   18m Climb up then LW to the largest black streak and horizontal break. Move up and LW to a PR, move R and up to widely spaced horizontal breaks, escaping L at the top. Large friends are useful.

Spring Fever   42m   E3   5b,5c   †
R.Thomas, G.Royle 1987
This takes the RH of the black streaks.
1   24m As for Black Looks.
2   18m Climb up and slightly R from the belay ledge to the base of the streak. Up the wall steeply, PR, to exit R.

Falsity   42m   E2   5b   *
P.Littlejohn, J.Mothersele 1977
Good steep climbing. Start at the obvious short corner crack on the R side of the wall. Climb the groove, then the wall RW to two flowstone bands and a break. Move L through an overhang to a ledge, PB possible. Finish as for Norwegian Wood.

Far City   42m   E2   5b,5c   †
L.Foulkes, D.Renshaw 1983
A serious route wandering up the R side of the Norwegian Wood wall.
1   27m Climb Falsity for 4m then traverse R for 6m and climb steep friable rock for 15m to a large ledge.
2   15m Walk RW until beneath a hanging corner. Climb it exiting L to finish up a short wall and diagonal ramp.

Third Slab

Easy Action   42m   VS   4b
T.Penning, P.Cresswell 1981
To the R is the third largest and loosest slab. Start 6m L of the prominent central crack 5 m from the slab's L side, below a crack 5m up. Climb to the latter crack from the L and climb it to its top, finishing up the wall above.

Sense Of Adventure   45m   VS   4a,4a
J.Harwood, P.Lewis 1980
Climb the crack in the centre of the slab, to its top and continue up a line of weakness moving L to finish.

Wimaway   45m   HVS   4a,4b
A.Sharp, J.Harwood 1980
This climbs the corner between Sense Of Adventure and the RH side of the slab.
1   30m Climb to a corner and follow this to a stance on the L.
2   15m Finish directly.

It is advisable to leave a rope in place down the finishing grassy gully for the next routes.

Surprise Package   36m   VS   4a
A.Sharp, J.Harwood 1980
Start just R of Wimaway at a boulder. Step off the boulder, move R to a groove, climb this and the wall above for 24m then move R to a grassy gully (poor belay) to finish carefully.

Gepe   30m   VS   4b
J.Harwood solo
Climb the deep chimney cleft on the R side of the third slab to a corner. Finish up the grassy gully.

Pontoon   24m   VS   4b
C.Horsfield, J.Harwood 1977
Climb the groove in the rib just R of the deep cleft of Gepe. Belay and abseil at 24m.

Simple Twist   24m   E2   5c
P.Littlejohn (unseconded) 1977
Start 4m R of Gepe, L of a short corner below the L side of a square cut roof. Climb the wall into the corner, then move R and around the arete to a crack. Climb it to its top. Abseil.

Twist   21m   HVS   5a
J.Harwood 1977
Start beneath a square cut roof 6m R of Gepe. Climb RW to the ledge on Sandstorm, then move up and traverse L above the roof to finish up a crack. Abseil.

Sandstorm   27m   VS   4b
J.Harwood 1977
This climbs the wide dirty groove R of Twist to a shallow cave, before traversing L to the belay of Twist. Abseil.

MITZY WALL
The cliff now turns a R-angle and provides better rock and routes. At the L side of this section is a set of huge overhangs split by two vertical breaks.

The Hunchback   30m   E1   4c,5a   **
P.Littlejohn, C.King 1978
An unusual and entertaining climb that has lost some of its lower pitch in the recent storms. Start in the recessed corner below the LH break.
1   18m Climb the chimney to the overhang, bridge outwards to the lip of the first roof and pull around onto a wall and a hanging stance.
2   12m Traverse R to an overhanging prow, climb the overhang and up a short wall to a stance. Abseil.

The Bills, The Bills   33m   E3   5b,5a
P.Littlejohn, C.Brookes 1981
This route replaces Cheap Tricks which has disappeared.
1   18m Climb the chimney R of Hunchback to the roof, traverse L across the steep wall, pull around the arete to reach the hanging stance of Hunchback.
2   15m Traverse R along the lip of the overhang, pull across to less steep rock. Belay as for Hunchback.

Mitzy   15m   E3   8b   †
A.Sharp, P.Lewis 1978
Start beneath an obvious split in the roof R of The Bills The Bills. This has lost part of its roof in recent storms and now looks impossible. Climb to the roof and struggle over it to a second roof. Abseil.

To the R is a deep depression starting from a small flat platform.

On its R side is an obvious arete. It is possible to traverse R along a large ledge to descend from these routes

Night Games   21m   E3   5c
M.Learoyd, R.Thomas 1985
Start from the platform and climb an undercut wall to gain a thin crack in the wall L of the arete. Climb this to a belay ledge. Abseil.

To Mitzy a Pup   30m   E3   6a   *
A.Sharp, P.Lewis 1980
This takes the arete. Climb the wall to a ledge, step L and climb the arete to its top (hex 10 belay). Traverse R or Abseil.

The Pod   27m   VS   4b   *
J.Harwood, C.Horsfield 1977
Climb the obvious pod-shaped chimney until a traverse R leads to the arete. Belay on the R.

Philosan   21m   VS   4b
C.Horsfield, J.Harwood 1977
Climb a crack, swing R to the arete and continue to a fault which is followed to ledges. Traverse R for the descent.

Fly Power   21m   VS   4b
J.Harwood, C.Horsfield 1977
Start just L of Duff. Climb a LW-leaning crack to a ledge. Continue to another LW-leaning crack, then the belay. Traverse R to descend.

Duff   21m   S   4a
J.Harwood 1977
Start 3m L of the R edge of the next wall. Climb the wall via a crack to a ledge. Continue RW to a ledge and traverse R to descend.

RIGHT HAND WALL
The cliff now turns to face the sea once more and contains some short routes that are useful when the tide is against you.

Against The Grain   18m   E2   5b
R.Thomas, G.Royle 1985
The large overhang where the cliff turns to face the sea. Climb a short problem wall on the L to gain a ledge then swing R over the roof, TR on the lip.

Via Normale   21m   D
J.Harwood 1974
Climb the crackline just R of the large overhang. A useful descent.

Moonlight Flit   14m   E1   5b
R.Thomas, G.Royle 1986

Start 3m L of the second crackline at a green, bulging wall. Make hard moves to start and gain a ledge. Finish up the overhangs above.

L'Escargot 14m VS 4h
J.Harwood, C.Horsfield 1976
The second crackline. Climb to a ledge and then a corner to more ledges. Traverse L to descend Via Normale.

Tri-Via 14m VS 5a
R.Thomas, G.Davies 1981
Climb the faint LW crack between the second and third cracks until bigger holds lead to a ledge. Finish up the overhangs above. Descent as above.

Overdue 14m VS 4b
J.Harwood, C.Horsfield 1976
Climb the third crackline to ledges, then over bulges to another ledge. Descent as above.

Overpaid 14m E1 5b
R.Thomas, G.Davies 1980
Start in the centre of the wall R of Overdue. Make a hard move to reach small holds and a ledge. Continue up overhanging rock on large holds.

Arkle 14m HVS 5b
A.Sharp, J.Harwood 1977
Climb the crackline above the edge of the rock pool of Becher's Brook.

Red Rum 14m VS 4c   *
P.Littlejohn, J.Harwood 1975
The RH crack line above the pool. Traverse R over the water to reach the crack.

Becher's Brook 27m VS 4b
P.Thomas, J.Harwood 1974
The narrow cleft at the back of the rock pool reached by an entertaining traverse or swim! Climb the crack, widening to a chimney, to ledges. Traverse R to the top of the seaward ridge. Descend easily to the R.

Foinaven 22m HVS 5a
C.Heard, A.March 1977
Climb Becher's Brook for 4m then traverse R to a crack. Finish direct. Descend RW.

WITCHES POINT OS ref 884726
R.Thomas
"If this is foreplay then I'm a dead man"

Cocoon

SITUATION AND CHARACTER
A Carboniferous limestone promontory at the S end of Dunraven Bay. It lacks the quality and intimidation of the main Ogmore cliff but is worth a visit.

APPROACHES AND ACCESS
See map 1. From Southerndown (Dunraven bay)(See Ogmore approach 1) "pay or be fined" car park, cross the beach E or walk over the headland. On the W side of the point facing Dunraven Bay are three areas:
1   At the back of the bay is the Stone Wing Cliff.
2   To the R is Dunraven Buttress characterised by overhangs and black stained rock. At the tip of the point is a cave with a solid white wall.
3   Facing seaward are the Sea Walls consisting of short but perfect rock. The LH area has a small bay with overhanging rock.

STONE WING CLIFF
Situated on the E side of Dunraven Bay. Belays are well back.

Stone Wings   36m   E4   5c,5c
P.Littlejohn, S.Robinson 1pt aid 1979
Start at the overhanging crack in the centre of the cliff.
1   15m Strenuously climb the crack to a ledge on the R.
2   21m A serious pitch. Traverse R to a ledge on the arete. Continue up R until steep moves lead to easy ground L of the nose and a grass slope.

Magic Touch   27m   E4   5c   †
P.Littlejohn 1979
This takes the clean white wall where it joins the earth slope. A serious route. Climb onto the wall from the R, traverse LW to a PR, and climb the wall on the L to an obvious handhold. Traverse L to a sloping shelf, move R to gain ledges and climb the groove and gully above.

The bulging black and white buttress R of Magic Touch is taken by:

Croeso i Cymru   18m   E3   6a   †
M.Crocker, R.Thomas 1986
Good climbing up the L side of the buttress. Start at a boulder filled gully. Climb the RH of two short grooves to a break, move R over a bulge to a ramp, PR, then move up the square-cut slim groove to gain a ledge above. Belay or traverse L to a TB.

The World-V-Gibson   21m   E5   6b   †
M.Crocker, R.Thomas 1986
The open groove in the L section of the buttress. From the boulder-choked gully, trend R to a smooth white wall, PR. Climb the wall to a break, NR, and traverse R over a bulge and into a groove, PR. Climb the groove, over a bulge to a ledge and belay or traverse L to TB on the way down.

Hanging by a Thread   22m   E3   6a   * †
R.Thomas, M.Learoyd 1986
Good sustained climbing. Start behind the tallest white-topped boulder. Climb to a break, move R onto a nose, over a bulge and onto a sloping ledge, PR. Traverse L to a pocket, TR, then move back R and up, 2TR's, and finish by swinging R to the arete and up to a belay.

WHITE WITCH CRAG
This is the W-facing, white crag with an undercut base, near the tip of Witches Point.

Evil Ways   21m   E5   6b/c   †
M.Crocker, R.Thomas 1986
A worthwhile route. Start at the L side of the cave. Climb an undercut, grooved rib to the roof. Move slightly L, pull over using a finger jug, PR, TR, and climb the steep incipient crack, PR, to good holds and an easy finishing wall.

Thin Lizzy   21m   E3   6a   * †
R.Thomas, M.Crocker 1986
Good climbing over the bulge and up the R side of the wall to a groove in the final wall, TR's, PR.

White Witch   27m   E5   6b   * †
M.Crocker, R.Thomas 1986
A R to L traverse across the white wall and lip of the cave. Start from a small stance in the corner, 6m up Thin Lizzy. Traverse L along the line of footholds and continue just above the lip, bold moves L gain the R end of a long and slightly descending crack line. Move down L to a niche and climb straight up to a horizontal crack, PR, then traverse L to join Evil Ways, PR. Finish up this.

SEA WALLS
These are situated on the tip of the point. Descend easily to the cave washed platform on the east side and walk R under the crag. The first route is encountered at an area of overhangs. Although used for many years by Outdoor Centres these are the first recorded climbs.

Paternoster   9m   E2   5c   †
R.Thomas, G.Royle 1987

Swing up L from the platform and take the overhang L of Fisherman's Friend.

Fisherman's Friend   11m   E2   5b
D.Meek, S.Robinson 1986
Climb up L to swing through the obvious crack over the overhang.

Jilter's Wall   11m   E2   5c
R.Thomas, G.Royle 1987
Start just R of Fisherman's Friend and climb the white wall past a PR.

Wanker's Crack   11m   VS   4b
J.Harwood c1970
Climb the crack 2m R past a rotten PR.
The following three routes are on the undercut wall 4m R.

Leg Over   7m   E2   6a
R.Thomas, G.Royle 1987
Swing L from the platform, TR, and pull over the small overhang, PR.

Pull Over   7m   E1   6a
G.Royle, R.Thomas 1987
From the platform climb directly past a large blue TR.

Hand Over   6m   HVS   5a
J.Harwood c1970
Take the faint rounded corner a metre R, starting from a slightly higher level.

R again is a higher level and an obvious thin , undercut black corner.

Undercut   9m   E1   5c
S.Robinson, D.Meek 1986
Gain the crack and climb it.

Step Aside   9m   E1   5c
R again, the obvious sloping crack is climbed painfully.

Cold Shoulder   9m   HVS   5b
J.Harwood c1970
Gain a ramp on the R, move up to a black spike and continue up the wall above.

Breakout   12m   HVS   5a
J.Harwood c1970
Gain the ramp from the R, then back R and up crozzly cracks.

Fast Flow   11m   E1   5b
J.Harwood c1970
Start 4m R of Breakout at a shallow scoop. Climb direct to and past a TR in the brown flowstone.

Surprise, Surprise   13m   E1   5b
M.Learoyd, R.Thomas 1986
Gain the faint flake 9m R again by moving up L, then back R.

Waiting Game   13m   HVS   5a
R.Thomas, M.Learoyd 1986
From a dip in the platform, prior to a corner, layback the obvious crack and climb the wall above.

Fools Rush In   15m   E3   6a
R.Thomas, G.Royle 1986
The arete R again, poor TR. Gymnastic to start.

Lasting Impression   15m   E3   5c
M.Learoyd, R.Thomas, 1986
The RW trending corner line. Move R at the roof and exit R.

Life and Soul   15m   HVS   5a
D.Meek, S.Robinson 1986
Cracks 4m R.

Relics   14m   HVS   4c
M.Learoyd 1986
Climb the wall 3m L of the end of the crag, past an old PR.

WENVOE (WHITEHALL) QUARRY OS ref 118735
R.Thomas
"Even when I made love to a girl, I did it in a press up position to
strengthen my arms"   Cesare Maestri

SITUATION AND CHARACTER
A typical bleak quarry setting, but its proximity to Cardiff and its
good limestone walls make it a useful crag for local climbers, until
they fill it in that is. The climbing is mostly steep slabs protected
by PR's and BR's.

APPROACHES AND ACCESS
See map 3. If approaching via the M4 turn off at junction 33 and
take the A4050. Leave at the first roundabout, junction with the
A48 and continue towards Barry past some TV masts to another
roundabout and a pub on the R. Turn R up a narrow lane and R
again to park at the quarry gates. A five minute walk through the
quarry leads to the back wall. In winter a large pool makes
approach to the central wall difficult and an abseil may be necessary. Permission to climb has not been gained. So please maintain
a low profile.

Rubble Rouser   27m   E2   5b
R.Thomas, S.Walsh 1987
Climb the black slab on the L side of the quarry back wall to the L
edge of an overlap, BR. Traverse R over the overlap, PR, and
continue, past horizontal breaks, PR, BR, to a small ledge and PB.
Abseil.

Clean Sweep   24m   E2   5b
R.Thomas, G.Royle 1987
This climbs the black wall to the L of Christmas Slab. Start just L of
the loose corner. Move up and slightly L to a horizontal crack, PR,
then up past more horizontal breaks, 3 PR's, BR, to gain a small
ledge and BB. Abseil.

CHRISTMAS SLAB
This slab is directly below the large gateposts to the L of Central
Wall.

Left On Ice   33m   E2   5b
R.Thomas, G.Royle 1987
Start 6m L of Here Comes The Sun. Climb the front of the shattered pillar, PR, TR to gain a rubble strewn ledge. Move up a thin
groove above, 2PR, to exit RW onto the slab, PR. Move up and L to
PR's then traverse R to the base of the final steep wall, PR's. Climb
this to reach a horizontal crack and easier climbing. SB.

Here Comes the Sun   33m   E1   5b
R.Thomas, E.Thomas 1986

Start 3m R of a loose chimney crack, up past a PR to the undercut flake, onto a ledge, PR, then up the slab, 2 PR's, to a small ledge, PR. Move up and RW, PR, to where the slab steepens, up this, PR, then follow the corner crack to belay on large posts.

A direct variation has been claimed but clipped all the runners on the normal route.

Horses Mouth   33m   HVS   5a
R.Thomas, S.Walsh 1987
Start 3m R of Here Comes The Sun. Climb to a PR, TR at 4.5m, continue up, 2PR's, and step onto a slab, then reach a small overlap, PR, and steeply up to several pockets, PR. Carefully using an undercut make hard moves up and slightly L to another pocket, PR, TR up the final wall steeply on small incuts, PR, and finish up the corner.

Before I Go   45m   E3   5b
R.Thomas, G.Royle 1988
Start slightly L of the shattered tower L of East Clintwood. Climb the centre of the black wall to a PR, trend up RW following the slab to a small roof, PR's, continue up to where the slab steepens, PR, and move R onto the arete, PR, to finish.

East Clintwood   33m   E3   6a   *
D.Meek, et al 1986
This takes a line up the steep slab immediately above the small pool. Start above a small tree making hard moves past a BR at 5m, continue to a shattered overlap, PR, then pull over and continue past a BR to gain good ledges at the base of the headwall, BR. Make hard moves up, BR, then move L, BR, exciting moves up and L lead to the arete and an easier finish.

The Way We Were   42m   E1   5a
G.Lewis, H.Griffiths 1987
Start at a sapling near a crumbling groove. Climb the groove and slab above, BR, to the overlap, PR, traverse L under the overlap to a ledge at the base of the corner, up this taking care with a death block at the top. A serious route.

Filoo   36m   E2   5c
R.Thomas, G.Royle 1987
Start at the toe of the slab by a tiny sapling. Climb up, BR, and move R to beneath the overlap, PR, step down and climb the overlap on the R using pocket holds. Move up, poor PR, then trend RW, PR, and continue directly to the top, 2PR's.

The Gingerman   36m   E2   5c
R.Thomas, G.Royle 1987
This climbs the RH side of the slab immediately L of the central wall. Approach by scrambling over the screes above the pool and

climb a corner crack to an overlap. Step R, PR, onto the slab, then move over onto the steeper wall, PR's, to gain a hidden borehole above, move L and up to a ledge, PR's, continue to a horizontal crack, BR, PR, then past more PR's to large finishing holds.

CENTRAL WALL
The largest area of rock up and R of the pool.

That's My Line   30m   E2   5c
R.Thomas, G.Royle 1986
Start at the L side of the wall, climb past a large PR to the R of the overlap. Follow this up and L, PR, until it is possible to make hard moves over onto a steep slab, PR. Move up the slab, PR's, keeping just to the R of an obvious borehole, TR.

The Meek, The Mad and The Ugly   30m   E3   6a   *
G.Lewis, S.Lewis, D.Meek 1986
R.Thomas, G.Royle (direct start)1989
The original route of the wall. Start just R of the last route. Move up, PR, then back L to those on the previous route, move R following the flake overhang past several PR's until it peters out on the upper slab. Up this to finish, 2BR, 1PR.
Direct Start: A direct start has been made but details are unavailable.

Highly Strung   36m   E3   6a
M.Crocker, R.Thomas 1986
A L to R girdle. Follow the last route to the first BR then traverse R, BR, PR's, until it is possible to take a hanging stance in the crack which bounds the far edge of the wall. Abseil.

The Big Leak   27m   E2   5b   *
M.Crocker, R.Thomas, M.Ward 1986
A very direct line. Reasonable climbing with spaced protection. Start 9m R of the last route and climb directly to the top, BR'S, PR's.

Slow Seduction   24m   E1   5b
M.Ward, R.Thomas, M.Crocker 1986
This takes a direct line up the slab which bounds the R side of the wall. Start high up on the rubble slope, climb to the grassy half way ledge, PR, continue directly, BR, to another BR and lower off.

Terminal   18m   E1   5a
H.Griffiths 1986
In the centre of the broken area to the R of the central wall is a narrow LW slanting slab, a very serious route. Start behind a buddleia bush just L of the slab, climb the wall until it steepens and move R to the L edge of the slab. Swing round onto the slab, and follow its L edge until it is possible to traverse up and L to the tree. Abseil.

Statement of Age 39m E2 5b
H.Griffiths 1986
A R to L girdle of the central wall, a lot of rope is needed for belaying. Start above the start of Slow Seduction at an obvious traverse line. Follow the traverse line L until it is possible to climb up to the L edge of a grassy ledge. From its middle climb slightly L to a PR and continue to another PR 9m below the top, traverse L past a PR to another PR on The Meek, The Mad etc. Continue up and LW to the borehole on That's My Line and finish.

TAFFS WELL OS ref 128827
P.Lewis

SITUATION AND CHARACTER
Taffs Well is a large quarried crag easily accessible from the M4 and therefore deserves more traffic (sorry). It is W facing and easily reached from Cardiff making it a popular venue for locals. Once quarried, it has a reputation for loose rock and poor protection but this is only true on some routes. The crag generally dries very quickly with a few exceptions and contains some good challenges.

APPROACHES AND ACCESS
See map 3. The crag is approximately 5 miles NW of Cardiff overlooking the S bound carriageway of the A470 between Tongwynlais and Taffs Wells (half a mile N on the A470 from junction 32 of the M4). Parking can be found at the base of the cliff, where it meets the roundabout. Immediately behind the crag is the landmark of Castell Coch clearly visible from the motorway.

THE SHIELD
This is the huge domed slab on the far L of the cliff.

Crimes of Fashion   24m   E4   6b   *
A.Sharp, P.Lewis, J.Harwood 1988
Start by scrambling up to the base of The Shield proper then move to the far LH end. Start 2m R of the L edge of the slab. Make difficult moves past a BR and climb direct, BR, PR, to a third BR. Climb diagonally RW, PR, then more easily to lower off a tree.

Promises   24m   E5   6a/b   *
A.Sharp, P.Lewis 1979
A serious and unforgiving pitch. Start 3m R of Crimes of Fashion, below a brown streak. Climb up with difficulty on small pockets to a resting ledge, continue to a hollow flake and follow it moving R on pockets near the top. Lower or abseil.

Spuriously Yours   24m   E5   6c   * †
M.Crocker, R.Thomas 1989
A desperate pitch with a committing start and runout upper section. Start 3m R of Promises behind a small hawthorn bush. Pull onto the wall on good but widely spaced finger pockets, then swing boldly R on a finger jug, BR. Trend desperately up R to better holds and a small ledge, climb direct up the slab ,TR, on good pockets to join Promises. Move up and traverse R to lower off a tree at the L end of Catwalk ledge.

Diamonds   36m   E5   6a   *
P.Littlejohn, S.Lewis 1979
Very serious. Start at the base of The Shield at 2 small trees, to the

R of Spuriously Yours. Follow the vague groove to a sloping shelf, TR, your first and only runner, a real clip!. Continue directly to a large crystal lined pocket, move 2m L then climb straight up the slab on widely spaced holds to another crystal lined scoop. Climb up slightly R to narrow ledges near the top and exit L by means of a hawthorn bush.

Skywalker 36m E5 6a   *
P.Littlejohn 1979
A equally serious relation to Diamonds. Start as for Diamonds, follow it to the sloping shelf at 12m, TR, traverse R and move up to a projecting ledge and continue R to a PR. Climb to a PR, then traverse R and continue diagonally to a smooth white slab which is climbed to a tree. Up for 3m then break R on good pockets to a PR, move up L, PR, to a shattered scoop which is followed to the top.

Sir Clive Dangerous 36m E5 6a   †
A.Sharp, C.Richards 1988
Start 12m R of Diamonds, below the shallow groove of Nero. Climb a bulging wall on sometimes friable holds, PR, step L onto a slab at 12m and follow Skywalker to the top.

Nero 61m VS 4b
K.Hughes c1960
Start at the highest tree, directly below a groove 18m R of Diamonds and 12m L of the R edge of the slab.
1 30m Climb the groove to a ledge on the R then climb a short wall to an earthy ledge, possible BB. Traverse R to two small trees, then R again to the arete of Pine Tree, continue up to a tree belay.
2 31m Climb up and R to the final short wall, traverse R onto the nose and finish straight up.

When in Rome 39m E2 5b
A.Sharp, W.Jewell 1985
Start as for Nero. Climb the wall R of the groove of Nero to the BB on Nero. Continue as for Cowpoke or Thin Air.

Cowpoke 51m E1 5a   *
J.Harwood, J.Richards 1975
FFA A.Sharp, S.Lewis 1975
A good route low in the grade. Start at the lowest point of the slabby buttress to the R of The Shield.
1 15m Climb the slabby buttress to its top, then move over L to belay at a tree near a small iron spike.
2 36m Climb the short shallow corner above, old BR, then move up and L to an earthy ledge, possible belay. Climb up to a break just L of a small bush (Catwalk), traverse L to a vegetated ledge then climb the wall above to the top.

The next two routes are alternative finishes to Nero and Cowpoke.

Thin Air   24m   HVS   5a   *
C.Hurley, P.Hurley 1972
Start at the earthy ledge on pitch 2 of Nero. Traverse L until it is possible to climb straight up, 2PR's, to the vegetated ledge on Cowpoke. Finish as for Cowpoke.

Flying Fresian   21m   E3   5b
S.Bartlett, H.Nicholls 1978
Start as for Thin Air. Climb up to reach the break and small bush as for Cowpoke, move R and climb straight up. Move up and R on loose rock to reach easier ground which is followed to the top.

The Hobbit   54m   HVS   4c
C.Hurley 1980
Belay as for Cowpoke pitch 1 at the small tree.
1   24m Climb over a small bulge just R of a short shallow groove and continue up the slab, passing twin trees on their R to a corner, climb this to a tree belay on the R.
2   30m Move up and R to the short final wall, traverse R onto the nose and finish straight up.

Pine Tree   73m   VD/S   ***
B.Powell 1961
An excellent and popular climb, possibly the best route of its grade in S.E.Wales. Start at the lowest point of the buttress.
1   39m Climb the slabby buttress to its top, traverse R then up a groove to a large pine tree belay.
2   34m Climb the wall behind the belay then follow slabs slightly RW, then diagonally R to the final short wall, "The Nose". Traverse round the corner to the R onto "The Nose" and up in a fine and exposed position to the top.

The following two climbs girdle The Shield in opposite directions.

Changes   30m   E3   5c   *
A.Sharp, P.Lewis 1979
A good girdle of The Shield from L to R. Start by scrambling up to a grassy ledge on the L, 3m to the L of Crimes of Fashion. Climb to the prow for a metre or two then step R onto the face, PR, climb across R to the hollow flake on Promises and step down to a small ledge. Traverse R more easily past a hole until a difficult move is made to reach easier ground, beneath Thin Air. Continue across to the vegetated ledge on Nero. Finish by any route.

Catwalk   36m   S
College of Advanced technology 1960
A R to L girdle. Start from the third tree on the second pitch of

Pine Tree. Step L around the obvious block to foot ledges and follow these down L. Continue the traverse along the moustache of ledges to the vegetated ledge of Cowpoke and finish up the wall above.

Sub Wall Gully 57m S
unknown c1960
Start in the trees 18m up R from the slabby buttress below and to the R of Pine Tree, beneath a small tree.
1 33m Climb to a small tree, then follow the obvious rising traverse line for 8m. Climb over the small bulge above and follow a shallow groove and short wall to a broken ledge. Continue up the slabs to one of the trees on pitch 2 of Pine Tree.
2 24m As for Pine Tree.

Rainy day Arete 73m VS 4c   *
P.Thomas, J.Harwood 1974
Start as for Sub Wall Gully.
1 36m Follow Sub Wall Gully to the rising traverse, move over the bulge, step L and climb up for 8m to a short corner. From a borehole above, move R and up to a large bulge which is turned on the L. Follow the arete until it is possible to reach a grassy ledge and PB.
2 36m Traverse L for 6m then climb straight up to finish as for Pine Tree.

Sub Wall 70m HS   *
B.Powell 1961
A good route slightly marred by a scrappy first pitch. Start at an obvious corner 15m up to the R of Sub Wall Gully.
1 33m Climb the corner until it steepens and step L to ledges. Climb up passing a huge block on its L to reach the grassy ledge of Rainy Day Arete, PB.
2 36m Climb straight up to the impending head wall, then traverse L to join Pine Tree.

Hot Moon 61m E3 4c,5c
T.Penning, P.Cresswell 1983
A serious climb up the crack in the head wall above Rainy Day Arete.
1 36m As for Rainy Day Arete
2 24m Climb up to the crack and follow it, PR, to finish out R.

Crime Minister 57m E2 4c,5b
T.Penning, C.Court, et al 1984
Start as for Rainy Day Arete.
1 36m Pitch 1 of Rainy Day Arete.
2 21m Move R to the start of a crack and swarm across it to the top of the cliff. Tree belay high up.

Noel Way   69m   VS   O
J.Noel 1960
A serious route on poor rock.
1   33m As for Sub Wall
2   36m Reverse the previous pitch for 13m until it is possible to reach the LH end of a gangway crossing the wall on the R, follow this to a final wall and pull over to ledges and a scramble to belays.

All Those Years Ago   12m   E4   6a
A.Sharp, R.Powles 1979
Hard but safe. This climbs a blunt rib in a short steep wall R of the start of Sub Wall. Climb a faint crack to a short bulge, TR, PR leading to a small roof, traverse 4m R to a PB lower off.

Hocus Pocus   21m   E5   6a
J.Harwood 1975 some aid
FFA P.Littlejohn, A.Davies 1982
A serious route. Start 3m R of All Those Years Ago, beneath a PR at 4m. Climb the short wall, PR, to small ledges above a bulge, then up to a second PR then traverse 3m L and move up to a sloping ledge. Climb diagonally L to a ledge, then move up R to the top, belay well back.

Focus   12m   E3   5c   *
P.Lewis, A.Sharp, J.Harwood 1986
A pleasant pitch. Start 3m R of Hocus Pocus. Climb the bulging wall to a PR at 9m, traverse 3m R to a PB. Lower off.

The Rib   36m   S
J.Noel c1960
Start at the foot of the buttress above and L of the car park and follow a gully and the line of least resistance to the top. The climbing above the steep wall is loose and poorly protected.

Red Square   24m   E4   6a
A.Sharp, R.Powles 1960
Start by scrambling up the gully of The Rib to a belay ledge at 18m. Climb the crack in the wall, PR, NR, to an awkward finish. Tree belay. Abseil.

Organised Chaos   21m   E4   6a   *
A.Sharp, P.Lewis, A.Swan 1988
A good route with fine technical climbing up the flowstone wall. Start on a pedestal 4m R of The Rib, BB. Climb directly, 4 BR's to a small vertical slot. Traverse L to finish as for Red Square.

Crowman   42m   E5   6a   *
P.Littlejohn, T.Penning 1983
A bold and strenuous route taking a central line up the wall R of

Organised Chaos. Beware of some poor rock at the top. Start by scrambling to a tree belay on a grass ramp under the line of overhangs high up on the wall. Climb up before trending R, PR, to black flowstone, climb this, PR, traverse L for a metre or two then up to a poor TR. Continue over the bulge above before moving across L then up to finish. Tree belay.

Painted Bird   42m   E6   6a   **
P.Littlejohn, T.Penning 1983
A good route with excellent climbing in the top half. Start below the white flowstone wall R of Crowman at a crack line. Climb the crack (sometimes damp) to a TR below the flowstone wall, possible belay. Climb onto the flowstone and follow it direct to the top, exhilarating. Tree belay.

Ghengis Khan   36m   E5   6b   *
A.Sharp, P.Lewis 1985
This has a well protected crux and a run out upper section. Start 15m R of Painted Bird. Climb diagonally L for 4m to a small overhang, traverse R for a metre, then climb directly up to a BR. Difficult moves, BR, lead to easier climbing RW on well spaced holds. A final difficult move at a small niche leads to a tree belay.

No Name   26m   VS   4b,-   *
unknown c 1960
A good first pitch. Start by scrambling to twin trees 8m R of Ghengis Khan and about 9m from the foot of the cliff.
1   26m Move up and LW to a corner/groove, then up and step L to the bottom of a slab, PR. Climb the slab and the shallow groove above to reach a final steep V groove, PR. Follow the groove to a large ledge and tree belay. Abseil.
2   -- O. For those wanting a wild experience it is possible to climb up LW across grass ledges and unstable rock until a final wall is climbed to tree belays.

Christendom   30m   E5   6a   †
M.Crocker, R.Thomas 1989
A delicate, sustained route on mainly sound rock, with regular but spaced protection. Start as for No Name. Scramble to the highest of a series of ledges below a sheet of rust coloured rock forming the L wall of Gladiator's corner.
Climb easily to a flake below the steepest part of the sheet, move across the bulge, BR, to better holds in a slight groove, BR. Climb straight up the rib to a vague break, BR, reach a good flake above, F 1 1/2, and mantleshelf onto a sloping ledge. Pull up the slab, BR, to jugs and a scoop, then to excellent pocket holds, PR, NR. Move LW to gain a ramp and hidden abseil station below the crumbling upper wall. Lower into the trees and abseil.

Gladiator   57m   E3   - , 5c   *
T.Penning, P.Cresswell 1983
Start below the obvious crack and groove line on the RH side of
the cliff. A bit more traffic would improve it.
1   12m Climb up before trending R to easier ground leading to a
large ledge below the crack, PB.
2   45m Climb the crack, strenuously and delicately, PR, then a
short V groove, PR. At its top climb up until 3m below the cliff
top, then move R to avoid killer blocks before finishing straight
up. Tree belay.

Western Traverse   45m   HS   4b
Pleasant climbing. Start as for No Name at twin trees.
1   21m Step onto the slab behind the trees and traverse R until it
is possible to climb up to a short groove. Follow the groove to
ledges on the R, then move up to a squarecut niche, traverse R to
PB and BB on ledges.
2   18m Move onto a short slab on the R, step R and traverse along
a ledge, PR. Climb down to some more ledges and continue past
a rib to another ledge. Climb up to a small tree and metal spike
belay, abseil. It is possible to continue by climbing over loose
rock passing various tree belays but it is not recommended.

Scram   30m   E6   6a   **   †
M.Crocker, R.Thomas 1989
A wild trip, extremely sustained with snappable holds. Start from
the large spike on the start of Western Traverse ledge system, PB,
BB. Climb a bulging groove system above the spike to its end,
2BR, then straight up to gain a good flat handhold. Move LW
across a smooth wall to gain good footholds, BR, reach L and pull
over a bulge above, PR, and step R onto easier angled rock. Climb
boldly up the rib, PR, and follow it LW in fine positions on the
edge of the wall, PR, to a stance with a small tree. 45m abseil from
the tree.

Rancho La Cha Cha Cha   21m   E4   5c/6a   †
M.Crocker, R.Thomas 1989
Another interesting excursion up the steep wall above the ledge
system of Western Traverse. Start from the PB, BB, on Western
Traverse. From the RH end of the ledge pull up onto the wall, BR
and move back LW to a short crack. Climb direct to a short
borehole, BR, then make hard moves L to a NR before climbing
direct to easier ground and a tree. Abseil off.

Underlying the horizontal ledge system of Western Traverse is a
steep solid wall seamed with shallow grooves providing the next
two routes.

Daggers   24m   E4   6a   * †
M.Crocker, R.Thomas 1989

A hard crux then spaced gear. If the rib to the R of the first BR is climbed it is E4 5c. Start at the LH side of the wall at the base of a LW slanting glacis. Gain a break above the glacis and pull straight over a strip of rock onto a steep wall. Climb slightly LW past a borehole, BR, to a shallow niche. Gain the shallow groove above, BR, and finish RW, PR, up a short groove. PB, BB on the ledge system. Abseil or blow your brains out on the upper wall.

New Day Today　20m　E5　6b   ** †
G.Gibson and R.Thomas 1991
Start from the belay of Daggers. Climb direct over the initial bulge, BR, to gain an obvious crack. Continue directly up the friable wall to a resting place, BR. Take the final wall directly to a tree belay. Lower off.

Look Over Yonder　24m　E4　6b   * †
M.Crocker, R.Thomas 1989
A good pitch on excellent rock. As for Daggers to above the strip of rock then step R to a short ramp. Climb directly up the shallow grooves, 2BR, 1BR, to reach better holds below a tiny roof, PR. Swing R onto a projecting shelf and finish up a short groove. PB, BB on a ledge system.

Southern Entry　24m　E1　5c
P.Watkin, C.Jones c 1960
FFA P.Littlejohn, J.Harwood 1983
Start 6m R of the start of No Name, below and just L of a groove 9m up the cliff. Climb a short wall to a ledge then the broken wall on the R to a grass ledge below a groove, climb over a bulge into the groove and follow it until it is possible to move R to a ledge. Surmount the short wall to reach Western Traverse, then move up to the tree and spike belay. Abseil.

The Id　30m　VS　4c
M.Fairlamb, G.Ashmore 1967
Start 8m R of Southern Entry at a tree stump. Climb to a ledge at 3m, then a crack until it is possible to move R onto a sloping ledge, PR. Climb up and R onto a doubtful looking block under an overhang and then gain the ledge above, PR, possible belay. Climb the groove behind the tree and gain a ledge on the L, continue L more easily and then up to a tree just above the belay on Western Traverse. Abseil off.

No Beer, No Fear　24m　E2　5b
R.Thomas, M.Learoyd 1990
Start as for The Id. Continue up the red groove, over a small roof then move L to the belay of Western Traverse. Abseil.

Foot and Mouth　18m　E2　5c
FFA A.Sharp, J.Harwood 1979

Start 6m R of The Id below a small overhang at 4m with a larger one at 8m. Climb up to a small overhang, step L then make hard moves up to and over the second overhang. Climb up until a move R can be made to the slender tree of The Id, finish as for that route.

Get Thee Hence   12m   E2   6a   * †
M.Crocker, R.Thomas 1989
A highly recommended problem, the only bombproof route on the crag. Climb up onto a broken pillar R of Foot and Mouth, then climb directly up a blunt rib on small holds, BR, PR to a deep break and tree, PB. Abseil off.

Talk About False Gods   24m   E6   6b   †
M.Crocker, R.Thomas 1989
An exceptionally steep and sustained route, with good in situ gear but some of the rock is akin to Weetabix. Start at the slender tree 12m up, which is the finish of The Id, Foot and Mouth etc. Gain a grotty break above the belay, pull onto the overlying slab, PR, via a thin crack, then climb easily to a big hold, where the wall rears up, PR . Now climb the wall, 4 BR's, moving R at the fourth to better holds leading LW, PR up the final headwall. SB, PB. Abseil.

At the RH end of the cliff is an obvious broken corner which can be climbed at VS but is definitely not recommended.

TAFFS WELL WEST OS ref 124827
P.Lewis

SITUATION AND CHARACTER
Neglected until the advent of 'sports climbing' this old quarry has become a popular venue for the bolt clippers. It contains some excellent technical routes but vegetation and its N facing aspect means that it stays wet after heavy rain.

APPROACHES AND ACCESS
See map 3. As for Taffs Well East to the roundabout beneath the crag. Turn L to Radyr, then R at the next roundabout. Half a mile along this road is a blocked off quarry track on the L, park in a small housing estate on the R. Follow a faint path up through the woodlands to gain a good track which is followed to a small pinnacle with the crag behind.

THE PINNACLE AREA
This is the three sided bay.

THE SOUTH WALL
This is the diamond shaped wall with a central leaning groove line.

Bristol Beat   13m   E5   6b
A.Sharp, P.Lewis 1988
Start 6m L of the central groove line, half way up an earth slope. Step onto the wall and huge jugs below a BR, trend R passing a pocket to a second BR, make difficult moves up the blunt rib until an easier traverse can be made RW, NR, to a ledge and 2 PB. Lower off.

Streaming Neutrinos   13m   E6   6B   * †
M.Crocker, G.Gibson, M.Ward 1987
A short, power packed pitch up the central leaning groove line. Start directly just R of a red patch to a good borehole, undercut up into the groove, BR, and climb it dynamically, BR. Slap the RH arete of the groove and climb it to a diagonal break, NR, move up to 2 PB and lower off.

It's A Black World   13m   E4   6a/b   * †
G.Gibson, M.Ward, M.Crocker et al 1987
The fine black wall R of Streaming Neutrinos. Start below the central groove. Trend RW above vegetation then move up to a borehole, BR, to gain good holds on the L, BR. Step L and go over a bulge to better holds, BR, continue directly to a ledge and 2PB. Lower off.

The West Wall
The next routes lie on the back wall of the bay and are gained by

abseil to avoid appalling vegetation below. Alternatively climb the recently cleaned easy angled slabs below the routes.

Party Animal   18m   E4   6a   * †
A.Sharp, P.Lewis 1987
This climbs a series of pockets on the L side of the wall. Climb a rib, BR, 2TR's to good holds then continue LW along the obvious line of pockets, TR, to a niche. Pull out of this, BR, and up R to a PB and situ rope. Lower off.

You Never Can Tell   18m   E4   6a   * †
G.Gibson, R.Thomas 1990
A fine wall pitch, well protected. Make the first moves of Party Animal, BR, to the 2 TR's, then press on via a trio of good pockets, to reach good holds above and slightly L, BR. Technical moves lead to better holds, BR, and a direct exit to a tree.

The next two routes need a prolonged period of dry weather to bring them into conditionand are best approached by abseil to a tree belay.

Palm Springs   18m   E5   6a   ** †
M.Crocker, R.Thomas 1989
Brilliant climbing up the short ramp just L of Stay Hungry. Approach by abseil to a tree belay on the underlying ledge. Climb up pockets, TR, F 2 1/2, until a hard move gains the ramp, BR. Palm up the ramp to good finger jugs in the bulge above, drilled PR. Continue direct, BR, step L and then finish direct, BR, on good finger holds.

A Million Destinies   18m   E5   6a/b   ** †
M.Crocker, R.Thomas 1989
A stupendous face climb, more sustained than its neighbour. Approach as for Palm Springs. Bear LW on pockets and crystal balls, NR, to reach the first of 3BR's, transfer onto tinies and climb the wall until an intricate move gains a projecting handhold. Move quickly up, PR, then LW to the final BR and exit up Palm Springs.

Stay Hungry   15m   E5   6a/b   *
A.Sharp, P.Lewis 1987
The crack on the R side of the wall provides sustained climbing. From a tree climb up on good pockets to a PR, technical climbing past 2PR's and a NR leads to a good hold and BB to lower off.

The Quartz Bicycle   16m   E4   6a   * †
G.Gibson, R.Thomas 1991
Really a direct start to Stay Hungry, combined with You Never Can Tell effectively eliminates it. Abseil in and take an awkward belay. Climb to a prominent undercut flake 3m L of Stay Hungry,

TR. Undercut L for 3m and pull onto the wall, BR, technical moves lead straight up, BR, to a large quartz hole, hex 6. trend RW on cleaned rock to a small shelf, PR and climb the headwall to a tree, TR and exit.

Digitorum Brevis   18m   E5   6b   ** †
G.Gibson, R.Thomas 1990
A superlative wall climb, high in the grade. Start by abseiling into a SB below the R side of the wall or, better, climb the easy angled slabs to the same point. Swing up and L to crystalline pockets, TR, then by a sustained effort climb the smooth wall, 2BR's, via a weird pocket, to reach a bucket at an undercut. Pull straight up onto the wall above, BR, then continue direct, PR, until moves L past a sapling lead to a root exit, TR.

THE NORTH WALL
The major part of this area is a grey wall topped with vegetation.

Ice Cream Sunday   18m   E4   6b   †
G.Gibson 1990
Climb the vague line up the wall 2m L of Scream For Cream, 2BR's, to reach a small layaway hold at a rock scar. Difficult moves up, BR, lead to a large layaway, BR, and a BB

Scream For Cream   18m   E4   6b   * †
M.Ward, M.Crocker, G.Gibson 1987
Good climbing with excellent protection up the obvious diagonal crack line. Start 3m L of Trailblazer up the bank and gain a bulge, BR, hard moves through it, BR, leads to a small ledge BR. Continue, BR, up to the diagonal crack, PR, up the wall, BR leads to a belay station.

Trailblazer   21m   E5   6b   ** †
M.Crocker, M.Ward, R.Thomas 1987
A sustained and direct line up the centre of the wall. Start 3m up and L from the lowest point on the wall. Move up and pull through a small roof, BR, stretch upwards, BR, and make long reaches to a diagonal crack, stake and sapling runner. Continue up a groove, PR, surmount the roof above with difficulty, BR, and step R to finish easily.

Security Plus   21m   E5   6b   * †
G.Gibson, R.Thomas 1990
Powerful, well protected climbing. Start 3m L of Norman Normal at the lowest point of the wall. Climb boldly up a faint rib to a good ledge, then step up and R to a small ramp. Delicate moves, BR, lead to powerful moves on undercuts, 2BR's, then to a small ledge and a final difficult move, BR. BB.

Norman Normal   18m   E5   6b   †
G.Gibson, R.Thomas 1987
Bold yet well protected when it matters, unless you fall off of
course. Start 4m L of where the diagonal crack meets the ground.
Gain a borehole then move up R to a ledge, continue straight up
passing 2 BR's and an overlap with difficulty to a vague rib, Follow
the rib and finish by moving R to a ledge and PB, BB. Lower off.

Taffy Duck   18m   E3   6a   ** †
G.Gibson 1991
Start as for All's Well. Move up for 3m before traversing L to meet
a crack past a bush. Climb the crack, stake, BR to gain Trailblazer,
stake and sapling. Continue across the crack, BR, PR and a high
BR in Scream for Cream to gain the chain belay on Ice Cream
sunday. Lower off.

All's Well   18m   E3   5c   * †
G.Gibson, R.Thomas et al 1987
Start just R of the diagonal crack/ground junction. Climb the
cleaned slab to an obvious overlap at 9m, pull out R and up a
shallow groove, PR, to gain a ledge. Step L to PB, BB, lower off.

Any Old Iron   15m   E3   6a   O   †
R.Thomas, J.Bullock et al 1987
Start at a cleaned strip, 27m to the R of Alls Well. Take a direct line
up the slabby lower wall, stake runner, 2PR's, to a good break,
take the headwall directly, BR, PR.

Bitter End   17m   E2   5c
R.Thomas, M.Learoyd 1991
Start at the R end of the Trailblazer wall. Climb mossy slabs to gain
an obvious flake. Move up this then make hard moves up and R,
BR, until it is possible to traverse L to the lower off on Normal
Normal.

THE SLABS
Continue along the track for 92m to reach a large slab

Can The Can   21m   E5   6a
A.Sharp, P.Lewis 1987
The line L of Palm, 3BR'S, move R to join Palm at its third BR.

Palm   21m   E5   6b   *
A.Sharp, P.Lewis 1987
A direct line up the centre of the slab. Climb a shallow orange
groove to small ledge, move up and R, BR, and continue to a deep
slot, BR. Finish directly, BR, PR and lower off a BB.

Chinese Whispers   24m   E5   6b   †
A.Sharp, P.Lewis 1987

This route climbs the RH edge of the slab. Start as for Palm and climb RW to a small ledge at 9m, move back L and climb the slab, 2BR's, PR to a BB and abseil.

CEFN COED OS ref 034080 to 038085
R.Powles, A.Long

SITUATION AND CHARACTER
The Crag is carboniferous limestone that has been extensively quarried. It has a total length of 157m, but over recent times the cliff has started to become very vegetated. This has meant that many routes from previous generations have been lost to the ravages of nature. Some should stay that way, but many others would benefit from a clean and may even regain their stars. There is quite a lot of scope for new additions, but only determined teams will find them. Many of the routes are of good quality on sound rock, but a brushing would improve them. There are some good routes here but they need some more ascents to regain their stars.

APPROACHES AND ACCESS
See map 3. The cliff lies just off the 'Heads of the Valleys road' (A465) at Cefn coed-y-cymmer, which is 1mile N of Merthyr Tydfil. When approaching from the S turn off the A470 at Cefn coed-y-cymmer onto the A465 (signposted Abergavenny). Park in the layby on the RH side of the road just after the junction. From the layby cross the road and step over a crash barrier and follow the fence RW for 50 m to a gap at a trench and an obvious descent path (Central Descent). Alternatively climb over the fence on the same side as the layby and follow a footpath along the top of the cliff for 68m and then break downhill until a steep descent route is found leading to the river, follow this upstream to the RH end of Bridge cliff.
From the foot of the central descent Main Wall East extends for 100m to the L to a grassy slope, a further 150m L is the Far East Wall. R of the Central Descent is Main Wall West and eventually Bridge Cliff.

Far East Wall
This is situated 145m L of a grassy slope, it is heavily vegetated but with a clean wall split by two chimneys.

Happiness is Clog Shaped   33m   HVS   5a
W.Hughes, I.Jones 1970
Start at a broken corner below and L of the LH chimney. Climb a corner to a tree and then a scoop, ascend the groove above and move R into the chimney to finish directly.

Rosie   33m   VS   4b   O
J.Kerry, A.Randall 1970
From a few feet up the groove on the previous route, move L and into another groove, up to the top.

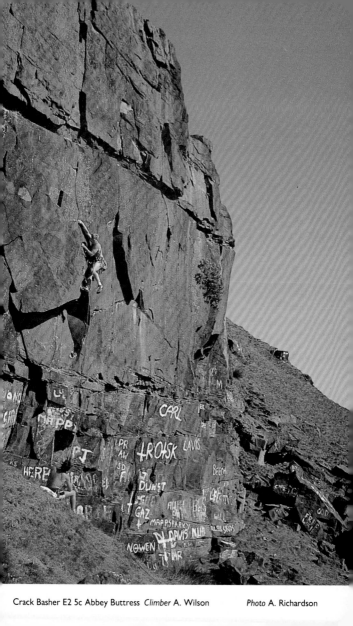

Crack Basher E2 5c Abbey Buttress *Climber* A. Wilson   *Photo* A. Richardson

Kicking Ass & Taking Names E5 6a 6b Deri Crag *Climbers* T. Forster & A. Sharp

Photo P. Lewis

Jelly Baby Lay By 33m VS O
W.Hughes, I.Jones 1970
The obvious RH chimney gained from the RH of two corners below.

EAST AMPHITHEATRE
The next climbs are to the R of the grassy slope mentioned above. Some of the climbs are overgrown but are included for completeness, they are best left for nature to reclaim. Only the best are described in detail. The ascentionists of the first 5 routes are unknown.

Styx 11m HVS O
Start at a hole on the first buttress and climb an indefinite groove/crack.

Groper 12m VS O
A prominent crack/chimney on the RH face of the first buttress.

Trundle 15m S O
Prominent grooves up the nose of the buttress opposite Groper.

Girdle of East Amphitheatre 61m VS O
L to R traverse starting up Trundle and finishing up Lumberjack.

Arthur Castle 19m HVS 5a
The overhanging crack at the LH end of the amphitheatre.

Viking 27m VS 4b O
P.Watkin, P.Thomas 1969
Climb cracks a metre R of Arthur Castle via an overhang to the top.

Odin 32m HS O
P.Watkin, P.Thomas 1969
The arete L of a prominent corner, into a groove, and the top.

The Blue Tailed Fly 33m HVS 4c O
J.Kerry, P.Watkin 1969
Start 3m L of a cave at ground level. Climb a groove to a small sapling, step L to an overhang which is taken directly to a bramble ledge. Climb a groove to cracks, then L to a slab then R to finish.

The Owl 33m VS 4c O
C.Horsfield, J.Kerry, P.Thomas 1970
Start just L of the cave. Climb to an overhang, pull over this and ascend the walls and grooves above to the top.

Gold block 35m HVS 5a   *
P.Watkin, C.Horsfield 1970

FFA S.Lewis, J.Harwood 1980
Start at a corner R of the cave. Climb the corner to a detached block in the overhang, pull over the overhang, move R then L to a V chimney. Climb this then move up RW to finish.

A variation on Gold Block has been climbed by P.Watkins, C.Jones 1970 but is completely overgrown. 7.5m further R a route has been climbed; Lumberjack first ascentionist unknown. It is completely overgrown.

MAIN WALL EAST
From the previous routes walk RW past a prominent hole and down into a depression. Here again many routes have become vegetated although all are mentioned only the best are described in detail. The area stretches from the hole to the Central Descent. Most of the ascentionists are unknown.

Manikin   35m   VS   4c   O
Climb a mossy corner R of the hole to a ledge, up a groove to overhangs then L to a tree . Climb a smooth groove and gain a crack to finish.

Squirrel   35m   VS   O
The groove 5m R of Manikin, avoid the overhang at the top.

Unter den Linden   35m   VS   O
A line joining the first tree of Squirrel with Champs Elysees.

Champs Elysee   30m   HVS   5a
S.Kerry, W.Hughes 1970
A series of walls and grooves 8m R of the prominent hole.

The area of rock as far as Spade has a number of routes that have become very overgrown. Godiva Groove P.Thomas, P.Watkin 1970, Hari Kiri unknown, Square Cut P.Watkin, P.Thomas 1970

Spade   36m   VS   O
Start at an obvious corner 26m R of the prominent hole. Climb a series of aretes and grooves to a chimney and the top.

Next is an obvious pond that is fed by the line Washing Machine Wall !!.

J.C.B   33m   VS   O
The shallow Corner.

Washing Machine Wall   30m   HS   4b   O
W.Hughes, G.Stainforth 1970
A dry weather climb up the obvious cracked waterfall above the pond to overhangs that are avoided to the L.

Cleavage 24m S
UWIST MC c1970
The obvious chimney 15m R of the pond, gained from the L.

Gethsemane 30m D Ω
A real monster taking the groove just R of Cleavage.

Excavation 27m S O
W.Hughes, D.Ellis 1970
The slab between Cleavage and the Central Descent.

Saes 27m VS O
Start at a borehole, and finish up a deep V chimney.

Sir Mortimer Wheeler 29m S O
D.Elias et al c1970
Climb a groove and crack 6m R of Excavation.

Draught Porridge 30m VD O
The indefinite buttress, groove and corner 9m R of Excavation.

The Flea 30m HS O
An indefinite buttress, groove and overhang L of the Fly.

The Fly 30m HVS 5a
P.Watkin, C.Horsfield 1970
Start 18m L of the Central Descent . Climb directly to a crack in an
overhanging wall L of a high square cut chimney, via a small tree
and a cave, climb it to a grass terrace, finish up the short wall
above.

The Flue 30m E1 5b
C.Horsfield, P.Watkin 1970
Start at a steep wall below the overhanging square cut chimney.
Climb the wall moving R to a tree and cave then back L to the
chimney, climb a corner and overhang above and continue up the
chimney to the roof. Step out L and finish directly.

Lily The Pink 30m VS 5a
C.Horsfield, W.Hughes 1970
Start 14m L of the Central Descent. Climb a corner beneath an
obvious high crack R of The Flue for a metre, then traverse L and
up a grassy groove to a tree. Move R and climb the crack to exit R
onto a wall which is followed to the top.

MAIN WALL WEST
To the R, the Central Descent is flanked by two prominent buttresses separated by a steep grass gully, R again is the start of
Main Wall West. 45m R of the Central Descent is a block overhang
high on the cliff followed by a shattered buttress with a cave at its

centre 6m up. Further R is a fence above which is the chimney of Bifid.

Diane   21m   VS   4c   O
M.Yoyce 1971
A poor route on the RH buttress. Climb a steep crack below a small tree to a ledge. Walk L then move up to an overhang. Traverse L, climb a corner for a metre or two, step R to a grassy ledge and finish up the grooved arete.

Aphrodite   21m   HVS   5a   O
J.Kerry, W.Hughes 1970
Loose. It climbs the wall L of the RH buttress.

Icarus Pillar   15m   VS   4c   O
J.Kerry, W.Hughes 1970
Start at the foot of the RH buttress. Climb to a ledge and hole then a large bay, climb an overhang then move RW up the overhanging crack to the top.

Finale   33m   VS   4b   O
C.Horsfield, E.Tebbert 1971
Start just R of the RH buttress at an indefinite groove below a small cave and tree. Climb to the cave and continue to a large ledge R of the tree. Cross slabs and step R onto the wall beneath an overhang with a hole, take it direct to the top.

The next section of cliff is like a scene from Gardener's World. It once sported 4 climbs Mr Noah, Strand, Embassy and Condor, ascentionists unknown.

Venus   30m   VS   4c
J.Kerry, C.Horsfield 1971
Start at a prominent open corner beneath a massive overhanging block 92m R of the Central Descent. Climb the corner to a grass ledge then climb a crack to another ledge. Continue up a corner to the block and move LW to finish up steep blocks.

Lyre   30m   HVS   5a
C.Horsfield, J.Kerry 1970
As for Venus to the grass ledge, then climb a grooved wall and short corner. Step L climb to the massive block and take the crack on its R to finish up the crack above.

Queen Bee   30m   HVS   5a   O
J.Kerry, C.Horsfield 1970
Start R of a large triangular overhang. Follow a crack, with walls and overhangs on its R, to a large ledge and climb the wall to another ledge. Finish up the final wall to a tree belay.

Lute   30m   D
D.Ellis, P.Watkin 1969
Start at Queen Bee. Climb to a small ash tree and follow a line of easy ledges up R to a wide crack. Step R onto a ledge then L onto a chockstone and finish up a crack line.

Land Waster   36m   VS   4b
T.Penning, P.Cresswell 1980
A R to L traverse. Start at the top of Lute at a hawthorn bush. Move to the L grassy ledge, step down to the horizontal break and follow this to the overhang of Finale. Finish over this. It is possible to belay after 19m.

Fred Carno   24m   HVS   5a
J.Harwood, J.Williams, F.Carno 1978
Start to the L of the shattered buttress at a short wall 4m R of Lute. Climb two short walls and two short grooves to the final overhang, move over this on the R then finish LW up a grassy slope.

Hells Teeth   24m   HVS   5a
J.Kerry, P.Thomas 1970
Start at a short corner just L of a cave. Climb the corner then step L to a ledge, climb onto another ledge and up a shallow corner for a metre or two, step L onto an overhung slab. Climb the overhang via its RH crack.

Knuckleduster   24m   HVS   5b
C.Horsfield, J.Harwood, J.Williams 1978
Climb to the first ledge on Hells Teeth then diagonally R past a tree to the cave. Climb an overhanging crack and chimney above to a roof, move back into the crack and over the roof then straight up finishing LW.

The Fang   26m   E2   5b
J.Kerry 1970
Start R of the shattered buttress, below and R of the cave. Climb a wall to the cave, traverse R and move onto the wall just R of a downward pointing spike. Climb a thin crack then a small corner to a horizontal crack, traverse R to the arete and finish via a sloping ledge.

Spelaean   30m   VS   4b   *
J.Kerry, C.Horsfield 1978
Start just L of a prominent bottomless corner. Climb a wall to a traverse line leading to the corner, climb it to the overhang and exit LW to a steep wall and the top.

What A Waste   30m   HVS   5b
S.Lewis, J.Harwood 1978
Start at a wall 3m R of Spelaean. Climb to an overhang, move L

and up to a small corner and up this until it is possible to move R to a ledge. Continue up a shallow corner and wall to the top.

Soup Dragon   29m   VS   4b   O
J.Kerry, C.Horsfield 1978
7m R of Spelaean is a thin crack now full of grass. Climb the wall L of this to a ledge then move up R into the crack, then a chimney and wall to the top. Needs a clean.

The Music Tree   27m   VS   4b
J.Kerry, C.Horsfield 1978
The short wall, corner and chimney just R of Soup Dragon.

The Iron Chicken   29m   HVS   4c   *
C.Horsfield, J.Kerry 1970
The obvious vegetated crack R of Music Tree, finishing L.

The Throwback   24m   E2   5c   *
P.Stott, R.Thomas 1980
Start just R of The Iron Chicken at an obvious corner capped by a roof. Climb direct to the roof, over it on the L, then step R to finish.

Walter Mitty   32m   HS   4a   *
C.Horsfield, J.Kerry 1970
Start just L of a prominent crack L of Linda's Wall. Climb to a ledge then move R into the crack and climb it, step L then up and R to a ledge. Finish up the steep wall to a tree.

Linda's Wall   33m   E4   6a   *
T.Penning, P.Cresswell 1pt aid 1980
FFA A.Sharp, P.Lewis 1983
As for Walter Mitty to the crack. Traverse R onto the wall to a ledge then climb up to the long shallow scoop, TR. Move up R to gain the horizontal break and traverse L to a PR below the over-hang. Now sprint for the ledge 3m above the overhang and then the top. Well done.

Alex In Wonderland   30m   E4   6a   *
T.Penning, C.Court 1984
A difficult route taking the grooves in the R side of Linda's Wall. Climb Bifid until halfway up the chimney. Traverse L to the grooves and climb them, PR, to the break, shake out, rev up and pull over the roof via a thin crack to finish up the wider crack above.

Bifid   32m   E1   5b   **
C.Horsfield, P.Thomas aid 1970
An old fashioned classic taking the big chimney just R of the fence. Climb the chimney to its top and climb the shallow groove,

PR, above to a small tree. Traverse L to a crack and up this LW to a ledge. Traverse R to the top.

The Great Arete   30m   E4   5c   *
T.Penning, C.Court 1984
A much fancied line eventually going at a reasonable grade! Climb up for a metre or two then move RW to the RH arete of Bifid's chimney. Continue to the break, have a shake, and move L to finish up the buttress.

The Art Of Motorcycle Maintenance   33m   HVS   5b
T.Penning, P.Cresswell 1979
A diagonal line on Great Wall. Climb Bifid for 3m then move R onto the L edge of The Great Wall, Move up RW to reach a crack which is climbed to an overhang. Finish L as for The Great Wall but the original way went R.

The Great Wall   32m   HVS   5b   *
J.Kerry, C.Horsfield 1970
A good popular route. Start at the R side of the wall beneath and R of a crackline. Climb the wall and step L to the crack which is followed to the overhang. Traverse L for 4m to an overhanging crack and climb to a ledge. Continue over the overhang on the R and finish RW.

Age of Reason   24m   E1   5b
R.Davies, O.Jones (with side runners)1988
Start as for Great Wall. Climb the narrow slab R of the crack of Great Wall using the arete. Pull over the small overhang and climb the wall above, TR's, moving L around the bulge to exit R at the second overhang.

The Fugitive   24m   VS   4b
P.Thomas, J.Kerry 1970
This takes the crack and chimney above and R of The Great Wall.

Sword of Damocles   24m   HVS   5a   *
C.Jones, D.Parsons 1970
The Sword has long gone. Start at a shallow corner just R of the previous route. Climb to a small overhang, then move up and R into a niche and roof. Move L and finish up R.

The West Amphitheatre
The amphitheatre immediately R of The Great Wall

Upidee   27m   HVS   5a   *
C.Horsfield, J.Kerry 1 pt aid 1970
Start beneath a huge detached block at 15m. Climb and traverse L to a shallow groove, PR, then move onto a small ledge and up to the detached block which is climbed via a V chimney to a flat

ledge. Climb up then traverse L across the overhanging wall to finish direct.

Apollo 13   26m   HVS   5a   *
C.Horsfield, J.Kerry 1970
Start just R of Upidee. Climb an overhanging wall to a step L, then R into a corner and a mantleshelf onto a ledge. Ascend the corner for 2m then step L to climb cracks in the wall to reach the top of the block on Upidee. Move R and climb the grooves to the top.

Agricola   24m   E1/2   5c   *
J.Kerry, W.Hughes 1pt aid 1970
FFA S.Lewis
A good sustained route. Climb Apollo 13 to the corner, continue up the corner, PR, traverse R under the overhang to the arete and a sloping ledge. Climb a crack then up diagonally R to a ledge and a small tree, move slightly L to climb the overhang directly to the top.

Three Nuns   21m   VS   4c
C.Jones, D.Parsons 1970
This climbs the obvious hanging corner at the back of the amphitheatre using the R wall. At the overhang traverse R and swing up the wall to a stance.

Peanut Butter   19m   VS   4b
W.Hughes, C,Horsfield 1970
The S shaped crack 4m R of Three Nuns.

The Pratter   19m   VS   4b   O
The groove near some blocks at the back of the West Amphitheatre.

There are two girdles of the Main Cliff.

Knackers Yard   59m   HVS   4c,4b,5a,4a
C.Horsfield, J.Harwood, J.Williams 1978
A R to L girdle.
1   18m Follow Queen Bee to the top of the prow, step down and hand traverse R past a bush and a borehole to the gully of Lute. Step R to belay.
2   7m Step R to a sloping ledge leading to short overhanging corners. Climb these to belay above the overhang on Hells Teeth.
3   24m Step down and traverse R on undercuts to a crack in the centre of the shattered buttress. Descend a metre or two and move R across large blocks to reach the hand traverse corner of Spelaean. Continue RW to a belay in Soup Dragon.
4   10m Step R and finish up Music Tree.

The Great Boer Trek   77m   E3   4b,5b,5b,4c
J.Kerry, W.Hughes 1970
A full expedition requiring a strong and competent party.
1   6m Climb Three Nuns to a ledge and belay.
2   ??m Traverse L across the wall to a crack, move down under
the overhang and traverse to the block on Upidee. Continue this
traverse to a stance in a chimney.
3   18m Hand traverse The Great Wall and move around the
corner to
the top of the chimney on Bifid. Follow the traverse line to the top
of Walter Mitty.
4   30m Step down and L to follow grass ledges to the foot of the
final corner of Spelaean, finish up this.

THE BRIDGE CLIFF
This is the short wall beneath the bridge with a small square
buttress at its LH end, it offers some very good technical pitches
on sound rock. The crag is sheltered with some route staying dry
even on wet days. This area is best approached via the descent
described at the start. It is useful to take a brush and abseil into
your route to give it a clean.

Parsons Pleasure   12m   D
The obvious corner L of John Henry.

Here And There   9m   E1   5b   †
G.Gibson solo 1985
Climb the centre of the wall L of Arris, starting from the R or direct
at 6a.

Arris   9m   E4   6a
A.Sharp 1982
Climb the blunt arete L of John Henry.

John Henry   12m   A2
P.Thomas, D.Davies 1970
The thin crack in the wall of the small square buttress.

Ere Lies Henry   12m   E5   6c   *
P.Littlejohn, A.Sharp, J.Harwood 1985
Start as for John Henry then climb the wall for 4m before moving
R to the arete. Step up then L to finish up a crack to a tree.

Tummy Ache   11m   E4   5c   †
G.Gibson solo 1985
The R arete of Ere Lies Henry. Wobble your way to the top on the
chipped holds.

Tough Of The Track   12m   E4   6a   *
A.Sharp, P.Lewis 1984

Start just R of the arete of Tummy Ache below a PR. Climb to the PR then move L to a rest, move back R with a few hard finishing moves just L of the small overhang. It is also possible to finish direct at 6b.

Grains From The Veins   12m   E4   6c
A.Sharp 1984
Start just R of the previous route. Climb the wall, to a good flake, continue with difficulty to good holds and finish up the crack R of the overhang.

Death Of A Salesman   12m   E3   5c   *
T.Penning, J.Harwood 1984
A good problem with some fine climbing, low in its grade. Start at a short groove just R of the last route. A thought provoking start, PR, gives way to thin moves up and L lead to a good hold. Move RW with a few hard moves to gain a dusty finish.

Trimmet   12m   E3   6a   *
L.Parsons, P.Wood A2 1969
FFA A.Sharp, P.Lewis 1983
Start just R of a tree stump. Hard moves up a cracked wall lead over the bulge, move L and continue up cracks to the top.

Daniel Baboon   12m   E3   6b
M.Danford, L.Parsons Ping A1 1970
FFA A.Sharp, T.Penning 1984
This route borders on the impossible for the short as two iron spikes are now missing. Start just R of Trimmet, step onto the top spike stump and using nonexistent holds reach around the roof for a big jug. Better still stand on your mate's shoulder and then muscle up the crack before stepping L to the layback crack.

Laughing Carrot   12m   E3   6b
A.Sharp, R.Smith 1984
A filler in. Climb the very short overhung corner to a good hold, continue to the break and finish more easily up the layback crack on the L.

Mad Dogs   12m   E4   6b
A.Sharp, J.Harwood 1984
Desperate climbing up the crack line R of Daniel Baboon. Levitate up the crack, then sprint up the wall to the top.

Santa Anna   12m   E1   5b
T.James, W.Williamson, M.Danford 1970
FFA C.Court, T.Penning 1984
Start just R of Mad Dogs. Climb the groove and wall above two iron spikes.

Bewitched   12m   E2   5c
A.Sharp, P.Lewis 1984
The cleaned line just R of Santa Anna, awkward at the top.

Rock Lobster   12m   F4   6a   ∩
O.Jones, R.Davies 1987
A real Polyfilla. Start just L of Gold Monkey. Climb direct to a large pocket at 7m, pull over the bulge, PR, and finish up Gold Monkey. Lower off BB.

Gold Monkey   12m   E2   5b
T.Penning, A.Sharp 1984
This climbs the obvious dirty corner above two iron spikes.

Singapore Girl   12m   E5   6c
A.Sharp, P.Lewis 1984
A finger stretcher. Start just R of Gold Monkey beneath a small overhang. Climb over it, PR, then follow some thin layaways to the L of two spikes.

The Brood   12m   E3   6b   1pt   aid
C.Heald, G.Stainforth (Gungami A1) 1970
A.Sharp, P.Lewis 1pt aid 1984
Start below the RH spike. Climb to a PA, and continue to the two spike runners.

Goblin Groove   9m   HVS   5a
J.Kerry, C.Horsfield 1970
Climb the clean corner just R of The Brood.

Sup 13   9m   VD
The wide crack just R of goblin groove

S'wet   9m   S
The cracks just R of Sup 13

Wee Willie Winkie   24m   E2   5c,5c
T.Penning, C.Court first complete traverse 1984
A R to L traverse.
1   12m Climb Gold Monkey to the obvious traverse line, move L and
belay on the last set of iron spikes.
2   12m Continue along the finger traverse to Death Of A Salesman
and continue around the arete to finish.

The cliff continues RW and although routes have been been recorded they are really no more than interesting bouldering.

MORLAIS QUARRIES OS ref 047098
R.Powles, A.Long

SITUATION and CHARACTER
These quarries are situated on the northern slope of Morlais hill about one and a half miles N of Merthyr Tydfil and overlooking the picturesque Taf Fechan Valley. The quarry consists of three tiers of limestone and the routes are characterised by the typical flat hold climbing common to many quarries. The area is very popular with groups and organisations teaching people the ins and outs of the vertical world so do not expect to be alone. Nevertheless it is easy to find an area away from too many people. It is a hideous place to climb when it is cold and damp, but when the sun is out there is a fine selection of routes to be done.

APPROACHES and ACCESS
See map 3. There are two possible approaches.
1   From the Merthyr Industrial Estate junction on the Heads of the Valleys road (A465) head for a T junction at OS ref 049092 where a track joins an unclassified road. Across the road a gate leads to an old tram road running N along the hillside. Follow the tram road for about five minutes to the R end of the Middle Tier. At the LH end of the Middle Tier is an obvious mound with a descent track leading to the R end of the lower tier. The Upper Tier can be seen above and R of the first rocks of the Middle Tier.
2   When approaching from the SW or N, leave the A470 or A465 and join the road which follows the Taf Fechan valley NE from Cefn coed y cymmer. Follow this for two and a half miles until the Aberglais pub is reached, about 225m up the hill is the Pont sarn pub. Park in the car park opposite. From the car park descend to the disused railway line and cross the viaduct (good bridge jumping territory!). On the other side ascend a steep bank to reach the Middle Tier of the quarry.
Don't leave any valuables in your car, there have been a large number of thefts.

THE LOWER TIER
In the centre of the cliff is an easy descent path leading down from L to R along grassy ledges. L of the descent is a long wall with a grassy terrace at 6m. Some 22m L of the descent are three short grooves, and 22m further L are three more grooves with a tree and bush at their foot. To the L of the tree is a cracked groove.

Novitiate   24m   S
C.Mortlock
Climb the groove to a grass ledge, step R and continue up the wall and a short groove to a mantleshelf. Finish straight up the wall.

Hawthorn Wall   27m   S
C.Mortlock

Climb the groove behind the bush on the R to a grass ledge, continue up the wall trending R to a ledge. Finish up a groove on the L.

Comici Special   27m   HVS   5a
J.Harwood, P.Thomas 1975
Climb a short corner and wall R of Hawthorn Special to a ledge, then walls via a grass ledge. Finish via a groove and crack.

Delivery   27m   HVS   5a   *
J.Harwood, S.Lewis 1976
Ascend the wall just L of a shallow R angled groove above a bush to a ledge, continue to a groove and the top.

Mainbus Abort   30m   VS   4b
Climb a shallow R angled groove above a bush to a grass ledge, then a frail tree. Traverse L to the groove of Delivery and then step R and climb a steep wall and the short walls above.

R.I.P   24m   VS   4b
A.Sharp, S.Evans 1974
9m to the R is a shallow groove just L of a trio of grooves. Climb the groove to a grass ledge, traverse L to a steep loose groove and follow this to the top.

The Sickle   24m   VS   4c   *
Start in the LH of the trio of grooves. Climb it to a grassy terrace, continue up for 3m, move R and follow a groove to the top.

The Grunt   7m   HVS   5b
P.Thomas solo
The RH groove is strenuously laybacked.

Greenmantle   27m   HVS   5a   *
Climb the borehole 3m R of the trio of grooves to a grassy terrace, mantleshelf onto a small high ledge 3m L of the arete and follow a line of ledges near the arete to the top.

Wall Street   7m   E1   5a
T.Penning, G.Horlier 1983
A protectionless route taking the wall L of Cerebellum above where Black Sabbath is written.

Half way down the easy central descent is a bush, above this are two thin cracks.

Cerebellum   7m   HVS   5b   *
J.Harwood, C.Horsfield 1976
A good pitch. Climb the LH crack to its top or step into a scoop on the R as soon as possible and climb this.

Khamil Rhouge   12m   E2   6a   *
L.Davies, P.Thomas 1986
Start as for Cerebellum. Climb the crack until it is possible to step
R into the scoop. Finish via the RH side of the nose.

Compact   7m   VS   4b
J.Harwood solo
Climb the RH crack past a tree.
To the R of the previous climb is a steep wall above a grass ledge,
in the middle of which is a RW sloping ramp.

Crisis What Crisis ?   12m   E4   6b
A.Sharp, P.Lewis 1985
Climb the prows/aretes between Compact and Exile with a hard
start.

Exile   12m   E4   6a
A.Sharp, L.Sharp 1981
Committing with no protection. Start L of the ramp and then
follow it to a red groove, go up this moving L (don't panic) to
reach good holds and the top.

Dead Red   12m   E3   5c   *
A.Sharp, L.Sharp 1981
As for Exile to the red groove but continue RW to a second groove
and climb this to the top.

Morlais Eliminate   27m   E3   5c
T.Penning 1984
Climb the wall immediately R of Dead Red with no protection, to
a poor PR at a thin overlap, continue via a short crack and a move
L to the top.

Triple Cross   27m   E3   5c   *
T.Penning, P.Cresswell 1983
Climb the groove line between Dead Red and The Go Between,
exit R to a small toe ledge then up L to the top.

The Go Between   27m   E2   5b   *
J.Harwood, I.Carney 1976
FFA A.Sharp, J.Harwood 1980
Start 3m R of a small tree beneath a hawthorn bush. Climb easily
to then up a small groove, PR, to the top.

Whispering Grass   33m   HVS   5a
J.Harwood, P.Thomas 1975
Start at a corner at the back of a small bay, 6m R of a tree. Climb
the wall and corner L of a hawthorn at 18m, move up and traverse
R above a bush to reach grassy ledges.

Busy Bee   33m   HS   4a
J.Harwood, S.Lewis 1976
Climb the buttress 3m R of the small bay, then follow the arete until it merges into a corner and crack, climb this to the top.

Gallery   30m   VS   4b   *
J.Harwood, P.Thomas 1973
Sparse protection. Climb a corner 4m R of the small bay and 6m R of a borehole past a small tree. Follow the next groove until a grass ledge can be reached on the R, move LW and follow a corner on the L side of the summit overhang to the top.

Narcotic   30m   VS   4b
S.Lewis, J.Harwood 1976
Ascend the groove 2m R of Gallery to a ledge, move slightly R and climb water stained rock to the R side of the summit overhang and the top.

Corset   36m   VS   4c
J.Harwood, J.Matthews 1976
A pleasant L to R traverse. Start at the RH end of the grass ledge from which Exile begins. Climb up and round the corner on the R to a ledge and continue to a small groove, PR, (The Go Between). Traverse across grass ledges around an arete and step down to a grassy ledge beneath the summit overhang. Step R and finish as for Narcotic.

Bore   12m   HVS   5a
Climb the borehole 4m R of Narcotic to a ledge. Follow water worn rocks above on the R until an easy traverse leads RW just below the top.

Green Corner   12m   S
N.Grant, N.Kingsford 1976
The obvious corner is climbed to a big ledge, move R to a groove which is followed to the top.

Flake Crack   12m   VD
The deep crack on the R wall of the corner is climbed to a big ledge, move R and finish up the groove.

Double Constraint   12m   S
D.Ellis
R of Green Corner is a small bay with a little groove in its L wall. Climb the groove to a ledge, then a tree. Move R and finish up a groove.

T.A.P.   6m   VD
Start 2m L of a borehole in the back of a little bay and climb a groove.

THE MIDDLE TIER
This can be divided into 3 sections. At the LH end is The Great Wall, RW the cliff is easier angled leading to, almost in the centre, Castle Bay. To the R the cliff is broken and easy angled, then steepens at a wall with an overhang at its L side, Windy Wall.

THE GREAT WALL

To The Batmobile   15m   HVS   5b   *
D.Hillier, A.Cummings 1982
Start on the L side of The Great Wall. Climb a crack with one hard move near the top.

Grace Under Pressure   E1   5b
A.Cummings c1980
A line has been climbed to the R of To The Batmobile, but no further information has been forthcoming.

Phobia   18m   E1   5b   **
P.Watkin
FFA P.Thomas, J.Harwood 1975
Direct Finish T.Penning, A.Sharp 1982
Climb the obvious water worn groove, to beneath the overhang, then traverse R along a sloping ramp before moving to the top.
The Rattling Finish: climb the overhang directly E2 5c

Blade Runner   18m   E3   5c   **
T.Penning, A.Sharp et al 1982
Good technical climbing. Climb Phobia for 3m then move R to a narrow ledge, climb straight up then R to a ledge, PR, follow the crack LW to finish as for Phobia.

Rogues Gallery   18m   E5   6b   *
G,Gibson 1984
Start just R of Phobia at a shallow groove. Climb the groove to a thin ledge on the L. Move up R, BR (missing), and continue boldly to a ledge at two thirds height. Move L to a thin crack and follow this to the top.

No Mercy   21m   E6   6c   †
G.Gibson 1985
The superb wall between Rogues Gallery and Partners In Crime. A faint thin crack leads to a ledge. Move up RW via ripples and no gear until a BR (removed) is reached and passed. Continue from a ledge above more easily.

Partners In Crime   18m   E5   6b/c   ** †
C.Jones (Partners A2) c1970
FFA A.Sharp, J.Harwood 1985
A superb and difficult climb. Start below a line of thin cracks on

the R side of The Great Wall. Climb the crack to where it fades, then make hard moves to pass a PR. Continue, PR, to reach a ledge at two thirds height. Traverse L to finish up a thin crack.

Fly Arete 18m HS
Start just R of the R arete of The Great Wall. Climb a wall to a groove on the R, step L onto the arete and follow this to the top.

Massascent Groove 18m VD *
A good but polished climb taking the groove and clean crack 2m R of the arete.

Ledge Way 18m VD
Start beneath two grooves 3m R of the arete. Gain the grooves and take the R or L one to the top.

Tiptoe 15m S *
Climb the shallow groove above a small grassy ledge 1m above the foot of the cliff.

Spectacle 15m VD *
Start 6m R of the arete at a borehole. Climb a shallow indefinite groove.

Serpent 15m VD
Start just L of an overhanging block. Climb over the small overhang and finish up easy slabs above.

Two Corners 15m VD *
Start 2m R of the overhanging block and L of a narrow prow. Climb a groove then move R to a short corner and finish.

S.T.E.P. 15m S
M.Danford, P.wood 1973
Climb the groove and short corner R of the prow.

CASTLE BAY
Castle Bay is the small bay 12m R of the narrow prow.

Gold Medal 13m VS 4b
A.Sharp, P.Hamer 1984
This takes the blank looking wall L of Top Cat.

Top Cat 13m S
Climb polished grooves at the back of the bay on the L. Different variations can be made

Name Game 13m HS 4a
P.Hamer, A.Sharp 1984
Interesting climbing up the wall R of Top Cat

Great Corner   13m   S   *
Climb the RH corner of the bay, often wet.

Castle Wall   11m   VS   4b   *
Climb the obvious crackline on the LH side of the R wall of the
bay.

Arisk   9m   VS   4b
Climb the crack in the centre of the R wall until it peters out at a
ledge. Then climb diagonally RW to the top. It is possible to climb
directly at 4c.

Squeeze It In   9m   E1   5a
G.Horler, N.Ward et al 1984
A contrived line. Climb to a small ledge then move across to the
crack of Arisk and climb up to a ledge. Finish straight up.

Wall Cracks   6m   HVS   5a   *
J.Harwood 1975
This takes the thin cracks on the RH side of the R wall.

WINDY WALL
The following climbs start from the large raised rock platform.

Griptight   7m   HS   4b
Climb the corner on the L side of the wall, L of two detached
blocks at 9m.

Gripfix   7m   HS   4b
Climb the centre of the short wall R of Griptight.

Parting Company   18m   S
Climb the groove on the L side of the two detached blocks.

Windy   18m   HVS   5b
J.Harwood 1976
Start beneath the R end of the detached blocks. Climb the serious
lower wall, then the crack splitting the two blocks.

Breezing   18m   HVS   5b
C.Court, K.Anderson, A.Jones 1984
Climb the groove just L of Pullover, PR(missing), and finish
through a gap in the overhang above.

Pullover   18m   HVS   5a
K.Hughes, D.Hillman c1970
Start just R of a borehole, beneath the big overhang, serious.
Climb up L to a shallow recess then continue over the overhang
and the wall above to the top.

Overdrive 18m E1 5a
Climb the wall between Pullover and Oxo to an overhang, which is climbed on its R to a belay ledge.

Oxo 18m V3 4b
Climb to the steep corner on the R of the overhangs, then traverse L to beneath blocks. Climb past the blocks L or R.

Philanderer 13m VS 4c   *
Climb the steep corner on the R side of the overhangs to the top.

Blue Buska 13m E3 5c   *
T.Penning, A.Sharp 1982
Start just R of Philanderer. Gain a hanging groove via a gymnastic move, 2 old BR's and follow it to the top.

Grease Monkey 12m VD
Climb the open groove 2m R of the steep corner of Philanderer.

Groovy 12m S
Climb the obvious clean cut groove just R of Grease Monkey.

Pull Through 12m S
Start beneath an overhanging block. Climb the slab passing the overhanging block on its L.

Blockhead 12m S
Climb to the overhanging block and pass it on the R.

Tree Corner 12m S   *
Climb the obvious groove to the R of the slab.

Split Buttress 12m VD
M.Danford, P.Wood 1971
Climb the shallow groove in the front of the small buttress then the L side of the wall above.

Fork Left 9m VS 4c
R of the small buttress is a groove that splits half way. climb the epancymously.

Fork Right 9m S 4a
M.Danford, P.Wood 1971
As for Fork Left but take the R fork.

Zig Zag 2a
P.Watkin 1970
This climbs the R to.
Stretch.

Sting 8m VD
Climb the groove at the LH end

Hair Of The Dog 12m E3 6a
T.Penning, C.Court 1985
The borehole between twin flakes 3m R.

THE UPPER TIER
The Upper Tier is easily reached from the T junction at OS ref

049092 by walking up and L or from the R end of the Middle Tier up and R.

The first climb starts about two thirds along from the L end at a hawthorn tree on the top ledge of a trio of ledges below a white wall.

Hiccup   15m   HVS   4c
J.Harwood solo 1975
Climb the wall R of a flake crack until it is possible to swing L on the upper blocks. Climb these and the wall to the top.

Morning Star   15m   E3   6a   *
T.Penning, J.Harwood 1985
The wall 3m R of Hiccup.

Clive's Crack   21m   HVS   5a
J.Harwood unseconded 1975
Start 3m R of the tree. Climb a wall to reach a borehole and follow this to reach a grassy ledge on the R.

Fairy Steps   27m   VD
This climbs the obvious diagonal line from L to R, starting at the bottom of a shallow rounded groove.

Evening Gem   18m   E4   6a   *
P.Littlejohn, J.Mothersele 1977
P.George, A.N.Other (direct finish) 1989
A good pitch. Climb the shallow rounded groove above the start of Fairy Steps and 3m L of an obvious brown stained groove. Exit L from its top, (or finish directly) and climb the short wall to a ledge and large tree belay.

Autonomy   18m   E2   5b
J.Harwood, W.Gray 1977
Climb a series of corners between the shallow rounded groove and the brown stain to a final wide crack.

Stretch   18m   VS   4b
Climb the brown stained groove.

Zig Zag   27m   HS   4a
P.Watkin 1970
This climbs the R to L ramp 4m R of the brown stained groove of Stretch.

Hair Of The Dog   12m   E3   6a   *
T.Penning, C.Court 1985
The borehole between twin flakes 3m R of Zig Zag.

is easily reached from the T junction at OS ref

Afternoon Delight   9m   E2   5c   *
C.Court, T.Penning 1985
Start at a tree stump 9m R of Hair Of The Dog. Climb the wall, PR,
then mantleshelf L to a faint corner at the top.

High Noon   9m   E2   6a   iii
C.Court, T.Penning 1985
The crack and short corner 1m R of Afternoon Delight, PR.

Snuff Stuff   9m   VS   4b
T.Penning solo 1985
A protectionless line up the LH side of the wall 9m R of High
Noon.

The East Tier
This is the Tier about one and a half kilometres SE from the main
climbing area. From the L side of Middle Tier walk up and SE to
OS ref 056096, to the obvious N facing buttress with two vertical
cracks and bounded on its LH side by a corner.

Little Owl   12m   S
A.Giles, R.Davies 1988
Climb the corner

One Between The Eyes   12m   HVS   5a
R.Davies, A.Giles 1988
The LH crack

Terminator   12m   E2   5c
R.Powles, A.Hughes 1988
Climb the RH crack.

TAF FECHAN OS ref 062105
C.Allen

SITUATION AND CHARACTER
Taf Fechan is one of several quarries situated to the S and E of Ponsticill reservoir, two and a half miles N of Merthyr Tydfil. The rock is carboniferous limestone that has been quarried, the upper part is weathered and there is a lot of loose rock on the ledges. It is advisable to abseil from the numerous tree belays.

APPROACHES AND ACCESS
See map 3. Leave the Heads of the Valleys road (A465) at the Merthyr Industrial Estate junction (also sign posted Mountain Railway). Follow the mountain Railway signs to the railway terminus. Continue towards Pontsticill to a layby on the L opposite a charred telegraph pole. Climb the steep bank behind the telegraph pole, cross over a railway line, to find the quarry.

Metalworks   18m   HVS   5a
A.Williams, P.Leyshon 2 pts of aid 1968
This takes the second thin crack of the waterspout. Climb over overhangs and follow a thin crack above to a ledge and a tree.

Take off   18m   D
D.Ellis, C.Taylor 1967
Start 6m R of a water spout. Climb to a ledge, traverse L on loose rock past a tree to belay.

Monument To Insanitary   21m   VD
D.Ellis, J.Parry 1967
Climb a short wall to a chimney, follow this to a ledge, then climb up R and scramble to a tree belay.

Anthrax   30m   VD
D.Ellis, P.Leyshon 1967
Start 2m R of the chimney. Climb the wall L of a small overhang, then step R to a groove. Climb this and the steep groove above on the R, finish up loose rock to a tree belay.

Thunder Crack   30m   VS   4b
D.Ellis, P.Leyshon, P.Minett 1967
Start in the corner R of the chimney. Climb RW to the foot of two cracks which join at the bottom. Follow the LH crack to a grass ledge, then scramble to a tree belay.

Lightning Crack   30m   VS   4b
P.Watkins, D.Parsons 1967
Start R of Thunder Crack, and climb the RH crack before moving L and scrambling to a tree belay.

Next are four corners.

The Godforsaken Gash   15m   E2   5c   †
M.Crocker, P.Thomas, M.Ward 1986
Start L of Thorny Problem. Climb a ramp to a ledge, follow a thin
crack and pull up L to a RW slanting crack, PR. Climb to a ledge
and abseil off a tree.

Thorny Problem   19m   S
P.Leyshon, D.Ellis, M.Berry 1967
The LH corner. Exit LW.

Renaissance   18m   E2   5b
M.Crocker, M.Ward 1986
This takes the L arete of Trilogy. Climb the awkward arete to a
ledge then move up the R side of the arete to a horizontal crack,
continue up the L side of the arete . Belay at a tree on the L.

Trilogy   20m   HVS   4c
C.Jones, D.Parsons 1967 1pt aid
The second of the four corners. Climb to an overhang and tra-
verse L to a tree belay.

Get A Load Of This   21m   E4   6a   †
M.Crocker, M.Ward 1986
The R arete of Trilogy. Start below Trilogy, scramble up to a ledge
and climb the smooth arete, PR, to a small ledge, then another
ledge to exit L above the arete's final step. SB.

Eulogy   36m   VS   4b
C.Jones, D.Parsons 1967
The third corner.

The Big Dipper   116m   VS
D.Ellis, L.Ainsworth 1967
A meandering L to R girdle of the LH section of the crag. Start in a
bay at the far L of the quarry, at blocks L of a big roof.
1   14m Climb loose blocks L of the roof and walk along a ledge to
a tree.
2   21m Go diagonally RW and cross R above an isolated wall and
down to a tree on the R.
3   21m Move R and down then traverse R and climb a chimney.
Move up and R to a wooded ledge.
4   15m Drop down and traverse R to a second groove, climb it
then move down under a roof. Exit on the R wall to a ledge.
5   24m Traverse R above a wall and up to a big ledge on the R,
continue R and climb down the upper part of a corner. Step R
around an edge and traverse RW then step down to a ledge and
belay.
6   Finish as for Eulogy.

Biology   36m   S
C.Jones, D.Parsons 1967
The fourth corner.

Diogenes   23m   VS   4b
D.Ellis, C.Taylor 1967
Start L of an arete with a small overhang near its base. Climb to a tree, follow the crack to a downward growing tree. Continue to a grass ledge and a short wall to a tree belay.

Point Five Arete   23m   VS   4b
D.Parsons, C.Jones, P.Leyshon 1968 2pts aid
Start at a short corner under a small overhang on the arete. Climb the corner, go L round the overhang then back R onto the arete. Move to a ledge then another ledge and climb the wall on the L to a ledge. Finish up the arete.

Father To Be   23m   E1   5b
C.Jones, D.Parsons 1968 4pts aid
FFA T.Penning, A.Sharp 1982
Climb a crack 3m R of the arete to a grassy ledge, traverse R and climb a short corner to a ledge and tree belay.

Rambler   35m   S
P.Leyshon, W.Evans, M.Shaw, A.Foss 1967
C.Jones, D.Parsons variation start 1967
Start at a large rectangular block (The Coffin). Climb to an overhang, step R and climb a corner to a ledge. Climb up R to a corner, follow this to grass ledges. Finish up the R wall of the corner, scramble to a belay.
Variation Start, The Coffin VS 4b: climb to the overhang, move L and climb a smooth corner to a ledge. Traverse R to join Rambler.

Hiatus   36m   HS   4a
C.Taylor, D.Ellis 1967
Start 4m R of a large rectangular block. Climb a groove to a small triangular slab and follow it to a grassy ledge. Move L and climb a corner to exit RW on poor rock.

Detergent   36m   HS   4a
D.Ellis, P.Leyshon 1967
Start 6m R of the large block. Climb a vegetated corner to ledges then L to a crack, finish on poor rock.

Prince Of Wales   36m   VS   4c
P.Leyshon, S.Lawton 1968
This takes the LH crack in the wall R of Detergent.

Nose Picker 36m S
P.Leyshon, D.Ellis 1967
The RH crack.

Grooved Arete 12m S
C.Jones, C.Taylor 1967
Start R of the arete. Climb a groove to a tree.

What's The Mara Boo Boo 12m E1 5b †
P.Bruten, L.Davies 1988
Start just R of Grooved Arete. Ascend a groove, move through a small overhang to a ledge, step R then climb a crack. Move L to finish.
Direct start, 6a: Ascend a small groove to climb the crack, PR.

That Was Then, This Is Now 15m E4 6a †
M.Ward, M.Crocker 1986
Start 3m R of Grooved Arete. From a ledge climb a thin crack to a narrow ledge system, TR. Move up R and climb the steep wall, PR. Finish RW. Abseil. BB.

Spitting Distance 15m E2 5c †
M.Ward, M.Crocker 1986
Climb a thin crack system 2m R of the previous route to a ledge, step R and climb a thin crack to finish RW. Abseil off a BB.

A.N.D 15m VS 4c
D.Parsons, C.Jones 1967
Climb the prominent clean corner in the centre of the cliff, R of a steep wall.

Sneak Preview 14m S
D.Ellis, I.Lazlo 1967
Start 3m R of A.N.D. at a borehole. Climb a shallow corner to an overhang, step L and up the short ramp to a ledge on the R. Step L and climb a groove then L again and up to a tree.

Thales 21m HS 4a
P.Nulington, D.Ellis, P.Leyshon 1967
The obvious corner in the R centre of the cliff, 30m R of A.N.D.

Andromeda 21m VS 4b
P.Leyshon, D.Ellis 1967
The wide crack to the R.

Decades Roll 15m E3 5c †
M.Crocker, R.Thomas 1986
Start 4m R of Andromeda. Climb up and move L round a bulge, climb the arete directly, PR, to a horizontal break and twin cracks. Move R onto the tip of the upper arete and then to a big ledge and trees.

Playtex   111m   HVS   5a
C.Jones, D.Parsons, P.Leyshon 1pt aid 1968
A L to R girdle. Start up Lightning Crack to an arete, step R onto a wall, traverse to a breakline at 15m. Belay as convenient. Finish as for Sneak Preview.

The cliff now becomes very broken and the routes are not recommended.

Curates Egg   21m   D   O
P.Leyshon, W.Evans 1967
Twin cracks R of Andromeda.

Rockfall   21m   S   O
P.Leyshon, D.Ellis, P.Minett, W.Evans 1967
The steep crack seamed wall L of the boulder scree.

Post Script   21m   VS   O
D.Ellis, M.O'Byrne 1pt aid 1967
FFA P.Leyshon, W.Evans 1967
Climb the steep stepped groove in the corner of the scree.

Severn Bridge   21m   HS   O
P.Leyshon, D.Ellis 1967
Climb a cracked slab at the L end of the debris covered platform.

Gardener   18m   VD   O
H.Ball, P.Leyshon 1967
Start at a borehole on the R of a pinnacle. Climb the groove to a grassy terrace, climb the niche and step R to a ledge and belay.

Cringe   12m   VD   O
P.Leyshon, P.Minett 1967
Start 6m R of Gardener. Climb to a ledge, step R and climb to a tree.

Nameless Crack   15m   S   O
The crack in the centre of the long wall, starting at a tree.

Nitwit   15m   M   O
P.Leyshon 1967
The break R of Nameless Crack.

Abandonment   12m   D   O
The grooved arete at the RH end of the long wall.

TWYNAU GWYNION QUARRIES OS ref 065105
A.Giles

SITUATION AND CHARACTER
Twynau Gwynion quarries lie on the hillside above Taf Fechan Quarry and provide some magnificent views of the Brecon Beacons. For many years it has been the secret location for many outdoor centres who wanted to avoid the crowded and polished crags of Morlais. It is an ideal crag for the middle grade climber who wants some seclusion. Many of the routes have been climbed before, but with names and grades there is now some order to the crag.

APPROACHES AND ACCESS
1   It is possible to reach the quarry by scrambling up the hillside from either side of Taf Fechan quarry.
2   By car, turn off the A465 'Heads of the Valleys Road' at Dowlais roundabout (Asda superstore). Miss the superstore's entrance and turn L, L again and then R. Follow the road/track through the buildings and horse boxes and turn R to follow a pot holed road for a mile until you come to the quarries.
3   A more pleasant way is to park in the Pant Cad Ifor car park. OS ref 062094. Follow the Garth lane (30m RW from the pub) through the farm, past a gas pumping station until the potholed track described in 2) is reached. Return the same way with the obvious reward.

BAY ONE
The smallest bay, glimpsed through the spoil heaps on the R of the track when coming from the Asda superstore. It is an 11m high wall of rough white rock and 30m in length.

White Groove   11m   HS   4b
The front of the clean buttress on the S end of the wall, move LW to finish.

Spare Rib   11m   HS   4b
The arete forming the R angle.

BAY TWO
150m N of Bay One is Bay Two forming a R angle and facing NW. An obvious feature is the arete of Corrugation. The routes are described from R to L.

Black Crack   VS   4b
The crack immediately R of a rounded groove, with an overhang at 6m, finish up the groove.

Flowstone   9m   HVS   5a
Start 1m L of two trees low down. Climb the flowstone wall

direct to the top.
Next are two cracks.

Two Half Quids   9m   VS   4c
The RH crack.

Two Fingers   9m   VS   4c
The LH crack .

Cystitis Eat Your Heart Out   9m   VS   4c
Start 3m R of a LH corner with a tree low down below a curving
crack. Follow it to the main horizontal break, step L then follow a
crack L of a small roof.

Suns Going Down   9m   VS   4c
Start just R of the LH corner and follow a crack to the top.

Corrugation   11m   E1   5b   *
The wrinkled arete of the great block either direct or on its R up
the corrugation in a shallow groove. The crux is difficult to
protect.

Frontal Wall   11m   S   4a   *
The front wall of the block has two cracks high up. Climb either
one, the RH one being harder.

Hawthorn Chimney   6m   D
The obvious chimney above a tree.

BAY THREE
45m N and at a lower level than Bay Two is Bay Three. It has a
single N facing wall, its RH end is two tiered and it's LH section
contains some fine crack lines. The lower wall of the double tier
contains a number of problems 5m high.
The first real route is:

Pete's Finish   12m   E1   5b
J.Harwood 1987
Just L of where the tiers merge. Follow a crack which is obvious
high up past a number of horizontal breaks.

Nut Wall Direct   12m   E1   5c
G.Evans, K.Wood 1975
Thin moves gain a ledge and tree at 3m, carry on up a crack to a
large grassy ledge. Move L to finish.

Unnamed   12m   E1   5b
J.Harwood 1987
Climb thin discontinuous cracks in the slabby wall.

Friends In Need 12m HVS 5a
Start 4m L. Difficult moves gain a crack line at 6m.

Little Owl 12m VS 4c
J. Harwood 1987
The distinct crack.

Pleasurance 12m HS 4b
J.Harwood 1987
Climb the wide crack.

BAY FOUR
The largest of the bays, offering less climbing than one would hope. The following routes lie on its S facing wall.

Balance 9m VS 4c
A crack on the L wall gives more trouble than anticipated.

The Block 10m VS 4c
3m R is a block. Climb it.

BALTIC QUARRY OS ref 063116
M.Crocker

SITUATION AND CHARACTER
Baltic Quarry lies high on the hillside, facing W and overlooking Ponsticill. Although part of the North Bay reaches 30m, the main interest lies in the extensive short cliffs. The rock quality is excellent and although many of the routes are more safely led the main value of the quarry lies in the fine soloing to be had. The cliff has been climbed on for many years by Outdoor Education Centre staff and locals, first ascentionists have not been included although it is likely that many of the harder routes were first climbed by M. Crocker.

APPROACHES AND ACCESS
There are two possible approaches:
1   Park in the layby as for Taf Fechan and follow the Brecon Mountain Railway N for half a mile before striking up the hillside to the Southern Bay.
2   Park at Ponsticill reservoir dam. Cross the Brecon Mountain railway and strike diagonally SE up the hillside to the Northern bay.

NORTHERN BAY

Minuscule   5b
The short arete . Start on the L.

Taff's Not Well   12m   VS   4b
The LH of two prominent aretes.

Rediscovery   10m   VS   5a
The RH arete.

Andy Borehole   6m   5a
The long borehole in the smooth wall.

Holiday Fever   9m   E1   5b
Start 9m R. Climb a thin crackline, under a sapling.

Exam Blues   9m   HVS   5b
Start 4m L of The Arch. Climb a wall and crack.

Temptress   9m   VS   5a
The thin crack 2m L of The Arch.

The Arch   9m   E1   6b
Pull through the arch with difficulty, then trend RW.

Slagged Off   9m   E1   6b
Climb the steep wall and short square cut groove below a tree.

Lonesome Pine   9m   E3   6a
The steep wall L of the arete.

Slight Alterations   9m   E3   6a
Follow the calcite cracks in the arete overlooking the S edge of the spoil heap. A super dyno gains the top.

Not So Plain Jane   9m   E2   5b
The groove L of Health Inspector.

Health Inspector   9m   E5   6a
The blunt arete between two grooves via the R side.

Sterilise   9m   E2   6b
The grooved arete provides a difficult problem. Finish up the LH side.

Light Speed   9m   E2   6c
Climb directly up the smooth flat wall of the quarry, 1BR.

Why Wimp Out?   9m   5c
Nice climbing up the centre of the short leaning wall towards the S end of the quarry.

SOUTHERN BAY

Iron Awell   9m   HVS   5b
Climb the centre of the rust coloured wall in the LH side of the bay, exiting RW.

Metal Mistake   9m   E3   6b
A direct line up the L side of the steep block wall via a projecting handhold at 3m. Replacing a bolt hanger reduces the grade to E1.

Harmony Of The Skies   9m   E3   6b
The next thin crack.

Smile   5a
The smooth grey wall topped by a small sapling.

Appear, Smear, Disappear Then Reappear   12m   E2   6a   *
Direct up the faint line of weakness in the calcite veneered slab L of the pod. Finish direct or traverse off R.

Bumbling About In Bhutan   12m   E4   6b
Enter a pod and pull straight over the bulge to finish RW.

Tortured   9m   VS   4c
The fine LH crack.

Traction   9m   VS   5a
The RH crack.

Curb All Intransigence   9m   E1   5c
The fine square cut arete on its RH side.

THE LLANGATTOCK ESCARPMENT OS ref 215147 to 173167
C.Court
"If I were a man who had no more dreams I should feel very sorry
for myself"
R.Messner

SITUATION AND CHARACTER
The escarpment extends for 3 miles on the S side of the Usk valley
overlooking Crickhowell. Most of the routes are in old limestone
quarries of a generally solid nature. It is an exposed cliff and can
be very cold when windy, but when the sun is shining it is a
picturesque and peaceful place to climb with some fine routes.

ACCESS AND APPROACHES
See map 1.
1   For the Eastern Edge (215147 to 205154) and Chwar Pant-Y-Rhiw
(203155 to 195158) there are several access possibilities. The easiest is via Gilwern, (just off the A465 'Heads of The Valleys Road').
Take a lane opposite the Corn Exchange Inn past Llanelly church,
over a cattle grid to a steep turn R onto a road contouring the
hillside. Follow the road for a mile to a track that forks LW, below
the Eastern Edge. Do not park on the roadside but follow the track
to a car park on the L. Further along, the road forks R at some
cottages (one is a caving hut). The Eastern Edge is directly above
the car park, Chwar Pant-Y-Rhiw is to the R and found by following the track to some old ruins, from here the RH fork leads to the
Pinnacle Bay.
2   For Craig-Y-Castell continue through Gilwern for about three
miles on the A4077 to Llangattock, then follow the Beaufort road
for about 3 miles uphill. Park just beyond a cattle grid. The cliff
can be seen above the bracken slope on the L.
***NOTE* The Llangattock Escarpment passes through Craig-Y-Cilau
National Nature Resereve. Climbing on Chwar Mawr and Craig Agen
Allewdd is by permit only.**

THE EASTERN EDGE

The Far Eastern Edge
This is the small buttress at the extreme LH end of the escarpment. From the car park a descent ridge can be seen splitting the
Eastern Edge. Grenoble Buttress is to the L and the Far Eastern
Edge 300m L again. The routes are found in the large central bay,
the LH end of which is very broken. It is easily reached by walking
from the car park.

Mirror   25m   VS   4c
J.Harwood, ANO 1983
Start R of grass ledges. Climb past a corner below a bramble in the
lower slabs, to ledges. Move R and climb cracks on the L to finish.

Reunion 22m E1 5b
J.Harwood 1986
Climb a corner L of a clean wall below a prominent tree, then a
second corner (borehole) to ledges. Follow finger cracks up the L
side of the wall.

Class Of 66 22m E2 5c
J.Harwood 1986
Start 3m R. Climb the centre of the clean wall to end at the
prominent tree.

Invert 22m VS 4b
J.Harwood, ANO 1983
Climb slabs below a prominent tree, then move R and climb the
wall just R of the smoothest part to a ledge. Move L to finish at the
tree.

Cotton Wood Cafe 22m E2 5b
J.James, S.Thompson 1986
Start at a small cave on the RH side of the bay. Climb a groove
above the cave to ledges at 10m, trend L to the arete and finish up
this.

GRENOBLE BUTTRESS
From the car park a descent ridge can be seen splitting the Eastern
Edge. To the L of this is a buttress with a wide chimney in its
centre, Grenoble Buttress.

Mistral 30m E2 5b
J.Harwood (with side runners) 1986
The face L of the obvious chimney. Climb a crack on the LH side
of the face to a grass ledge, then climb the centre of the face
above to the top.
Two climbs have been made L of Grenoble: Bite Size and Little
Jerk but they are loose and dangerous and not described.

Grenoble 30m VS 4c
T.Penning, J.Harwood 1986
Climb a crack below a chimney and move LW to gain the chim-
ney. Follow this to the top. SB.
The next route is to the R of the descent ridge.

Bitter Bark 33m E2 5b   *
T.Penning, J.Harwood 1982
Start beneath a groove, just L of a wall with a semicircular chimney in its upper half. Climb the wall to a ledge, move R, then L to a
hollow. Pull into the groove and follow it, PR, to the top.

Z.X. 33m E1 5b
T.Penning, J.Harwood 1981

A worthwhile route. Start beneath the semi circular chimney. Climb a groove and wall then the chimney to exit RW.

Space Between My Ears   33m   E2   5b
T.Penning, J.Harwood 1982
Start as for Z.X. Climb trending RW to a tree, continue on poor rock and climb a short corner to a hawthorn. Step L and climb to the top.

Penwood Special   23m   E1   5a
T.Penning, J.Harwood 1982
R of Z.X. is a line of overhangs at 12m. Climb a crack to the RH end of the overhangs, traverse L a metre and pull into a wide groove which is followed to the top.

Wall Of Glass   30m   HVS   5a
T.Penning, J.Harwood 1982
Start on the L side of a long wall broken by a grassy ledge at one third height. Climb cracks to a grassy ledge, then move up and L to climb a short corner at two thirds height, traverse R for 3m then gain the top.

No Ref   30m   HVS   5a
J.Harwood solo 1983
Climb a thin crack R of Wall Of Glass to a grass ledge, move R then L to join Wall Of Glass. Finish LW up the slabby corner.

The Gambler   30m   HVS   4c
T.Penning, J.Harwood 1982
Start beneath a slanting crack in the centre of the long wall. Climb thin cracks to a grassy ledge, step L and climb up to the slanting crack and then to the top.

Bruten Lee   26m   HVS   5a
P.Thomas, L.Davies, P.Bruten 1984
Start 3m R. Climb a thin crack and a brown groove in the upper wall.

Azolla   26m   VS   4b
T.Penning, J.Harwood 1981
Start at a pair of obvious deep cracks. Climb the L crack, step L, then continue straight to the top.

The Backsliding B   26m   VS   4b
J.Harwood roped solo 1983
Climb the crack just R of Azolla and continue to the top.

Wonderful Life   30m   HVS   4c
T.Penning, J.Harwood 1981
Climb up to and above a tree at 5m, traverse R to a shallow groove and climb this to the top.

Fighting Cock Buttress
The cliff now becomes broken with a long steep wall to its R,
Winning Wall. R again is a cliff with a large overhang near its base.
On the L side of Winning Wall is Fighting Cock Buttress with the
obvious groove in its R side of Fighting Cock.

Vendetta   33m   E3   6a   * †
M.Crocker, M.Ward 1985
Fine climbing. Climb the groove L of Fighting Cock, TR, then a rib
to a sloping ledge. Pull over a roof and pull up R into a short
groove, move up LW then pull round a bulge and up a steep wall.
Climb a slim groove exiting R at its end.

Fighting Cock   26m   E3   5c   *
T.Penning, G.Gibson et al 1984
A good climb with a bold move at the top. Climb a short crack
below and R of an obvious groove line, then move across L to gain
the groove. Climb it to the top. Belay well back.

Race Against Time   14m   E1   5b
L.Davies, P.Thomas 1986
Start 3m R of Fighting Cock. Climb to an overhang from the R, PR,
pull over to finish via a crackline above.

WINNING WALL
This long steep wall contains some of the hardest routes at llangattock.

Wonderlands   27m   E5   6b   *
M.Crocker 1987
Extremely thin and sustained. Climb a shallow groove at the LH
end of the wall. Move L across an unstable ledge, TR, and climb
directly up the grey flowstone wall, PR, TR and 2 BR's. A long
reach from a projecting hold gains a long and dirty grassy ledge,
continue easily to a good tree.

Mad Hatter   20m   E5   6a   *
G.Gibson, H.Gibson 1984
A fine serious route. Start below an obvious grey streak in the wall
L of Stay Sharp. Climb, TR, to a nose, TR, and continue with
difficulty, PR, stretch for a small hold and then finish RW.

Stay Sharp   27m   E4   6a
A.Sharp,   T.Penning 1982
Start below an obvious water worn groove. Climb up and trend R
to a grassy ledge, then move L to beneath a short slanting corner,
poor PR. Climb straight up, PR, to good holds, and continue up
the corner to the top. SB.

Winning   27m   E3   5c   **

T.Penning, J.Harwood, C.Court 1984

A classic, one of the best routes at Llangatock. Climb cracks in the centre of the wall to a loose band, step up and L into a shallow groove line, 2PR's. Climb this to a small pocket, move up, PR, and trend RW to finish.

Hitman   27m   E4   6b   *

G.Gibson 1987

Start 6m R of Winning at crack lines leading to the top of an easy ledge system. Climb to the top of the ledges and move straight up, TR, step L, BR, then climb direct by a series of extending moves to the top, PR.

Culmination Crack   27m   E3   6a

G.Gibson, T.Penning, C.Court 1984

A tough finish. Start as for Hitman at easy climbing below and L of a crack high on the cliff. Climb straight up over ledges, then traverse R to the crack, PR. Finish directly.

Cold Snatch   33m   E1   5b   *

P.Littlejohn, D.Renshaw 1979

Start 4m L of a large overhang at the base of the cliff beneath and L of a grassy ledge. Climb thin cracks, move R and up to a grass ledge and a band of shattered rock. Step back L to a thin crack and follow this to the top.

The Big Bright Green Pleasure Machine   40m   E2   5c   *

T.Penning, P.Cresswell 1pt aid 1981

Climb Cold Snatch to the band of shattered rock, traverse R to a ledge, PR, below a short corner capped by a small overhang. Pull into the corner, 2PR's, then move RW and up to a ledge. Traverse L and finish up cracks.

Mean Green   40m   E4   6a

A.Sharp, P.Lewis 1983

A short direct start to the previous two routes. Climb a short groove R of Cold Snatch to gain Cold Snatch.

Liberator   40m   E3   6a   **

C.Court, L.Davies 1986

Start 2m R. Climb a thin crack, PR, until forced R into a shallow corner which leads, PR, to an overhang. Swing L to a good ledge, move up and R into the short corner of The Big Bright etc, 2PR's, and climb the crack above taking its LH branch to finish.

The cliff now has a large overhang at its base.

The Roaring Eighties   43m   E5   6a   **

M.Crocker, R.Thomas 1985

A magnificent challenge through the roofs between Pleasure Machine and West Wind. Long slings are useful. Start 7m R of Liberator. Climb a shallow groove past a roof to a break at 8m, traverse R to steep rock, PR, Move up to a good hold, PR, and pull over a roof and the next roof, PR, using a tree. Traverse R until difficult moves gain a good flat hold up and R, climb a shallow groove above, PR, and finish up a thin curving crack on the R.

West Wind   36m   HVS   5a   *
P.Littlejohn, D.Renshaw 1979
Start 3m R of the large overhang. Climb the wall bearing slightly LW to a horizontal break, move L and up to a narrow ledge. Climb the wall via a flake, before moving R to a groove which is climbed to the top. Belay well back.

Tramp   8m   HVS   4c
L.Davies solo 1986
The small groove, flowstone and scoop R of West Wind.

R of Winning Wall, the cliff is broken, then there is a large area of flowstone, with a cave at ground level. L of the cave is a loose looking corner and L again a shallow corner with flowstone cracks above.

Domino Theory   38m   HVS   4c
T.Penning, J.Harwood 1982
Climb the shallow corner, step R then up deep cracks to the top.

Sister Sledge   33m   E1   5b
C.Court, T.Penning, J.Harwood 1984
This follows the curving crack corner L of the cave at ground level.

Angel In My Pocket   33m   E3   5c   *
T.Penning, A.Sharp et al 1984
Serious. Start 5m R of the cave. Climb a LW trending ramp leading to an overhang. Pull over it and continue, TR's, to the top.

The Dark Ages   30m   E2   5b   *
M.Crocker, M.Ward 1985
Start on a block below a scoop at 7m. Climb LW to a break, move up R into the scoop and step back L onto a ledge. Climb the sheet above via a crack, TR, move L and up to finish.

Sir Hammer   33m   E1   5b
T.Penning, J.Harwood 1982
Loose! Start beneath a chimney/crack line on the RH side of the wall. Climb a thin crack and a small overhang on its R then up the chimney to exit RW.

Second Generation 33m E2 5b
T.Penning, P.Cresswell, C.Court 1984
Start just R of Sir Hammer. Climb a corner onto the wall above, then a shallow corner to the top.

At the far RH end of the Eastern Edge is a square shaped slab above a small ruin.

Nerve Test 22m E2 5c
T.Penning, J.Harwood 1982
Start by scrambling up to the L side of a slab. Traverse R, with feet on poor rock, to a ledge, then climb sloping ledges and a thin crack to the top of the slab. Scramble off RW.

Shock Dose 30m E2 5b
M.Crocker, M.Ward 1985
The slab R of Nerve Test. Climb the RH of twin cracks in the initial wall and step L to a ledge. Move up, then LW to gain twin cracks and the top.

Egina 20m HVS 5a
L.Davies, D.Leitch 1986
As for Shock Dose to the ledge, step R and continue up the wall, TR, moving R to finish up a corner.

CHWAR PANT Y RHIW
The most popular section at Llangattock. From the car park follow the track, as for The Eastern Edge to the RH end of the cliff and the small ruin. At this point take the RH fork in the track to the Pinnacle Bay of Chwar Pant Y Rhiw.

Pinnacle Bay
At the extreme LH end of the bay, high up on the grass slope is a small buttress of unquarried limestone. Below and R of this the cliff starts in earnest. At the LH end is a broad shallow recess between two noses, with a muddy pool to its R. Further R is a large chimney with a blank looking wall to its R.

The Pinnacle 10m S
Climb directly up the centre of the small buttress on the LH end of the bay.

Scoop 16m VD
Start at the recess between the noses. Climb on the R for 3m, then traverse L to gain a ledge above the LH nose. Finish L or R.

Spirogyra Corner 20m HS 4a
In all but the driest weather there is a muddy pool at the foot of the wall R of Scoop. Start 3 m L of the pool. Climb a groove with

a small overhang at 5m to gain a nose, then a ledge and tree. Move up to a rock tower and take this on the R.

White Wall Direct 20m VS 4b *
Start just R of the pool at three grassy ledges. Scramble to the second ledge, then climb to a nose, which is taken on the R. Move L then climb a rib on its R to finish.

Little Red Rooster 20m HVS 5a
C.Court solo 1983
Climb the shallow corner 6m R and continue direct to the top.

Excalibur 20m E1 5b
C.Court solo 1983
A difficult start. Climb the steep wall R of Little Red Rooster to finish on easier ground.

Switchblade 20m VS 4b
C.court solo 1983
Climb the obvious short corner R of Excalibur to a small overhang. Pull over this and climb the short wall above. Finish as for Straighter.

Straighter 20m S
Start 9m R of the pool to the L of some grey rubble. Climb a blunt pillar and short wall to a ledge, finish up the rib.

Diagonal 22m S
Start 4m R of Straighter at a corner/crack beneath a nose. Gain a slabby scoop, then traverse L and up to a very short rust coloured corner. Continue to a tiny overhang and finish LW.

Ornithology 22m S
Climb to the slabby scoop as for Diagonal, then move R to another scoop. Exit R and follow ledges up L to finish up a corner above a small cave.

Apollo X1 22m S
Climb a short steep crack R of the corner crack of Diagonal to a ledge. Continue over small ledges to a short chimney leading to a good ledge below a bulging nose. Finish up the corner R of the nose.

Bespoke 22m VD
Start at a steep wall R of a short open chimney and L of an overhang. Climb a crack system and steep wall before moving R to a scoop. Finish direct, via a cracked wall.

Spiral Stairs 23m D
Start as for Bespoke. Climb R over short steps to a blank wall, and

continue R to easy ground. Scramble back L and finish via mossy blocks and a cracked wall.

Original Route 23m D
R of Bespoke the cliff projects to form a blunt toe. Climb over easy steps and a short wall, then trend R to various finishes.

Piton Traverse 21m VD
Start 6m R of Original Route, 12m L of a large chimney. Traverse L to ledges then back R to a recess below the final wall. Cross a nose to a ledge and finish by a corner/crack.

Raven Route 21m VD   *
Climb the shallow groove 4m R of Piton Traverse and step R onto a steep wall. Move up R then L to a large ledge. Climb the black wall on its R and finish up the corner/crack.

Crusty Wall 21m S
Climb a grey wall just L of a large chimney to a ledge. Finish straight up.

Sad Groove 21m S
Climb the large chimney, finishing up loose looking cracks.

Johns Jaunt 19m HVS 4c
J.Harwood 1977
Climb a thin crack 4m R of the large chimney, then a short wall to a ledge R of a hawthorn. Finish straight up.

Dus 19m VS 4b
J.Harwood 1977
Start at shallow groove 9m R of the large chimney. Climb up and L to a ledge at 6m, move R and up to a grass ledge. Finish straight up.

The Pedestal 19m VS 4b
Start at the R edge of a blank wall. Climb a shallow corner leading to a shaley ledge, with a small pedestal. gain the shale band above and finish via a mantleshelf and a short crack.

R of the blank wall is a break in the cliff. To the R, the lower wall is marked by a line of overhangs.

Man About The House 9m HVS 5c
L.Davies solo 1985
C.Court direct 1985
Start below and L of the overhangs at a steep slab, 2m R of an obvious crack. Climb the wall to pass a small overhang.

Jailbird   19m   HVS   5a
C.Court solo 1983
Climb the crackline in the centre of the slab past a small overhang. Finish as for The Creaking Flakes.

The Creaking Flakes   19m   HVS   5b   20m
Start 3m R. Climb a steep rib and trend L to flakes, move L and up to a hawthorn. Climb the corner behind, and finish by either of two cracks.

Entertainer   19m   E2   5b
P.Bruten, L.Davies 1985
Start 2m R of The Creaking Flakes. Climb an inverted V and surmount a small overhang, PR, to finish up an arete.

Wildest Dreams   20m   E2   5c   *
D.Hillier, S.Edwards 1982
Climb a crack in a shallow corner R of Entertainer. Step R and pull over two bulges, PR, to a hawthorn. Finish up the corner L of a nose.

Visions In Blue   9m   E2   5c
L.Davies, P.Bruten 1985
Climb the wall and bulging crack, PR, R of Wildest Dreams.

Ramblin Sid   19m   S
The first break in the overhangs, above a cone of grass. Climb a corner and short wall to a tree, then follow a sloping corner to a choice of cracks to finish.

Hideaway   18m   S
Start R of the line of overhangs. Climb an overhanging corner, moving R at a yellow block and finish up the wall above.

R of Hideaway the wall projects and passes a cave at ground level.

Hidden Rib   18m   VD
Climb a grey groove and broken slab on the L to a yellow block. Climb over this and finish up the wall above.

Nice One   19m   HS   4b
L.Davies solo 1986
The groove between Hidden Rib and Fingernail Crack.

Fingernail Crack   19m   S
Start 3m R of Hidden Rib. Climb a thin jagged crack in a corner and go L via steps to a grass ledge. Finish up the wall above.

Cuticle   19m   HS   4a
R of Fingernail Crack and L of a cave entrance is a smooth 4m wall.
There are many ways up it.

Hymns And Arias   7m   E1   5c
L.Davies 1985
A boulder problem with a good landing. Climb a steep wall,
round the corner from Cuticle, with a small overhang at 4m.

Purple Putty   19m   VS   4c
D.Hillier solo 1982
Start at an obvious crack 2m L of a cave entrance. Climb up over a
bulge at 4m to a shale band, traverse R to a crack and finish up
this.

High Frequency   19m   E1   5b
C.Court, M.Davey 1983
Committing. Start at the L side of the cave. Climb up slightly R,
over the loose band to finish just L of a shallow corner.

Heat Of The Moment   19m   E1   5b
D.Hillier, P.Jones 1982
Start 2m R of the cave. Climb up and step L over the cave to a
block at the shale band. Finish via cracks and a flared corner.

Little Overhang   19m   HVS   5a
Start 12m R of the cave at a crack in a corner with a small block
overhang at 4m. Climb above the overhang to a resting ledge on
the R. Move L to reach a shale band and finish up L via steps and
the final wall.

Puraka   18m   HVS   4c   *
Start as for Little Overhang. Climb to the resting ledge, then go
up R to reach the shale band. Finish up a short corner.

Gold Rush   18m   E1   5b   *
C. Court, L. Davies 1984
A good climb. Start 9m R of Puraka. Climb a corner, and then at
9m an overhang on its L. Continue up the wall above, and finish
through the break in the top overhang.

Apache   18m   HVS   5a
C. Court, M. Shepherd 1983
Start 12m R of Puraka. Climb an obvious arete with a triangular
block at 4m, then the corner above.

Cowboy   14m   VS   4b
Towards the RH end of this section of cliff, 2m R of Apache,
before a small buttress where the cliff turns, there is a sharp rib,
projecting forward. Climb a corner on its L to gain the top of the

rib, then follow steps to the upper wall which is climbed via some thin cracks.

Passage to Andrea 18m E3 6a *
I. Waddington, Gwent M.C. 1986
An alternative start to Julie Andrea. Start 2m R of Cowboy. Climb a shallow groove and crack line, PR, then move up and R to the tree. Finish as for Julie Andrea or abseil.

Julie Andrea 18m E3 6a *
C. Court, T. Penning 1984
Sustained and technical. Start 3m R of Passage to Andrea. Climb a bulging crack line to the tree at half height, then step up and R to a small ledge. Trend L to a shallow corner, PR, and straight up to finish.

White Tiger 17m E3 5c *
C. Court 1983
Bold climbing. Start at a large corner 9m R of Julie Andrea. Climb the corner to its top then move R over the bulge, and easily up to a ledge at half height. Climb the wall above, trending R, poor PR, to a small ledge. Move back L to gain the finishing cracks.

The next 13 climbs start from a ledge halfway up the cliff, easily reached from the R. At the back of the ledge is a loose looking corner (Brere Rabbit) above a spiny bush, with 4 corners to its R. The first climb starts 15m L of Brere Rabbit, at the far L end of the ledge, below a thin crack in the wall above.

Wildlife 8m E2 6a
C. Court, L. Davies, P. Thomas 1986
Start below the thin crack. Climb a ramp then trend R to a narrow ledge below the thin crack, PR. Finish straight up the crack.

Don't Walk Over My Head 8m VS 4b
This takes the obvious crack line 3m R of Wildlife.

No Sh-t 8m VS 4b
C. Court, N. Haines 1982
Start 3m L of Brere Rabbit below a rib. Climb the wall to take the rib on its R.

Brere Rabbit 8m VD
The loose looking corner.

Rotten Wall 8m S
Climb the obvious crack R of Brere Rabbit.

Night Shift 8m HVS 5b
L. Davies, P. Thomas (with side runners) 1986

R of Rotten Wall is a crack, and R again of this is a line up the wall. Climb the wall to the top.

To the R are three corners.

Limbo 9m S
Climb the LH corner.

Misty Haze 9m HS 4a
P. Thomas (solo) 1984
The arete R of Limbo.

Missing Link 9m S
The second corner, finishing at a rusty chain hanging from the top of the cliff.

Dunno 9m HS 4a
P. Thomas (solo) 1984
The third corner, finishing L. The corner direct is VS 4b.

Corner Buttress 12m D
A useful descent. From the toe of the buttress, where the cliff turns, scramble up to the R corner and climb this.

Corner Buttress Arete 12m VS 4b
Climb the buttress, where the cliff turns.

Flowstone Wall
At the extreme RH end of Pinnacle Bay, around the corner from Corner Buttress Arete, is a long steep wall covered in flowstone.

I Can See Clearly 17m VS 4c
L. Davies, P. Bruten 1986
Start as for Corner Buttress Direct. Traverse the flowstone wall from L to R at 12m height. Finish up Perk.

Man of Mystery 12m VS 4b
C. Court, N. Haines 1982
Start 3m R of Corner Buttress Arete. Climb cracks to the top.

Suddenly Last Summer 14m VS 4c
T. Penning (solo) 1981
Start on the slope leading down from Corner Buttress Arete, under the steep flowstone wall at a small recess. Climb cracks above the recess, traverse R a metre. Finish straight up past a diagonal web of flowstone.

Christmas Spirit 15m VS 4b
L. Davies, P. Thomas 1983

Start at a crack just R of Suddenly Last Summer. Climb the crack to finish up Suddenly Last Summer.

Perk   18m   VS   4b
J. Harwood 1977
Direct Finish L. Davies, P. Bruten, P. Thomas 1984
Pleasant climbing on good rock. Start on a block at the lowest point of the flowstone wall. Follow the line of least resistance to the steep headwall, and either traverse R into the large crack to finish or move L at the headwall before finishing straight up.

Knight Flyer   18m   VS   4b
C. Court, N Haines 1982
Start 4m R of Perk.
Climb a crack and wall above, then trend L to finish as for Perk.

Free Runner   18m   VS   4c
P. Thomas, L. Davies 1984
Start 3m R of Knight Flyer.
Climb flowstone, R of a small tree, to finish up a faint crackline.

Bridlevale Wall   21m   E2   5b   *
T. Penning, J. Harwood, M. Learoyd 1984
A good introduction to the harder flowstone climbing. Start at a short, wide, crack, almost in the centre of the wall. Climb the crack to the flowstone, and follow this directly to the top.

Wild Touch   24m   E3   6a   *
C. Parker, A. N. Other 1983
The hardest route on the flowstone wall. Start about 4m L of the crackline of Passage of Time. Climb flowstone directly, to a faint crackline and finish up this.

Cry Havoc   24m   E2   5c   **
T. Penning, P. Cresswell 1980
Direct: T. Penning, J. Harwood, C. Court 1984
Excellent climbing with good protection. Start just L of Passage of Time . Climb to a disjointed crackline and follow it to a small hole. Then either traverse R to join Passage of Time or continue directly to the top.

Passage of Time   24m   E1   5b   **
An excellent climb marred only by its exit. Start on the R side of the flowstone wall at a block with a fine crack above it. Climb the crack and finish up L.

Edge of Time   33m   E1   5b   *
T. Penning, J. Harwood 1984
This climb takes the arete R of Passage of Time. Climb Passage of

Time until level with a small overhang. Traverse R to the arete and climb it easily, but in a fine position, to the top.

MAIN AREA

To the R of Flowstone Wall, the cliff is dominated by a series of daunting overhangs, where only the bold dare to venture.

Hangman   30m   E4   6a   *
P. Littlejohn, D. Renshaw 1979

A difficult climb. Start on the R of the flowstone wall below and R of a big corner, R of a huge boulder. Climb a groove to the overhang, then traverse L to beneath the corner. Move up L over the overhang into the corner, and climb this to exit R. Belay well back.

More Fool You   30m   E4   6a   **
A. Sharp, P. Lewis 1979

Start as for Hangman. Climb the groove to the overhang, then traverse R to a ledge. Pull over the roof and move R to a resting place, PR's and BR's. Step back L and climb the wall, PR, to the top. Belay well back, or leave a rope in situ.

Fool's Executioner   33m   E3   6a   *
T. Penning, P. Cresswell 1983

This climb takes the diagonal crack leading out R from More Fool You. Follow More Fool You to beneath the overhang (possible belay). Pull over the overhang and then move across R to the crack. Climb the crack to the top and belay well back.

Johnny Cum Lately   33m   E3   6a   *
T. Penning, A. Sharp 1982

An impressive route. Start at a crack below the red coloured overhang to the R of the corner of Hangman. Climb the crack to its top. Swing R, PR, to a ledge beneath the centre of the overhang. Climb up to the overhang and traverse L on undercuts to a good resting place. Continue up the crack above to exit L. Belay well back.

Acid Rain   30m   E5   6b
A. Sharp, J. Harwood (1pt aid) 1982
FFA C. Parker 1983

The start is exceptionally hard. Start R of Johnny Cum Lately, at a shallow corner crack. Climb the crack to the overhang. Pull round this into the short V-groove (crux), which is followed to a ledge beneath the main groove. Climb this groove to exit L. Belay well back.

I.Q. Test   42m   E5   5c
T. Penning, J. Harwood (5 pts aid) 1988

A powerful pitch taking the awe inspiring groove line at the L end of the central overhangs. Climb the groove past a small tree to a PR at 7m. Move L using PA, F 1-1/2, and NA, until the wall can be climbed to the main overhang. Two PA's are used to cross the roof to the foot of the groove, PR, TR. Climb into the main groove using a large flake on the R and continue past the yellow rock band, PR. Traverse L at the top of the yellow band for 3m. Climb easier ground to the top.

Heaven Can Wait 21m E4 5c   *
T. Penning, J. Harwood (2 pts aid) 1988
An impressive pitch. Start at a groove below the central over-hangs. Climb the groove to a break (Friend 4) and traverse R until a ledge can be gained. Climb the grey wall, 2 PR's, move L and up to below the roof. 2 PA lead to spectacular moves via two large flakes to the end of the roof, PR. Move up and L to the belay on Children Of The Moon. Finish up this or abseil.

The Hundred Years War 30m E3 5c   *
T. Penning, J. Harwood 1982
Fine climbing above the overhang. To the R of Acid Rain the cliff has an even wider band of overhangs at 9m. Just R of the centre of this section is a break in the overhangs. Start below and R of two slanting grooves, at a corner. Climb the corner to exit L at a shale ledge, beneath the overhang. Pull over the overhang, step L, then climb straight up, PR, to exit R. Belay well back.

Obsession 30m E4 5c   **
T. Penning, J. Harwood 1988
An alternative finish to the Hundred Years War.
Follow the Hundred Years War to just above the overhang, then continue up the groove to the R of the twin grooves, 2 PR's.

Children of the Moon 75m E3 6a,5b   *
T. Penning, P. Cresswell 1984
A sensational R to L traverse above the main overhangs.
1   36m Climb The Hundred Years War to just above the over-hang, and level with the lip of the big overhangs. Traverse L, 2 PR's, (crux) to easier ground. Climb up L to a good ledge and belay. There is a logbook here for fellow lunatics to sign and make comments.
2) 39m. Continue L, over detached flakes into the big V-groove of IQ Test. Step across L on to the wall and move up, PR. Continue L around the arete and on to a steep wall. Climb past a sapling to the top.

American Mi Mi 33m E4 6a   *
T. Penning, J. Harwood, C. Court (1pt aid) 1983
A. Sharp, P. Lewis 1983
Start beneath a large detached block at 6m up and to the R of the Hundred Years War. Climb (carefully!) onto the block from the L.

Pull over the overhang and climb to an overhang with a groove on its L. Climb the groove to the top.

Split Second Rhyming   30m   E3   6a
A. Sharp, P. Lewis 1983
A difficult climb. Start below an obvious curving crack, 6m up and to the R of American Mi Mi. Climb a wall to boulders, make hard moves into a groove, and layback out L. Continue up the groove above to the top.

To the R of the overhangs are two grooves.

Average Hand   30m   E2   5c   *
T. Penning, J. Harwood 1982
Start below the LH groove. Climb a crack, move slightly L and pull over a bulge into the groove which is followed to the top.

5 Miles Out   30m   E2   5b   *
T. Penning, P. Cresswell, A. Sharp 1982
Start at a shallow L facing corner, below the RH groove. Climb the corner into the groove and follow this with interest to the top.

Animal Eric   30m   E2   6a   *
A. Sharp, J. Harwood 1982
A hard start. Start just R of 5 miles out. Climb a short wall (crux), PR, to the LH of two cracks. Follow this crack to exit R then L.

Singapore Sling   30m   HVS   5a   *
T. Penning, J. Harwood 1982
Start at a shallow corner leading to the RH of two cracks. Climb the corner to a small ledge at 4m. Climb the steep wall on the R, and the crack above, to exit L.

Belshazzar's Dream   23m   VS   4b
Start at a shallow corner just L of a grassy cone. Climb the corner to a deep groove with a sapling. 3m above the sapling, move R to a small ledge. Finish up the wall.

Thread Bear   21m   HS   4b
T. Penning, J. Harwood 1981
This climb takes the L side of the flowstone wall R of the grassy cone.

Hairy Bear   18m   HVS   4c
T. Penning (solo) 1984
This climb takes a line up the white flowstone just R of Thread Bear.

BLACK WALL
This is the steep black wall of flowstone at the RH end of the Main Area, with a large corner at its RH end.

Funky Flowstone Route   18m   E3   6b   *
M. Crocker, G. Jenkin 1985
Start on the L side of Black Wall. Climb into a niche and up on to a
ledge above. Climb straight, TR, to some pockets, then move up
R on to a rounded ledge. Step back L, then straight up to the top.

The Black Adder   18m   E3   5c   *
T. Penning, P. Cresswell, C. Court 1984
Serious with a hard move high up. Climb the line of black
flowstone on the RH end of the wall.

Skin Tight   21m   E4   5c
M. Crocker, R. Thomas 1985
Serious. The arete R of The Black Adder. Climb straight up and
continue just L of the arete to easier ground. Belay well back.

Spindrift   18m   HVS   5a
C. Court, T. Penning 1984
To the R of Skin Tight is a large corner. This climb takes the
obvious crack in the RH wall.

Crack Down   18m   E2   5c
C. Court, L. Davies 1984
Around the corner from Spindrift are two prominent cracks. This
strenuous climb takes the one on the L.

CHWAR MAWR OS ref 195157 to 185158

**THIS CRAG IS WITHIN THE CRAIG-Y-CILAU NATIONAL NATURE
RESERVE CLIMBING IS BY PERMIT ONLY.**

CRAIG AGEN ALLWEDD OS ref 185158 to 183165

**THIS CRAG IS WITHIN THE CRAIG-Y-CILAU NATIONAL NATURE
RESERVE CLIMBING IS BY PERMIT ONLY.**

CRAIG Y CASTELL
From the lay-by, just beyond the cattle grid, cross the road and
follow the obvious track up to the L end of the cliff. OS ref 173167.
At the L end of the cliff is a small buttress. Some 25m R of this is a
small bay below a hawthorn at the top of the cliff. 15m further R is
a small brown wall, below abseil bars on the clifftop, then the cliff
leads past a small cave (Catacomb) to a bay with a vegetated R
corner (God's Teeth). The cliff is then overhanging, and R of the
overhangs is a polished buttress (Rowan Route). The cliff continues to a grassy rise at its base with a vegetated corner (Green
Corner) to its R. Further R is an ivy covered overhang, and 50m R
of this is an obvious corner (Stupid Sapling). 20m R of this corner
is a large overhang at 6m, and 30m further right is a short chimney
which marks the end of the routes described. To the R of this

chimney are some small walls which may be climbed from D to VS.

Crackin Wall   12m   E1   5b
C. Court, M. Bishop 1984
The obvious crack on the L side of the small buttress at the LH end
of the cliff.

The Left Twin   15m   VD
Start 6m R of Crackin Wall, on the R side of the buttress.
Climb the crack.

The Right Twin   15m   VD
Start 3m R of The Left Twin. Climb cracks to a ledge, then the cracks
above to the top.

Stromboli   23m   HS   4a
Start below a hawthorn bush at the top. Climb the wall to the
corner and follow this to the top.

Rebecca   24m   VS   4b
The thin crack R of Stromboli. Finish R of the hawthorn bush.

Storm   24m   E2   5b   **
P. Littlejohn, S. Lewis 1979
Start 6m R of Rebecca. Climb to a block overhang at 6m and move L
through this to a ledge. Step R and follow the crack direct.

Tempest   17m   E1   5b
C. Court, M. Bishop 1984
A worthwhile climb. Start 6m R of Storm. Climb a crack line and the
obvious gap in the overhang to finish direct.

The Ascent of Rum Doodle   18m   VS   4b
Start R of Tempest and L of the small brown wall, below a corner on
the upper wall. Climb a crack, step L to the corner, and follow it to
the top.

Daedalus   17m   VD
Start R of the small brown wall. Climb a crack curving beneath an
overhang, then pass the overhang on the L and finish easily.

Heaven's Gate   17m   HVS   5b
L. Davies, P. Thomas 1985
Follow Daedalus to beneath the overhang, then pull over this to
gain a thin crack.

Cool Touch   17m   E2   5b
L. Davies, P. Thomas, M. Henry 1985
A faint line to the R of Daedalus. Climb to an overhang (loose rock),
then finish via the ledge above.

Fleet Feet 17m E1 5c
C. Court, M. Bishop 1984
Climb the centre of the steep wall between Cool Touch and Catacomb. A difficult start leads to easier ground above.

Next the cliff leads past a small cave.

Catacomb 17m VS 4b
Climb out of the small cave. Finish L of an overhang.

Accidentally Right 17m VS 4b
J.P. Hamill-Keays, J.L. Hamill-Keays 1989
Climb Catacomb to an overhang, traverse R along a ledge to finish up the corner of Orang Utang.

Orang Utang 17m VD
Start R of the cave and L of a large tree growing out of the rock. Climb a crack and corner above to the top.

Sheisskopf 17m S
N. Grant, N. Kingsford 1978
Climb up behind the large tree to a hawthorn. Climb the wall and overhang above to finish.

Jackorner 17m VS 4b
N. Grant, N. Kingsford 1980
Climb cracks to the R of the large tree, and continue over ledges to a hawthorn stump. Then climb flowstone and the corner above, to the top.

Tales Of The Unexpected 17m E2 5c
L. Davies, P. Bruten 1985
Start beneath the overhang 4m R of Jackorner. An easy, but poorly protected start leads to the overhang, PR. Pull over this to finish straight up.

God's Teeth 17m VS 4c
A poor climb keeping just L of a vegetated corner.

Rockfall Climb 17m VS 4b
N. Grant, N. Kingsford 1979
Start 4m R of God's Teeth. Climb a shallow crack, then trend R to a sandy corner which is followed to easy ground.

Duty Free 21m VS 4c   *
C. Court, M. Bishop 1984
Start 9m R of Rockfall Climb. Climb a shallow corner crack to ledges below a large corner. Move R and finish up a corner.

How To Stuff A Wild Bikini   20m   E2   5c   *
C. Court, P. Bruten 1984
Start to the R of Duty Free, at a thin crack. Climb easily to a band
of overhangs, and pull over these, past a completely detached
flake.

Right of the overhangs is a short polished buttress.

Trading Places   15m   HS   4b
L. Davies, J. Smith 1986
Start to the R of the overhangs, but L of a grassy cave. Climb a
steep crack in a short polished buttress until it merges with
Rowan Route.

Rowan Route   20m   VD
Start above the grassy cave. Climb direct, past small rowan trees,
to the top.

Tarzan Boy   15m   E1   5b
P. Bruten, L. Davies 1986
Start at a small cave 2m R of Rowan Route, below a small corner in
an overhang at 5m. Climb to and above the overhang, trend L to a
flake crack, and finish up the steep wall above.

Split Indifferences   18m   HVS   5a
L. Davies, J. Smith 1986
Start at a shallow crack line above, and 3m R of, Tarzan Boy.
Follow the crack to reach grassy ledges, then trend up and L to
the centre of a small wall. Climb straight up via a thin crack, PR.

Canyouhandlit   17m   S
N. Grant, N. Kingsford 1979
Start 4m R of Rowan Route below a corner high up. Climb the wall
via grassy ledges to finish up the corner.

Irrelevant Grope   17m   VS   4c
Climb a crack R of Canyouhandlit, step R, and finish up
flowstone.

Lime Juice   17m   E1   5c
C. Court, P. Bruten 1984
Start R of Irrelevant Grope. Climb a steep wall, then an obvious
crack.

Fresh   17m   E1   5b
L. Davies (solo) 1985
A variation start to Lime Juice taking a thin line to its R.

Castell Main XXXX   15m   E2   5b
C. Court (solo) 1986

Climb the obvious corner R of Fresh to its top, and exit via some holds on the RH side. Step L then up and R onto the flowstone wall above. Finish straight up.

No Peg Route   17m   VD
N. Grant, N. Kingsford 1978
Start just R of Castell Main XXXX. Climb flowstone to a ledge, then the wall above.

Once Shy   17m   S
N. Grant, N. Kinsford 1978
Start at an overhanging crack, R of No Peg Route, and just L of a flake in the ground. Climb the crack, step R and finish up the wall or, after 4m, traverse R to a sandy groove and follow this.

Lucky Nut   15m   VS   4b
N. Grant, N. Kingsford 1978
Start R of a flake in the ground, but L of a green corner. Climb through a break in a small overhang, past a hawthorn, and finish direct.

Green Corner   15m   VD   O
Climb the obvious vegetated corner.

R is an ivy covered overhang and 40m R again is the prominent corner of Stupid Sapling.

Once Bitten   17m   VD
Start 6m R of the ivy covered overhang. Climb a broken corner, move R, and finish up the RW leaning groove.

Valhalla   17m   VS   4b
Climb the broken corner of Once Bitten until it is possible to take the crack on the L.

Central Slab Direct   15m   VD
N. Grant, N. Kingsford 1980
Start just R of Once Bitten. Climb the centre of three slabs.

The Needle   15m   VD
Start below a tottering flake at half height. Climb a corner to the flake, and climb this to a small cave. Finish up L.

Mountain Hash   15m   S
Start below and R of the tottering flake of The Needle. Climb broken rock to a ledge, then the thin crack above, to finish between two rowan trees.

Fisher's Folly   17m   VS   4c
Start at a V-groove, L of Stupid Sapling. Climb to a break, traverse

R, and move up to a large ledge. Trend R to a grassy ledge, then finish up the broken crack.

Stupid Sapling 15m VD
Climb the prominent corner.

Flash 15m HS 4a
C. Court (solo) 1986
Climb the obvious crack 2m R of Stupid Sapling. Step R to finish.

Castell Craig 15m E1 5b   *
C. Court, M. Rosser 1986
Follow cracks in the wall 2m R of Flash. 2 PR's.

S Route 15m S
Start 4m R of Stupid Sapling. Climb a corner to a flake crack, then climb this to finish up flowstone.

Chicken 17m VS 4c
N. Grant, N. Kingsford 1979
Start at a tree 9m R of Stupid Sapling. Climb up behind the tree, then traverse R to a bush, and finish direct

Next is a large overhang.

Red Mike 17m VS 4c
T. Penning, P. Cresswell
Start below the R end of the overhang at 6m, below a groove. Climb to the groove, via the wall on its L, and finish up it.

I Should Smile 17m E3 5c
P. Thomas, L. Davies 1985
Climb the weakness in the wall R of Red Mike, finishing up the thin cracks in the headwall above.

To the R of the overhangs are three cracks.

Diarrhoea Crack 17m VS 4c
N. Grant, N. Kingsford, 1pt aid, 1979
T. Penning (solo) 1981
Climb the LH crack and finish up the wide groove above.

Road to Nowhere 17m E1 5c
L. Davies, P. Bruten 1985
Climb the centre crack.

Crack of Gwent 17m E1 5b
Members of Gwent M.C. 1985
Climb the RH crack.

Developing World   18m   E2   6a
L. Davies, P. Thomas 1988
An eliminate. Follow a shallow groove (between Crack of Gwent and Quiet Hero) for 6m, BR, to join Crack of Gwent.

Quiet Hero   17m   E2   5b
P. Thomas, L. Davies 1986
Start 2m R of Crack of Gwent, at some iron sticking out of the ground. Climb an arete to a flake crack above, then move up to finish more easily.

Peaches and Cream   18m   E2   5c   *
C. Court, L. Davies 1985
Start below the obvious corner, 6m R of the cave. Climb the wall, PR, to the overhang. Pull over this and into the corner on good jams. Finish L.

Slurry   17m   S
N. Grant, N. Kingsford 1980
Start 4m L of Briar Crack, where the overhangs end. Climb a groove to a bramble, move up R, and climb a corner to finish R.

Only Yesterday   15m   HS   4b
L. Davies, D. Leitch 1986
Climb the grooves above the start of Slurry.

Briar Crack   6m   VD
The short chimney, just before the cliff becomes very scrappy.

Jug Thug   8m   E2   5b
C. Court (solo) 1986
Start 6m R of Briar Crack. Climb the broken crack line through a series of overhangs.

Redstart   8m   HVS
Start 13m R of Jug Thug at a hawthorn. Climb to a ledge L of the hawthorn. Move out L at the same level to beneath the corner of the overhang. Move up and L to a crack, then finish up the steep headwall.

SANDSTONE

INTRODUCTION

"I think that there is a great change taking place in the attitudes of present day climbers to their activities and although there are those who believe that certain changes and new ideas are not really in the best interest of the sport, this is probably prejudice"

L. Tjeda-Flores 1968

Since the last edition of this guide book there has been a vast increase in the number and quality of sandstone crags let alone routes, such that it deserves a section all of its own. It will probably require a guide of its own within the next five years. Every valley has several quarries from which rock was removed to build the terraces which housed the increasing workforce required by the burgeoning coal and iron industries. There is no better place to study industrial archaeology than in the valleys. Neglected for almost a century these hillside scars are now being sought out and developed by small teams of sandstone activists. Sandstone climbing is in the early stages of its evolution and is slowly beginning to gain the status it deserves.

Jim Perrin wrote in 1973 ... "Perhaps someday the sandstone crags which line the valley rims will be hailed as major discoveries". Many are already singing the praises but only time will tell if the prediction is correct.

The majority of the highest quality routes take blank looking walls or aretes but after a lot of work some truly classic easier lines have been produced. The first ascentionists have put a lot of hard work into their routes but with few exceptions they were not done 'on sight'. Various tactics have been employed on the first ascents, red pointing, pinkpointing and in a few cases down right frigging. Early ascentionists should beware of the grades and stars and realise that in many cases they are making the first true onsight ascent. Prospective ascentionists should also note that the technical grade can often be lowered if the route has chalk on it, half the problem on sandstone walls is finding the holds. The routes have not been marked with a dagger as in the previous sections

Protection is mostly fixed and every effort has been taken to ensure that it is still in place, however a recent spate of gear thefts have made it wise to check visually that gear is still there. Most of the fixed gear and lower off points are recent and some of the PR's are stainless steel so many years will pass before they need replacing. However some of the fixed gear is home made and its safety and longevity must be suspect. Unpleasant and dangerous exits have often been equipped with lower off or alternatively an escape rope is advised.

Many of the sandstone crags appear scruffy but, there are many excellent climbs, so do not be put off if, on your first visit, you do not land the quality you wish, search again it does exist ....
honestly. Do take a brush and be prepared to abseil and clean pockets and holds, be it on your head if you do not.

Visitors not familiar with the complex valleys road systems should carry an OS map; sheet 170 "The Rhondda" and 171 "Cardiff and Newport" and use it!

On the following page is a starred list of sandstone crags. This will no doubt cause some consternation amongst the local activists whose favourite crag is not triple starred. It is however intended to give the first time visitor the best chance of finding the plum lines on Sandstone.

STARRED LIST OF SANDSTONE CRAGS

Three Stars ***
Definitely worth a visit, containing a good concentration of starred routes and nearly all the three starred routes on sandstone.
Llanbradach; Navigation Quarry; Cwmaman Main Quarry; Cwm Dimbath; Abbey Buttress; The Gap.

Two Stars **
Worth a visit if in the area or if you have worked out the other crags. Some may have an isolated excellent route.
Gladys Quarry; Penallta; The Darren; Mountain Ash; Ferndale; Punk Rocks;

One Star *
Of interest only to locals or adventurous climbers from afar. The inclusion of a starred route has saved some of these from the next category.
Gelli; Llwynypia; Roadside Quarry; Deri Crag; Bargoed Quarry; Quarry Mawr; Cwmcarn Quarry; Cefn Pennar.

No Stars
No stars and little climbing, only the people who discovered them will rave about them. The place to send your worst enemies in search of that Gem.
Glynfach Crag; Penrhiwceiber; Cwmavon; Blaenllechau; Ystrad; Crag Craig Fawr.

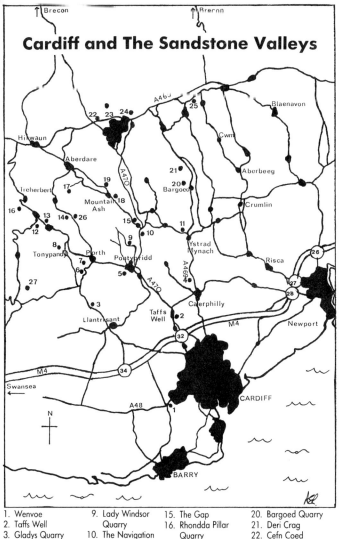

Cardiff and The Sandstone Valleys

1. Wenvoe
2. Taffs Well
3. Gladys Quarry
4. Llanbradach Quarry
5. The Darren
6. Roadside Quarry
7. Punk Rocks
8. Llwynypia Quarry
9. Lady Windsor Quarry
10. The Navigation Quarry
11. Penallta
12. Gelli
13. Ystrad
14. Ferndale
15. The Gap
16. Rhondda Pillar Quarry
17. Cwmaman Main and West Quarries
18. Mountain Ash Quarry
19. Cefn Pennar
20. Bargoed Quarry
21. Deri Crag
22. Cefn Coed
23. Morlais Quarries
24. Taf Fechan
25. Quarry Mawr
26. Blaenllechau Quarry
27. Cwm Dimbath

HISTORY
J.Harwood

"Go with the flow man" a young upstart

"Only dead wood goes with the flow" an ageing rock jock.

The sandstone crags had been climbed upon by previous generations as the following quote proves: "One party recently spent a memorable day on one of the most impressive of the monolithic middle grit quarries at Cross Keys, north of Newport. Motivated by a strong sense of one upmanship they ascended 70 feet climbing on coal seams, packs of cards and piles of pennies, before abseiling off from a doubtful five ton pinnacle after one of their ropes was sliced by a falling rock" (from Rock Climbing in South Wales, Rocksport 1969). It was not until the 1980's however that it really came of age, prior to this sandstone was virtually unknown in South Wales. The first significant development was Pat Littlejohn's attack on the crumbling horrors of Llanbradach to give The Expansionist in 1978. During 1984 Gary Lewis, Charlie Heard, Mick Learoyd and other S.W.M.C. members spearheaded the development of Cilfynydd and the Darren. One or two other routes had probed into gloomy corners but these efforts such as Alun Richardson's Load of Rubbish and Phil Thomas's Sennapod Corner remained unrecorded and largely neglected.

The new wave of activity started in 1988, Lewis and his team had shown the way with their use of bolt protection on the blank walls of Cilfynydd. Vigorous gardening and the use of lower off points has helped to reduce the perils of loose rock. The pace of activity became frenetic as every man and his dog sought out his own secret crag and picked the plums before going public. There were heated exchanges when parties turned up to try lines cleaned by others. However in the midst of all this some really fine pitches were put up. Once the dust has settled and an objective view is taken, some of the climbs will be viewed along with best in South East Wales.

Several different parties have been responsible for the development but the largest contributions have come from three teams. There were the original protagonists, Gary Lewis, Mick Learoyd and Haydn Griffiths, the "outsiders" Martin Crocker and Roy Thomas and the valley's team of Andy Sharp and Pete Lewis. Support to these teams has been given by many.

The boom began when rumours spread of Crocker's ventures into dankest Mountain Ash Quarry. The slumbers of previous generations were rudely awakened as the Right wall yielded Whiter than White. Other climbs quickly followed and over to the left Crocker added all manner of problems mostly with the hard to clip bolt.

Sharp and Pete lewis rose to the challenge and launched a Welsh counter attack with the discovery of Cwmaman. The superb south facing wall took a bit of drying to reveal the gems of Propaganda, Science Friction and Mother of Pearl. In his turn Sharp let the secret out allowing Crocker in to pick up the remnants of which Hot Beef Injection should become popular.

Crocker then returned to the more traditional Cilfynydd and with the acceptance of bolts mopped up the remaining lines to produce some hard test pieces. Next on the agenda was Llanbradach, described by more than one pioneeer as a 'Lost World' because of the festering swamp at its base. Since Littlejohn's pioneering venture, Expansionist, nothing had been done due to the unstable and forbidding nature of most of the buttresses and cracks. Once Thomas, Ward and Jenkin had set to gardening however the stage was set. Naturally 'steel fingers' Crocker produced such desperates as Slip Into Something Sexy and the superb Caerphilly Contract.

Sandstone crag x's were appearing fast and furiously from obscure valleys and coal tips, all claiming to be the best yet.

Lyndsey Foulkes and Learoyd developed Punk Rocks with several pitches including Completely Punked and the Waiting Game. unfortunately for them the crag was in view from Sharp's house and he swooped in to climb The Mona Lisa.

The roamings of Roy Thomas and Crocker led them to Treherbert and Thumbsucker, a harder equivalent of North Wales' The Mau Mau and well worth searching out. Exterminate All Bolt Thieves was a route that highlighted a not uncommon problem in the area.

Next on the agenda was Ferndale where several adventures had been experienced in the past. Crocker anticipating a holiday in the sun added pleasent lines such as Seashells In The Seychelles. Sharp then added more serious and testing fare in the form of By Appointment Only, Physical Presents and Race You Up The Wall Bars.

The teams moved on. At Cilfynydd Giles Barker added Elastic Retreat while Crocker added Innuendo to Cwmaman. The latter prompted a return visit by Sharp who replied with Le Rage and a testing girdle, Rab. Anyone who has driven from Cardiff to Brecon could not fail to notice the chunk of rock missing from the hillside like a giant bite and it was not long before the dry weather prompted a blitz on The Gap. The best find was the arete of One Track Mind although desperates like Pleasent Valley Sunday and Forsters Momentary Lapse Of Reason gave more value for modern sports climbers.

The list of new crags was never ending. Deri gave a spectacular overhanging arete, Kicking Ass And Taking Names to Sharp and a reachy crack and wall, Menage a Chien to Crocker. The Sharp Team opened up Bargoed with climbs like Blowing For Tugs. But secrecy was the order of the day and it was an obviously put out Gary Lewis, who while preparing to do battle on The Campaign For See Through Bikinis, was suddenly joined by Sharp's team who proceeded to put up some sterner stuff. The Uninvited being a aptly named effort.

The hillsides of South East Wales produced more sandstone crags and will for many years to come. Crocker and Thomas developed Sirhowy, Sharp and Harwood added the difficult Valley's Initiative to Mountain Ash and Thomas Learoyd and friends explored Gelli and Cefn Pennar. The sandstone crags continue to yield their fare to the various teams and as the guide goes to print the race is still on for those elusive crags that will keep the pace of development at full steam for years to come.

CWMCARN QUARRY OS ref 221940
M.Crocker
"Climbing well depends on who you drink with" A. Austin

SITUATION AND CHARACTER
The quarry is situated on the forested SW facing spur above Cwmcarn to the N of Risca. It is a worthwhile venue in winter because it gets any sunshine going and dries instantaneously.

APPROACHES AND ACCESS
From a point half a mile N of Cross Keys turn R to Cwmcarn. At the Cwmcarn Pub turn R into Park Street and then turn next L to a parking spot. From a lane between garages, go up a path tracking LW to the Quarry.
In the centre of the quarry is a fine orange coloured promontory face providing the following routes.

Where There's A Killer   19m   E3   5c
M.Crocker 1990
Serious. Start at the first arete L of the words Killer Wall. Go up a short rib to a ledge. Continue up the RH side of the main arete until a quick pull on a tiny oak tree gains a small ledge. Move up the final arete and step R across a grotty corner to the large ledge above the promontory.

Face The Rap   19m   E2   5b   *
M.Crocker 1990
A bold lead up the LH arete. The initial arete leads easily to ledges. Climb straight up the arete, avoiding the pillar to the R, PR, and run it out to the top.

Rap Crap   19m   E2   5b   *
M.Crocker 1990
Start at the centre of the face below the initials MC. Clamber up
ledges then follow disjointed thin cracks to a ledge atop a massive
flake. Ascend the headwall steeply with a long reach to finish.

To the R is a steep red coloured wall. The next routes commence
from a ledge at 6m reached via a short arete below its LH end.

Squeaking Bats   12m   E1   5b
M.Crocker 1990
The striking slim corner leads over a tricky bulge to a single BB.
Abseil.

Red With Rage   12m   E3   5c
M.Crocker 1990
Climb the wall R of Squeaking Bats past two horizontal slots to
reach a long layback edge. Follow the edge until jugs lead to the
single BB. The grade assumes that the large ledge on the R is not
touched.

QUARRY MAWR OS ref 205910
M.Crocker

SITUATION and CHARACTER
This broad and largely broken sandstone quarry is situated on the S
bank of the Sirhowy River, near Newport, 1/2 mile into the eastern
limit of Sirhowy Country Park.
The main attraction is a 20m high leaning wall (the Rust Curtain) at
its eastern end, plus a number of shorter walls at its western end.
Most of the quarry faces W and presents an afternoon/evening sun
trap.

APPROACHES AND ACCESS
See map 3. Sirhowy Country Park is reached by taking the Risca
road at junction 27 of the M4 at Newport. A written request to the
owners of the quarry did not succeed in obtaining permission to
climb, presumably because of concerns of liability. Climbing has
however proceeded to take place and problems are unlikely to be
encountered providing climbers maintain a low profile and act
responsibly. The climbing is easily accessible from the picnic area.

THE RUST CURTAIN
Within seconds of the picnic area is a red wall of fine sandstone.

Butcher Heinrich   15m   E5   6b   *
M.Crocker, R.Thomas 1989
Probably the best pitch on the wall, sustained and fingery with an
almighty reach at the crux. Start at the LH end of the wall below a

broad orange scoop. Climb direct via a scoop, 2BR's, to a thin overlap. From a finger jug above, BR, stretch over the roof and finish direct on large holds, PR.

Strange Little Girl   15m   E3   5c
R.Thomas, M.Crocker 1989
Start 3m R of Butcher Heinrich. Climb a crack, BR, to gain a horizontal break, PR. Step L at a tiny sapling and climb the flake above, PR, to a lower off.

Skanderberg   15m   E5   6b   *
M.Crocker, R.Thomas 1989
This takes the centre of the wall. Climb up then move R and finish directly, BR's, to a BB. Lower off.

King Zog   15m   E5   6b   *
M.Crocker, R.Thomas 1989
Climb the crack cutting the roof, on jams, then continue, 4BR's, to the BB on Skanderberg.

THE WEST WALLS
These are reached by following a faint track W(R) for 61m through the woods.

Deaf As A Post   12m   E4   6b
M.Crocker, R.Thomas 1989
A worthwhile technical problem. Start below the centre of the wall. Scramble to the highest of a series of ledges below a very narrow strip roof. A big reach, BR, leads to a good short crack. Climb the crack, swing L to much better holds and an abseil station.

BARGOED QUARRY OS ref 153006
G.Lewis
"A climber was nearly killed when a washing machine fell past him" . . .
"What route was the washing machine on"
A conversation between local climbers.

SITUATION AND CHARACTER
A typical urban quarry setting. Apart from the hazards of tangled bedframes and burnt out cars there is also a large menacing local who is very protective of nesting hawks, both should be given a wide berth. Climbed on many years ago it has been rediscovered. In the centre of the quarry is a sweep of slabs decreasing in height to the L. R of this is the tower of Blowing For Tugs. A metre up and R is a ledge system with an obvious corner.

APPROACHES AND ACCESS

See map 3. This quarry is situated on the outskirts of Bargoed. Drive through Bargoed past the railway station and the viaduct on the l. The road now turns R over a river bridge, after 100m turn L into Quarry Row and park on waste ground.

Mister Gorrillas Got a Big Nose   11m   E3   6b
M.Crocker, R.Thomas 1989
Good technical climbing. Start on the LH side of the slabs. Gain the horizontal break at 3m, climb up on small holds, BR, and finish via a good pocket, PR.

Pepperatzi   15m   E2   5b
L.Foulkes, M.Learoyd 1989
Climb the obvious groove on the L edge of the tower.

Blowing For Tugs   15m   E4   6b   **
A.Sharp, P.Lewis, J.Harwood 1989
The fine slab bounding the L side of the corner. Start below the steep wall in the centre of the slab. Climb the wall to good ledges on the arete. Pull through the overhang, BR, hard moves lead to good holds, PR. Finish direct to a tree belay.

Hawk's Cheep   15m   E1   5b   *
J.Harwood, P.Lewis, A.Sharp 1989
The obvious corner is climbed direct, 2 PR's, to a tree belay.

Our Man in Bargoed   12m   E4   6b
A.Sharp 1989
Start 6m R of Hawk's Cheep. Climb the steep wall with hard moves passing a BR at 5m. Continue with ease to a PR. Lower off.

Black Dog   12m   E2   5c   **
P.Lewis, A.Sharp, J.Harwood 1989
Start 3m R of Our Man in Bargoed. Climb the steep wall and a thin crack, to a good ledge. 2 PR.

Up For Grabs   20m   E3   6a
M.Learoyd, L.Foulkes
Climb the groove R of Black Dog via an overlap. 3PR.

LLANBRADACH QUARRY   OS ref 146895
M.Crocker, R.Thomas
"All you need is balls and chalk" P.Jewel

SITUATION AND CHARACTER

This huge rambling sandstone quarry is Wales' answer to Roraima, without the poisonous spiders. It is situated close to Caerphilly and offers a surprisingly good collection of routes, varying from short, technical testpieces to substantial undertakings of a length unmatched on local sandstone. The secluded, 'Lost World' atmosphere makes this a pleasant place to climb in the summer, but take long trousers and Wellington boots. Many of the climbs are well worth doing, with the Expansionist Buttress routes taking pride of place. Indeed this wall houses some of South Wales' finest sandstone routes.

Though situated on the eastern side of the mountain, the Northern and Eastern walls receive plenty of sunshine. Rock quality is typically variable but is especially good on the more highly recommended climbs.

On a final note; Peregrine falcons are known to nest here so please try to avoid their nesting areas.

APPROACHES AND ACCESS

See map 3. The quarry is reached by following the A469 N from Caerphilly. Turn L into a short steep lane at the signpost for Llanbradach (this is easy to miss) and park, room for 3 or 4 cars. Walk under the railway line and turn L along another track which soon leads to the quarry on the R.

The quarry comprises a massive tree-filled bowl with its back wall divided by a slanting vegetated terrace. In its northern end is a swamp which despite its harmless appearance should not be crossed!

WESTERN WALLS

These are the low level discontinuous walls on the L (W) side of the quarry, they are easily approached by following the track S from the quarry entrance and crossing through trees. The LH walls are characterised by a striking arete taken by Bas Chevaliers and to its R, across a gully, a 15m sheer wall.

Bas Chevaliers   21m   E3   5c   *
M.Crocker, R.Thomas 1988
The arete provides a nicely structured pitch. Clamber over the roof, bear L and climb an easy groove in the arete to a break on the R. Get established on the smooth wall above, PR, move up, and diagonally LW, to finish up the arete. It is possible to reverse to, and lower off a tree just below the top.

Hush Money   12m   E3   6b   *
M.Crocker, M.Ward 1988
The arete on the L side of the sheer wall provides some good moves. Start up the easy groove of the L arete but quickly swing R onto the arete, BR. Pass a small roof with difficulty, BR, and finish steeply up the arete, PR, to a good tree. Abseil off.

Contraband   15m   E6   6b/c   ***
M.Crocker, R.Thomas 1988
A masterpiece of technical intricacy up the centre of the sheer

wall. Devise and execute the long sequence necessary to gain a superb hold at half height. Continue directly on better holds and then easily RW to a tree. (3 PR's, 2 BR's).

The following routes are R of a waterfall. There is an obvious groove (Exhumation Corner) marking this section.

Boston Strangler   21m E5 6b
M.Crocker, R.Thomas † Patch 1991
Sleek climbing L of Exhumation Corner. Climb the corner for 7m. Step L onto the fine sheer wall, PR, and gain a good ledge. Climb the centre of the wall, 2BR's, and finish by a finger traverse, NR, to an abseil station or easier direct to a weak tree.

Exhumation Corner   21m E3 5c
R.Thomas, M.Learoyd 1989
Start at the obvious cleaned corner. Climb ledges and the corner until it is possible to step L. Lower off.

Expense Account   21m E3 5c
R.Thomas, M.Learoyd 1989
Climb the centre of the wall R of Exhumation Corner until it is possible to step L and lower off. (3PR's,1BR)

Balance Sheet   24m E3 5c
M.Learoyd, R.Thomas 1989
Start below the obvious steep groove in the lower wall. Climb it and follow the flake crack to a ledge. Climb the final groove in the arete to an exit RW and tree belays.

THE UPPER TIER
The upper walls are best approached by taking a small track up the LH ridge which winds its way above the western walls of the lower quarry. The track levels out and passes beneath impressive walls. The first recognisable feature is a very steep green tower, split by a crack high up. To the immediate R is a chossy corner and small retaining wall and arete. R of this rounded arete is a good steep wall with a groove on the R.

SMALL WALLS AREA
A series of walls immediately before the green tower

Once Bitten   13m   E1   5c
R.Thomas, M.Crocker 1991
Climb easily to a small ledge at the base of the wall, up this, 3 BR's to a tree lower off.

7m R and up through some trees is another small wall.

Hollow Feeling   13m   E2   5c
M.Learoyd, R.Thomas 1991
Climb the rattling L arete of the wall to a BB. 2 BR, 1PR.

Practice What You Preach   13m   E3   5b
M.Crocker, R.Thomas 1991
Start from the same patch of jungle and climb the centre of the wall to the same lower off.

7m R is a wall

You Change Me   30m   E4   6a
M.Crocker 1991
Gain a small footledge below the smooth lower part of the slab from the L or R. A delicate step up, BR, leads to undercuts and a thin crack on the L, climb over a bulge and continue direct to jugs, BR, PR. Move up and R to a footledge, continue boldly up the scoop above and exit onto the arete. Scramble to the top.

3m R is a prominent tower.

Torch The Earth   26m   E5   6b/c
M.Crocker, R.Thomas 1991
A direct line up the centre of the L wall of the tower. Start below the arete. Climb a borehole, TR, and the slabs above to a flake top ledge below the wall. Take a ragged crack, 2PR's, and a protruding flake to gain a resting position on the L. Swing L onto the headwall and climb it until an undercut move leads to finger holds and an abseil station above. 3 BR's.

Dirty As A Dog   26m   E2   5c
R.Thomas, G.Royle, M.Learoyd 1991
Climb to the flake top, as for Torch The Earth, then move R onto the arete. Follow cracks in the arete to a prow, PR. Swing L over the roof, PR, and continue up the wall with difficulty, BR, to a BB.

Desert Storm   26m   E5   6a   ***
M.Crocker, R.Thomas 1991
Start on the RH wall of the tower. Climb a short groove and then a sustained line up the lower wall, 3 BR's, to reach a resting place in a niche in the central crackline. Follow the crack, 2 PR's to a jug on the R, drilled PR. Swing back L and pull up the final wall to reach a BB.

R of the grotty corner bounding the RH side of the tower is a sheer face.

Twenty Second Chance   20m   E4   6c
M.Crocker, R.Thomas 1991
The blunt LH arete. BR, PR.

Sixty Second Go See   20m   E4   6b
M.Crocker, R.Thomas 1991
Fingery climbing on good rock. climb the centre of the black
facet to the R of the arete,2 BR's, to a junction with Roaring
Forties.

Roaring Forties   21m   E3   5c
R.Thomas, J.Bullock 1989
This climb takes a line up the L side of the steep wall. Climb a
flaky crack, BR, and make hard moves using small incuts to gain
a flake, PR. Move up L, PR, to gain a thin crack. Follow this, PR,
to gain a lower off point.

Between The Lines   21m   E3   5c
R.Thomas, G.Royle. 1989.
Start as for Roaring Forties. Move R into the centre of the wall,
climb direct until it is possible to move L to the lower off point
of Roaring Forties, 2PR's, 1BR.

Dirty Day Out   21m   E3   5c
J.Bullock, R.Thomas 1989
Climb the dirty groove, 3PR, 1BR, to the R to a single lower off
point. (Abseil rope back-up advised).

Saboo   21m   E3   5b
M.Learoyd 1989
Climb the middle of the steep wall 5m R of Dirty Day out, to a
ledge. Climb the obvious groove to a small roof which is sur-
mounted on the R Lower off. 3 PR's.

R of a damp corner is an arete directly behind a solitary birch tree.

Blinded By Love   24m   E4   5c   **
R.Thomas, G.Royle, M.Learoyd 1991
Climb the arete, PR, to a small ledge system. Move up the steep
wall, PR, then go R onto the upper arete, BR. Continue up this,
2PR's to gain a flake on the R. The easier but run out top section
leads to a tree.

Aptitude Test   13m   E3   6a
M.Crocker 1991
The blunt green arete 6m R, 2 BR's.

To the R is a slabby wall, an old quarry spike can be seen projecting from the top, and a pile of debris lies below (from the
original exploration!).

You Are What You Is   21m   E3   6a   **
G.Barker, R.Trevitt 1989
An excellent climb, with some lo . . . ng reaches, rapidly losing

any of its remaining loose rock. Follow a line of cleaned holds and ledges up the R side of the slab to an interesting finish onto a grass ledge. Abseil off. 2 PR's, 3 BR's.

NORTHERN WALLS
In the lower NW corner of the quarry is a massive 45m buttress dominated centrally by a vertical crack and bounded on its L by a superb arete. Approach the routes by turning R into the quarry and following a faint track below the western wall and around the outside of the swamp.

The Caerphilly Contract   45m E5 6a,6b   **
M.Crocker, R.Thomas, M.Ward 1988
A route of great character with a particularly steep, exposed and generally mind-blowing second pitch. Well protected but do not pull too hard on the holds on the first pitch. Start as for The Expansionist.
1   27m 6a. Climb the groove for 6m to a large PR and swing L to a rib, climb the rib, BR, and then its LH side, NR, PR, to ledges, PR. Gain a shallow groove in the rib, PR, swing out L onto the leaning wall, BR, and climb it to a small slab. BB.
2   18m 6b. Climb the impending wall R of the now well sculptured! arete, PR, to a good undercut on the arete, PR. Make a very difficult sequence back up R, BR, and continue rather frenetically past 2PR's to better holds and the top of the arete. Scramble up the grass ledge past a stake. Walk off RW.

Little White Lies   45m E4 6a,6b   *
M.Crocker, R.Thomas 1988
Fine, steep wall climbing up the exposed face between The Expansionist and The Caerphilly Contract.
1   27m 6a. Climb pitch 1 of The Caerphilly Contract to the twin bolt belay.
2   18m 6b. Step R to a short groove and pull over a bulge onto the wall. Go straight up the wall with a particularly stubborn move to gain a good horizontal slot. Continue direct on better holds to and awkward exit onto a short slab. 5 PR's, 1 BR. BB abseil.

The Expansionist   45m E3 5b   *
P.Littlejohn, J.Harwood, C.Horsefield 1978
The original climb of the cliff. A serious groove and an excellent crack in the upper buttress, that is also accessible via pitch 1 of The Caerphilly Contract if the state of the lower section repels. Start at a small groove in the L arete of a corner, below and L of the crackline. Climb the groove, bear R into a corner and move up to the overhang, PR. Pull over to another groove leading to a shale band. Traverse R to large dubious flakes and the wide crack line (possible belay). Climb the crack to the top. Belay well back. Scramble up to belay as for the previous route.

EASTERN WALLS

This is the low wall gradually increasing in height as it runs SE from the quarry entrance above the swamp. On entering the quarry turn R where the first ridge meets the quarry floor. Scramble through the bushes to a pool; behind the pool is a prominent corner and rounded rib and to its L an unusual bulging wall up which Slip Into Something Sexy forces its way.

Slip Into Something Sexy   18m E5 6b   *
M.Crocker, R.Thomas 1989
A forceful pitch with some poor gear. Clamber up ledges to the wall L of a vegetated corner PR. Climb up the centre of the wall to finish at a tree. Abseil. 2BR's, 1PR, 1NR.

Slipping Into Luxury   18m E2 5c   *
M.Ward, G.Jenkin, R.Thomas, M.Crocker 1988
Well protected edge pulling. Start just to the R of the vegetated corner and just L of the arete. Climb the initial wall to jugs then move to the arete and continue finishing at an abseil point. 4BR's, 1PR.

Sadness   24m   E1   4c
G.Jenkins, R.Thomas 1988
Poor rock, but an attractive line. Climb the open groove to the R of Slipping Into Luxury to a ledge, PR, TR. Step onto the R side of a groove and continue to a second ledge, BR. Pull carefully onto a smaller ledge above. Move R, PR, TR, to better holds leading to the safety of a tree. Good belay up L.

PENALLTA OS ref 138952
T.Penning

SITUATION AND CHARACTER

Set on the hillside overlooking Ystrad Mynach it is natural Pennant sandstone of a generally firm nature and is a very popular venue for the lower grade climber.

APPROACHES AND ACCESS

See map 3. The crag is situated at Ystrad Mynach and can be seen behind the National Coal Board Computer Centre, on the Ystrad Mynach to Nelson road (A427).
When approaching from Ystrad Mynach, pass under the railway bridge (visible from either direction), take the first R after the bridge, (or if coming from Nelson, the L turning just before the bridge) into a housing estate. Take the first L again into Griffith Street and park on a rough road at the end of the street, on the R. A well worn path now leads up to the R end of the crag (5 mins.).
Almost in the centre of the crag are two large amphitheatres about 6m up, with a massive pinnacle dividing them. L of the L amphitheatre, the cliff is undercut at its base.

At the extreme LH end of the crag is a short arete leading to a ledge, and a crack in the wall above. The first climb takes this arete.

Limbo   15m   VS   4c
Climb the arete without any real protection to the ledge. Continue up the crack on the L to finish.

Cornflake   8m   HVS   4c
This short climb takes the wall just R of the arete.

Afterthought   15m   VS   4b
A poor route, which climbs the obvious, overgrown corner to the overhang before moving L to finish up the crack above.

Cadet's Route   12m   VD
Climb the wall to the R of the corner and exit via a crack in the wall above.

The Wolery   12m   S
I.Jones
Start just L of a huge boulder at a crack beneath a holly tree. Climb the wall L of the crack past the tree to a chimney. Finish up the slab on the L.

Spiny Norman   13m   VS   4b
I.Jones
Start on the huge boulder. Pull over the overhang moving R and then up to a ledge. Traverse L and finish up the chimney.

Y-Fronts   20m   S
I.Jones
Around the arete to the R of the boulder is a corner with a large white streak. Climb the corner by the Mensa members VD move then traverse L under the overhang to a ledge. This point can be reached by climbing the bulge to the L of the corner at about 5b. Walk L to the chimney and climb this to the top.

Split Crotch Variation and Continuation   18m   E1   5b   *
C.Hurley 1978
Interesting climbing. Climb the corner of Y Fronts and the overhanging crack above to a ledge . Traverse L a metre and then climb the wall above to a sloping finish.

Maginot Line   9m   E1   5b
S.Lewis
Immediately R is a short arete. Climb the arete for a metre before making a diagonal traverse L into the overhanging crack up which the climb finishes. The wall just L of the arete can also be used to start this climb, but is desperate.

Klingon 8m E2 5c
S.Lewis 1976
This takes the short arete direct to a hard finish, unprotected.

Eeyore's Gloomy Place 15m VD
I.Jones
Start in the corner to the R of the short arete. Climb the corner
and then the chimney on the R in the L amphitheatre.

Pinnacle Chimney 15m D
Start below a tree growing out of the L amphitheatre, just R of the
corner. Climb up past the tree and finish up the chimney above.

Dinsdale 15m S
I.Jones
Start at the crack line to the R of the tree on Pinnacle Chimney.
Climb it into the L amphitheatre, and continue up the crack in the
wall above.

Too Risky 13m HVS 4c
T.Penning
Start at the crack as for Dinsdale. Climb the crack for 5m to the
obvious break. Traverse R above the bulge to a ledge and then
climb up to the ledge above.

The next two climbs start in the L amphitheatre above the start of
Eeyores Gloomy Place.

Hell for Pleasure 9m E1 5b
C.Court
Climb the L wall of the amphitheatre, in its centre, to the top.

Sheer Pleasure 9m E1 5b
T.Penning
This climb takes the LH wall of the pinnacle which forms the R
wall to the L amphitheatre. Start on the L side of the wall and
climb up and then R across the wall.

Stiches n' Scars 12m E5 6b
M.Crocker, R.Thomas 1989
Gymnastic roof climbing. Start just L of Scabs. Move up to the
roof and surmount it, PR, to gain the break, then climb the wall to
the large platform. Effectively eliminates Too Risky.

Scabs 12m E3 5b   *
P.Littlejohn solo 1982
A good climb with no protection, taking the obvious bulging wall
to R of the crack of Dinsdale, and just L of a boulder.

Shriekback   12m   E5   6a
A very strenuous climb taking the overhang just R of Scabs and directly above the boulder.

Shag Rat   21m   E1   5b
P.Thomas 1976
Start about 5m to the R of the large overhang, at a rock ledge. Climb the wall on pockets into the L side of the RH amphitheatre. Continue up the wall just R of the pinnacle's arete, to the top.

The next five climbs start in the R amphitheatre, easily reached by a short crack directly beneath it.

The Last Waltz   8m   D
Traverse L on the pinnacle face to the arete and climb this to finish.

Bold Finger   10m   HVS   5a
A strenuous climb up the short overhanging crack, on the R side of the L wall. A nice struggle to finish.

The Sighting   9m   VS   4c
This climb takes the crack in the back of the amphitheatre, just L of a corner.

The Gibbon   9m   S   4a/b
Some suspect rock on this climb which follows the corner at the back of the amphitheatre.

Sheer Hell   9m   E2   5b   *
J.Harwood
An enjoyable climb up the middle of the R wall of the amphitheatre.

Sennapod   22m   HS   4b
L.Parsons, I.Jones
A worthwhile climb. start at the short crack leading into the R amphitheatre. Climb to a ledge on the R, beneath an overhang. Climb the overhang and then the arete above to the top.

The Horticulturalist   22m   S
Start at a short crack 5m R of the short crack leading into the R amphitheatre. Climb the crack to a ledge and then the wall above to another ledge. Continue to a tree, traverse R and climb the arete, to finish.

The Herbiculturalist   22m   S
P.Watkin
Start just R of the short crack of the Horticulturalist. Climb the wall to a ledge, move L over a bulge and then up to a large ledge. Continue up the corner above, finishing L or R at the top.

Free Wall   22m   S
I.Jones
Nice climbing. Start just L of the obvious flake crack (Devils in Hell). Climb the wall to a ledge and then pull over the bulge to another ledge. Bear R to a large ledge (the Prow), and climb the corner above finishing L or R.

Devils in Hell   22m   VD   *
A popular climb. Start at the obvious flake crack. Climb the crack to a large ledge at the top of the Prow. Continue up the corner to a move R at its top.
Direct Finish 22m VS *: From the large ledge climb the wall directly above the Prow to the top.

Western Roll/Free World   27m   HVS   5b   *
G.Lewis 1975
Good steep climbing. Start just R of the obvious flake crack.
Climb the wall to a horizontal break, pull over the bulge on its L and continue up the wall to a large ledge. From the L end of this pull over a small overhang to the large roof. Swing out R and climb to the top.

Aaron the Amorous Aardvark   18m   S   4a
I.Jones
Worthwhile if only for the stomach traverse. Start at a short wall below the L of twin overhanging cracks.Climb the wall to the break and stomach traverse L into a crack (Devils in Hell). Climb the crack for 5m, then move R on a diagonal crack. Continue up to a sloping ledge and then move R to a large ledge.

Pushover   18m   VS   4b
This climb takes the LH of the twin overhanging cracks. Climb the crack to a ledge. Step L and continue up the corner crack to the large ledge.

The Pusher   18m   HVS   4c   *
I.Jones
This climb takes the R of the twin overhanging cracks. Climb the crack to a ledge. Step R and climb the crack above to the large ledge.

Alley Crack   18m   S   4a   **
M.McMahon
This takes the LH of two obvious cracks at the RH end of the cliff. Climb the layback crack just R of The Pusher and then move R over a bulge into the crack. Climb it to the large ledge.

Alley Oop   18m   S   4a   **
This takes the RH crack. Start in the centre of a short wall directly below the crack. Climb the wall to the RH crack and follow this to the large ledge.

The Flying Fonzarelly   5m   E2   5b   *
Follow the line of old BR's and PR's through the roof from the large ledge.

Thin Chimney Finish   5m   HVS   4c
The masochists way to the top from the large ledge. Pull over the chimney and squirm to the top. Fun to watch from the top.

Gigglers' Arete   18m   E1   5b
J.Harwood
Climb the arete R of Alley Oop, to a move R or L at its top, just below a small tree. Protection in Alley Oop at this grade.

The Higher the Fewer   51m   VS   4c
I.Jones
A good traverse, from R to L, with a nice finale across the R wall of the R amphitheatre. Start at the R end of the crag beneath the RH crack of Alley Oop.
1   40m Climb a short wall to a ledge beneath the crack, and then traverse L to the arete, before moving L again in a corner. Continue to large tree, then climb up to a large ledge and belay. **2**   21m Climb up to a holly tree and then traverse L across the R wall of the R amphitheatre to a corner (The Gibbon). Climb the corner to finish.

A low level girdle at 5c is worthwhile, from the Y-Fronts' area to Alley Oop.

DERI CRAG OS ref 129012
R.Thomas

SITUATION AND CHARACTER
A small sandstone quarry overlooking a pleasant valley. It contains a small number of good quality routes.

APPROACHES AND ACCESS
See map 3. The crag can be seen on the hillside when approaching Deri from Bargoed. (See Bargoed Quarry for more details). The easiest way to approach the crag is via Heolddu Comprehensive School (in Bargoed). Go over the first cattle grid then R over another grid, then L. Follow the road for approx half a mile to a stile on the R. Park here.
The crag can be reached in a few minutes by following the foot path then contouring R along the hillside.
The first climb takes the obvious overhanging arete in the centre of the quarry.

Kicking Ass and Taking Names   15m   E5   6a/b   **
A.Sharp, P.Lewis et al 1989
A superb arete, strenuous and technical, with ample fixed protec-

tion. Gain the arete from the R and continue up the R side via long moves to a good ledge. An easy 3m remains. Belay on the platform.

R of the arete is a leaning wall having a rounded arete and at its R end a fine crack.

Menages A Chien   12m   E5   6b   *
M.Crocker, R.Thomas 1989
Great climbing. Very strenuous, with a big reach at the crux. Climb the lower wall firstly on jugs and then with more difficulty, PR, to an obvious slot. Span L for the arete, PR, and climb it exiting LW over the capping roof.

Troilism Trouble   12m   E2   5c   *
R.Thomas, M.Crocker 1989
Start in the dirty corner crack and step L into the obvious steep jam crack (or climb direct at 5c). Continue steeply to the top.

THE DARREN (LAN QUARRY) OS ref 072 912
G.Lewis
"Win without boasting, lose without excuse"
A.P.Terhune

SITUATION AND CHARACTER
The cliff is situated above Pontypridd in pleasant woodland surroundings. The rock is fairly sound Pennant Sandstone. Although the cliff may be of little interest to climbers visiting South East Wales, it is important for local climbers, particularly for afternoons and evenings.

APPROACHES AND ACCESS
See map 3. From Cardiff or Merthyr Tydfil take the Ynysybwl exit from the A470. Drive into the centre of Pontypridd (first signposted Town Centre then Graigwen), to St. Catherine's Church. Turn R just before the church, (again signposted Graigwen), and follow the road over a metal bridge before turning R, then L (signposted White Rock Estate) to reach Graigwen Place at the top of a short road. Turn L into Graigwen Place, then take the first R and follow the road up the hill before turning R into White Rock Avenue. Take the first L again into Lanwood Road. Park about 50 yards up on the L at a path way between a bungalow and a house. Follow the path through a swing gate then follow the RH fork for a few minutes to a bay at the end of the cliff.

LEFT HAND BAY
This is the rather gloomy bay on the L. At the back on the L is a corner and L of this is a steep blank wall.

Striking Twelve   11m   E3   6a
A.Sharp, P.Harding, A.Forster 1989
Climb the wall. 1 PR.

Midnight Express   13m   E2   5b
G.Lewis, T.Penning 1980
Climb the corner for 3m. Step L and climb the crack above.

New Sensations   13m   HVS   4c
T.Penning, J.Harwood 1982
Climb the corner direct.

Uphill Walker   13m   VS   4b
T.Penning, G.Lewis 1980
Start just L of an overhang on the back wall of the bay. Climb the groove and cracks above to the top.

Sheik Yerbouti   13m   E1   5b
P.Harding, A.Forster, A.Sharp 1989
Climb the crack and overhang R of Uphill Walker.

Trillian Crack   13m   HVS   5a
H.Griffiths, G.Lewis, C.Heard 1980
Climb the obvious crack R of the overhang of Sheik Yerbouti.

Behind the Bike Shed   12m   E4   5c
A.Forster (solo) 1989
Climb the "well cleaned" slab R of Trillian Crack.

CENTRAL BAY
The small central bay.

Lotta Bottle   6m   E3   6a
A.Sharp 1982
The crack in the L wall of the central bay, gained from the L.

Smack   9m   E3   6a
A.Sharp, P.Lewis 1989
Climb the arete to the R of Lotta Bottle, 1PR.

Hear No Evil, See No Evil   20m   VS   4c
G.Lewis, S.Mundy, J.Card 1980
Climb the groove at the back of the bay.

Reach For The Sky   23m   E2   5b   *
C.Heard, G.Lewis 1980
Start at the R of the bay. Climb to a slab via a flake, which is climbed to a ledge. Follow the flake crack on the R to finish.

THE RIGHT HAND BAY
This is more imposing, and flanked on the L by The Terminal Overhanging wall and on the R by BAT wall.

Enter The Darren 18m E4 6a *
P.Lewis, A.Sharp 1989
The best route up the wall. Climb the slabby arete to finish strenuously up a big crack, 1PR.

Rise 18m E5 6a/b
A.Forster, P.Harding 1989
The obvious line in the middle of the wall. Climb to a PR at 9m. Hard moves lead to a niche, move R, PR, BR on the L. Finish up the wall with difficulty.

Arizona Stan 18m E6 6b *
A.Sharp, P.Lewis 1990
A strenuous route. Start 5m R. A difficult pull up an arete leads to good holds, continue desperately until a short traverse L leads to a PB, 2BR's, 4 PR's

Alive and Kicking 18m E5 6a
T.Penning, J.Harwood 1989
Climb a thin crack to the R of a triangular block to a good break. Hard moves, BR, NR, lead to a niche and an easy finish up the obvious crack.

BAT WALL
The RH groove seamed wall.

Autumn Leaves 24m E3 6a
T.Penning, J.Harwood 1990
Climb the slab and corner L of Sorry Lorry Morry, stepping L onto an arete to finish, 2PR's.

Sorry Lorry Morry 23m E3 6a *
G.Lewis, M.Harber, L.Foulkes, S.Blackman (La Grande Cruise) 1982
A.Sharp, P.Lewis 1989
This replaces a more wandering line. Climb the LH of 2 obvious grooves, then the wall and crack directly above. 3 BR's. Lower off a tree.

Juvenile Justice 23m E4 6b/c *
A.Sharp, P.Lewis 1989
This climbs the bald slab R of Sorry Lorry Morry, with a very hard start. 3BR's. Lower off a tree.

Boulevard De Alfred Turner (1926) 23m VS 4c **
G.Lewis, H.Griffiths 1981

Climb the groove in the centre of the wall with an inscription at the bottom to a tree then R and up a crack to finish.

Alfred's Variation   23m   VS   4c
T.Penning, P.Cresswell 1981
Climb Boulevard De Alfred Turner to the tree, step L and climb the crack direct.

Andrew The Zebra   23m   E1   5b   *
G.Lewis, C.Heard, S.Robinson 1981
Start at a white Z painted on the wall 3m R of Boulevard De Alfred Turner. Climb the wall via two ledges, then a bulge on the R. Finish up the crack above.

Calling Card   23m   E3   6a
T.Penning, A.Sharp, P.Lewis 1990
Climb a crack on the LH side of a pillar. Hard moves, 2PR's, lead to a small ledge. Climb the crack above.

Stow Crack   18m   HVS   5a
G.Lewis, C.Heard 1980
The obvious flake crack on the R side of the wall. Gain the crack from the R and finish on the wall above.

The wall terminates in a very steep arete.

Shaken But Not Stirred   E4   6a
A.Sharp, P.Lewis 1989
The wall L of the arete, BR, PR, to a tree.

Madame X   E4   6b
A.Sharp, P.Lewis 1989
The arete, BR, PR, to a tree.

Antelope Migration   36m   HVS   4c
T.Penning, G.Lewis 1981
A Girdle of Bat Wall from R to L. Start at the short arete on the R of the wall. Climb to the arete using blocks on the R for 6m, then traverse L to a flake crack. Climb this to ledges and traverse across L to a tree. Step L and climb the crack to a hole, then traverse L to a small tree and finish up the groove above.

THE NAVIGATION QUARRY OS ref 090935
G.Lewis
"If they invent a glue that will hold me, I will use that aswell"
C.Maestri

SITUATION AND CHARACTER
This sheltered, sunny quarry is hidden from view, on Cilfynydd

Common. Its seclusion may be one of the reasons for the profusion of graffiti. Kestrels have nested in the quarry for several years and their nests should be avoided between March and August. Most of the climbs follow steep slabs where protection is well spaced and there are some brittle holds, although these become less as its popularity increases. Climbers should stick well within their grades on these less well protected lines. Assorted belays are to be found on the top but you may have to search for them. Notwithstanding the comments just made, it is an excellent place to climb.

APPROACHES AND ACCESS
See map 3. From Cardiff take the A470 to the turning signposted Abercynon. At the top of the slip-road turn L. Go a short way down the road to the Navigation Inn; do a U turn and drive back up to a set of traffic lights leading on to the old road. Turn R and park in a lay-by a short distance along this road on the L. Walk back up the road to the traffic lights; go through a gate on the R which opens onto an old road. Walk along this road (above the parking place) until it disappears into gorse bushes. From here a narrow path with some old cables protruding from it, leads up onto an incline leading onto The Common. Follow the incline for about 100 m until the quarry entrance is visible on the L, between some tips.

At the LH side of the quarry is a right-angle corner with NOG written at the bottom.

Leftover 21m VS 4c
G.Lewis, S.Blackmore 1989
Climb a groove at the LH end of the L wall to an arete finish.

3m L of NOG is the start of two climbs:

Expanded Mole Groove 21m HVS 5a
G.Lewis, C.Hurley 1984
Climb past a niche, then move L into a grass bay. Climb the LH groove and crack to finish.

Gold Block 21m E2 5b   *
G.Lewis, M.Learoyd 1984
Variation G Lewis (solo) 1984
A good climb. Climb up to a small groove at 5m, TR. Gain the arete above and climb it direct (no protection) to a ledge at 15m. Finish up a steep groove and crack to the L.
Variation: Kestrel Groove HVS 4c: From the ledge at 15m move R to ledges then back L to finish.

To the R of NOG is a frequently wet wall topped by a large grass ledge at three quarter height. Above this is a short, clean wall sporting a prominent overhang. Here lurks a little meany:

The Elastic Retreat   9m   E4   6b   *
G.Barker (unseconded) 1989
Gain the ledge either by abseil or from Squash Match. Belay at a
thin RW slanting crack. Climb straight up the centre of the wall,
PR, to the overhang. Pull up (good protection in pockets) to reach
some micro edges and crank for the top.

Code of the Road   21m   E1   5a
M.Learoyd, C.Hurley 1984
An interesting pitch with an awkward finish. Climb the blunt nose
directly above the words LEGIN GRIFF. Gain the RH crack, PR, and
climb to the grass ledge. Climb the stepped corner on the LH side
of the ledge then a RW slanting crack. Finish directly.

Rock Over Beethoven   21m   E2   5b
B.Brewer 1988
From a ledge 2m L of the words WALLY make some thin moves,
then go up the slab with a rock-over to finish. Finish up Squash
Match. Poor protection.

Where Did You Get That Bolt   22m   E3   6b
A.Sharp, P.Lewis 1989
Just above the words WALLY is a BR. Gain the prominent pocket
below the BR, use a no. 4 trampoline to dyno for a big hold (yes
that one!) and continue more easily, but with no protection, up
the slab to join the Squash Match finish.

Squash Match   22m   E2   5b   *
G.Lewis, M.Learoyd, L.Foulkes 1983
Start above THE ANT. A good slab climb which has suffered from
the peg thieves, and is at present badly protected. Gain an
obvious hole at 3m and follow a vague crackline to easier ground
below a V groove to the L. Move up to the grass ledge, walk L, PR,
then climb back up R into a scoop and an easy finish.

Geeny   22m   E2   5b
G.Lewis, G.Barker 1989
Worthwhile, apart from an easily handled loose band at 13m.
Climb straight up the pleasant slab directly above GEENY to a
ledge. Follow the shallow groove above, BR, to the loose band
(Friends above) and finish up the excellent top wall just R of a
prominent R angled groove.

Death Wish   22m   E2   5b
M.Learoyd (solo) 1984
Not as dangerous as it sounds. A side runner in the first crack of
Fly Me To The Moon is needed at this grade. Climb the blunt
arete above the words NOG JOHNNY with a hard move at 8m.
Continue to the loose band, then take the steep wall above on
superb jugs.

Fly Me To The Moon 22m HVS 5a **
G.Lewis, S.Blackman 1982
Excellent. Climb the wide crack L of CHOC MAVNIC to gain a
ramp. Move up to the loose band then swing up the headwall on
superb holds.

Man Or Mouse 22m E4 6b *
A.Sharp, P.Lewis 1989
Fiercely thin, but with protection where it counts. Climb the
blank slab 2m R of CHOC MAVNIC, BR, to a shaley ledge. Con-
tinue up the sustained slab above with a long reach to clip a BR.
Finish up the wall above.

Let Me Play Among The Stars 24m E2 5c *
G.Lewis, S.Blackman, C.Heard 1982
An entertaining pitch with a stubborn crux. Start below two paral-
lel cracks at a short crack. Follow the crack to the shaley ledge
(Friends in large pockets). Climb the RH crack, BR, to a ledge.
Climb direct, passing three boreholes to move across the overlap
above.

Black Magic 24m E3 5c
A.Forster 1988
A vague line which makes use of the rock between the previous
route and Ladybird. Climb the thin crack next to IAN, PR, and go
up a short wall to a ledge at 6m. Continue directly passing 2
horizontal breaks, PR, to finish just L of the overhang.

The remaining climbs have belays on the short back wall (2 BR,
SB, PB, near the edge at the top of Eastern Bloc. Various wires also
offer back-ups.

Ladybird 25m E3 5c *
L.Foulkes, G.Lewis 1983
A good pitch which traces the line of least resistance up an
uncompromising wall. Start above STEVE PLOD. Climb to a horizontal slot, then to a ledge, (BR can be lassoed). Move diagonally
LW, PR, up a ramp/crack, an awkward move gains a PR and
ledges. Move back RW, PR, and finish up the shallow groove to
the R.

Totally Relaxed 25m E4 6a/b *
A.Richardson, G.Lewis (Relax)1984
M.Learoyd, G.Lewis 1988
This replaces a more wandering line. A good climb but escapable.
Start just R of Ladybird. Gain a vague layback crack, BR, then
directly to a ledge, Friend 3, PR. Difficult moves up, BR, lead to a
resting ledge. Climb to the bulge then swing L to a slot just below
the top. A strong pull finishes the job.

Western Front   24m   E4   6a   *
M.Learoyd, G.Lewis 1983
A strenuous problem in a fine position. Now superseded, but
worth doing as the original solution before bolts. Climb a groove
between JIMMY and SPUD. Go up easily RW, PR's missing, to a
ledge. Move back LW above the overhangs passing a hole to
climb a crack in the headwall, PR. Finish at a small tree.

Western Front Direct   25m   E5   6b   ***
M.Crocker, R.Thomas 1988
The superb modern solution. As for Western Front for 8m then
gain a small ledge on the L below a roof, PR. Make hard moves
over it, BR, and join the crack of the original route.

Tears For Smears   28m   E1   5b
G.Lewis, R.East 1984
A wandering line starting just R of Western Front. Climb to the
missing PR's! move RW and continue onto the ledge of Let Me
Know What Life Is Like. Climb its corner for 6m until on the arete.
Traverse R to finish up the arete by The Owl & The Antelope.

Eastern Bloc   24m   E5   6b/c   **
M.Crocker, R.Thomas 1988
Steep and technical but safe, the prudent will carry two Friend 2's.
Start just L of SPUD. Climb steeply to reach a small slab and
continue to a large spike runner. Pull up over the small overhang
to reach the slot on Western Front. Now proceed straight up the
headwall on small edges, 2 BR's. The final overhang on monster
holds makes a spectacular finish.

Goblin Girl   25m   E3   6a   *
G.Barker, G.Lewis 1989
A short, sustained sequence up the slim groove R of Eastern Bloc.
Start at Ol NOG, climb the arete to the tree and then into a
groove above, gain the niche to the L and then a ledge. Do not
climb the corner above but move L into a groove. Climb this, PR,
to an overhang, BR, pull round it and accelerate to the top.

Let Me Know What Life Is Like   24m   HVS   5b   **
G.Lewis, S.Blackman 1982
A fine introduction to the cliff. As for Goblin Girl to the ledge at
15m then continue up the steep corner (crux) onto the arete and
then back L to finish.

Evening Light   24m   E3   5c
G.Lewis, H.Griffiths 1984
Exposed. Start below the arete R of Let Me Know What Life Is Like.
Gain the arete above the tree and climb up the edge, PR low
down. (a number of PR's were stolen after the first ascent at E2).

Save A Mouse Eat A Pussy   25m   E2   5c
G.Lewis, G.Barker 1989
An entertaining problem requiring the use of an excitingly dubious hold. The BR is fortunately close by. Start up Evening Light to
the PR, then directly up the scoop on its R, BR, over the bulge and
finish directly.

The Owl And The Antelope   26m   E2   5b
G.Lewis, C.Heard, M.Learoyd 1983
The route of the crag. Superb, climbing up a magnificently positioned slab. Start at a groove 2m R of OL NOG. Climb up a small V
groove to ledges leading R to the roofs. Climb to a small hole
directly above a prominent borehole (long thread). Gain the slab
and glide up to a hidden slot and ramp. Gallop up LW to finish up
a shallow groove.

On Jupiter And Mars   28m   HVS   5b   *
G.Lewis, S.Blackman 1982
Another fine route, with technically interesting moves. Well pro-
tected. Climb the R wall of OL NOG to beneath the stepped
roofs. Climb RW under the roofs to a hard move, PR. Continue
RW round the final overhang, large thread, to finish.

Crash Landing   26m   E3   5b
G.Lewis, D.Renshaw 1983
One short difficult section which is unprotected; the rest is easy.
Start 5m R of the stepped roofs below a groove at 6m. Climb the
wall to the ledge and continue L of the groove. Gain a small ledge
at 12m then step R and finish up the slab R of On Jupiter And
Mars.

Ol' Blue Eyes   24m   E2   6a
G.Barker, M.Kidd 1989
A couple of hard moves, but quite a stretch! Safe. Climb directly
up the wall between Crash Landing and Heart-throb, BR. Finish
up the slab just L of a faint crackline.

Heart-throb   21m   E1   5c   *
G.Lewis, D.Hart 1989
A good, technical bridging problem. Short, but worth doing. Start
below the prominent R-facing groove 6m L of a tree the base.
Climb the wall to a ledge below the groove. Make some delicate
moves up the groove, BR, to a ledge on the L. Easier climbing
follows to the top.

Sheepbone Wall   23m   HVS   4c
G.Lewis, M.Learoyd 1983
Start at a tree. Follow a crack/groove with care over a small
overhang to a ledge. Finish up the slabs on the R.

Big Spider Groove   18m   HVS   5a
G.Lewis, L.Foulkes 1983
The obvious cleaned corner directly opposite Sheepbone Wall. At the top move L to finish up the wall.

Acid House Trip   E2   5c   **
G.Lewis, D.Hart, G.Barker 1989
A superb traverse taking in the best situations on the cliff. A good knowledge of the routes is essential to follow the description. Follow Heart-throb until it is possible to move L to the final overhang of On Jupiter And Mars. Make a couple of moves over this to a prominent hole above to the L, Friend 3. Move back down and traverse along the lip of the overhang to the slot on The Owl and The Antelope. Step down to a ledge and traverse round to the BR on Save A Mouse, Eat A Pussy. Swing round the arete at this level on hidden holds to the ledge on Let Me Know What Life Is Like. Belay.

The Gang Of Four   42m   E3   5b   *
M.Learoyd, G.Lewis, C.Pound, T.Jordan 1985
A traverse of the main wall. From the tree on Let Me Know etc, move L to PR's on Tears For Smears, continue up L to a small block, make hard moves on small finger holds to the ledge on Ladybird, 2PR's. Move up and L, PR, then down the crack, PR, on Let Me Play etc. Continue up this route to the ledge, move L and up to finish diagonally L of a vague crack in the headwall.

THE GAP OS ref 080693
R.Thomas

SITUATION AND CHARACTER
This is the obvious square cut notch in the skyline on the W side of the Taff Valley overlooking Quakers Yard. This natural sandstone crag has been quarried in parts and provides a variety of climbing styles, ranging from sandstone walls to "grit like" jamming cracks. Some of the holds are extremely friable and the grades can vary from ascent to ascent. It should however prove to be one of the more popular sandstone crags.

APPROACHES AND ACCESS
See map 3. Although the crag is clearly visible from the A470 (Cardiff to Merthyr road) the easiest approach is not obvious. At the Abercynon/Mountain Ash roundabout take the third exit R and then L at the next roundabout to Quakers Yard. Just before the first set of traffic lights take a narrow L turn over a bridge, go up a steep hill until the road passes over the A470 then immediately right along a single track road. The Lower Quarry is soon visible up to the L. Park in a layby 3 minute walk from the Lower Quarry.

LOWER QUARRY
This is the obvious bowl shaped quarry just above the parking area.

Yikes 9m E4/5 6a
M.Crocker, R.Thomas, M.Learoyd 1990
Weak edges and a potentially long (and stony) tumble will probably render this an unjustifiable 'on sight' lead! Start below a short crack commencing at 4m in the LH wall of the quarry.Climb direct with a giant reach to gain the crack. Go up the crack, PR, to an abseil station.

Just Hanging Around 15m E1 5b   *
R.Thomas, G.Royle 1990
The twin crack in the L side wall is climbed until a move over a small roof leads to a more broken crack and an exit L, 2PR's.

Bluster 14m E3 5c
P.Donnithorne, E.Alsford 1991
Start 3m R of Just Hanging Around, on a grassy mound. Climb up LW, BR, to good holds, move up and RW, BR, to ledges and an abseil point.

The back wall of the quarry has two obvious diagonal cracklines and is bounded on it's R by a startling arete.

Loctite 19m E4/5 6c
A.Sharp, P.Lewis, A.Forster 1989
Start at an obvious earth mound on the L side of the face. Climb the wall desperately, BR, to a rest at the second BR. Move over the overlap and continue up the arete. Lower off.

Land of the Dinosaurs 19m E2 5b   *
R.Thomas, G.Davies, M.Learoyd 1990
A strenuous pitch. Climb the obvious slanting crack 2m R of Loctite to a lower off.

Momentary Lapse of Reason 20m E5 6b/c
A.Forster unseconded 1989
Climb the wall 3m R of Land Of The Dinosaurs to a rounded ledge. Continue more easily to the final overhang, hard moves L past this lead to a lower off. 4 BR's.

Rattle Those Tusks 20m E2/3 5b   *
R.Thomas, M.Learoyd 1990
Start 3m R. Gain a low pod, pull over into a wide jam crack, then climb to a small cave beneath a roof. Exciting moves over the roof, BR, lead to a BB.

The Gap: Lower Quarry

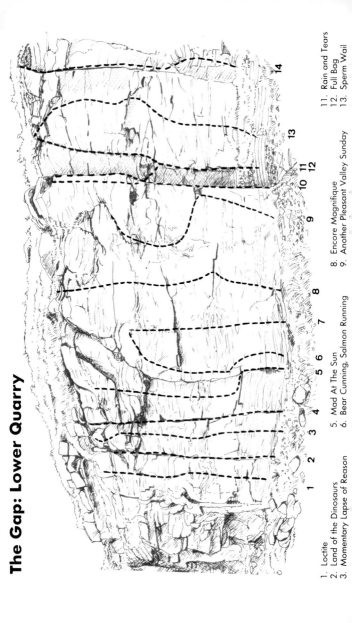

1. Loctite
2. Land of the Dinosaurs
3. Momentary Lapse of Reason
4. Mad At The Sun
5. Mad At The Sun
6. Bear Cunning, Salmon Running
7.
8. Encore Magnifique
9. Another Pleasant Valley Sunday
11. Rain and Tears
12. Full Bag
13. Sperm Wail

Mad at the Sun   21m   E6   6b/c   **
M.Crocker, R.Thomas 1990
A blistering pitch. One of the most difficult on sandstone. Start R of
the second crackline below an overhang capped groove. Climb the
groove, PR, to good holds above the jutting roof. Now follow a
diagonal edge LW, BR, into the centre of the face and boldly pull up
to a superb slot hold, PR. Continue directly up the sustained face,
BR, to the capping roof, BR. Overcome the roof on superb holds,
BR, and continue, NR, to a BB. Abseil.

Bear Cunning, Salmon Running   18m   E4   6a
P.Lewis, A.Sharp 1990
Climb the arete R of the capped groove moving R onto the wall
above, 3BR's. BB to the R.

Anything You Can Do   18m   E6   6b
A.Sharp, P.Lewis 1990
Start 3m R of Bear Cunning. Climb the wall to the same BB, 3 BR's.

Encore Magnifique!   18m   E6   6b   ***
M.Crocker, R.Thomas 1990
A tremendous, sustained pitch at the lower end of its grade.
Perhaps the best in the quarry and possibly on Sandstone. Start 6m
L of a hanging arete. Climb up to and over a thin strip roof.
Continue via a shot hole to twin jugs and a shakeout. Proceed
directly up the wall until a final stiff pull gains the final jug. 4BR's, 1 PR.

Another Pleasant Valley Sunday   18m   E5   6b   **
A.Sharp, P.Lewis 1989
Climb the wall, just L of the hanging arete on the R side of the wall,
direct to a BR. Hard moves L lead to good holds, BR. Continue via a
desperate lay-back, PR, to a lower off.

One Track Mind   18m   E5   6a   *
A.Sharp, P.Lewis 1989
The superb hanging arete. Serious to start but with a well protected
hard move at 6m. Climb the arete to the overlap. Hard moves out R,
PR, and an awkward rockover lead to the final arete which is
climbed easily to the top. TB lower off.

Rain and Tears   18m   E1   5b   *
R.Thomas, M.Learoyd 1990
Climb the striking corner crack R of the arete, 1PR.

Full Bag 18m E2 5b
R.Thomas, M.Learoyd 1990
The obvious cleaned crack 3m R. Start as for Rain and Tears

Sperm Wail   21m   E5/6   6b   *
M.Crocker, R.Thomas 1990

Forceful climbing. Start 5m to the R of Rain and Tears. Climb directly to a large pocket and surmount the bulge slightly RW to good ledges. Pull over the roof and climb the overhanging slab! on tiny holds, 2 drilled PR, to gain better holds leading LW to a final bulge, PR. Abseil station on the L.

Naked Truth   21m   HVS   5a
R.Thomas, G.Royle and a cast of thousands 1990
The crackline 3m R of Sperm Wail.

Perfect Scoundrels   18m   E4   5c
T.Penning, P.Lewis, A.Sharp 1990
Climb the roof of the obvious cave and the arete above, 2PR's, 1TR.

THE NATURAL OUTCROP
This is the obvious skyline buttress up and R of the lower quarry and consists of a jumble of large blocks split by chimneys and short cracks.

RECTANGULAR WALL
This is the first wall seen as one approaches from the lower quarry and has a distinctive rectangular front face.

First There Is A Mountain   8m   E4   5c   *
M.Crocker solo 1990
Start on the R of the unprotected L arete of the rectangular wall and continue by means of a finger pocket on the L.

Then There Is No Mountain   8m   E4/5   6a
M.Crocker solo 1990
The RH arete of the leaning, natural sandstone block. Start in the centre of the wall, trend diagonally RW on fingerholds and reach the arete with difficulty . . . bold!

Next is a small buttress with a prominent overhang.

Juggery Pokery   6m   E3   6a
D.Viggars, P.Donnithorne 1991
Climb the black wall on its R side to the overhang, TR, cross this at its widest point.

R of Juggery Pokery is a hidden descent chimney and then:

TALL STORY WALL

Old Dog   6m   VS   4c
R.Thomas, M.Learoyd 1990
Climb the short jam crack just R of the earthy descent chimney.

New Tricks   7m   E1   5b/c
R.Thomas, M.Learoyd 1990
The steep wall between the jam crack and the green undercling,
1PR, move L to exit.

Tall Story   11m   E2   5c
P.Thomas, T Hall 1987
Climb the shattered rock to the roof, undercling and traverse RW
to gain a chimney and the top.

In Over My Head   11m   E3   6a/b
M.Learoyd, R.Thomas 1990
Start at the obvious rock fang. Climb directly on tiny holds and pull
over the overhang, 3PR's, move R to exit.

Mister Natural   9m   E1   5b
R.Thomas, M.Crocker, M.Learoyd 1990
Climb the bulging crack starting from a shallow hole at its base and
join the chimney of Tall Story.

Surprise Surprise   9m   E2   5b
M.Learoyd, R.Thomas 1990
This takes the crack starting from the R of the shallow hole to gain a
scoop just below the top, PR. Finish direct.

Audio Pornography   9m   E4   5c   *
M.Crocker, M.Learoyd 1990
Superb climbing, well protected above half-height. Start R of the
shallow hole. Climb the centre of the flat quarried wall to reach
good horizontal holds, PR, leading to a sloping mantelshelf exit.

THE UPPER QUARRY
R again, one enters the upper quarry, its L wall has an obvious deep
jamming crack. The following route takes the wall 2m L of this.

Newtons Apple   11m   HVS   5a
R.Thomas, G.Royle 1990
Well protected climbing up the centre of the wall 2m L of the crack.
3PR's.

Dirty Gerty   11m   HVS   4c
G.Royle, J.Bullock et al 1990
Climb the wide jamming crack on the L wall.

Acceleration Due To Gravity   11m   HVS   5a
G.Royle, J.Bullock, R.Thomas 1990
Climb the curved thin crack a metre R of Dirty Gerty.

Tangent   11m   E3   5c
P Thomas solo 1988

Climb the green corner crack, 1PR.

The following four routes take the back RH wall of the quarry.

Scared Seal Banter   12m   E5   6b   **
M.Crocker, R.Thomas, M.Learoyd 1990
An enthralling and unremitting pump up the blank LH side of the
RH wall (The BR's are missing). Stand on stones to reach a jug and
make desperate moves up and slightly LW, BR, to gain a slot, BR.
Now climb directly up the wall on mostly good edges, BR, PR's, to
exit slightly to the R.

The Mastic Mick   12m   E4   6a
M.Crocker, M.Learoyd 1990
Steep climbing with one hard move, immediately L of the off-
width crack. Start as for Scared Seal Banter. Trend RW from the
initial jug to an undercut roof. Crank over the roof, BR, to reach
an enormous pocket. Continue on fairly comforting holds 2PR's,
to exit direct.

Cled's Crack   12m   E2   5c
P.Thomas, T.Hall 1987
Climb the obvious wide crack in the RH wall.

The Grouts Of San Romano   12m   E3   6a   *
M Crocker unseconded 1990
A fine and fingery pitch up the wall R of Cled's Crack. Go up a
steep slab on tiny edges to reach a big jug. Continue up the
headwall, BR, PR, to exit on good holds.

Brush Up   12m   HVS   5a
R.Thomas, J.Bullock, G.Royle 1990
Climb the RH corner crack, 1PR.

Step Up   12m   E1   5b
M.Learoyd, R.Thomas 1990
Climb the thin S shaped crack on the R wall of the quarry, 1PR.

Godfather   12m   E2   5b
G.Lewis, H.Griffiths 1990
Climb the arete, PR, to finish direct.

Up Yours   11m   E1   5b   *
R.Thomas, M.Learoyd, et al 1990
Climb the flying arete R of the upper quarry entrance, 2PR's.

Smoothie   9m   HVS   5c
M.Learoyd, J.Bright, G.Royle 1990
Takes the lower bulge R of Up Yours then takes a central line over
the lip, PR.

Windy Edge   7m   E1   5a
M.Learoyd, R.Thomas 1990
Climbs the obvious arete using the L edge, PR.

On the opposite side of the notch (The Gap) is the following route.

O Solo Mio   7m   HVS   5a
M.Learoyd solo 1990
Climb the short wall on the opposite side of The Gap.

QUAKERS YARD OS ref 090963

Several climbs have been recorded here, but its proximity to the railway line and the presence of an unfriendly householder make it a 'no go area'. The lower part of the cliff has been smeared with axle grease and a 100 lb anvil hangs like a sword of Damocles over a groove line which might have proved the crags main attraction.

MOUNTAIN ASH QUARRY OS ref 057985
G.Lewis

SITUATION AND CHARACTER

Despite the proximity of the industry of Mountain Ash, this quarry is secluded behind oak woodland, it is therefore very difficult to spot from the road. Most of the quarry is rather broken, with terracing breaking up the continuity of walls. However there are a number of unbroken walls which provide some good climbs especially the Whiter Than White Wall. Unfortunately it faces the wrong way, and remains wet for several months of the year. Even so the fine quality of the routes is worth experiencing in the summer months. The other walls face the right way. Not an outstanding crag, but worth a visit.

APPROACHES AND ACCESS

See map 3. The quarry is situated alongside the A4059 Abercynon to Aberdare road. When driving from Abercynon a row of houses on the RH side of the road is the beginning of Mountain Ash. Take the first turning R at these houses, and park in the first row of terraces. There is a small path into the woods and the quarry from the end of this street. Please park considerately; this is a residential area.
Because of its trees it is difficult to get an idea of the situation of the various walls. On the LH side of the quarry there is a natural buttress which can be climbed with good protection in various places. There is a small bay in the centre of the buttress; the first climb takes a crack in the L arete of this bay.

Little Bruiser   8m   E1   5b
Climb the crack and overhang to a tree.

First Orifice   8m   HVS   4c
The crack on the L side of the central bay

Getting Closer   8m   VS   4c
The crack just L of The Fanny.

The Fanny   8m   VD/S
The monster orifice is negotiated to reach a large tree.

The next climb is on the RH side of a small bay.

Another Choss Monster   8m   VD
The groove and slab above to a large tree.

Crockery Pot   8m   VS   4c
Climb the centre of the RH buttress.

Pork Pie Killer   8m   S
The arete just R of the overhangs.

Further R are two bright orange-coloured, S facing walls. The LH
wall has two very steep routes on good rock.

Outspan   12m   E5   6b/c   *
M.Crocker, R.Thomas 1988
The scoop in the L side of the wall provides engrossing climbing.
Climb the scoop directly, but intricately, 2BR's, then scramble to
tree belays above.

Ripe 'n Ready   12m   E4   6b/c   *
M.Crocker 1988
Steep, well-protected climbing up the RH side of the wall. Make
one move up the easy corner and swing L to a good hold on the
wall. (Or gain this point directly - much harder). Move up to a tiny
overlap, pull over (hard if short) and continue straight up the
centre of the headwall to the top.

The RH wall has only one route.

Pastis On Ice   12m   E4   6b   **
M.Crocker, R.Thomas 1988
From a ledge below the RH side of the wall follow a line of jugs in the
centre of the wall to a steepening, PR. A massive reach gains a pocket
and further hard moves must be made up the arete to finish, BR.

The Cut   8m   E2   5c
P.Donnithorne, A.Price 1988
A few metres R is a crack starting on a terrace system. Climb it.

Molybdenum Man   6m   E3   6a
M.Crocker, R.Thomas 1988

Climb the RH side of the short arete, 15m R of Pastis On Ice in the base of the quarry, 1 BR.

Ferndale Revisited 8m E4 6b   *
A.Sharp, P.Lewis 1989
Climb the wall on small holds, BR. Hard moves past a BR lead to a nervous LW finish. Tree belay.

In the centre of the quarry is a sweep of slabs (taken by Narcissi) made obvious by their continuity to the top of the cliff. Immediately L of these slabs is a steep wall defined by a fine arete.

Tragedy 12m E1 5a   *
M.Crocker, M.Learoyd, R.Thomas, P.Lewis 1988
Climb the LH side of the arete exiting RW to tree belays.

The Future Holds 12m E4 6b   *
M.Crocker, R.Thomas 1988
Superb climbing up the centre of the orange wall R of Tragedy. Gaining the pocket at three quarter height is the crux. 2BR's. Abseil off.

Belgium 45m VS 4c
M.Capron, G.Lewis 1987
The groove system bounding the L side of the sweep of slabs. Climb with true pioneering spirit passing several trees.

Narcissi 36m E1 5b   *
G.Lewis, J.Boyle 1987
An excellent pitch. Start directly beneath the prominent V groove at the top of the sweep of slabs next to a R-facing corner.Climb easily up the side of the corner to a borehole in a scoop. Move R, mantleshelf onto a ledge and surmount a bulge above, PR. Step L to a crack and continue straight up to gain a small ledge on the L. Pull over the bulge on it's R and climb the V-shaped groove, exiting RW.

The quarry is bounded at its RH end by the impressive R-angled Sennapod Corner, with the Whiter Than White Wall to its R. To the L of the corner is an unclimbed wall bounded by an arete. Further L the cliff becomes more broken and vegetated, with a corner filled with some particularly savage bushes marking the L end of this bay. 9m R of this corner is a clean, slabby arete.

Homebase 21m E1 5b
G.Lewis, G.Barker 1989
Climb the arete without protection to some ledges. Finish up the steep wall at the top, with better protection.

Little Polvier 21m VS 5a
G.Lewis, A.Keward 1989

Climb the R facing groove between Homebase and Certain Peace to a ledge on the L. Move up to a higher ledge on the R and climb the obvious crack to a tree.

Certain Peace   24m   E2   5c
R.Thomas, M.Crocker 1988
Start below the arete L of Sennapod Corner. Climb a short wall, then swing R onto an arete. Climb it on its front face, BR, PR, to a ledge. Follow the flake crack above to finish up the slab.

Jetlagged   21m   E3   6a
M.Crocker 1990
Start 2m L of Sennapod Corner. Climb straight up passing a sandy pocket and a hard reach, BR, to reach ledges, drilled PR. Finish directly.

Far Cry From Squamish   21m   E4   6a
M.Crocker 1990
The central, LW slanting, crackline in the LH wall of Sennapod Corner. From a sandy recess layback the crack to a ledge, continue pensively up the crack to reach an abseil tree at the top.

Sennapod Corner   27m   HVS   5a   *
P.Thomas, R.Partridge 1970s
Climb the big corner direct.

Whiter Than White Wall   21m   E5   6c   ***
M.Crocker, M.Ward 1988
A brilliant pitch, one of the best hard routes on sandstone. Climb the blank wall R of Sennapod Corner, with an especially long reach to pass a blank section at 9m. Reach R to a tree and lower off. 3 PR's, 1 BR, Friends useful.

A Load of Rubbish   24m   E2   5b   *
A.Richardson, A.N.American 1984
The original route of the wall taking the LH crackline. 4 rusty PR's protect it.

Valleys Initiative   E4   6a/b   *
A.Sharp, P.Lewis 1988
Climb the centre of the wall between A Load Of Rubbish and Ain't As Effical, 2BR's, 2PR's.

Ain't As Effical   21m   E3   5c   *
M.Crocker, M.Ward, G.Jenkin 1988
Sustained climbing, but with adequate protection. More traffic is required to clean up the ledges. Climb the crack R of A Load Of Rubbish.

The Entrepreneur   17m   HVS   5a
M.Ward, M.Crocker, G.Jenkin 1988
Pleasant climbing up the wall 6m to the R of a vegetated corner. 2 PR's and a large oak tree are the landmarks.

PENRHIWCEIBER QUARRY OS ref 053978
P.Donnithorne

SITUATION AND CHARACTER
A small N facing quarry overlooking the Cynon Valley, with nice views of Mountain Ash Quarry.

APPROACHES AND ACCESS
Approach from the A470, take the A4059 and turn L over a railway and river bridge towards Penrhiwceiber, until at the end of the one way system. Turn R at the Mount Pleasant Inn and follow the road up hill to its end. A five minute walk gets you to the crag.
At the LH end of the quarry is a huge vegetated corner, the following route climbs the arete 8m L of the corner.

Pickhead Arete   18m   E1   5a/b
E.Alsford, P.Donnithorne 1991
Start 3m R of the arete. Scramble up ledges LW to the arete, PR. Climb the arete on it's R for 4m then swing round and finish just L of the arete. BB.

Edgewhere   16m   E4   6a/b
P.Donnithorne 1991
Start just R of the large vegetated corner at a blocky corner. Climb the corner for 4m to a grassy ledge. Probe directly up the wall past 3 BR's, then traverse R to PB and BB.

Landfill Project   18m   E3   5c
P.Donnithorne, E.Alsford 1991
As for Edgewhere to the grassy ledge, then traverse R past a PR along a grassy ledge until below BR's. Climb the wall past 2 BR's until a toe traverse LW leads to the belay.

CEFN PENNAR OS ref 034013
M.Learoyd

SITUATION AND CHARACTER
A small crag offering an enjoyable 6m high bouldering wall with numerous problems and a steep compact 11m wall.

APPROACHES AND ACCESS
See map 3. From the village of Mountain Ash turn R at the traffic lights and follow a minor road passing through Cwmpennar. At

Cefnpennar, park in the bus turning circle, one and a half miles from Mountain Ash. The crag is reached along a lane, beneath a radio mast, which ends in a field.

Old Gringo   11m   E1   5b
R.Thomas, M.Learoyd 1989
This takes the series of cracks and pockets on the L side of the wall. Start beneath a ledge at 3m with a crack and groove above and a steep finish.

Pickpocket   11m   E3   6a
M.Learoyd, R.Thomas 1989
Climbs the wall R of Old Gringo, using small pockets, PR. Move R to a crack, PR, and continue, using pockets, to the top.

Root 66   11m   E1   5b
M.Learoyd, R.Thomas 1989
An obvious crack and tree is reached directly using a crack and pocket in the lower wall, PR on the R. Interesting moves gain the sling on a high branch!

Wacka Day   11m   E4   6b
M.Learoyd 1989
An eliminate, keeping to the wall R of Root 66 and avoiding the wider crack on the R. Gain the steep wall using a vertical crack to reach a small ledge, PR on the L. A long reach gains a flake, PR. Continue directly up the wall.

CWMAMAN MAIN and WEST QUARRIES OS ref 998992
R.Thomas

SITUATION AND CHARACTER
These sheltered sunny crags will no doubt become popular with those seeking high grade sandstone climbing. The main attraction is the S facing wall of Cwmaman Main quarry which despite a seepage problem offers good steep rock and solid protection. The N facing slabs on Arete Buttress have excellent routes at their best in the summer months. Described by some as "The jewel in the sandstone crown".

APPROACHES AND ACCESS
See map 3. Cwmaman Quarries are best approached from Aberdare if approaching from the N, and Mountain Ash if from the S. Gain the A4275 road between Aberdare and Mountain Ash. From Mountain Ash drive for 3 km and take a L turning to Cwmaman. From Aberdare take the Aberaman road to reach the same turning. Drive up the road to reach a cross roads, turn L then take the third turning on the L after the Shepherd's Arms, (The crags are visible to your L and R). Now take the first L into Llanwonno road.

Cwmaman Main Quarry: Drive up the hill and turn L at a sign for the Pwllfa water treatment works. Park near two cottages and walk along the path away from the cottages (N) for 100m until a path is reached on the R just after an electricity pylon. Strike up the hillside to the quarry.
Cwmaman West: Instead of turning L into Llanwonno Road continue up the hill, park and walk along a track to derelict cottages where a faint path leads up and R to the quarry.

CWMAMAN MAIN QUARRY

South Wall
This is the S facing wall on the LH side of the quarry.

Good Tradition   12m   E2   5c
P.Lewis, A.Sharp 1988
Start on the L side of the S wall 2m R of a corner. Follow flakes and pockets up the steep wall, 2PR. SB well back.

Clear Head And A Blow Lamp   15m   E2/3   6a   *
A.Sharp, P.Lewis 1988
A sustained well protected pitch. Climb the thin crack just R of Good Tradition, 3PR. SB.

Mother Of Pearl   18m   E4   6b   ***
A.Sharp, P.Lewis 1988
A "mega" pitch with one very hard section. Start 2m R of the previous route. Climb the wall via a series of flakes, edges and breaks, 3PR's, 2BR's. SB.

Two For Tuesday   18m   E4   6a
A.Sharp, P.Lewis
The cracks up the RH side of the wall.

The World Is My Lobster   18m   E4   6a
A.Sharp,P.Lewis
The arete L of Propoganda.

Propaganda   23m   E6   6b   ***
A.Sharp, P.Lewis 1988
Start 8m R, below a small ledge with a BR at 6m. From the ledge make hard moves, BR, to a break, PR, then a series of finger wrenching moves, PR, to a shattered crackline. Finish up this 2PR. Lower off.

Science Friction   23m   E5   6b   ***
A.Sharp, P.Lewis 1988
Another finger wrecking monster. Start 2m R at a crackline with a BR at 6m. Desperate moves, BR, lead to hard moves between the horizontal breaks, PR, BR, and a final nerve wrecking finish. 3BR, 2PR. SB.

Le Rage   18m   E5   6c   **

A.Sharp, P.Lewis 1988

A stunning line. Start 5m R of Science Friction. Swagger up to a PR, technical climbing, 2BR's, leads to good holds. Continue up the wall, 2PR's, to the final blank section, BR. One hard move gains the lower off.

Innuendo   18m   E5   6b   **

M.Crocker, R.Thomas 1989

Superb climbing. Start L of the vegetated corner at the RH side of the wall. Climb the wall via a good ledge, 2BR's, to breaks below a narrow roof, PR, and then to a chimney. Climb direct on good holds, 2PR, to a good exit.

The Numbers Game   24m   E4   6a   ***

A.Sharp, P.Lewis 1989

A L to R girdle with good protection, low in the grade. Follow Good Tradition to its first PR, traverse R to a chimney, PR. Step up the arete for 3m, PR, to a good break, then traverse to the finish of Le Rage, 3PR's.

MIDDLE WALLS

The cliff now turns a R angle

Instead Of This   12m   E1   5b

R.Thomas, G.Gibson 1990

Start at a short approach wall just L of centre on the wall R of Innuendo. Climb an arete to a ledge, then climb the L side of the face above, 2BR's, BB.

Zoo Time   11m   E1   5b

R.Thomas, G.Gibson 1990

Climb the R side of the wall, BR, PR, to the same lower off.

Crack Line Man   11m   VS   4c

SWMC 1989

Climb the obvious groove crackline then the wall above.

ARETE BUTTRESS

40m R is another steep N facing wall with a prominent RH arete.

Hot Beef Injection   18m   E3 6a   **

M.Crocker, R.Thomas 1988

Elegant climbing. Start on the LH side of the wall. Climb a short ragged crack to a break, make an outlandish mantleshelf, PR. Step L then climb direct passing 2BR's to bigger holds and an abseil station.

Spam Javelin   18m   HVS 5a

R.Thomas, E.Jones 1990

Climb the crack in the centre of the crag.

Neo Maxi Zoom Weenie   18m E3 5c   **
M.Crocker, R.Thomas 1988
Sustained technical climbing on good rock. Start on the R side of
the wall a metre L of the arete. Follow a good crack and pull over a
bulge onto the wall, PR, move up and RW, PR and then continue
just L of the arete to an abseil station.

Anniversary Stroll   17m E1 5b
R.Thomas, M.Crocker 1989
Climb to a shallow cave 3m R of the arete. Move up and R then
directly up to an abseil station, 3PR's.

Hey Mister   17m E2 5b   *
R.Thomas, M.crocker 1988
A good pitch. Follow a rising crackline up the slab R of the arete,
then back L. Lower from an abseil station.

Pete's Route   17m E2 5b
P.Lewis 1989
The wall 3m R.

CWMAMAN WEST
The arete and steep slabs clearly visible on the R on passing out of
the village.

Cwm To Papa   11m VS 4b
R.Thomas, G.Gibson 1990
Climb the arete easily but with little protection to a lower point.

Cwm To Mama   11m E2 5c
G.Gibson, R.Thomas 1990
Climb the centre of the slab, 1BR. Lower off.

Cwm Mammon   11m E3 6a
G.Gibson, R.Thomas 1990
Climb the R side of the slab, 2BR, 1PR to the same lower off.

BLAENLLECHAU QUARRY OS ref 004968
P.Lewis

SITUATION AND CHARACTER
A small slabby quarry overlooking the industrial dereliction of
Ferndale.

APPROACHES AND ACCESS
See map 3. The crag is situated on the road between Blaenllechau
(opposite Ferndale) and Llanwonno. It is best to view the crag from
the road through Ferndale, then to pinpoint the parking spot
above the quarry, as the quarry cannot be seen from that road. Park

above the crag at a small pull in opposite a rock cutting. A two minute walk LW takes you to the main slab in the centre of the quarry.

Away With The Mixer   12m E3 5c
P.Lewis, A.Sharp 1988
Good climbing up the LH line of the slab. Lower off a PB.

Away With The Fairy   12m E3 6a
P.Lewis, A.Sharp 1988
The thin crack R of Away With The Mixer.

FERNDALE OS ref 994969
M Crocker

SITUATION AND CHARACTER
Prominently situated above Darren Park in the small Rhondda town of Ferndale it has become quite popular. The escarpment runs for some distance, but the existing climbs are concentrated in a small amphitheatre of quarried rock directly above the lake in Darren Park. The climbs are short, but usually on clean rock with good protection. Unfortunately the cliff faces E, and is out of the sun for most of the afternoon, making it a poor choice in the winter.

APPROACHES AND ACCESS
See map 3. In the centre of Ferndale there is a prominent four way junction. When approaching from Porth turn L here and drive up the hill past the Working Men's Club to a parking place where the houses end. The quarry can be reached in five minutes by walking up the hill from here.
On the L of the quarry there is a prominent pillar, with an obvious descent route in the gully to its R. Further R is the prominent crackline of Silent Movies bounded by another pillar. The quarry is flanked on the R by blank walls split by a crackline.

Just Good Friends   9m E3 6a
A.Sharp 1989
The sustained thin crack in the wall L of the easy descent. 1PR.

Culture Vulture   17m E3 6a
A.Sharp, P.Lewis 1989
Start at the RYE. Climb a slab, BR, with awkward moves to a good hold, BR. Power up the steep wall to a lowering-off point.

Race You Up The Wall Bars   14m E4 6c   **
A.Sharp, P.Lewis 1989
Highly technical and fingery. Climb a blank slab L of an obvious finger crack, BR, lay-away on dinkies and eventually reach a good hold, BR. Make desperate moves L to a crack and up to a good ledge, PR. Lower off the tree.

Silent Movies   14m HVS 5a   *
A.Sharp, P.Lewis 1989
A good crack, which is unfortunately short-lived. Climb the crack
in the centre of the wall. Lower off the tree.

The Loony Left   11m E3 6b
A.Sharp, P.Lewis, P.Harding 1989
Start on a slab 6m R of Silent Movies. Climb the slab, PR, to a loony
move L enabling good holds to be reached. Lower off.

The next feature is another pillar with a tree growing out of the wall
three quarters of the way up.

Blondes Have More Fun   18m VS 4b
G.Lewis, F.Barrett, G.Barker 1989
Scramble onto a grass ledge on the R of the pillar. Take the easiest
line up to the tree. Stand on this and reach the top.

Rhondda Born   18m E2 5b   *
A.Sharp, P.Lewis, P.Harding 1989
An elegant pitch. Start 6m right of Blondes Have More Fun. Climb
easy ledges to the blunt rib, continue up this, BR, to the final crack.
SB.

Physical Presents   20m E4 6b   *
A.Sharp, P.Lewis 1989
This takes the L line up the central wall. Climb a groove in the
centre of the wall, BR, traverse L for 3m then climb the wall, 2 BR, to
good holds, PR. Step R to finish up the crack. Lower off.

By Appointment Only   20m E3 6a   *
A.Sharp, P.Lewis 1989
A good pitch, low in the grade. As for Physical Presents to the first
BR. Move LW to a good hold, then lurch over the overhang via a
hidden jug, BR. Continue straight up the wall, PR. Lower off.

Ten Green Bottles   20m E3 6a
A.Sharp, P.Lewis 1989
Start 3m R Physical Presents. Climb up a nose, PR and continue up a
slab to hard moves past a pocket, BR, step L and finish on big holds.
Lower off.

One Size Fits All   12m E4 6b
T.Forster, A.Sharp 1989
Very fingery. Climb the smooth slab 6m R of Ten Green Bottles, BR.
Lower off.

To the R is the final wall split by the crack of Sea Shells On The
Seychelles:

La Digue   18m E3 6a   *
M.Crocker 1989
The wall L of the crack line is climbed, 2BR.

Sea Shells On The Seychelles   21m E1 5b   **
M.Crocker 1989
The superb central crackline is climbed with good protection to
finish up the wall, PR.

Gregorie's Island Lodge   21m E2 5c   *
M.Crocker 1989
Start and finish as for Sea Shells etc, but make a worthwhile trip
onto the R wall, PR, BR. Return LW, PR, to finish.

LADY WINDSOR QUARRY OS ref 061943
G.Lewis

SITUATION AND CHARACTER
See map 3. This little roadside crag had been described as pleasant
and a bag of rubbish. This is no longer debatable as the area has
been landscaped and the crag no longer exists.

GLADYS QUARRY OS ref 021856.
G.Lewis
"You've got it wrong Andy, What you must do is climb the worst
looking routes first then it can only get better"
M.Learoyd 1991

SITUATION AND CHARACTER
Only twenty minutes from Cardiff this pleasant little crag faces W
and once again has easy access. The main lines dry quickly after
rain and they should become popular.

APPROACHES AND ACCESS
See map 3. Leaves the M4 at junction 34 and take the Road to
Llantrisant, then follow the A4119 towards Tonyrefail after approx 5
miles turn R to Gilfach Goch and Coed Ely. The crag can be seen
above and R immediately after the roundabout. Take the first
turning R as you enter Coed Ely, at the top of the road turn R
(parking available) and walk to the end of the road. Climb over the
gate and follow the path to the crag.
The main feature of the crag is a central crack system, bounded on
its L by short walls and grooves and on its R by the 11m Leaning
Wall. The first routes are on the short wall to the L of the central
crack.

The Beer Monster Goes Gardening   6m VS 4c
D.Hart, J.Davidge, J.Hart. 1989

Climb the disjointed crack on the extreme L of the crag, finishing via the tree.

Lager Lout 8m E2 5c
D.Viggars, E.Alsford, P.Donnithorne 1991
The wall just R of The Beer Monster Goes Gardening, 1 BR.

The Old Way 8m HVS 5a
H.Griffiths, D.Hart 1989
Start at a hole. A boulder problem start leads to a slight depression in the crack above. Traverse L and finish via the tree.

Alements 9m E2 5c
P.Donnithorne, E.Alsford 1991
The wall 1m R, 1 BR, 1PR.

Scandal 9m E3 6a
A.Sharp, J.Harwood. 1989
Climb the wall on the R side of the 'Cannabis leaf', 1BR.

My J C B's Exploded 13m HVS 4c
G.Lewis, D.Hart, S.Blackmore. 1989
Climb an arete R of the words Pink Floyd, between two groove lines, then step into the RH groove with twin trees above. At the top of the groove traverse R to a good belay on a large tree.

Bush Wackers' Groove 12m VS 4c
G.Lewis, M.Alley 1989
Climb the groove directly to the twin trees and finish RW. A must for the budding Bellamy!

THE LEANING WALL

Tall, Dark And Handsome 11m E4 6a
A.Sharp, P.Lewis, J.Harwood, H.Griffiths 1989
The leaning wall L of Campaign For See-Through Bikinis is climbed to a ledge. Continue steeply, 2 BR's, to a tree. Lower off.

Campaign For See-Through Bikinis 12m E2 5b   *
G.Lewis, H.Griffiths, D.Hart 1989
The crack system in the centre of the crag is climbed on increasingly large holds, PR. Just below the top pull onto a ledge and traverse R to a belay.

Young, Free and Single 11m E5 6a   **
A.Sharp, P.Lewis, J.Harwood 1989
A test of strength and endurance. Climb the wall R of Campaign For See-Through Bikinis, 3 BR's, to finish up pockets below a small tree.

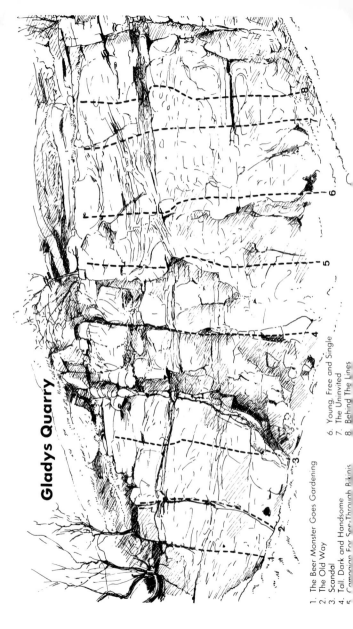

Gladys Quarry

1. The Beer Monster Goes Gardening
2. The Old Way
3. Scandal
4. Tall, Dark and Handsome
5. Campaign For See-Through Bikinis
6. Young, Free and Single
7. The Uninvited
8. Behind The Lines

The Uninvited   11m   E4   6a   ***
A.Sharp, J.Harwood 1989
The centre of the leaning wall is climbed, 3 BR's, to finish up an obvious crack, NR.

Behind The Lines   11m   E4   6a   **
A.Sharp, J.Harwood 1989
Climb the RH line on the main wall to a hard finish either LW or RW, 3BR's.

Buffalo Hunter   13m   HS
J.Harwood (solo) 1989
Climb the arete on the RH side of the wall to a large tree.

ROADSIDE QUARRY (TREBANOG)   OS ref 013904
G.Lewis

SITUATION AND CHARACTER
See map 3. This SW facing crag is situated next to the road in Trebanog. It is exposed to the wind and dries quickly. The climbs are short and it is a useful venue for local climbers. Belays are quickly arranged on an old fence at the cliff. Top roping is easily arranged making it a useful little training cliff.

APPROACHES AND ACCESS
Turn L off the A4233 (Porth to Tonyrefail road) in Trebanog, signposted Williamstown. The crag can be seen on the RH side of the road just after the Working Mens club. Also see the approach to Punk Rocks.
The very short crag on the L has a number of problems. Just to the R is a gently overhanging wall with a corner on its R.

Oneupmanship   6m   E1   5b   *
M.Learoyd, C.Nash, G.Lewis 1988
Climb the obvious line up the LH side of the overhanging wall.

The March Of Progress   6m   E5   6b
A.Sharp, P.Lewis 1990
Takes the wall L of For Your Hands Only, 1BR, 2PR's.

For Your Hands Only   9m   E4   6a   *
A.Sharp, P.Lewis 1984
The obvious steep line up the centre of the wall.

Banog's Barmy Army   6m   E5   6b   *
A.Sharp, P.Lewis 1990
Follows a devious line up the centre of the wall R of For Your Hands Only finishing LW, 1BR, 1PR.

Aunty Pasty   9m   HVS   4c
G.Lewis, H.Griffiths 1988
The obvious overhanging corner is climbed by a crack in the R wall
at first until a steep finish is made.

Air Play   9m   VS   4c   *
G.Lewis, H.Griffiths 1988
Climb the arete with increasing interest.

Playing Away   9m   HVS   5a
H.Griffiths, S.W.M.C 1988
A harder variation of Air Play by staying just R of the arete.

Bushbaby   9m   HS
Start in a hollow 3m R of Playing Away. Climb the LH line to the top.

Simon's Crack   9m   S
Take the RH line out of the hollow to finish up a crack.

Jaffa Buttress   9m   HVS   5a
H.Griffiths, G.Lewis 1988
Climb the buttress as directly as you dare and gain the grass ledge
on its L side. Finish easily up the reddish arete.

Terry's Crack   9m   VS   4b
Terry and Howell 1988
The obvious curving crack L of the words Philip Weel painted on
the rock.

Howell's Horror   9m   D
Howell (solo) 1988
The easy groove between Blagdon and Terry's Crack.

Blagdon   9m   VS   4c
P.Hamer, R.Smith 1984
The obvious corner to the L of the blank wall. (Poor protection).

Fire Water   9m   E3   6a
A.Sharp, R.Smith 1984
Climb the centre of the wall R of Blagdon.

Hair Of The Dog   9m   E3   6a
A.Sharp 1984
Climb the wall R of Fire Water past the letters PC.

Barlamb Abuse   9m   D
A five year old local was seen descending this groove, solo, to drag
off an injured sheep.

Ledge Climb   9m   V   D
Start by making a rising traverse RW onto the ledge of Sunday
Swing. Finish up the crack in the arete.

Sunday Swing   9m   VS
G.Lewis (solo) 1988
Climb the very steep but juggy arete which is L of the Fire Down
Below chimney. Easier climbing after the ledge.

Out With The Boys   9m   E2   5c
L.Foulkes, G.Lewis, M.Learoyd 1988
Climb the bulging L wall of the large chimney to reach a thin crack.
A good ledge is reached just above this. Finish directly.

Fire Down Below   9m   HVS   5a
G.Lewis, T.Howell, H.Griffiths 1988
The large chimney is climbed to good holds leading steeply L.
Finish with a long reach for good holds at the top.

Kiwis Can't Fly   9m   E2   6a
L.Foulkes, M.Learoyd, C.Nash
A steep little crack in the R wall of the chimney.

I Spy Arete   9m   HS
M.Learoyd 1988
This pleasant arete can be climbed for a sneak preview of the
harder climbs to the L and R.

I Spy Direct   9m   E1   5b
M Learoyd, S.W.M.C. 1988
The wall R of I Spy is climbed direct.

Eastend Groove   9m   HS
H.Griffiths solo
The next groove.

Mick's Little Viper   9m   E1   5b
M.Learoyd 1988
The LH crackline, direct.

Eastend Crack   9m   VS
The RH crack.

Desperate Arete   9m   S
Climb the arete direct with little protection.

Descent Route   9m   D
To the R of the arete is a crack which provides an easy way up or
down. Start on the arete, climb up and R to the crack.

Last Arete   9m   HS
Climb the last arete direct; poor protection.

PUNK ROCKS OS ref 019909
M.Learoyd

SITUATION AND CHARACTER
This is a small E facing Quarry situated above the village of
Cymmer. There are actually two quarries, the RH is the better of
the two and sports a few good routes.

APPROACHES AND ACCESS
See map 3. The easiest approach is to leave the M4 junction 34,
A4119 to Llantrisant. At Tonyrefail turn R at the roundabout signposted Porth (A4233). At Trebanog descend about one third of a
mile then take the first L after The Farmers pub, and the third R to a
playing field. Follow a track to the L trending RW to the quarries.

The Left Hand Quarry
The centre of the crag has an obvious ledge at 5m.

James Bond   12m   E1   5b
L.Foulkes, M.Learoyd 1989
Climb the thin RH crack to the ledge and from its RH end climb the
wall to good pockets. Move L into a shallow groove beneath the
finishing overlap. PB.

Eddy Edwards   12m   HVS   5a   *
M.Learoyd, L.Foulkes 1989
Climb the crack with an inverted spike near the bottom. PB.

Edwina Curry   12m   E1   5b
L.Foulkes, M.Learoyd 1989
Start just R of Eddy Edwards, join it and finish up it.

To Distant Friends   12m   VS   4c
M.Learoyd, L.Foulkes 1989
Climb an obvious crack 6m from the R edge of the wall. PB.

Black Looks   12m   E2   5b
M.Learoyd, L.Foulkes 1989
Climb the wall R of To Distant Friends, PR. Finish Direct.

The Right Hand Quarry
The quarry offers some excellent steep problems especially on the
central walls.

Scoop   9m   VS   4b
M.Learoyd, L.Foulkes 1988
Climb the obvious chimney crack at the L end of the wall.

Dai Swastika   9m   HVS   5a
M.Learoyd, L.Foulkes 1988
This takes the thin block choked crack on the LH side of the main wall. PB, lower off.

Call My Bluff   12m   E2   5b   **
M.Learoyd, L.Foulkes 1988
The thin crack and small pod are climbed trending LW at the top.

Mona Lisa   12m   E5   6b/c   *
A.Sharp, P.Lewis 1989
Climb the wall L of Completely Punked. Hard moves lead to a long reach to clip a BR, more hard moves lead to a long reach, NR. Continue to a break traverse R and lower off (situ belay).

Completely Punked   12m   E2   5c   **
L.Foulkes, M.Learoyd 1988
A strenuous route taking the obvious jam crack in the centre of the wall. Lower off, NR, PR.

Waiting Game   12m   E4   6a   **
M.Learoyd, L.Foulkes 1988
Start R of the central crack line. Climb to a flake, move up, PR on the R, step R and up, PR, and reach a hanging flake crack. Move L to finish. Lower off, PB.

Ferret Wall   15m   E1   5c
M.Learoyd, L.Foulkes 1988
Long arms are useful on this one. Climb the wall R of a chimney crack, just L of Amen Corner to a ledge at 3m, PR, move R then back L, PR. Finish direct via a pocket in the upper wall.

Amen Corner   12m   VS   4b
L.Foulkes, M.Learoyd 1988
Climb the corner to the RH edge of the wall.

The Enterpreneur   12m   E1   5b
L.Foulkes, M.Learoyd 1988
Climb a crack in the lower wall on the RH end of the crag trending L to finish directly over a bulge.

To the R is another bay. The back wall of which is split by an obvious jam crack.

False Protection   12m   E3   5c
G.Lewis, M.Learoyd 1989
Climb the jam crack passing a loose band to gain the steep headwall above, BR. Move L onto the arete to finish.

GLYNFACH CRAG OS ref 026905
A.Sharp

SITUATION AND CHARACTER
A small crag tucked away above the village of Porth.

APPROACHES AND ACCESS
From the A4058 in Porth bear L at the YMCA. Continue up the steep hill and take the second turning on the L into Glyn Street. Park at its end on a small hill and follow the path up the hillside passing a football area, then take the track to the obvious quarry, 10 mins. The routes are at the far end of the quarry in a small hollow.

Killers Arete   15m   E4   5c
A.Sharp, P.Lewis 1990
The thin crack up the overhanging arete on the LH wall, 2PR's, SB.

Moses Supposes His Toes's Were Roses   15m   E4   5c
P.Lewis, A.sharp 1990
Climb onto a large flake in the centre of the wall, then trend LW to a break, climb strenuously to finish, 1BR, 2PR's.

Nervous Ninties   15m   E4   6b
A.Sharp, P.Lewis 1990
As for Moses etc onto the flake then step R and up to the break. Hard moves lead to good holds and the top.

Psychotherapy   9m   E5   6b/c
G.Henderson, J.Obradowica 1990
Climb the white wall on the RH side of the quarry. PB.

Yaks Back   9m   E1   5b
G.Henderson, J.Obradowica 1990
Start 4m R. Climb a slabby brown streak.

LLWYNYPIA QUARRY OS ref 994940
M.Crocker

SITUATION AND CHARACTER
Situated 90m up the SE facing wooded hillside above Llwynapia it is one of the most picturesque sandstone quarries in South East Wales and a delightful place in which to climb. Though lacking any really outstanding routes, the good quality rock, sunny outlook! and absence of seepage makes a visit worth while.

APPROACHES AND ACCESS
See map 3. For visitors to South Wales the Rhondda Valley crags are best approached by leaving the M4 (junction 34) and heading towards Llantrisant then the A4119 towards tonyrefail. Continue along the new road across several roundabouts following signs for

Rhondda and Llwynypia. 200m past a large Victorian Engine house and Gasometer the road bends to the R. Park in a bus stop and walk up Station Terrace until it is possible to follow a track which runs parallel to the stream draining the pool beneath the crag.
Across the 'dam' is a wall with a distinct pillar and an off-width chimney on it's R side. The following routes take lines up this wall.

Bernard's Balls Up   12m   E4   6a
M.Crocker, R.Thomas 1989
Climb the steep wall, immediately L of the chimney, to a tree. Lower off.

Calling The Shots   12m   E4   5c   *
M.Crocker, R.Thomas 1989
The fine arete of the pillar is climbed direct with gradually decreasing difficulty. A PR at three-fifths height provides inadequate protection!

Well Heeled   12m   VS   4c
M.Crocker, R.Thomas 1989
Climb the obvious thin crack in the wall directly behind the pond. Scramble down RW to descend.

Calcanium Crunch   11m   E2   5b
M.Crocker, R.Thomas 1989
An enjoyable pitch on superb rock which takes a line up the smooth RW section of the steep slab above the previous route. A PR at 6m provides the only protection.

Free Wales Army   18m   E1   5b
M.Crocker, R.Thomas 1989
Start at the words 'Free Wales Army'. Move up the roof-capped groove and pull onto the rounded arete, PR. Climb the arete past a sapling on the L and finish steeply up its R side.

Towards the RH side of the quarry, and to the L of where the stream descends over the crag, is a fine 12m, south-facing wall.

Alibi   12m   E3   5c
M.Crocker, R.Thomas 1989
Fine technical climbing on good rock. Start in the centre of the wall. Follow widely spaced holds to a jug at the base of a crack at half height. Climb the crack awkwardly and mantleshelf to finish. Poor protection for the first 6m.

The Brawl   12m   E3   6a   *
M.Crocker, R.Thomas 1989
An excellent and problematic finish after a thin crack to start. Climb straight up the thin crack in the R side of the wall. Finish up the steep arete with a couple of long reaches.

GELLI OS ref 984946
M Learoyd

SITUATION AND CHARACTER
A quarried NE facing escarpment overlooking Gelli Industrial Estate, offering numerous short routes in the middle grades. The quarry faces the evening sun.

APPROACH AND ACCESS
See map 3. Approach from the M4 as for Llwynapia. Where the road bends R after the engine house take the L fork (signposted Gelli) passing the entrance to the YHA. Follow this road (B4223) passing the Gelli Industrial Estate. Park in a turning on the L which leads to the Mid Glamorgan Landfill Site. Take the steep path on the L leading up past stables and a fenced compound. It is a steep ten minute walk to the quarry.

GREEN ARETE
On the L of the quarry is a prominent green arete.

Green Arete   12m   VS   4c
G.Lewis 1989
Climb the green arete moving R to finish.

Red Wall 1
6m to the R is a red wall.

K.E.S.   12m   VS   4c
M.Learoyd, R.Thomas 1989
Climb the slabby wall centrally, 3m R of the previous route, PR.

Wot No Metal   9m   E1   5b
R.Thomas, G.Royle 1990
A prominent Y shaped crack on the L edge of the red wall.

Little Treasure   9m   E1   5c
M.Learoyd, R.Thomas 1989
The scooped wall is climbed directly, BR, with a long reach to finish.

Toil   9m   HVS   5a
G.Lewis 1989
Climb the twin crack on the R edge of the red wall without using the chimney crack.

Galvanised   11m   E1   5b
R.Thomas, G.Royle 1990
Gain and climb the obvious curving flake crack to a ledge then move L onto the upper wall, 2PR's.

RED WALL 2

The centre of the quarry has another red wall bounded on the R by an obvious slab with an arete above.

Titanium Man   9m   E1   5b
G.Royle, R.Thomas 1990
Climb the steep crack immediately R of a prominent grassy chimney.

Tobacco King   9m   E3   5c
M.Learoyd, R.Thomas 1989
Start a metre or two to the R. Climb the prominent curving crack, PR.

Cigarillo   9m   E4   6a
M.Learoyd, L.Foulkes, R.Thomas 1990
Climb the wall to the R, 1BR.

Down Under   15m   VS   4c
R.Thomas, M.learoyd, et al 1989
Climb the obvious slab until harder moves lead R to the arete.

To the R is a green wall bounded by a grassy corner and narrow retaining R wall.

Little Taff   12m   E1   5a
R.Thomas, L.Foulkes, M.Learoyd 1990
Climb the thin crack in the centre of the wall L of the vegetated crack, PR. Continue to the small overhang at the top of the crag. Pull over this to gain the top. SB well back.

A Little Something I Prepared Earlier   12m   E1   5b
R.Thomas, M.Learoyd 1989
Climb the wall L of the grassy corner, 4PR's.

Unearthed   12m   HS   4b
R.Thomas solo 1989
Climb the crack L of the arete of the retaining wall to a ledge and continue up the groove to finish.

Ice Station Gelli   12m   E2   5c
M.Learoyd, G.Lewis 1989
Climb the steep wall 4m R of the word Buzzy, taking the upper wall direct, 3PR.

Send In The Specials   12m   E1   5b
R.Thomas, G.Royle 1990
Start 3m R of Ice Station Gelli. Step L off a grassy step to gain a wall, PR, continue steeply up this, 2PR's.

Hole In One   12m   HVS   5a
G.Lewis, M.Learoyd 1990
3m up and R again is a grassy ledge, step L from this to a finger hole
and threaded PR. Move diagonally up R to finish, 2PR's.

YSTRAD OS ref 975955
R.Thomas

SITUATION AND CHARACTER
This sheltered SE facing quarry is situated in the Rhondda Valley
overlooking the villages of Ton Pentre and Ystrad. A 10m length of
rope might prove useful for lowering off although most routes are
equipped with lower off points . . .

APPROACHES AND ACCESS
See map 3. The crag is located above the A4058 which passes along
the N side of the Afon Rhondda Fawr (Rhondda river). When
travelling from Porth pass through the village of Ystrad and turn R
at a large church with a fountain outside. Take another R and follow
a straight road uphill to reach a parking area. Walk SE along vague
tracks for 300m until a field is reached. Skirt this field on the R until
at the top of the quarry.
The following routes are on the overhanging back wall of the
quarry and are described from L to R.

Alone And Blue   12m   E3   5c
R.Thomas, G.Royle 1990
Climb the L side of the wall, PR, to a horizontal break.
Finish up the steep headwall. Lower off.

Help The Aged   12m   E1   5b
R.Thomas, M.Learoyd 1990
Climb the obvious crackline 2m R of Alone And Blue.

Road To Nowhere   12m   E1   5b
R.Thomas, M.Learoyd 1990
The next crackline R, slightly harder than its companion, 1PR.

April Fool   12m   E3   5c
M.Learoyd, R.Thomas, L.Foulkes 1990
A strenuous route. Start 3m R of Road To Nowhere and climb the
steep crack to gain a narrow ledge, PR. Move up and L, PR, then
climb steeply, 3PR, until it is possible to gain a lower off.

Spirit of Ystrad   12m   E4   6a
M.Learoyd, R.Thomas 1991
Climb the wall 2m R of the previous route. 4 PR's.

Tom Tom Club   12m   E2   5b
E.Jones, R Thomas 1990
13m R is a depression at the base of the quarry. Climb steeply from the base of the depression, PR, to a broken system of ledges. Continue up the final wall, 2PR's.

RHONDDA PILLAR QUARRY OS ref 937977
R.Thomas

SITUATION AND CHARACTER
See map 3. This crag has an excellent pillar well worth visiting. It is situated in a wild moorland setting with superb views of the surrounding Rhondda Valley. It is clearly visible 210m up the hillside W of Treherbet.

APPROACHES AND ACCESS
Park at Treherbet railway station. Cross the railway and a stream on the L to follow a track, take the first R then follow a smaller path back L until above the crag. A distinctive feature is the leaning pillar on the RH side of the crag. The L side of the pillar consists of a slabby wall, the RH side is gently overhanging. The finishes are still not clean and a rope left in place would make some of the exits enjoyable.

BLOCK WALL
Up and L of the pillar area is a grassy descent gully. L of this is a crack seamed green wall with large blocks under it and large overhangs above.

Little Big Ego   8m   E2   6a
M.Crocker, R.Thomas 1989
Climb the thin crack by stepping from the jumble of boulders.

Submerged By Blubber   7m   E2   5b
M.Crocker, R.Thomas 1989
Climb the back wall of the cave then pull over the roof crack on jams. Rope advised for exit.

Baker Day   9m   HS
R.Thomas, M.Learoyd 1989
The obvious chimney/crack line on the RH side of the wall is climbed to a SB up and L.

R of these is the short back wall of the pillar gained by a faint track that follows the pillar round its base. Follow the track RW to gain the pillar area.

Lamb Leer Disease   15m   E1   5b   *
M.Ward, M.Crocker 1988

The enjoyable crack in the slabby L wall of the pillar. Take care with the exit or Lower off.

Bizzare Geetar   18m   E3   5c   *
M.Crocker, M.Ward 1988
Fine exposed climbing up the wall R of Lamb Leer Disease and the RH arete. Gain the arete from the L, PR missing, climb the wall to the L then swing back R, PR, to a small ledge. Finish directly until the 'Nosepicker' exit is made.

Nosepicker   18m   E5   6b
M.Crocker, R.Thomas 1989
Powerful climbing up the RH side of the L arete of the leaning R wall of the pillar. 2PR's, 1BR.

Thumbsucker   18m   E4   6a   **
M.Crocker, M.Ward 1988
Climb the impressive finger crack R of the arete, until difficulties ease and it is possible to step L to ledges and a nail biting finish.

Nailbiter   18m   E4   6a
M.Crocker, R.Thomas 1989
Climb the wall R of the finger crack, 1BR, 1PR.

Beneath the pillar a faint track leads LW around the back of the mountain to a small crag characterised by having trees at its top

Lynch'Em   12m   E5   6a
M.Crocker, R.Thomas 1989
Climb the unprotected groove on the L side of the wall.

Exterminate all Gear Thieves   15m   E4   6a
M.Crocker, R.Thomas 1989
Climb the R side of the wall, poor PR to a large tree.

CWM DIMBATH OS ref 951896
R.Thomas

SITUATION AND CHARACTER
The most secluded of all the sandstone crags situated in Ogmore forest close to Blackmill. It was first climbed on in the 70's by the late Charlie Heard and was then lost to SWMC folklore until now. The crags are located in a large natural rift but there is some evidence of quarrying. Dense oak woodland excludes direct sunlight so the crag may remain damp after a heavy downpour. It is a delightful and peaceful place in which to climb and is well worth seeking out.
The aretes at the entrance to the rift will provide a day's entertainment for the VS/HVS climber.

APPROACHES AND ACCESS

See map 3. Turn off the M4 at junction 36 and take the A4061 Bryncethin road to Blackmill (5 miles). Turn R in Blackmill (A4093 sign posted Tonyrefail) just past the Ogmore Junction pub and proceed to the village of Glynogwr. Turn L between the village school and the church into a steep and narrow lane. Park at the bottom of the lane after passing over a ford. Enter the forest and follow the track upstream, past a gate, when it meets another road turn R up the hillside. At some trees marked by graffitia small path L leads through the trees until the main rift is reached. On the R, at the entrance to the rift, are a series of aretes which although short are sunny and dry quickly. Further into the rift on the R is the main crag split by a roof crack, Where The Power Lies and higher still is the upper quarry.

ENTRANCE ARETES

Across The River   7m   VS   4c
R.Thomas, G.Royle 1990
The first, undercut arete.

Into The Trees   8m   VS   4c
R.Thomas, G.Royle 1990
The next sharp arete up and L.

Groucher   7m   VS   4c
R.Thomas 1990
The rounded arete 3m L of Into The Trees.

Whinger   7m   HVS   4c
E.Jones 1990
The cleaned wall just L.

Moaner   5m   VS   4c
R.Thomas 1990
The sharp stepped arete 3m L.

Teaching Granny   5m   E2   6a
R.Thomas, G.Royle 1990
The steep wall between the arete and crack exit RW. PR.

Huff And Puff   7m   HVS   4c
R.Thomas, G.Gibson 1990
The rounded arete 2m L.

Sucking Eggs   10m   E3   6a   **
R.Thomas, G.Royle 1990
The exciting arete 14m L of Huff and Puff. Start directly below the arete. Climb the arete and R wall, 3PR's, step L at the top to join At Your Convenience.

At Your Convenience   10m   E3   6a   **

R.Thomas, G.Royle 1990

The steep wall 2m L of Sucking Eggs. 4 PR's.

THE MAIN CRAG AREA

The main feature of this area is the large overhanging wall and roof split by a crack. The first routes are to the R of this feature.

Phil's Ammonia   10m   E1   5b

R.Thomas, G.Davies 1990

Climb the arete of the green wall cut by two cracks, 7m L of Sucking Eggs. 2PR's.

L is a vegetated wall, the next route is on the wall facing out of the rift.

Teddy Bears Picnic   13m   E1   5a

R.Thomas, G.Davies 1990

Climb the centre of the slabby wall, 2PR's.

Coming on Strong   23m   E5   6b   ***

A.Sharp, P.Lewis 1990

Superb. Start on a small ledge on the RH side of the overhanging wall. Step L into an off width crack, that is hard to get into, hard to stay in, but easy to get spat out of! Climb to the roof, PR, and move strenuously but more easily through it, 2PR's. Climb boldly up the leaning wall, PR, to a belay ledge. The prudent will carry a Friend 1/2.

Where The Power Lies   23m   E6   6b   ***

A.Sharp, P.Lewis 1990

Start 3m L of Coming On Strong beneath the imposing crack splitting the centre of the overhanging wall. Climb the crack with increasing difficulty to reach good jugs below the roof. Powerful moves through the roof, or a flying leap, leads to good holds on the lip, PR. Strenuous climbing up the leaning wall, 2PR's, leads to a final hard move onto the belay ledge. All very uphill.

The Knowledge   20m   E4   6b   ***

P.Lewis, A.Sharp 1990

Excellent climbing. Start below the arete just L of the previous routes. Difficult moves past a BR leads to good holds. Perplexing moves past a BR brings good holds at the base of a slab. Gain the slab, PR, and climb diagonally onto the arete and up to a tree belay. Lower off.

If You Go Down To The Woods Today   20m   E4   6a   ***

C.Heard, A.N.Other (A1) c1975

P.Lewis, A.Sharp 1990

An Excellent crack climb. Start 3m L of The Knowledge at a thin crack. Climb the crack and short slab above finishing as for the previous route.

Day Of The Mastodon   12m   HVS   5a
R.Thomas, G.Gibson 1990
This climbs the sharp arete at the L end of this section via a pull over a small roof at its base.

On the L side of the lower rift opposite The Knowledge is the following route:

Burdizzo   10m   E1   5b
R.Thomas, J.Bright 1990
Climb the wall 2m L of the earthy chimney.

The path now rises steeply up and over a grass col to the top and the Upper Rift.

UPPER RIFT

Trickie   10m   VS   4b
G.Lewis 1990
Essentially an easier finish to the next route. Climb onto a small ledge in the centre of the buttress, traverse R under the overhang to finish.

Tieksodeeophobia   10m   HVS   5a
G.Lewis, A.Burke 1990
Climb onto the small ledge as for Trickie but climb up and L on good holds.

10m L of the last route is a prominent dirty blind groove with a slabby L wall

No 7 Climb   12m   VS   5a   O
G.Lewis, A.Keward 1990
The filthy groove with a step L onto the slabby wall.

Just to the L is a fine wall with a R to L sloping ramp running up its centre.

Consuming Passion   20m   HVS   5a   *
H.Griffiths, L.Travers 1990
A good route. Climb the prominent and well protected crack to the R of the ramp, finishing directly.

Never Mind The Bollocks share The Knowledge   20m   E3   5c   **
A.Burke, E.Jones, H.Griffiths 1990
Climb the ramp until level with the underside of the capping roof. Step R over the roof and finish up the centre of the buttress. Friends will be found useful

Wild Pussy   20m   E1   5c
H.Griffiths, E.Jones
Bold at first. Climb the narrow pillar to reach the top L side of the ramp.

Grit Expectations   15m   E4   5c   *
E.Jones, H. Griffiths 1990
Bold and strenuous. Climb the wall set back 8m L of wild Pussy via a break and a blind flake to a rounded break. Make a hard move up to the overhang and finish over this more easily.

CRAG CRAIG FAWR OS ref 799867
A.Freem

SITUATION AND CHARACTER
The is the lower of the two crags clearly visible from the M4, junction 38, high up on the hillside. It is of interest to locals only, the routes are steep and gritstone-like in character a rope from the top may help with some of the finishes. The view from the top is superb.
The crag is one buttress with a central overhanging area split by two obvious cracks.

APPROACHES AND ACCESS
See map 1. From junction 38 on the M4, follow signs to Margam Abbey and park on the Forestry track at the base of the hill. Walk up and LW, through the wood to reach the crag (10 mins). The land is owned by the Forestry Commission and is a conservation area. "High profile" climbing will probably lead to a ban, so avoid damage to plants and do not disturb the upper (very loose) cliff which is a nesting site.

Silf   11m   HVS   5a
P.Boyd, A.Freem 1986
This climbs the obvious RW curving crack starting next to a grassy gully. At half height an awkward move onto a ledge is followed by a crack just L of the arete.

Left Edge   11m   E1   5b
A.Freem, P.Boyd 1986
Artificial but enjoyable. Follow the R-angle arete on the L of the main face mainly on its R side then join Silf to finish.

Quercus   21m   HS   4a
A.Freem, A.Freem 1986
Climb the crack containing a tiny oak tree and the groove above and R. Finish over the summit rocks. PB.

Antonia's Route   21m   VS   4c
A.Freem, A.Freem 1986
Climb directly up the slightly fragile wall merging with Owl Groove at the top of the wall.

Owl Groove   21m   VS   4c   *
A.Freem, D.Owens 1986
Follow the impressive groove, L of an overhanging wall.

Derbyshire Hiraeth   24m   E2   5b
A.Freem 1982
Climb onto a jutting block at 2m then up a small V groove to the LW trending crack. Move up and L easily to the top.

The Orangery   24m   E1   5b
A.Freem, N.Gould 1986
Follow the straight crack up the wall moving R to finish.

Gorsedd Groove   24m   S
A.Freem, D.Owens 1986
The RW facing corner, capped by a small roof. Enter and leave it RW.

Gibbon   21m   VS   4b
P.Boyd, D.Owens 1986
Start 3m R of Gorsedd Groove, near the R end of the crag. Climb directly up via cracks and ledges.

ABBEY BUTTRESS OS ref 785882
R.Thomas
"Are you going to write that route up"
"I'll write it up with a point of aid"
"Which point is that"
Overheard conversation between two local activists after a dubious first ascent.

SITUATION AND CHARACTER
This was the crag that everyone had seen and intended to visit but never had, and will wish that they had. It is clearly visible from the M4 motorway as it passes the Abbey Steel Works Port Talbot. This makes the view somewhat esoteric but nonetheless spectacular. The crag is good solid sandstone and although not extensive, contains some excellent routes exclusively in the higher grades. Its exposed position makes it a cold place when the wind is blowing but it does catch the sun from midday onwards. There are stake belays situated well back from the top.

APPROACHES AND ACCESS
See map 1. Leave the M4 at junction 40 and head for the steelworks. At the traffic lights turn L. At the Old Surgery pub (on the R) turn L

up the road opposite (The Incline). Follow it past a school under the motorway and park carefully on some grass in front of two bungalows. A Path on the L (W) of the bungalow leads up the hillside to a track , the crag is to the R (E).
The crag consists of a main face with a horizontal break at two thirds height, smaller broken buttresses at each end and lots of graffiti.

Closed Shop   21m   E2/3   5c   *
R.Thomas, J.Bullock, G.Evans, L.Moran 1986
Start at a LW ramp, 3m R of an obvious corner, on the LH side of the main face. Climb the LW ramp and crack to the horizontal break. Pull onto the upper wall, PR, gain a thin crack and then the top. SB.

Restrictive Practice   21m   E2/3   5c   **
R.Thomas, G.Royle 1986
Start as for Closed Shop. Follow the ramp for a few feet until a thin crack leads to the break. Pull onto the upper wall moving slightly R, NR, move back L and follow cracks to the top. SB.

Crack Basher   21m   E2   5c   ***
R.Thomas, G.Royle 1986
The classic of the crag, hard for its grade. From the start of the last route climb RW into a pod. Go L over the roof and follow a thin crack to the break, TR. Make perplexing moves up the wider crack above to the top.

Sign Of The Times   21m   E5   6b   ***
R.Thomas, G.Royle 1986
FFA M.Crocker, R.Thomas 1986
Start just R of Crack Basher. Gain a large PR and TR, then climb a crack to reach a flake out R, PR. Move up and R, if you can, to gain a shallow crack and the break. Follow the crack above, PR, then up the wall above.

P.R.Job   21m   E4   6b
M.Crocker, R.Thomas 1986
An alternative start to Urban Development. Start just R of Sign Of The Times below the initials PR. Make hard moves past a PR, move L then R to gain the flake crack of Urban Development. Finish as for that route.

Urban Development   21m   E4   6b   **
R.Thomas, G.Royle 1pt aid 1986
FFA M.Crocker, R.Thomas 1986
Start R of P.R.Job and just L of an obvious L slanting groove at mid height. Gain a PR, then climb a crack, PR, until hard moves lead LW to a flake crack. Gain the horizontal break and follow the crack on the L to the top.

Writings On The Wall   21m   E3   5c
G.Royle, R.Thomas 1986
Start as for Urban Development. At the first PR make hard moves R
to the base of a hanging groove. Climb this to the break and pass
over a leaf of rock to the top, PB,SB.

Split The Equity   12m   F2   5b
R.Thomas, G.Royle, J.Bullock 1988
The steep flake line R of Writings On The Wall. Gain the small cave
below and R of a small tree, pull out and follow the flake to the top.

Industrial Relations   23m   E1   5b
G.Royle, R.Thomas 1986
Start below the tower at the RH end of the crag. Climb the corner
and follow a crack splitting the tower to a small ledge and final
short wall. PB, SB.

Bargaining Counter   E1   5b
G.Evans, L.Moran 1986
A L to R Girdle across the break. Start as for Closed Shop and finish
up Writings On The Wall.

CWMAFON QUARRY OS ref 769914
R.Thomas

SITUATION AND CHARACTER
This small crag is located at the bottom of the Afan valley overlooking Port Talbot. It is visible high on the hillside as one passes
along the M4 towards Swansea

APPROACHES AND ACCESS
See map 1. Leave the M4 at junction 40 (travelling from the east).
Head for the steel works and at the traffic lights turn R. Follow the
main road past the railway station and continue around to a
roundabout virtually beneath the motorway. coming from the W
leave the motorway at junction 41 and reach the same roundabout.
Follow signs for Cwmafon until it is possible to park in a layby on
the L.

Amicable Settlement   8m   E2   5c
R.Thomas G.Royle 1990
At the L side of the crag is a short crack seamed wall above a scree
slope. Climb the central crack to a stake belay well back in the
grass.

Slack Alice   17m   E1   5b
G.Royle, R.Thomas, M.Learoyd 1990
At the bottom of the scree slope on the R is an obvious slab and
arete. Gain the arete from the L and climb it to the top.

MINOR CRAGS

Many of the crags described as minor crags in the previous guide book are now "major" crags. The following cliffs have been climbed on by previous generations and are awaiting their promotion to the major league.

DAREN FAWR OS ref 022098
A long escarpment of generally loose rock situated 5 kilometres N of Merthyr Tydfil on the E side of the A470.

Wuthering Heights 23m S
The centre of the long wall at the LH end of the cliff by an obvious flake crack.

Thunderguts 21m VS
Towards the RH end of the cliff there is a large gully with a tower on its R. Climb the front of the tower via a prominent crack.

Scalar 23m VS
Climbs the steep face 3m R of Thunderguts.

DAREN FACH OS ref 019104
This is a natural limestone cliff 11m high, which lies on private land. It is situated a little further N than Daren Fawr and the best approach is towards the RH end via the screes.

Lightflight 10m VD
A groove 45m L of thwe boundary fence at the R (S) end of the crag.

Grappler 11m VS
Take a curving corner moving R on a slab below some hanging blocks.

Undertaker 11m S
This climbs the obvious overhang-capped groove using a dubious block to exit R at the top.

Towards the centre of the crag there is a clean corner crack graded Moderate with a VD on the RH wall and a S climb in a groove to the R via a tree at half height.

INDEX